THE ENCYCLOPEDIA OF
DOG BREEDS

JULIETTE CUNLIFFE

p

Contents

How to Use this Book

This book contains a number of important features:

- **Eight chapters of detailed information** on all aspects of owning and looking after a dog, the history of dogs and their place in the human world. Photographs, illustrations, informative captions and 'dog-fact' boxes provide extra detail on every page.
- **Descriptions of over 400 dog breeds.** The first section lists British Kennel Club registered dogs in A–Z order within one of seven allocated groups, such as the Working Group or Toy Group. The second section lists dog breeds in A–Z order according to their country of origin.
- **Icons** provide additional information about weight, height, diet, maintenance and appearance of each breed.
- **'Breed Information' boxes** cover alternative names for specific breeds, details of kennel club registration and permissible colour variations within the breed.
- **The reference section** comprises a reading list, useful contacts such as the Kennel Club, a glossary of vital canine terms and an extensive index.

KEY TO SYMBOLS

The four symbols used throughout the breed sections of the encyclopedia provide the reader with extra information at a glance.

The generic group to which a dog belongs – Gundog, Hound, Pastoral, Terrier, Toy, Working, Utility

Gundog

GROUP **COAT CARE**

Maintenance required for the coat, ranging from one brush for little care to four for high maintenance

The size of a dog, being small, medium or large

SIZE **FEEDING**

The amount of food required by a breed, ranging from one bowl to four bowls

Introduction

THE AIM of *The Encyclopedia of Dog Breeds* is to give to readers general information about dogs and an insight into the majority of breeds which are recognised by leading kennel authorities throughout the world.

Almost unbelievably, it is estimated that there are somewhere between 700 and 800 breeds of dog across the globe but many of them are either hardly known outside their own country or are not officially recognised. Some of these are newly created breeds, others are of long standing; in some cases their devotees have not even tried to obtain official recognition.

Different countries operate under diverse ruling bodies and there are many interesting breeds of dog found throughout the world which are not known in the UK. Because Britain is an island nation, and the fact that quarantine laws have been so stringent until now, freedom of movement for dogs to and from Britain is not as easy as in the majority of countries.

In this book I have attempted to outline all breeds recognised by the English Kennel Club, American Kennel Club and the Federation Cynologique International (FCI), under whose rules many countries operate, and in addition I have included a few interesting breeds that are not official recognised. Because different countries organise dogs into different groups, and often call them by completely different names, it has not been easy to decide the best way of outlining them in a book of this nature. I have therefore included all breeds recognised in Britain and a few only recognised in the USA, in one section, but readers should bear in mind that the majority of these are also found elsewhere. Others have been divided primarily by country, so that if readers do not know a breed's name they might at least know its country of origin, giving them another way of locating a particular dog which interests them.

As I have already said, the naming of breeds varies enormously, so whilst the majority of alternative names have been given for each, the main breed name given is that which I believe is most easily recognisable. Indications have also been given regarding size, coat care and feeding, although these are only a very general guide. It is important to understand that the amount of coat care required varies considerably, depending on whether one keeps a dog as a pet, a working dog or as a show dog. Someone showing a Lhasa Apso in full coat needs to allocate a maximum amount of time to maintaining such a long

coat in tip-top condition, whereas if the same breed is kept purely as a pet it may be professionally trimmed two or three times each year, requiring less grooming in between these times.

As years move on, the world grows smaller and smaller, and our knowledge of dogs increases in return. There are many judges who, like myself, have the opportunity of travelling to different countries; through sharing our interests and experience in dogs, information is disseminated and slowly we have come to learn and appreciate more and more about the many species of dog which share our planet.

Writing this book has given me enormous enjoyment and I am delighted to be able to include so many photographs of excellent examples of breeds portrayed. The majority of photographs are of dogs which have won high accolades in the show world, including at Crufts, and so readers have the chance to see truly representative pictures, which I feel is very important in a book of this kind.

My especial thanks are due to the talented canine photographer Carol Ann Johnson, who provided the vast majority of the photographs. Thanks go also to Harry Baxter, Serge Sanchez of Vos Chiens, Samsung, Zena Thorn-Andrews, Meg Purnell-Carpenter, Marianne Kruger, Dr Daniel Taylor-Ide, Angela Racheal, Diane Philipson, Gaye Sansom, Alyce Ingle and all the others who have been of assistance in contributing photographs and information about of some of the breeds which are hardly yet known in Britain. I am also most grateful to the artist and dog-lover Deirdre Ashdown.

Meriel Taylor kindly assisted Carol Ann in locating less well-known breeds on the continent and Sue McCourt talked me through the coat-care procedures used in the terrier world. Yves de Clercq, Secretary General of the FCI, and Michael R.

Darwin of the Kennel Union of South Africa provided me with a huge amount of help. As usual, my sincere thanks are due to the English Kennel Club and its staff for their invaluable support, especially Brian Leonard and Gary Johnston, whose assistance is always much appreciated.

Lastly I owe very special thanks to the *Kennel Gazette* for having put forward my name as author of this book, and to Polly Willis, The Foundry's Project Editor, who listened patiently to my trials and tribulations throughout the many hours of writing and research I carried out. This book has been a pleasure to write; I hope it is now a pleasure to read.

JULIETTE CUNLIFFE

A World of Dogs

THOUSANDS OF YEARS AGO, man and dog teamed up together, each benefiting from the other's company. As the years progressed, different types of dog evolved, some to hunt with man, others to work in different ways and yet others purely as companions.

THE TASKS WHICH DOGS have performed throughout the centuries are many and varied. They have guarded man, protected his flocks, chased and retrieved game, pulled heavy burdens, sought out and saved lost souls from snowy and difficult terrain – even from the sea – the list is endless. Now, we are

Top

Dogs were working animals before they became pets. This Antwerp dogcart was photographed in 1900.

Above and Right
The relationship between man and dog is celebrated in an eighth-century manuscript and a scene on a 425 BC Greek vase.

thoroughly familiar with the important work carried out by police and sniffer dogs. Some dogs act as 'eyes' for the blind, others as 'ears' for the deaf and many help to make life a great deal easier for those who are disabled in other ways.

PEDIGREE GROUPS

PEDIGREE DOGS ARE THOSE which have been bred to conform to a Kennel Club breed standard: a written 'blue-print' for each breed recognised in a particular country. As more and more foreign dogs are introduced to Britain, additional breeds are frequently added to the Kennel Club's long list, currently numbering 189 breeds. Until the end of 1998 the various different breeds were divided into six groups, but from the beginning of 1999 they were re-organised to form a seventh group, the Pastoral, which was added to Gundog, Hound, Utility, Terrier, Toy and Working Groups.

In other countries Kennel Clubs also recognise different breeds, although in most countries the majority of breeds recognised in Britain are included in their own official breed lists too. Grouping differs from country to country. In the United States there are again seven groups: Sporting, Hound, Non Sporting, Terrier, Toy, Working and Herding; whilst the Federation Cynologique International (FCI), the World Canine Organisation, recognises 329 breeds divided into 10 different groups. In consequence, several of the breeds which belong in a certain group in one country find themselves differently grouped elsewhere.

MONGRELS AND CROSSBREEDS

OF COURSE, NOT ALL DOGS are pedigree-bred – there are also cross-breeds and mongrels. Crossbreeds are those of which the parentage is known, a term used generally when one pure-bred dog is mated to another pure breed. A mongrel usually describes a dog with at least one parent of mixed breeding, but pedigree, crossbreed or mongrel, all are dogs and all have worked their way deservedly into our affections.

IN THE BEGINNING

WHEN WE LOOK AT THE DOG which shares our fireside today, it is sometimes difficult to imagine how it has evolved over millions of years. Early mammals fed only on vegetation but in time meat eaters came about – they were able to survive by eating the vegetarians. History takes us back to mouse-sized, flesh-eating mammals called *Creodonts* which lived at the same time as dinosaurs, some 100–50 million years ago. Although climatic changes brought about the death of the dinosaurs, the *Creodonts* survived and from these developed *Miacis*, between 54 and 38 million years ago in the Eocene period. Believed to be tree and den dwellers, the *Miacidae* were small, with long backs, short legs and long tails. Several characteristics of *Miacis* have been passed down to the dogs we know today.

EARLY ANCESTORS

CATS WENT ON TO DEVELOP from *Miacis* but the next evolutionary link in the history of the dog brought *Hesperocyon*, with an inner-ear anatomy characteristic of the canine family. By now, time had moved on to 26 million years ago and by 19 million years before our time, the successful carnivore *Cynodictis* had come into being, but opinion is now changing about whether or not the modern dog developed from this or more directly from *Hesperocyon*. Either way, possibly, dog's early ancestors developed in North America, then spread from there into Eurasia.

By this time. a running animal had developed, the fifth toe of which having been shortened into what later became the dog's dew claw; a type of animals had now evolved that had dog-like feet and had also increased in size.

THE *CANIDAE* FAMILY

AROUND 12 MILLION years ago, during the *Miocene* period, came *Tomarctus*, a wolf-like creature which hunted in packs and had the beginnings of a modern dog's tooth anatomy, so that by the end of the *Pliocene* period, around two million years ago, the foundation stock for all modern carnivores had evolved and with it the family of *Canidae* from which came jackals, foxes, hyenas, wolves and the dog.

Over recent decades, various theories have been put forward regarding the precise evolution of the dog and much valid debate has ensued. Doubtless, with the passage of time, new discoveries will be made, leading to further theories being put forward. Meanwhile, science and history have combined, allowing us to look back in time and to see the development of that remarkable animal we know and love as the dog.

Top
A dog is known as a mongrel if it has one mixed-breed parent.

Left
The modern dog was well established by the time of this Egyptian relief from 3,500 BC.

Above
This mosaic from Pompei shows that the dog had become a domestic pet by then.

The Anatomy of Dogs

A DOG'S SKELETON IS PERHAPS BEST described as a framework for the body, but whilst the bones are alike in terms of the general shape and number, there are variations which cause the differences in construction and function from breed to breed. Of course, the skeleton of a long, low-legged breed such as the Dachshund is markedly different from that of a Deerhound. Both are hounds, but they have very different functions and so need to be appropriately constructed to suit their breed requirements.

THE SKELETON

HOWEVER LARGE or small a breed of dog, all have an equal number of bones making up the skeletal structure, with the exception of the bones in the tail. It is the length, thickness, quality and strength of bones which causes breeds to differ, added to which deviations in bone structure can cause dogs within individual breeds to look or to function slightly differently.

Surrounding the brain is the skull with deep pockets as protection for eyes and ears, but skulls vary considerably in shape, again according to the breed.

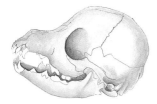

Above
From the top; the skull of a collie, a bulldog and a terrier.

THIRTEEN RIBS

LONG RIBS FORM a protective cage around heart, lungs and liver and in a well-constructed dog these need therefore to extend well back along the body. There are nine ribs connected to the sternum by cartilage, three pairs of asternal ribs which join each other at the base, and one pair of floating ribs. Contrary to popular belief, all dogs have these thirteenth, floating ribs which are the shortest of

all and remain unattached below. In some dogs, the ends of those ribs is visible, in many it is not.

The neck is fitted to the head by a ball and socket joint and the vertebrae extend right along the back to the tip of the tail, but according to the breed there can be between three and 26 vertebrae in the tail itself.

CONSTRUCTION OF THE SKELETON

PERHAPS SURPRISINGLY, the shoulder blades are not attached to the rest of the skeleton but this is an advantage as it allows for greater flexibility for movement, especially when running. This is especially useful for racing dogs such as the Greyhound. Below the shoulder blade is the humerus or 'upper arm' which has a knob at its head, preventing the complete

DOG FACT:
The skeleton of dog and man are remarkably similar, although man's posture is upright. However, a dog has no collar bone.

straightening of the shoulder joint, thereby limiting the forward reach of the front leg. At the hip, the femur should fit neatly into the pelvis by a ball and socket joint.

Elastic tendons, fibrous ligaments and powerful muscles hold the skeleton together; with the joints, each surrounded by a capsule filled with lubricating fluid, acting as shock absorbers.

MOVEMENT

TO ENABLE A DOG TO MOVE in the first place, the brain has to send messages down the spinal cord. These subconscious messages then travel out through peripheral nerves to the various muscles, some instructed to contract, others to relax. Involuntary movements, such as the twitching made by a dog whilst it is sleeping, that makes it look as though it is running, are controlled by the autonomic nervous system, another part of the peripheral nervous system.

Damage to the spine or peripheral nerves results in the inability of muscles to receive and send messages efficiently, and spastic movement usually indicates damage either to the spinal cord or the brain itself. Muscles can become rigid if blood supply is lost, or they can shrink through lack of use or because there has been damage to the nerve supply. All these factors can be reasons for lack of co-ordination, partial or even complete paralysis.

REGULAR EXERCISE

EXERCISE AS A MATTER of routine is important for ease of movement. Equally, over-feeding, especially if coupled with under-exercise, results in restricted movement at an early age. In a balanced gait there is complete synchronisation between two halves of the body, be it that those two halves are assessed in profile, or from front or rear. The hindquarters provide the propelling or driving force while the forequarters, although they provide support and act as a stabiliser, play a smaller part in the actual propulsion. Of course, to move correctly a dog has to be soundly constructed, but different breeds, by their design, move in differing ways.

Although there are some intermediate types of movement, the main gaits are the walk, trot, canter and gallop. A gallop often used by sight hounds amongst others, is the double suspension gallop, a gait in which there are two distinct periods of suspension during the sequence of movement, giving an increase in speed over the normal gallop. It is possible to observe all times when all four legs extended at the same time, and then all legs contracted together.

Some gaits are specific to certain breeds. The amble is one in which front and hind legs on the same side move together as a pair, used sometimes when a dog is tired, but seen quite frequently in the Old English Sheepdog when moving at slow speed. The hackney gait, with an exaggerated lift of the front pasterns and feet, is correctly seen in the Miniature Pinscher but is a common fault in the movement of most other breeds.

Left and Below
The hindquarters of this Basset Hound and Bulldog are clearly providing the propelling force while the forequarters provide stability. Most breeds have a characteristic gait, which stems from the construction of the skeleton.

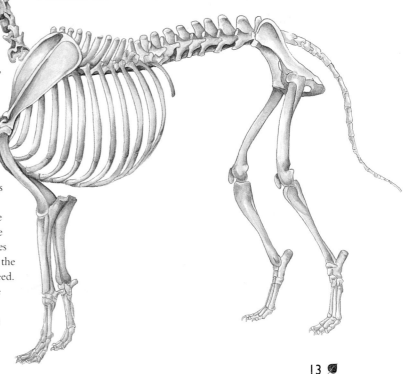

Teeth and Nails

incisors in both the upper and lower jaws. Located behind them are premolars, designed for cutting and shearing. The teeth at the very back of the jaw are molars, these have more flattened surfaces, used for grinding and chewing.

Between the canines are the small incisors, usually six in number in the upper and lower jaws. These are used to nibble meat from bones and also to groom the coat and skin.

There are 42 teeth in total, two more in the lower jaw than the upper because of an additional pair of pre-molars. Roots on a dog's teeth are extremely long.

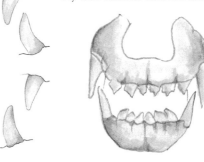

NAILS

NAILS ARE ACTUALLY A MODIFIED skin structure that grow at a constant rate and cannot ever be retracted and extended at will. How frequently or infrequently nails need to be clipped depends largely on the texture of ground on which a dog spends most time. A dog living in the home on carpet is likely to need much more attention to its nails than one spending many hours each day on a concrete run. The forefeet

Right
In order: correct incisor bite, a level bite, an over-shot mouth and an under-shot mouth.

Above Right
Front view of puppy's mouth at three months.

Right and Below
Side view showing teeth and roots.

Far Right Below
Front view of adult dog's mouth.

TEETH

BECAUSE DOGS ARE CARNIVORES their mouths and teeth are constructed to allow them to eat meat. In the wild, dogs scavenge and sometimes kill so they need long canine teeth with which they can stab, enabling them also to catch and hold their prey when necessary – these are the four very large teeth, one placed on either side of the

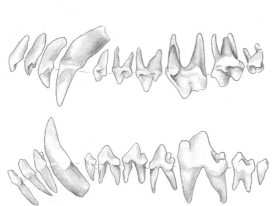

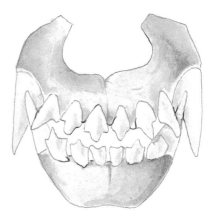

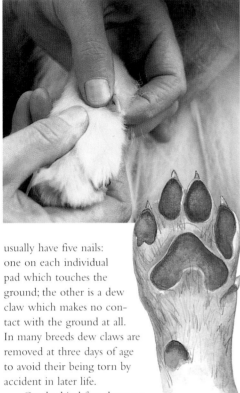

usually have five nails:
one on each individual
pad which touches the
ground; the other is a dew
claw which makes no con-
tact with the ground at all.
In many breeds dew claws are
removed at three days of age
to avoid their being torn by
accident in later life.

On the hind feet there are
often only four nails, but some-
times five if hind dew claws exist. There are exceptions to the general rule as some breeds have double dew claws and one breed, the Norwegian
Lundehund, even has an extra toe.

Because of selective breeding, some dogs have
particularly long coats, and hair may grow inside
the ear and between the pads of the feet. This
would not have happened to dogs in the wild, so
attention needs to be paid to these areas and excess
hair removed if necessary so as to avoid ear infections building up and
painful tight knots of coat
forming between the pads.

SKIN AND COAT

DIFFERENT AREAS of a dog's
skin vary to suit specific
purposes. The pads of the
feet are thick and durable, a
necessity in order to bear
weight and because they
come into contact with
rough ground. Ears are
made up of much thinner

skin for they are used for social signalling and so
have to be sufficiently flexible to be moved about
at will. Dogs' anal glands are also made of skin, and
this needs to be flexible enough when passing
stools to allow secretion of a substance which plays
an important role in territorial marking.

In general the surface of skin – the epidermis
– is not very strong; however, it continually lays
down new cells allowing it to serve as a protective
layer. Beneath is the dermis which is much
stronger, elastic and flexible.

HAIR GROWTH

THE WAY IN WHICH a dog's hair grows depends
upon its breed, but whatever it actually looks like,
it grows in cycles. Following a growth stage it goes
through a transitional period and then rests. When
a dog's coat sheds, more hair is then ready to
replace it. The cycles of growth are influenced by
outside factors. Temperature plays a part and this is
not just seasonal temperature but also temperature
within the home, something which is now more
likely to remain fairly constant in centrally heated
homes. In a natural environment, dogs typically
shed hair in spring and autumn.

Other factors which affect the
cycle of coat growth are the
increase and decrease in daylight
hours and also hormones,
female ones tending to decrease
hair density and males ones
usually increasing it. This is the
reason why many bitches which
have been spayed (neutered) develop a more abundant coat and
conversely bitches are frequently
said to 'drop coat' during or
following a season.

Sight, Sound and Smell

SIGHT

ALL DOGS ARE BORN BLIND and deaf but both ears and eyes begin to open between roughly the ninth and fourteenth days. Although head shapes vary considerably, eyes are always relatively widely spaced, providing good lateral vision, enabling the dog to see even slight movement through the corner of the eyes, much more easily than can a human. Conversely, dogs cannot adjust their focal length as easily as humans.

Dogs' eyes are flatter than those of humans, and more sensitive to light and movement. Via the optic nerve the retina sends information to the brain and, hidden by the lower lid, is the nictitating membrane or 'third eyelid' which sweeps across the eye to keep it clean. To keep the eye moist, tears produced by the lachrymal glands and their ducts flow into the nasal cavity.

Above

Widely spaced eyes give dogs better lateral vision than humans, but the focal length of dogs does not adjust as easily.

DOG FACT:
A dominant dog tries to make itself look as bulky as possible with hackles raised and head and tail

Bottom and Right
Bassets' long ears help them to pick up scents from the ground, while the flexible ears of a Whippet help them hear.

SOUND

DOGS' EARS are especially sensitive to sound, capable of hearing sound four times further away than a human can. They are also able to locate the source of sound incredibly quickly, at six-hundredths of a second. Sound is captured by the outer ear and funnelled down via the ear canal into the ear drum where vibrations stimulate the middle ear to amplify and transmit sound. Part of the inner ear then converts sound into signals which are sent to the brain.

The ears of dogs are incredibly varied in shape, largely dependent upon function, and all are very mobile with the ability to scan for sound. One often sees a breed such as a Whippet moving the ears into the most extraordinary positions in an attempt to hear even better. Often a long ear gives protection and is found especially on dogs which go to ground, while long ears can also sweep up scent, helping in scent detection.

SCENT

IN ANY BREED, smell is a dog's most advanced sense, and there is even a sex-scenting organ in the roof of the mouth transmitting information to that part of the brain which relates to emotional behaviour. Helped by moisture on the nose, scent is captured on this major organ of smell, passing then to the nasal membranes, which detect even the smallest scent.

Along the nasal membrane are sensory cells, which convert the scent to chemical messages, interpreted within the brain. To bring the dog's acute sense of smell into perspective, whilst a human has around five million scent receptors in the nasal folds, a dog has about 200 million.

BODY LANGUAGE

ALTHOUGH dogs utter sounds they do not have the speech ability of humans and so, coupled with the noises they make such as barking, growling and whining, they use body language to better convey their mood and feelings.

Much of their body language is learned from the dam, and the youngsters practise on their siblings from a very early age. Puppy play looks comical and can sometimes appear frighteningly over-boisterous but at this time important lessons are being learned and put into use. Even in a young litter of puppies a careful observer can

distinguish which members are dominant and which more submissive. Usually this strength of character will continue into adulthood, so a that a dominant dog will need more human control and a less confident one more encouragement.

INSTINCTIVE BODY LANGUAGE

A PUPPY JUMPING UP TO LICK a mother's mouth is prompting the dam to regurgitate what she has

eaten to produce food, a natural instinct in the wild and one which is carried through to adulthood in dogs' behaviour with humans.

Puppies and older dogs show power by stalking others, the hindquarters slightly raised, the ears erect. They stare at

another dog or stand over the more submissive individual, possibly even baring the teeth. The less dominant of the two will try to avoid eye contact, may press the tail between the legs and flatten the ears. This dog will probably take up the posture of lying on one side, ears held back and lips retracted to what is often termed a 'smile'. Lying on the side, or even the back, exposes the stomach and genitals, again indicating submission. A puppy may even urinate slightly in the process. Of course, there are many intermediate stages of communication, each important in its own way.

Those who keep more than one dog will usually know which is the pack leader, but the leader may change, often as a dominant dog grows old or a strong puppy matures. For this reason, it is always important for the owner to keep control of the situation so that no unpleasant fights ensue. In a successful canine household, the human should always be the supremely dominant party for only if this is the case will a dog respect the owner and abide by house rules.

Left
The body language of this puppy clearly shows submission when faced with an aggressive cat.

Bottom
An adult Griffon Bruxellois dominates a tiny Bulldog puppy – the situations may be reversed when the puppy is fully grown.

DOG FACT:
Because of their incredibly fine sense of smell, most dogs can detect one part of urine in 60 million parts of water.

A Dog's Life

no stipulation as to the age at which males are used for breeding purposes but they can be sexually active from around six months, so again care is needed. Males are sexually mature well into old age and in some breeds, dogs of 11, 12 and even more perform successful matings.

GESTATION PERIOD

AN AVERAGE GESTATION period is 63 days, but bitches can whelp as much as a week early or late without experiencing any problems, although veterinary advice is of course needed at this time. At whelping, a bitch goes through the first and second stages of labour, at which time complications may arise and in certain cases assistance or even a caesarean operation might be necessary. Under normal circumstances, puppies are fed totally by their dam for the first three or four weeks, following which they begin weaning. By the time they are six or seven weeks old they are no longer reliant on their dam for food, although they will willingly still suckle from her if given the opportunity.

Puppies should never be allowed to leave their dam and siblings before the age of eight weeks – 10 weeks is more usual.

A bitch usually first comes into season between six and nine months, but it can be earlier

Above and Right
Puppies are kept with their dam and siblings until 8–10 weeks.

Bottom
Embryonic puppies in the womb.

BREEDING AGE

IN BRITAIN, the Kennel Club does not normally allow the registration of any puppies born to bitches under the age of 18 months, nor to bitches over eight years. However they are certainly capable of producing pups outside these limits so care must be taken that males do not come into contact with bitches in season (on heat). The Kennel Club makes

and is frequently later. After the first couple of seasons, she usually settles down into a regular cycle of twice a year or slightly less frequently, but there are dogs, especially in certain breeds, which come on heat only once a year.

Some breeds mature later than others and have different life spans, so reach their 'prime of life' at different times, too. As a general rule, smaller breeds tend to live longer than very large ones. Some of the giant breeds, such as Great Danes or Mastiffs, may live only until the age of seven or eight, whereas a Lhasa Apso or Shih Tzu, for example, has an average life span of 12–15 years, many live even longer.

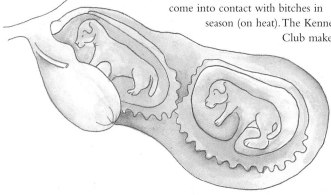

INSTINCT AND LEARNING

THE DOG'S CLOSEST ANCESTOR is the wolf, but now, many generations on, different breeds of dog have developed, each with their own particular skill. Different senses are more highly developed in some breeds than others, according to the dog's main function. In the wild, dogs are pack animals and some domestic dogs have retained a greater pack instinct than others.

TRAINING DOGS

ALTHOUGH MAN HAS DEVELOPED breeds in different ways in order to best meet his own needs, much of the behaviour we see in dogs has become instinctive over a very long period involving many generations. Training is also important, but usually training and inherited traits go hand in hand. A dog which has an instinct to herd sheep needs to be trained how best to do the work because an untrained dog can all too easily create havoc by using inborn skills in which the dog sees fit, but not the owner. One which has an instinct to work well with the nose again needs assistance in learning exactly what to do. Some dogs are specialised at scenting out truffles, others at following the scent of animals or even criminals, or perhaps finding those who have become lost in the snow. Each breed has its own special talent, this inborn talent having, to a large extent, been developed through selective breeding by man.

THE RETRIEVING INSTINCT

SOME OF THE GUNDOG breeds and the Newfoundland are instinctively good swimmers and even without any special training will retrieve things from water. However, such dogs need to be taught what needs to be retrieved or rescued and what does not: for large dogs have been known to 'rescue' people swimming happily and safely!

Dogs have long been used to guard people, their homes and belongings. In Tibet, for example, the country's Mastiff guards not only domestic animals but also women and children whilst the menfolk are away from home. Inside monasteries, other, smaller dogs instinctively give a warning bark to the monks to let them know that visitors or intruders have passed the Tibetan Mastiffs chained outside.

Dogs have been designed for many specialised purposes such as pulling heavy carts or giving chase to game. Today many of dogs' skills, whether instinctive, bred or taught, are put to use in a variety of ways to fit in with modern life.

Left
The dog's hunting instinct was put to good use by man from earliest times.

Bottom
Training and inherited traits play equal roles in developing the behaviour of a breed. The natural instincts of pointers and sheep-dogs, for example, have to be controlled to suit their owners.

DOG FACT:
If a bitch produces a very large litter, or if she cannot supply sufficient of her own milk, supplementary hand feeding is necessary.

Coat Types

JUST AS THE STRUCTURE and outline of dogs varies, so does the coat, and in many cases a coat is a dog's crowning glory. A well groomed coat in good condition is not only a pleasure to look at – it also makes a dog feel more comfortable and less prone to skin complaints and external parasites.

The outercoat is generally longer and of a harder or harsher texture but there are numerous variations on this theme – breeds such as the long-coated Lhasa Apso, the shaggy-coated Old English Sheepdog, the wiry-coated Welsh Terrier and the Hungarian Puli with its corded coat are all breeds with double coats.

SINGLE COATS

BREEDS SUCH AS THE ITALIAN Greyhound and Maltese which have no undercoat are termed single-coated. So it is not only smooth-coated breeds which have no undercoat.

COAT VARIATIONS

Top
The little Italian Greyhound has a single coat.

Centre
Many terriers, including the Cairn, have broken coats.

Bottom
The Hungarian Puli has a corded coat that is difficult to maintain.

AN INTERESTING ASPECT of coats is that they vary so much and what is a correct coat colour or texture in one breed may be totally unacceptable in another. The reason behind this usually lies in the function of the breed, but fashion has also played an important part.

DOUBLE COATS

MANY BREEDS OF DOG ACTUALLY have two coats, an outercoat and an undercoat. This is generally termed a double coat but can also be correctly termed a two-ply coat. The undercoat is usually short, soft and dense, or moderately so. It acts as a protective layer against water and the elements while also being a support for the outercoat. Some dogs, particularly those which come from cold climates, do not shed their coats so the undercoat gets thick and matted if it is not regularly groomed out.

COAT TEXTURES

CRINKLY, HARSH and wiry coats are described as 'broken', a term applied to many dogs in the Terrier Group. In texture it rather resembles coconut matting but when reaching its maximum length it softens and needs to be removed, preferably by hand-stripping. When such coats have reached their maximum length, the outer coat is said to have 'blown', meaning that it has softened. In order to allow the new, harsh coat to grow in, the old coat needs to be removed at this point, often by hand-plucking.

Some coats are described as bear-like, meaning that they consist of a harsh outer jacket, usually 7.5–15 cm (3–6 in) in length, with a short, woolly undercoat which is 2.5–5 cm (1–2 in) long. Other coats may have a dense mane, sometimes called a shawl, of what is usually fairly coarse hair around the shoulder. This is often more prominent in dogs than in bitches.

Curly coats are typical of breeds such as the Curly-coated Retriever and the Irish Water Spaniel. In such breeds the curly coat is created by a mass of thick, tight curls which rather resemble astrakhan. Because of this the coat traps air and, in doing so, protects the dog against both water and cold.

Breeds with stand-off coats have a long, heavy, harsh jacket comprised of hair which stands out from the skin, rather than lying flat against it. In most cases such a coat is supported by a dense undercoat of shorter, soft hair. Breeds with coats of this type include the Keeshond and Pomeranian. Some breeds have long coats, others are called smooth-coated and both are fairly self-explanatory. An Afghan Hound is obviously a long-coated breed, whilst dogs like the Manchester Terrier and the Bull Terrier have smooth coats. The term 'taut coat' actually applies to a coat on a sleek, tightly

natural intertwining of both the top coat and the undercoat. These cords can vary in width from quite narrow to broad, but they should always be distinct from one another and should never be matted or joined. It is important to realise that breeds with corded coats are in need of constant attention so that the coat remain corded and do not become tangled or matted.

Other variations include the linty, soft, downy coat typical of the Bedlington Terrier, and the Bergamasco's extraordinary long, abundant coat, which tends to form into strands or loose mats. The crisp coat of the Dandie Dinmont Terrier is called a 'pily' coat. It comprises a dense, harsh outercoat and a soft, very close innercoat which is almost fur-like. Certain breeds have varied coat textures, creating different types within the breed, as seen in the Dachshund, a breed with three coat types.

Left
The Boxer has a smooth coat.

Far Left
A Shar Pei has a bristly, harsh coat.

Centre Left
The Curly-coated Retriever has a coat of tight curls.

Below
The Dandie Dinmont Terrier has a 'pily' coat.

stretched skin, which has absolutely no wrinkles, folds or creases.

There are rather special coats on some breeds, such as that of the Shar Pei, in which the short, bristly coat should be harsh to the touch. Many might say a longer coat looks more glamorous, but a coat of the correct texture is necessary to maintain true breed type. Other breeds need a longer 'stand-off' coat, a heavy, harsh jacket which stands out from the body as opposed to lying flat against the skin.

Corded coats such as those found on the Hungarian Puli and Komondor are created by the

Above
A English Toy Terrier has a short coat.

Left
The Shetland Sheepdog has a long, fairly coarse coat.

Colours and Markings

ONE OF THE CONFUSING aspects of colour is that a specific word used to describe colour in one breed may describe a subtly different colour in another. Red and gold are prime examples, as both can range through various different hues. Grey is another colour which varies widely, ranging from light silver-grey to dark grizzle.

UNDERSTANDING COLOURING

TO EXACERBATE the problems of defining colour, some breeds change colour with age. The Kerry Blue Terrier does not acquire its typical blue colour until maturing from puppyhood, while in a number of breeds black dogs turn grey with age. Bitches may change colour due to hormonal change within the course of a year. Some breeds have coats in a wide variety of colours, but if their breed standard requires nose pigment to be black, effectively liver and chocolate coats cannot be accepted. This is because the dogs' genetic make-up means that pigment will be of a corresponding colour and not black.

Right
The Kerry Blue Terrier does not gain its distinctive colour until maturity,

Then there are colour combinations such as black and tan, liver and white or tri-colours which are black, tan and white. A parti-coloured dog is one which has white with another colour broken up in fairly equal proportions, whilst pinto, also termed piebald, indicates irregular black patches superimposed on a white background.

MERLING

MERLING, AS SEEN IN THE SHETLAND Sheepdog, is due to a dominant colour pattern expressed as irregular dark blotches against a lighter background, both being of the same general basic pigment. The term 'merling' is usually applied to breeds with long coats but there are some short-coated breeds so coloured. One such is the Smooth Collie, another the Cardigan Corgi. The term 'dapple' is often used as an alternative. Perhaps blue merle is the colour one most associates with this particular colour type, but there can also be other variations such as liver merle or red merle.

TICKING

TICKING IS A TERM OFTEN used in relation to Gundog and Hound breeds. It means that very small areas of hair are of a different colour to the basic ground colour. Ticking is usually distributed throughout the coat and often indicates dark spots on a lighter ground. Ticking, sometimes called ticks, can also be referred to as flecks or speckles.

SABLE

SABLE IS A SPECIFIC COAT colour pattern which is produced by black-tipped hairs overlaid on a differently coloured background. Sables can be of various colours, such as grey-sable, silver-sable, gold-sable and so on. The undercoat is usually light in colour and dogs with sable coats frequently also have dark masks.

BRINDLE

A BRINDLE-COLOURED COAT is one in which a subtle striped effect is produced by black or dark hairs against a background of lighter coloured hair.

SADDLE MARKINGS AND BLANKETS

BOTH SADDLE MARKINGS and blankets are areas of usually dark or black coat over the region of the back, but blankets are marking that extend further down the flank of the dog than

do saddles. These terms are frequently used in relation to hound breeds.

MASK

A MASK IS USUALLY DARK HAIR on the head, forming a pattern which is like a mask. Often, as for example in the Boxer and Great Dane, it affects only the region of the muzzle, but in other breeds it can be a mask around the eyes and on the top part of the head, as can often be seen in the Alaskan Malamute. Apart from colour, the term 'mask' is also sometimes used when the length of coat varies, being shorter on the head than on the rest of the body.

PIPS

PIPS ARE SPOTS ABOVE the eyes of most breeds which are black and tan in colour. This term is not used universally for all breeds but such markings can be seen typically in the Dobermann, Rottweiler and Gordon Setter. In black and tan Basenjis these marks are frequently known as 'melon pips'.

PENCILLINGS

PENCILLING IS THE TERM usually used to describe the black markings which run along the top of each toe, as in the English Toy Terrier.

STOCKINGS AND SOCKS

THE TERM, 'STOCKINGS' IS used for areas of usually white coat covering most of the leg and creating a striking contrast from the main coat colour. When the colour only covers the feet or

reaches up the pastern no further than the wrist in front and/or behind hocks, it is referred to as the 'socks'.

SPLASHED

A SPLASHED COAT is one which has irregular markings, usually white ones, on a more deeply coloured background. Often splashing is an undesirable type of coat marking, but not in all breeds.

SPECTACLES

THE CIRCULAR, LIGHT-COLOURED AREAS around each eye, typically in the Keeshond breed, are usually called spectacles.

LOZENGE MARK OR SPOT

THE TERMS 'LOZENGE MARK' or 'spot', which can sometimes also be known as the 'kissing spot', are used for single marks positioned in the centre of the skull, which is highly typical of the Blenheim-coloured Cavalier King Charles Spaniel. Although usually relating to marks on the head, these lozenges or spots can also be found on other parts of the dog's body, such as the chest.

Left
A gold-sable Lhasa Apso puppy poses proudly.

Centre
A Boxer puppy has a dark mask round its muzzle and eyes.

Bottom
Shetland Sheepdogs show a variety of different shades of merling.

Canine Terminology

ONE OF THE DIFFICULT THINGS about trying to get to grips with canine terminology is that very frequently the same expression is used to mean different things. Sometimes this is because a word or expression is used in a slightly different context from breed to breed, but very regularly it is because it has been misconstrued at some time in the past and so the completely wrong term has been copied, at least verbally, and worse still sometimes in writing. All this leads to great confusion.

UNDERSTANDING TERMINOLOGY

Right
A Maltese show dog should have a black nose.

IN THE FOLLOWING PAGES readers will find some of the terms in frequent use, although many have been omitted, primarily because they are terms used when describing a fault and this book is intended to give an overall impression of what good dogs are like.

Right
The Tibetan Spaniel clearly illustrates the bowed front or the ten to two position.

However, many of the expressions you will find outlined constitute a fault in some breeds but are perfectly acceptable in others. To cite an example, a Rottweiler with bowed front legs would look strange indeed, although slightly bowed legs are required of, among others, the Tibetan Spaniel. Similarly Dachshunds and Basset Hounds may have front feet which point straight ahead, but it is also acceptable for them to turn out very slightly, the reason for this acceptance being because of their

Right
This Wire Fox Terrier clearly shows the brick-shaped head.

construction. On the other hand feet which are turned out, often called an 'east west front' or 'ten to two' is a bad fault in the majority of breeds.

So much changes from breed to breed, after all that is why each breed has its own distinct stamp, but additionally structure and things such as pigment can be different within a breed. In the latter cases pigment often goes hand in hand with coat colour, and likewise eye colour is often affected in the same way. A Weimeraner would look awfully strange with a black nose, and yet if a Maltese did not have a black pigmented nose it would be severely penalised in the show ring. To further complicate matters, some breeds should ideally have black noses but in lighter coat colours within the same breed a correspondingly lighter coloured nose is acceptable.

PIGMENT

WHERE PIGMENT is concerned the possible complications and variations do not end there. Some dogs' nose pigment is affected by the weather or by hormonal activity. What is commonly known as a 'winter nose', or a 'snow nose' in some breeds, is when pigment reduces to a much paler shade, usually in winter, but resumes its normal dark colour when the weather warms up again.

HEAD SHAPE

THE TERM 'BRICK-SHAPED HEAD' would be very detrimental if one described an Afghan Hound as having one, but in some breeds, such as the Wire Fox Terrier, this is exactly what is required of the head and trimming even helps to further enhance this appearance.

EYE SHAPE

EYES ARE ANOTHER rather confusing part of a dog's anatomy where descriptive terms are concerned. In certain breeds 'almond eye' has been altered to 'oval eye' so as not to encourage too small an eye which may have been leading to problems in the breed. There are breeds which are known to have problems with their eyes, caused in many cases by the excess quantity of skin or hair around the eye. In such cases, as in that of the Shar Pei, inclusions have been made in the Kennel Club's breed standard to prevent this, the clause in this particular standard saying: 'Function of eyeball or lid in no way disturbed by surrounding skin, folds or hair'. This is a practical and sensible inclusion and one can only hope that breeders abide by such clauses when they have been written into a standard with sound reason.

Left
Shar Peis have excess skin around the face.

TAILS

TAILS OF COURSE are often held differently when a dog is standing than when on the move and when judging breeds it is important to know how high a tail may be carried correctly when moving. Also, when standing there a few breeds where the tail may be held either up or down, neither of which is to be penalised.

EAR SHAPE

WHERE EARS ARE CONCERNED the descriptions are many and varied, with sometimes more than one description relating to a single breed. Some ears are held differently when a dog is alert as most dogs move their ears to a greater or lesser extent when wishing to hear more accurately. Even the development of teeth can affect ear carriage, so in some breeds this is taken into consideration when

assessing youngsters. Certainly Whippets are capable of doing most extraordinary things with their ears until they have reached maturity.

Lastly, one has to consider that breed standards differ sometimes from country to country, sometimes just a little, but that small difference can be enough to lay emphasis on a certain aspect of a dog so that a breed can vary slightly in different countries as one travels around the world.

Far Left
A Beagle with a flagpole tail.

Below
A Whippet puppy with drooping ears.

Back and Underline

LEVEL BACK

IN A DOG with a level back, technically the height at the withers is identical to that of the height at the loins.

LONG BACK

A LONG-BACKED breed is one in which the distance from withers to rump is appreciably longer than the height of the dog at the withers, as in the Dachshund or Corgi breeds.

ROACH BACK

IN THE VAST MAJORITY of breeds, a roach back is considered a fault but some breeds actually require a slight arch over the loin, which some consider a slightly roached appearance. It is therefore important to ascertain whether such an arch is correct, or the result of faulty construction.

SLOPING BACK

A DOG WITH A SLOPING BACK is generally higher at the withers than at the loins because the back slopes downwards toward the rear, as in the German Shepherd Dog. However, a sloping back

BACK: ARCHED OVER THE LOINS

THE TERM 'arched over the loins' refers generally to a level back which arches to a greater or lesser extent over the loin area, this arch usually being due to muscle development, hence denoting strength in this area. The Rhodesian Ridgeback and Dachshunds are two examples of breeds which require this arch.

Top Right
This German Shepherd Dog shows a sloping back that is higher at the withers.

Above
Although smaller than the Ridgeback, the Miniature Wire-haired Dachshund also is 'arched over the loins'.

Right
The Rhodesian Ridgeback has strong, muscular loins typical of dogs that are 'arched over the loins'.

can, technically, also be one which slopes in the opposite direction, being higher at the loins than at the withers. In a few breeds this is correct, as in the Old English Sheepdog and the Chesapeake Bay Retriever.

STRAIGHT BACK

A STRAIGHT BACK need not necessarily be a level back; it is one which runs in a straight line and in which there is no dip or arch at any point between the withers and loin. Such a back can be found in the English Toy Terrier.

WHEEL BACK

A WHEEL BACK is an exaggerated form of roach back, and is one which forms a continuous arch from withers to tail. The Borzoi and Bedlington Terrier are both typical examples of breeds with this shape of back.

Left
The English Toy Terrier has an archetypal straight back.

Centre and Centre Left
Both the Borzoi and the Bedlington Terrier have the arched-shaped wheel back.

Bottom
The Whippet illustrates the exaggerated tuck-up with its accentuated chest.

UNDERLINE: TUCK-UP

TUCK-UP, OR CUT-UP as it is sometimes called, is the shape that is produced by the underline of the abdomen as it sweeps up to the region of the hind-quarters. In some breeds this is highly exaggerated, such as in the Whippet, and it is further accentuated when the chest is deep. In other breeds tuck-up can be only moderate, or barely noticeable.

Ear Shape and Set

the tips of the ears are clearly rounded, rather than forming a point.

BAT EARS

THE TERM 'BAT EARS' as used in Europe, has a similar meaning to tulip ears, being fully erect, wide and forward facing. They are broad at the base, set fairly wide and rounded at the tips, as in a Cardigan Welsh Corgi.

BUTTON EARS

BUTTON EARS are semi-erect, the lower portion standing upright and the upper section dropped downward or folded down in a forwards direction so as to obscure or partially obscure the orifice to the ear canal.

BLUNT-TIPPED EARS

BLUNT-TIPPED EARS, also described as round-tipped ears, can be seen in breeds such as the French Bulldog and Chow Chow. In these

CANDLE-FLAME EARS

THE DESCRIPTION, 'candle-flame ears' is specific to the ears of the English Toy Terrier.

Top Far Right
The Shetland Sheepdog has keenly cocked ears.

Top Centre
The Border Terrier has button ears.

Top Left
The Welsh Corgi has bat ears.

Far Right
The Bedlington Terrier has filbert-shaped ears.

Centre Right
The Skye Terrier can have dropped or pricked ears.

Centre Left
The English Toy Terrier has candle-flame ears.

Above Right
Blunt-tipped ears are seen in the French Bulldog.

COCKED EARS

COCKED EARS can also be called semi-drop, semi-prick or tipped ears. In these the tip is bent just slightly forwards, not so much as in button ears. Shetland Sheepdogs' ears are typical of this type.

CROPPED EARS

CROPPED or crop ears are made to stand erect as a result of surgical removal of a section of

the ear lobe, a practice forbidden in Britain and in a few other countries. Such ears can give a quite different expression to the head and in some countries ears are cropped to enhance the imposing appearance of the heavier breeds.

DROP EARS

THE TERM drop ears can be expressed in many different ways: as dropped, full drop, folded, pendant or pendulous ears. They are all ears which hang down from their junction with the side of the head. The Skye Terrier is a breed in which ears may be dropped or pricked.

PRICK EARS

ALSO CALLED erect, upright or pricked ears, prick ears are those which are standing up stiffly, and can be seen in German Shepherd

Dogs, the Siberian Husky and also the Pomeranian. Dogs with prick ears may, however, have either rounded or pointed tips to the ears, according to their individual breed.

FILBERT-SHAPED EARS

THIS IS A particularly unusual shape of ear; the term is used most often to describe the ears of the Bedlington Terrier and the term is taken from the shape of a hazel nut or filbert.

FLYING EARS

FLYING EARS ARE those which stick out or fly away from the sides of the head. In many breeds this is a fault and can be in just one or in both ears. However, in gazehounds this is considered to be perfectly acceptable for, when something catches their

attention, they lift their ears to hear sounds better. Flying ears, to a greater or lesser degree, can also be temporary; they are often caused by teething.

FOLDED EARS

EARS WHICH ARE folded are pendant ears, but the lobes of the ears hang in downward folds rather than hanging flat. Such ears are seen typically in the Bloodhound and the Field Spaniel.

HEART-SHAPED EARS

ALTHOUGH THE heart-shape of the dog's ear cannot really be seen due to the coat which covers the ear, it can be felt. Breeds such as Portuguese Water Dogs and Pekingese have ears shaped like this.

HIGH-SET EARS

HIGH-SET EARS are those which start from relatively near to the top of the skull, certainly higher than the level of the eye. Such an ear set is associated with quite a number

of different types of ear formation.

HOODED EARS

HOODED EARS ARE relatively small,

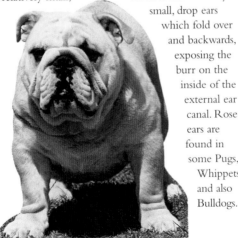

with both edges of the ear curving forward, as in the Basenji.

LOBE-SHAPED EARS

LOBE-SHAPED OR lobular ears describes the shape of ear required by breeds such as English Springer, Irish Water and Cocker Spaniels. Again this can be felt but not so easily seen due to the ear furnishings (fur).

LOW-SET EARS

THE OPPOSITE of high-set ears, these are ears which begin from a reasonably low position on the skull, as in the Bloodhound.

ROLLED EARS

ROLLED EARS ARE long, pendant and folded, associated with hound breeds; the lower tip and edge of the ear are curled inwards.

ROSE EARS

ROSE EARS ARE fairly small, drop ears which fold over and backwards, exposing the burr on the inside of the external ear canal. Rose ears are found in some Pugs, Whippets and also Bulldogs.

TRIANGULAR EARS

TRIANGULAR EARS are those in which the three sides form an equilateral triangle. They may be pricked or dropped. Breed examples are the

Siberian Husky, the Norwegian Buhund and the Pyrenean Mountain Dog.

TULIP EARS

TULIP EARS are often described differently in different countries. In Britain, they are generally rose or semi-drop ears which, for some reason, are erect and as such are faulty. However, in some countries 'tulip ears' is terminology used to describe ears which are stiffly erect, with edges curved slightly forward, as in the French Bulldog.

V-SHAPED EARS

V-SHAPED EARS are triangular and are usually dropped, though not always. There is good length from tip to base, as with the ears of the Bullmastiff or Hungarian Vizsla.

Left
The Siberian Husky has triangular ears.

Centre Far Left
The Bloodhound illustrates a breed with folded ears.

Centre Left
The ears of the Basenji curve forwards, giving them a hooded appearance.

Below Left and Bottom
This Bulldog has rose ears which fold over and backwards. The larger ears of the Hungarian Vizsla are V-shaped.

Eyes and Expression

Top Right
A Gordon Setter has pips above its eyes.

Right
The haw is a thin fold of skin below the eye, as visible in the bloodhound.

Centre Right
The Keeshond's unusual coat markings around the eyes are called spectacles.

Centre Far Right
The Tibetan Mastiff is said to have a propensity for foreseeing evil due to its markings.

Top, Above Right and Right
Chow Chows have deep-set eyes, while the eyes of the Bulldog and the Malamute are upturned.

ALMOND EYES

ALMOND EYES are effectively oval in shape but bluntly pointed at both corners and can be found in breeds such as the Irish Water Spaniel, Finnish Spitz, German Shepherd Dog and Borzoi.

OBLIQUELY PLACED EYES

OBLIQUELY PLACED eyes, which are sometimes referred to as Mongolian eyes, have the outer corners situated higher up in the skull than the inner

DEEP-SET EYES

DEEP-SET EYES, also sometimes called well-sunken eyes, are those in which the eyeballs are seated well back into deep eye sockets, making the eyes well-recessed into the skull. The eyes of a Chow Chow are deep set.

corners. Breeds in which such eye placement is correct include the Alaskan Malamute, the Bull Terrier, the

GLOBULAR EYES

GLOBULAR EYES are round in shape and somewhat prominent, although they are not bulging in profile.

HAW EYES

HAW EYES are specific to breeds in which the haw (inner lining of the lower eyelid) is visible, as in the Bloodhound.

Finnish Spitz and the Flat-coated Retriever.

OVAL EYES

MANY DIFFERENT breeds have oval eyes and this term can, in most cases, also be described as an oblong eye. Dachshunds have typical oval eyes.

ROUND EYES

ROUND EYES ARE set in apertures which are circular in shape, as can be seen in breeds such as the French Bulldog, the Griffon Bruxellois and the American Cocker Spaniel.

TRIANGULAR EYES

TRIANGULAR EYES are more angular in their contours than oval or oblong eyes and they can be found in correctly shaped Afghan Hound eyes.

DESCRIPTIVE EYE MARKINGS: SPECTACLES

THE TERM 'spectacles' is used to describe the circular, light-coloured area surrounding each eye in the Keeshond, which has a darker colour of coat on most of the head.

PIPS

MANY BREEDS which are black and tan in colour have tan spots above the eyes. This descriptive term is applied to short-, or relatively short-coated breeds such as the Dobermann, Gordon Setter, Rottweiler and Basenji, in which breed they are usually called 'Melon Pips'.

FOUR EYES

A TIBETAN MASTIFF, or any other Tibetan breed with tan markings above the eyes, is called 'four eyes'. It is believed that such dogs can foresee evil as much as three days in advance.

DOMINO

DOMINO IS actually a reverse facial mask pattern occasionally found in some breeds. This can frequently give a somewhat different appearance to the eyes.

EYE COLOUR: WALL EYE

A WALL EYE is created by the incomplete, flecked or spotted distribution of melanin deposits on the background of a blue iris. This is a common eye colour in dogs with a merle coat colouring and can also be called fish eye, jewelled eye, china eye, marbled eye or silver eye.

EYELASHES

THE EYELASHES of the Lhasa Apso are exceptionally long, to keep the veil of hair which falls over the eyes from entering them. This combination provides protection from the glare of sun and snow in the rarefied atmosphere of Tibet.

EYEBROWS

LIKE HUMANS, dogs also have eyebrows which are formed by the skin and hair which cover the ridges of the skull's frontal bones. The development of the eyebrows varies greatly according to the breed, but can be seen particularly clearly on the Wire-haired Dachshund.

EYE RIMS

IN MANY BREEDS the colour of the eye rims are important, as is the relevant tightness of the rims. The colour of the eyerims indicates the pigment and in the majority of breeds this pigment around the eyes should be unbroken. Most breeds are required to have dark eye rims, but there are exceptions.

THIRD EYELID

THE THIRD EYELID is actually the nictitating membrane, which is the protective cover located at the inner corner of each eye to protect the eyes from injury and to act effectively as a 'windscreen wiper'. This is usually pinkish in colour but the outer edge may be pigmented, so blending with the eyelids. When unpigmented this is more noticeable, even when a dog's eyes are open, although in some breeds it is not faulted. The third eyelid can be seen beginning to cover the eye from the inner corner while a dog sleeps.

EXPRESSION: EASTERN

A TYPICAL expression found in the Afghan Hound, this is also known as an Oriental expression, and is created by a combination of the head structure, eye shape and placement, colour and the masking on the face.

GRUFF

GRUFF DESCRIBES the typical facial expression of the Bouvier des Flandres, the tough, hard-bitten appearance being enhanced by beard, moustache and bush eyebrows.

MONKEY-LIKE

A MONKEY-LIKE expression is highly descriptive of the distinctive faces of the Griffon

Bruxellois and the Affenpinscher

APE-LIKE

AN APE-LIKE expression is typical of that of the Tibetan Spaniel, full of ape-like character.

SAUCY

THE CHIHUAHUA'S face is described as saucy, which indicates the pert facial qualities created by the combination, placement and size of the various components of both the structure of the breed's skull and the characteristic features of the dog.

Top Left
The Shetland Sheepdog sometimes has a domino pattern around the eyes.

Left
The monkey-like Affenpinscher.

Centre Left
Pronounced eyebrows can be seen in the miniature Wire-haired Dachschund.

Below Centre Left
The Afghan Hound's expression has been described as typically 'eastern' or 'oriental'.

Left
The Griffon Bruxellois, like the Affenpinscher, has a monkey-like face

Bottom Left
The Lhasa Apso has very long eyelashes.

Bottom
The Chihuahua's pert face gives it a saucy look.

Fronts and Feet

GUN-BARREL FRONT

A GUN-BARREL front is one which is straight when viewed from the front. Both forelegs and pasterns are straight, positioned vertically to the ground and also parallel.

HORSESHOE FRONT

THIS IS A SPECIFIC description of the front of a Bedlington Terrier, in which the forelegs are straight but should be wider apart at the chest than at the feet.

STRAIGHT FRONT

THE DESCRIPTIONS STRAIGHT front and gun-barrel front are sometimes interchanged as in both descriptions the forelegs are perpendicular to the ground and parallel. In both, this straightness continues through wrists and pasterns, down to the feet.

WIDE FRONT

SOME BREEDS, notably the Bulldog, should have a wide front assembly, while in most breeds 'wide front' indicates that it is wider than is normally accepted in the breed.

BOWED FRONT

Top
Bowed feet are frequently found in Tibetan Spaniels.

WHEN VIEWED FROM the front, a bowed front is one in which the forelegs curve out from the elbows, and then in toward the wrist. Although faulty in most breeds this characteristic is required in the Tibetan Spaniel and the Pekingese.

Centre
The feline-footed Pointer.

CROOKED FRONT

Bottom
These Miniature Smooth-haired Dachshund have a crooked front.

A CROOKED FRONT is an essential construction of the forequarters of breeds such as the Dachshund and Basset in order to accommodate the forward portion of the chest in these very short-legged breeds. When viewed from the front, the forelegs incline inwards and are sometimes slightly curved.

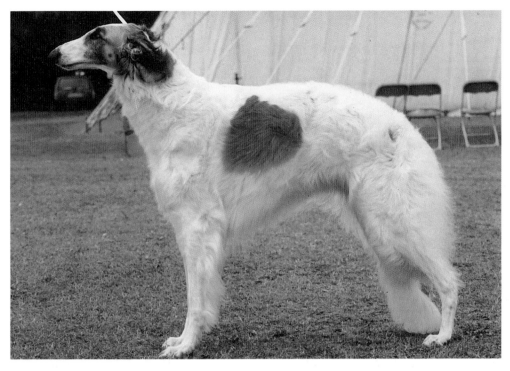

CAT FEET

CAT FEET IS THE TERM most usually used for feet which are round and compact, with well-arched toes and toes tightly bunched together, the two centre ones being only very slightly longer than the others. The pads on such feet are deeply cushioned and covered with thick skin. A few breeds specify circular, close-cupped or compact feet which are basically the same, all leaving a round impression rather than an oval one.

HARE FEET

IN HARE FEET THE CENTRE toes are longer than the outer and inner ones and toe arching is less marked giving a longer overall appearance, as in the Tibetan Spaniel and the hind feet of the Borzoi.

OVAL FEET

OVAL FEET ARE sometimes called spoon-shape feet and although much like cat feet in other respects the centre toes are just slightly longer. Such feet can be found on the Pointer and this is the accepted shape of the normal canine foot.

WEBBED FEET

BREEDS WHICH RETRIEVE FROM water often have webbed feet, which means they have strong webbing between the toes. This is also found in some of the arctic breeds which have historically and traditionally had to work in snow.

Left
The Borzoi dog has hare feet.

Bottom
Cat feet on a Bulldog.

Head and Skull

other ways, technically a balanced head is one in which the skull and foreface are equal in length. A typical example is the head of the Gordon Setter.

BRICK-SHAPED HEAD

WHEN VIEWED from

above, a brick-shaped head has a skull and muzzle approximately equal in width. A Wire Fox Terrier is a prime example, often accentuated by careful trimming. The description 'rectangular' head also applies to this shape.

CLEAN HEAD

A CLEAN HEAD, also

termed a dry head, is free from wrinkles and lumps caused by bone or muscle. The term 'gaunt head' is also used to describe some other breeds such as Belgian Shepherd Dogs.

CONE-SHAPED HEAD

A CONE-SHAPED head, also known as a conical head, is the head shape found in Dachshunds, and is triangular in outline, both from the side and from above.

EGG-SHAPED HEAD

A BULL TERRIER has a typically egg-shaped head, the very word 'egg' being descriptive of the way the terrier's head tapers in towards the nose.

FOX-LIKE HEAD

SPITZ BREEDS are renowned for their fox-like heads. The heads are elongated

*Top Right and Centre Right
A Smooth-haired Dachshund has a cone-shaped head, while a Spitz has a fox-like head.*

*Top and Centre
A Chihuahua's head is apple-shaped, and a Wire Fox Terrier has a brick-shaped head.*

APPLE HEAD

AN APPLE HEAD or apple skull is synonymous with a domed skull. The roof of the skull is shaped like an inverted hemisphere, rounded in all directions, albeit to varying degrees according to the breed. The most extreme example of this skull shape is found in the Chihuahua.

*Right and Centre Right
The balanced head of a Gordon Setter and the gaunt head of a Belgian Shepherd dog.*

*Far Right
A Bull Terrier has an egg-shaped head.*

BALANCED HEAD

ALTHOUGH THE TERM is sometimes used in

and triangular in shape, with a relatively fine foreface.

OTTER HEAD

THIS COLOURFUL term describes the way in which the head of the Border Terrier is shaped like that of an otter.

PEAR-SHAPED HEAD

PEAR-SHAPED is the term that describes the contours of the head of a Bedlington Terrier.

LONG OR TAPERING HEAD

THE BORZOI has a typically long, narrow head which tapers. This description is usually used for those breeds in which the stop is only slight or imperceptible.

RAM'S HEAD

THE DESCRIPTION, Ram's Head, covers

the combination of the contours of skull and foreface when viewed in profile, which appear convex, as in the Bull and Bedlington Terriers.

SHORT OR ROUND HEAD

EITHER OF THESE terms is used to describe the overall head shape of a foreshortened head with a broad, square skull which, combined, give a rounded appearance.

SQUARED-OFF HEAD

SQUARED-OFF refers to the muzzle or lip shape of a head which is not V-shaped, as in breeds like the Borzoi, nor rounded as in breeds such as the French Bulldog. A Pointer head is an obvious example of a squared-off head.

WEDGE-SHAPED HEAD

THE DESCRIPTION, V-shaped head, can also be used for one which is wedge-shaped. When viewed either from above or in profile the head forms a triangle,

although the wedge shapes need not be of equal dimension. Because of this, the description can be used for a wide variety of different breeds.

SKULL SHAPES

THERE ARE three divisions in skull formation:

Brachycephalic: the skull of breeds with shortened forefaces, such as the Pug.

Dolichocephalic: found in the Borzoi, which has a skull of great length.

Mesocephalic: the skull of breeds including those of Spaniel type.

Breeds such as the Lhasa Apso, which have a short foreface, are described as partial-brachycephalic.

ARCHED SKULL

AN ARCHED skull can either arch from side to side or sometimes in a lengthways direction.

BROAD SKULL

BROAD SKULL describes the width between the ears in relation to the actual length of the skull. The Golden Retriever is an example of a breed that is broad in skull.

FLAT SKULL

A FLAT SKULL is flat in both directions, both from ear to ear and from stop to occiput. Dogs such as Bearded

Collies, Clumber Spaniels and Pointers are breeds with this type of skull.

OVAL SKULL

AN OVAL SKULL has gentle, curved contours from ear to ear, as in the English Setter.

ROUNDED SKULL

NOT AS exaggerated as a domed or apple skull, in a rounded skull the top of the skull is arched in both directions, from ear to ear and from stop to occiput. The skull can be more or less arched, according to the breed. The Japanese Chin and the French Bulldog are both breeds with rounded skulls.

Top Left
The attractively shaped head of the Border Terrier is named after the otter.

Centre Left
The French Bulldog has a rounded head.

Above Left
The Japanese Chin has a rounded face.

Far Left
Bedlington Terriers have a pear-shaped head.

Bottom
Golden Retrievers are broad in the skull.

Noses

BROWN NOSE OR LIVER NOSE

Right
The Clumber Spaniel breed has a flesh-coloured nose.

A BROWN OR LIVER-coloured nose is a perfectly acceptable colour in some breeds, usually coupled with a corresponding coat colour because of the genetic make-up. Breeds such as the German Short-haired Pointer have a brown nose; the Irish Water Spaniel's is dark liver and that of the Sussex Spaniel, liver.

BUTTERFLY NOSE

A BUTTERFLY NOSE, sometimes called a spotted nose, is considered an undesirable nose colour in many breeds as it is a partially unpigmented nose of irregular appearance. However, completion of full nasal pigmentation does take time so this cannot always be truly assessed in a young puppy. Such broken pigmentation is permissible in harlequin-coloured Great Danes, though it is not desirable.

FLESH-COLOURED NOSE

A FLESH-COLOURED NOSE has an even colour but of a rather light shade, as in breeds such as the Weimeraner, Clumber Spaniel and Pharaoh Hound. In breeds where this colouring is a fault it is generally termed a 'dudley nose'.

Above
The German Short-haired Pointers' brown nose is acceptable because of its coat colour.

Right
Harlequin-coloured Great Danes may have varying pigmentation on their noses.

RAM'S NOSE

A RAM'S NOSE IS also called an aquiline nose. When viewed in profile the topline of the foreface is almost straight except that the nasal cartilage at the end dips down, as in the Deerhound.

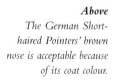

ROMAN NOSE

THE PROFILE OF A ROMAN nose is one in which the nose curves in a convex manner. The Bull Terrier is a typical example.

SELF-COLOURED NOSE

A SELF-COLOURED NOSE is of the same or similar pigmentation to the coat colour, as for example a chocolate-coloured nose in a dog which is chocolate and tan.

WINTER NOSE

A WINTER NOSE is also frequently called a snow nose or smudge nose and is seen more in some breeds than in others. This is effectively a nose which is normally solid black in colour but which, in the winter months, takes on a pinkish hue or streak. It is acceptable in some breeds such as the Siberian Husky and is also often found in the Labrador Retriever.

FLARED NOSTRILS

FLARED NOSTRILS ARE WIDE open to allow for the maximum intake of air. Typical are the nostrils of the Bouvier des Flandres, whose breed standard requires nostrils to be well developed.

Left
An archetypal Roman nose is found in the Bull Terrier.

Below
The ram's nose is typical of the Deerhound.

PINCHED NOSTRILS

PINCHED NOSTRILS ARE a fault in any breed as they do not allow sufficient air into the lungs, leading to breathing problems. The breed standard of the Shih Tzu specifically mentions that pinched nostrils are highly undesirable.

Left
The Chesapeake Bay Retriever has a self-coloured nose.

Far Left
The flesh-coloured nose of the Pharaoh Hound is normal in the breed.

Tails

*Top Right
A Husky has a
curled tail.*

*Top
An Old English
Sheepdog with
a bobtail.*

*Centre
A Cocker Spaniel's
tail is cocked, a
Poodle's is docked,
and a Bull Terrier
has a crank tail.*

*Below and
Bottom Right
A Siberian Husky
and a Chihuahua.*

BEE STING TAIL

THE DESCRIPTION 'bee sting tail' is used in connection with the Pointer, indicating a strong, straight tail which tapers to a point.

BOB TAIL

A BOB TAIL OR bobbed tail is that of a dog which is either born tail-less or in which the tail has been docked close to its connection with the body, as in the Pembroke Welsh Corgi or the Old English Sheepdog, the latter being familiarly known as 'Bobtail'.

BRUSH TAIL

A BRUSH OR brushed tail is one which is covered in a stand-off, brush-like coat, the hairs of which are roughly the same length all over, giving the tail the appearance of a brush, as in the Siberian Husky.

CARROT-SHAPED TAIL

THE SCOTTISH Terrier has a typical carrot-shaped tail, namely in the shape of this well-known vegetable.

COCKED-UP TAIL

A COCKED-UP tail is one which is raised up at right angles to the backline, as in the Cocker Spaniel.

CRANK TAIL

A CRANK TAIL, also called a crook tail, is one in which the root is arched out, following which it hangs down vertically, with the end angled out like an old fashioned crank. This tail can be found in the Staffordshire Bull Terrier. Sometimes,

however, the term crook tail is applied to a malformed tail

CURLED TAIL

THERE ARE two basic varieties of curled tail, one a single curl, the other double, but there are many different variations within these two.

DOCKED TAIL

A DOCKED TAIL is one from which a part has been removed. This is usually done surgically at four or five days of age. However, this is an issue which has been the subject of much heated debate in Britain in recent years. Historically, Boxers, Dobermanns, Poodles and many Terriers have had their tails docked.

FLAGPOLE TAIL

A FLAGPOLE TAIL is long and carried erect, directly upwards like that of the Beagle.

FLAT TAIL

A FLAT TAIL IS SPECIFIC to the Chihuahua. It is

flattish in appearance and broadens slightly in the centre, then tapering to a point.

GAY TAIL

A GAY TAIL is carried higher than the horizontal line of the back and is considered a fault in many, indicating that it is being carried much higher than it should be, usually while the dog is on the move. However, in some breeds this is normal carriage, as in the Fox Terrier. In others it is a requirement while the dog is working.

HOOK TAIL

A HOOK TAIL hangs down but has an upward swirl at the tip, as in the Pyrenean Sheepdog or Briard.

HORIZONTAL TAIL

THE TAIL OF the Bull Terrier typifies a horizontal tail, which can also be called a whip tail and is very similar to that known as a 'bee sting'.

KINKED TAIL

A KINKED OR KINK tail has a sharp bend or an acute angle somewhere along its length. In some breeds, such as the French Bulldog, it is a normal feature, in others it may be a fault or can have been caused through injury.

LOW-SET TAIL

A LOW-SET TAIL is one which begins from a sloping croup or from a point which is lower than the topline.

OTTER TAIL

AN OTTER TAIL is a strong one, thick at the base and tapering towards the tip. It is covered in dense, thick coat and is flat on the underside, designed especially to act as a rudder when the dog is swimming. The Labrador Retriever has such a tail.

PLUMED TAIL

A PLUMED TAIL is one in which a plume of hair cascades downwards in the shape of a plume. It may just be plumed toward the end or may grow in this way from the entire tail, the hair being

carried like a plume over the back. A Chinese Crested Dog has a plumed tail, as does the Pomeranian and Pekingese.

POT-HOOK TAIL

THE SHIH TZU has a pot-hook tail, which is held over the back like a teapot handle, thereby forming an arc as opposed to lying flat over the back.

RAT TAIL

A RAT TAIL has a thick root which is covered in soft curls, and yet the rest of the tail is only sparsely coated or can have no hair at all. An Irish Water Spaniel has a typical rat tail.

RING TAIL

A RING TAIL, or ringed tail, usually indicates a long tail in which either all or part of the tail forms a ring. In some breeds this is considered a fault, but a truly typical Afghan should have a ring at the end of the tail.

SABRE TAIL

A SABRE TAIL may be carried upwards or downwards, depending upon the breed. It has a gentle or slight curve, as in the Basset Hound or German Shepherd Dog.

SCIMITAR TAIL

A SCIMITAR TAIL is similar to a sabre tail but has a more exaggerated curve, as in the Dandie Dinmont Terrier and English Setter.

SCREW TAIL

A SCREW TAIL is a short one in which there is a twist, kink or spiral turn, as in the Boston Terrier.

SICKLE TAIL

A SICKLE TAIL is carried over the back loosely, like a semi-circle, not lying flat against the back. A Siberian Husky has such a tail.

SNAP TAIL

A SNAP TAIL is carried over the back but towards the tip comes into contact with the back itself, as in the Alaskan Malamute.

SQUIRREL TAIL

A SQUIRREL TAIL is long and angles forward sharply, as in the Pekingese. It follows the line of the back but does not touch it.

STUMPY TAIL

A STUMPY OR stump tail is a short one, correctly found in breeds such as the Schipperke. This term, however, is also used for dogs whose tail is shorter than is required in certain breeds.

SWORD TAIL

A SWORD TAIL is one which hangs straight down, as in the Basset Griffon Vendeen and Labrador Retriever.

TAPERING TAIL

THIS TAIL is long, and short-coated, tapering to a point, as does the tail of the English Toy Terrier.

TUFTED TAIL

A TUFTED tail may be long or short and with either a plume or trimmed hair at the end. A Chinese Crested is an example of the plumed, whilst a Poodle's pom-pom is a trimmed example.

WHIP TAIL

A WHIP TAIL is pointed and carried out stiffly in line with the back, as in the Bull Terrier.

Top and Bottom Far Left
The Pekingese and Pomeranians both have a plumed tail.

Above Left
The Basset has a sabre tail.

Above
The Schipperke has a stumpy tail.

Above
English Toy Terriers have tapering tails.

Above Left
An Irish Water Spaniel has a pot-hook tail.

Left
Alaskan Malamutes have snap tails.

Other Features

BALANCE

ALTHOUGH BALANCE can refer just to one section of the anatomy, such as the head, it is more generally used to describe overall symmetry – a harmonious and well-proportioned blend of the various parts which go to make up a dog of the breed in question.

BREECHING

THE TERM breeching is also called breeches, culottes, pants, trousering or trousers, according to the breed. Added to the difference in terminology are variations in meaning, because whichever term is used it can refer to the fringing of longer hair on the thigh region, the ridge-like pattern of hair on short-coated breeds such as the Dobermann, or just colour, as in the case of the Manchester Terrier, when it relates to the tan-coloured hair on the outside of the hind legs.

CHEST

THERE ARE SEVERAL different chest types, again according to the breed, so that a barrel chest (a chest of rounded contours) in one breed may be exactly what is required, whereas in another breed, such as a sighthound, it is a serious fault as such a shape of rib does not allow the breed to function as it is intended. An oval chest (egg-shaped) chest is the shape

required in most breeds of dog but some are deep in chest, others less so.

CHISELLING

CHISELLING, sometimes also called modelling, is clean-cut contours and lines, primarily around the head and foreface, although different degrees of chiselling can be required, according to the breed. In a Smooth Fox Terrier, for example, part of the foreface is described in the breed standard as 'moderately chiselled out'.

COBBY

A COBBY DOG is one which is strong and yet compact, a term taken from the horse known as a cob. A typical cobby breed is the Pug.

COUPLING

THE COUPLING is the area which joins the chest to the hindquarters. In most breeds long-coupling is a fault, although a reasonable length assists turning ability. In many breeds the distance between the last rib and the start of the hindquarters is relatively short (short-coupled), which gives strength in this region.

CREST

ALTHOUGH SOME BREEDS can have a crest of hair on the head, the term 'crest' usually refers to the area of the neck between the nape at the junction of the head and neck, and the withers.

DEWLAP

DEWLAP IS THE LOOSE, pendulous skin in the area of the chin, throat and neck, typically found in breeds such as the Basset and the Bloodhound.

FURROW

A FURROW OR FLUTE is more accurately described as the median line which is a longitudinal groove formed either by bone or muscle. This runs from the centre of the skull toward the stop and is a requirement in some breeds such as the Hungarian Vizsla.

GAIT

GAIT IS THE WORD GENERALLY used to describe the action, motion or movement of a dog, clearly something which alters not only according to the structure of the breed and the speed with which it moves, but also whether or not the dog concerned has sound conformation.

HINDQUARTERS

THE HINDQUARTERS COMMENCE at the pelvic girdle and encompass the area of the dog from there downward. The angulation of the hindquarters varies very much according to the breed, extreme comparisons being those of a German Shepherd Dog and of a Chow Chow.

KEEL

THE OUTLINE OF THE FOREMOST PART of the lower chest of a Dachshund is described as a keel, as it resembles the keel of a boat.

OCCIPUT

THE OCCIPUT, occasionally called the occipital crest, peak or apex, is the ridge formed by the occipital bone where, at the back of the skull, it joins with the parietal bones on either side. Many breed standards have some reference to the occiput and it is usually from this point that head proportions are measured.

RACY

A DOG WHICH is racy is one which is streamlined and elegant in appearance, quite the opposite of a cobby dog.

SHOULDERS

DIFFERENT BREEDS are required to have slightly differing shoulder placement. The most frequently used terms are 'good layback of shoulder' indicating that the shoulder blade is positioned correctly to allow adequate or good forward extension of the forelegs, and 'steep in shoulder', in which case the angle at which the shoulder blade is placed is too upright, hence restricting forward movement.

STOP

THE STOP IS the depression in the topline of the head, situated almost centrally between the eyes

and varying in depth according to the breed. It is much more prominent in short-nosed breeds than in breeds such as the Rough and Smooth Collies and the Borzoi.

WELL RIBBED-UP

A DOG WHICH IS DESCRIBED as being well ribbed-up has a rib cage that extends well back along the length of the whole body.

Top and Left
The variations of dogs' hindquarters can be seen on comparing a German Shepherd with a Chow Chow.

Bottom
Greyhounds stream-lined appearance may be described as racy.

Dog Care and Management

 DECIDING TO BECOME the owner of a dog is a commitment not to be undertaken lightly, a decision to be made with the involvement of all close family members and something which should have been discussed at length. It is likely that one member of the family will be primarily responsible for looking after the dog but everyone concerned must be genuinely enthusiastic about the coming of a new family member, for that is what a dog should be.

DISCUSSING DOG OWNERSHIP

A DOG JOINING a new home against the wishes of one or more people in the immediate family can cause argument, often leading to the dog having to be re-homed - distressing for all concerned and, most importantly, for the dog. It is absolutely essential that a dog is not left at home alone all day. Ideally one member of the family should generally be based around the home, and this does not just apply when the puppy is young and adjusting to a new environment but for the entire life of the dog. Of course a dog can be left for short periods and there are many homes where, for example, the wife works part-time to no major detriment of the dog. There are even cases where an owner's lunchtime at home can break the boredom of a dog which would otherwise be left alone for too long. The dog needs to relieve itself, stretch its legs and have some human companionship to break the monotony of an otherwise over-long day.

Neighbours also have to be considered. A dog left alone can not only be destructive, due to boredom, but can also be noisy. A dog's owners may easily not notice the noise because when the family returns home the dog will be quiet, so if one lives in a built-up area, or indeed has any neighbours at

Top Right
All dogs, including working dogs, enjoy spending time indoors, in a domestic environment.

Right
Dogs easily suffer from boredom which can manifest itself as constant barking or disruptive behaviour.

all, they will probably be telling the truth if they complain that your dog is barking all day.

It should always be borne in mind that most dogs have happier lives if they are allowed to live in the house and take part in the routine of everyday life. Even working dogs appreciate some time in a domestic environment and absolutely no dog should be tethered outside all day. One tends to think that such treatment of our canine friends is in the past, but regrettably in many cases it is not.

Consideration must also be given to holiday time, as depending which country you live in, a dog may not be allowed to travel with you abroad and return to the country of domicile. This is currently the case in Britain because of quarantine laws. There are some extremely good boarding kennels but these must be investigated carefully and ideally taken on personal recom-

mendation. Having said that, no dog should constantly be sent in and out of kennels just for the owner's convenience.

No one should ever give a dog as a gift, for much as the receiver may have enthused over the idea of having a dog, the ultimate decision and responsibility to buy and look after a dog must rest with that person alone. Indeed, most genuine breeders will refuse to sell a puppy during the few weeks prior to Christmas, for fear that the dog may have been purchased as a surprise gift. Added to that, the festive season is always a time of great activity and a time at which normal household routine rather falls by the wayside. A new dog needs to be brought into a stable environment, so that they can have every possible opportunity to learn how to adapt to a new home easily. This should be done at a time of the year when there is less frenetic activity in the household, for the sake of the new dog.

Top and Top Left
All members of the family have to want a dog and be able to look after it for the foreseeable future.

Centre Left
Dogs need exercise and it is important to take this into account before getting a dog as a pet.

QUESTIONS TO ASK

When deciding whether or not you should have a dog, there are some important questions you should ask yourself:

• Is it likely that I will still be able to look after a dog many years from now?
• Would all my close family members like a dog to join us?
• In the knowledge that a dog cannot regularly be left alone all day, will someone be at home for a large proportion of each day?
• Is my home and garden suitable for a dog? If not, can I carry out any alterations or repairs which may be necessary?

• Is the area I live in built-up? Will I have complaints from neighbours?
• Food, vaccinations and veterinary bills will need to be taken care of. Can I afford the upkeep of a dog?
• Should I take out a pet insurance policy, in the knowledge that routine vaccinations will not be covered by this?
• Is a new baby expected in the home? If so, would it be wiser to wait until the baby is a little older?
• Is any member of my immediate family asthmatic or likely to be allergic to dogs?

Finding a Dog

PLANNING TO SPEND the next 10–15 years with a dog means your initial selection must be made carefully, ensuring that your new-found friend has had the best possible start in life. Never be tempted to buy from a pet shop or other retail outlet, as in doing so you will only encourage irresponsible breeders to produce yet more litters, purely for cash gain.

WHERE TO FIND A DOG

IF THERE IS AN ADVERT in the press for the breed or type of dog you have chosen, be sure to check this out very carefully and never be tempted to buy a dog unless you feel certain it is in good health and the circumstances are exactly right. You should be able to see the puppy's dam as you do not wish, albeit unwittingly, to purchase through a third party who may be selling the dog on behalf of someone else. Put yourself in the breeder's shoes for a moment. If you had brought

Below
Dog shows are excellent places to find out more about the breed you are interested in and also the breeders.

up a litter of puppies with dedicated care and attention, wouldn't you want to meet the people who were buying one of your puppies?

If possible visit a dog show where you will have opportunity to come into contact with breeders, discuss the breed more fully and find out who is likely to have suitable puppies available for sale to you in the coming weeks or months. You may have to wait a while but this should not deter you. Many of the best breeders have waiting lists.

If you have given careful consider-ation to the breed of dog you would like, in the unfortunate event of a suitable puppy not being available don't change your mind instantly to another breed, just for the sake of introducing a new dog to your life at that particular time. There would be nothing worse than ending up with a dog which will always be compared to the breed upon which you had set your heart.

ADULT OR PUPPY?

A PUPPY WILL GIVE ENDLESS hours of enjoyment with the pleasure of knowing that your canine companion has spent virtually all its life with you. However, a puppy is very demanding, and unlikely to be fully house trained, nor even fully vaccinated upon arrival. A young puppy will add greatly to one's workload, especially during the first few weeks, when there will be training, frequent meals and a lot of tidying and mopping up, particularly if the newcomer is too young to take out on a

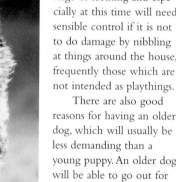

lead for walks. A puppy will also go through the stage of teething and espe-cially at this time will need sensible control if it is not to do damage by nibbling at things around the house, frequently those which are not intended as playthings.

There are also good reasons for having an older dog, which will usually be less demanding than a young puppy. An older dog will be able to go out for walks immediately and should be house trained, although any new dog will have to learn house rules.

TAKING ON A STRAY

IF YOU TAKE ON A STRAY, find out as much as possible about why a new home is needed, because you will not wish to have any unpleasant surprises which cause you to have to rethink your decision when it is too late. Always remember, too, that in Britain anyone finding a stray dog is not at liberty to claim ownership of that dog without first reporting the dog to the police, giving the original owner chance to come forward. There are numerous dog rescue organisations, both large and small. If you would like to give a

home to a dog of a particular breed, you would be wise to make contact with rescue officers for that breed only. To find these you will need to telephone the secretary of the breed club, whose number can be obtained from the country's Kennel Club. Dogs find themselves in a rescue situation for many reasons, all too frequently because insufficient thought was given to taking on a dog in the first instance, or perhaps family circumstances have changed. Indeed, often when a new baby arrives on the scene the family pet is the first to go. Of course there are other very genuine reasons for dogs needing to find new homes; owners die or are taken into long-term care, some even have to move abroad and are not in a situation to take the dog along too. However, even rescue societies have waiting lists, so do be patient and always be honest about your reason for wanting to take on an older dog, in this way rescue officers can place dogs in the most suitable homes as it would be awful if a dog had to move on yet again.

The same rule applies if you decide to get a dog from one of the larger re-homing organisations. Always try to find out as much as possible about the dog's history and, in return, be honest about your own suitability as an owner.

Dogs in the Home

SPECIAL ARRANGEMENTS WHICH MAY have to be made to accommodate a dog in your home will depend to a large extent on the type of dog you have, its size, activity level and, surprisingly enough, whether or not it has a tail. The enthusiastic tail of a large dog can do untold damage to precious ornaments neatly displayed on a low table, so do bear this in mind and keep precious items out of harm's way.

DOGS AND SAFETY

Right
Puppies are naturally inquisitive and will eat objects found in the house or garden that could either poison or harm them.

Below and Opposite
Dogs take up room, need feeding and want attention. Make sure you have the time to give to a dog.

WHATEVER THE SIZE of your dog, anything which might do harm should be kept out of reach, remembering that puppies can be especially inquisitive and have no idea what constitutes danger and what might just prove to be fun. Electric cables must be kept safely concealed for these can cause death, as can poisons left carelessly around the home within easy reach. Remember that inquisitive dogs in the bathroom can find all manner of things, not all of which are safe. Remember that poisons are a danger, some plants are harmful to

animals and domestic cleaners frequently contain toxins. These are often packaged in plastic containers which are punctured all too easily by sharp teeth. Take care, too, that heavy objects cannot be pulled or knocked down, or sharp objects stolen and chewed up before they are noticed. Broken glass and other sharp objects can not only cause tragedy if swallowed, or at least an expensive veterinary bill, they can also injure feet and pads.

THE GARDEN

YOUR GARDEN MUST BE entirely secure. Some dogs are climbers, others turn out to be diggers, and dogs with long muzzles seem to have a crafty way of enlarging a tiny gap in wooden fencing. Numerous items used in and around the garden can also be highly dangerous so garden sheds should be inaccessible. Many slug pellets, weed-killers, fertilisers and the like contain substances that can cause illness and even death. When in the garden take especial notice if your dog is carefully washing the pads of its feet for it may have trodden in or dug up something toxic. Swimming pools and deep ponds in the garden must also be given careful consideration for safety's sake. In swimming pools, although most dogs can swim, they may find no easy means of escape.

EQUIPMENT

FOOD BOWLS MUST ALWAYS be kept clean and fresh water available at all times. Sleeping quarters should be slightly raised from the ground to avoid draughts. Although wickerwork beds look pretty they are not at all suitable as most dogs are tempted to chew them, creating dangerous edges. A bed which can be cleaned easily is much more appropriate and can be lined with washable veterinary bedding for comfort and hygiene. A collapsible dog crate can also be very useful both for travelling and use around the home. A dog must never associate this with a place of punishment, rather as a refuge for a few quiet moments.

The home in which you live, your lifestyle and surrounding environment will all play important parts in your selection of a

breed. Even your own age and strength, and that of close family members, will have to be considered. Many people love large dogs but are simply not able to cope with them. A large dog needs plenty of space both inside the house and outdoors and owners will need sufficient strength to control the dog and to walk it on a lead, as large dogs need road work to build up muscle, not just free run.

SECURITY

DOGS, BOTH LARGE and small, are capable of jumping great heights and running at great speed, so this is another consideration when deciding whether a dog is suitable for your own garden, or whether your garden can perhaps be adjusted to suit the dog. Always remembering that most dogs can move swiftly, safety is of prime importance. Gates must be secure and exterior doors to one's house should be considered carefully so that your dog can only get outside to a safe and secure area. This means that if doors need to be kept closed all members of the household must be relied upon in this regard. Sadly one hears of far too many dogs coming to a tragic end. Some dogs are small enough to make their way through cat-flaps, so that also needs consideration to prevent accidents and mistakes. A notice on the gate to prevent people from

walking up the garden path and leaving the gate open can also be a wise precaution.

Inside the house, doors are also a subject for debate and consideration. Stable doors are always useful, especially leading to a kitchen area, where it is often neither safe nor convenient to allow dogs to be around.

Below
Make sure that a dog cannot escape from the garden.

Training a Dog

TO HAVE A HAPPY MUTUAL relationship with your dog, then training, at least to some degree, is a necessity. Although some breeds are more responsive to training then others, most are capable of absorbing the basics. If they do not, then the fault is likely to be that of the handler. Lead training is a must because when away from home your dog will need to be on a secure lead in public places.

OBEDIENCE

BEFORE ALLOWING YOUR DOG freedom in certain suitable, safe places you must be sure that your dog is sufficiently well-trained to come back to you upon command. Not everyone likes dogs and yours should learn not to jump up at every passing stranger. Any dog mess must be cleared up by you immediately and disposed of in a safe place. Hygienic poop-scoops can be bought, or a plastic bag serves the purpose just as well and is easy to carry in your pocket.

Above
Rewards are a good way of training a dog.

Right
Dogs can learn various commands, such as 'no', come', 'sit' and 'stay'.

Your dog will soon be able to learn simple commands. The word 'No' is an essential command, as is 'Come', 'Sit', 'Down', 'Wait' and 'Stay', all of which can be taught to good effect. Dogs should be socialised, both with other dogs and with people, but supervised when meeting young children, who are often tempted to approach an animal suddenly and may take a dog by surprise. I do not advocate the use of a muzzle except in special cases when a dog is untrained or untrainable, in which case professional advice must be sought.

Training classes are a useful and enjoyable means of learning how best to teach a dog to behave as you would expect, and the Kennel Club now operates a 'Good Citizen' scheme giving even a novice a relatively easy goal at which to aim. Training classes are often advertised in local veterinary surgeries but you will need to decide whether you wish to attend obedience or show training classes, the latter called 'ringcraft'. For optimum performance in the show ring, most owners of show dogs do not agree with combining the two.

TOILET TRAINING FOR YOUNG PUPPIES

WHEN A PUPPY ARRIVES at its new home, it will most probably not have been house-trained, or if it has it will be confused by its new environment and will not know what is expected of it so teaching will have to begin again.

Without fail, as soon as a puppy has awoken from sleep or has had a meal it should be taken outside. It is best to lift the puppy up to begin with because until it is familiar with the door it will

they were still with their dam. A piece of newspaper, several sheets thick, should be placed on the floor and progressively moved closer and closer to the door, until it can eventually be moved outside. From that point on the puppy will usually be happy to ask to go out into the garden. In training some people prefer to leave a little soiling on the paper so that the puppy associates this with where it is meant to urinate again.

REWARD AND PUNISHMENT

WHEN A PUPPY OR ADULT DOG has done something to please the owner, a reward must be given. This need not necessarily be a reward in kind, but there should be plenty of praise which gives the dog great pleasure and encourages the same good deed to be carried out again on future occasions.

Titbits are often given in training but, if used, these must be suitable and must not lead towards allowing a dog to become obese – some breeds are more prone to this than others. However, a dog carrying out physical training will work off the odd extra calorie.

Conversely, if a dog misbehaves, there should be some punishment. However, it is essential that punishment is only given out when a dog is actually caught in the act. If punished subsequent to a misdeed, neither a puppy nor an adult dog will associate the two, and will wonder why it is being punished. Punishment at the wrong time causes total confusion.

Verbal reprimand is usually quite sufficient and at no time should a dog be treated violently. The simple words: 'Bad dog', will suffice following which the dog should not be petted for a short while or again confusion will ensue in the dog's mind. Most dogs respond to a direct look in the eyes, combined with verbal reprimand. Provided that there is no fear of the dog biting, one can grasp the scruff of the neck and hold the head in front of one's own, though not too close please.

Left
Professional dog training classes can help dogs that seem untrainable and relieve the owner's frustration.

Below
Grabbing the scruff of a dog's neck in reprimand is sufficient punishment.

Bottom
Only reprimand a dog if caught in the act; otherwise they will not understand the punishment.

probably stop to 'spend a penny' en route. Stay outside with your puppy, or keep a careful eye through a window, but do not play games with the youngster at this time as the puppy must learn the reason why it has gone outside.

Training with paper is also a useful method, especially for very tiny puppies who will generally prefer to urinate on paper rather than on the floor. They may well have has paper lining on the floor of their whelping pen and puppy play area when

one should be able to assert one's influence by way of direction from the very start.

Initially a dog should always be trained to walk on one's left although later, for show training, it will also be necessary to walk on the opposite side as sometimes a judge will need to see the dog from a different angle, probably because of the shape of the showring. Once a dog has begun to walk without incident on a lead, it can be taken to a safe place on the roadside, but this must be on a sensible collar and lead, not a show lead which is used for show-training but can all too easily be slipped.

Only when one has absolute confidence that a dog will not run off, with danger of accident, should a dog be trained to walk without a lead. A lead must always be attached when walking the dog near traffic.

LEAD TRAINING AND OBEDIENCE

TRAINING A YOUNG PUPPY to get used to the lead can be a trying time, especially with some breeds. Some youngsters almost seem to take to a lead like a duck to water, while others certainly do not. To begin with, the young puppy should just be allowed to get used to the feel of a collar around its neck. This should just be kept on for a few moments, always under supervision, and the spans of time should then be increased so that the puppy stops trying to scratch it off which will most probably happen on the first two or three attempts.

GETTING YOUR PUPPY USED TO THE LEAD

A LEAD SHOULD THEN BE ATTACHED, and the puppy taken somewhere safe, ideally just in the garden, and if possible in an area which is not associated with play. Different owners have different methods of getting a dog used to a lead and a lot depends upon the size of the dog and the breed in question. With small breeds I always like to allow my puppies to 'take' me along to begin with, holding the lead very lightly so that the puppy hardly knows anyone is attached to the other end. Then, slowly, I start to take control, inevitably with some resistance from my canine companion. Larger dogs generally seem more amenable to lead training so

Top Right
Lead training is essential for the dog's safety and the owner's patience.

Centre Right
Hand signals are often useful in teaching a dog to stay.

TEACHING A DOG TO STAY

DIFFERENT PEOPLE have slightly different methods of training a dog to sit and to stay. The lead needs to be a long one for this exercise. First the owner gets the dog to sit and then moves slowly away, repeating the word: 'Stay'. A hand signal can often also be useful in order to reinforce the verbal command. If the dog moves, it should be verbally reprimanded, placed back in its original sitting position and the exercise repeated again.

The distance between dog and owner should gradually be increased, and initially when the dog responds well the owner should return to the dog, rather than the other way around. Soon enough the time will come to teach the dog to come when called, although at this stage the dog should still be on a long lead. For this the handler tugs gently on the lead, with the word: 'Come'. When the dog is proficient in the commands 'Sit', 'Stay' and 'Come', the time has come to work without a lead, always in a safe place.

Rewards, by means of fuss and attention or in kind, will have been given throughout the training process. One will build up to other, more advanced obedience training, and 'Down' and 'Fetch' are the next lessons which are usually taught. Again the trainer will initially need to give assistance in gently pushing or placing the dog into the required lying position and once one has reached this stage the time during which the dog is left can be substantially increased, with the handler moving further and further away, possibly even out of sight. A dog must have complete confidence in its trainer, and vice versa, before this can work successfully.

When training a dog to fetch and retrieve an object, difficulty can be encountered at first in persuading the dog to drop the item as requested. For this, carry some titbits during the exercise; they will come in especially useful as the dog will nor-

mally be perfectly happy to exchange the object retrieved for a tasty morsel.

Some owners also teach their dogs to go to the toilet on command, and although the author has rarely had much success in this department, it is a highly useful training exercise for anyone whose dog masters it.

Below Left
Initially, owners may have difficulty in persuading their dogs to drop a retrieved item.

Bottom Left
Dogs should be led on the owner's left, although this is sometimes reversed in the show ring.

Feeding Dogs

ALTHOUGH DOGS ARE carnivores and enjoy meat, they are actually omnivorous and usually both willing and able to eat and digest various types of food. They do not require such a high protein content in their diet as cats do. However, although a dog can live perfectly well on a completely balanced but unvaried diet there is evidence that dogs enjoy some variety in their food.

ESSENTIAL ELEMENTS

WHETHER choosing to feed one of the many complete diets or create one's own food combinations, the diet must be well-balanced, containing both protein and carbohydrates. A certain amount of fatty acids, vitamins and minerals are also needed for healthy skin and coat and a variety of body functions. Fruit and vegetables are beneficial to a dog's diet, and for the convalescent dog boneless chicken or fish with boiled brown rice are highly digestible.

An active dog obviously needs a higher protein content in his diet than the dog which lazes around all day, and likewise overweight dogs should have fewer calories. All packeted, ready-prepared foods contain comprehensive lists of ingredients and these should be studied carefully before you make your selection.

Top Right
Stainless steel feeding bowls are the most hygienic ones to use.

Right
A dog's appetite can vary depending on hormonal changes or external influences, such as climate.

WHEN AND WHAT TO FEED

NEVER CHANGE SUDDENLY from one type of diet to another for this can give a dog loose motions. Instead, introduce the change gradually, mixing the new one with the other in increasing quantity over a few days. Fresh and tinned foods should be removed and disposed of if left uneaten, but dried foods can remain available all day. Adult dogs will usually require one main meal daily, with a light

snack given at the other end of the day. On the other hand, this may be divided into two smaller meals if preferred.

Under no circumstances should a dog be allowed to exercise energetically within half an hour following a heavy meal. Also, as an aid to digestion, large or tall dogs should ideally have their food dish raised off the ground so that they do not have to bend down so far to the bowl.

Bones can be dangerous for dogs as they are liable to splinter and cause them internal damage. However, marrow bones are usually considered safe, but even these must be discarded if they begin to break up in the packet. Fresh water must be made available at all times. Non-spill bowls are available and can prevent spillage, and stainless steel dishes are the most hygienic both for food and drink.

OBESITY AND OVERFEEDING

A HIGH PROPORTION OF DOGS suffer from obesity and this is primarily due to the most common dietary problem – overeating. Some breeds are more prone to problems of obesity than others – the

Cocker Spaniel and Labrador are two prime examples of breeds affected, whereas most of the terrier breeds are less susceptible than others.

If a dog has a weight problem, ensure that he only eats what you give him. Stop other people feeding tit-bits between meals. Sometimes there is a medical reason for the dog carrying too much weight, so speak to your local vet before putting a dog on a diet.

If a dog is given an especially enjoyable meal it may eat more than it might otherwise have done, but with regular appetising meals, it reduces its intake accordingly so there is no harm in feeding tasty but sensible food all the while. There is a social factor related to a dog's appetite. If puppies are fed in a group, on average they eat more than if they are fed alone. This rule applies in adulthood also because of the competitive element involved.

In general, dogs that are particular about their food have fewer problems of obesity, it is the breeds which are habitually less choosy in their feeding habits that suffer most. Other factors which can cause dogs to put on excess weight are hormonal. A bitch that has been spayed, or a castrated dog, undergoes hormonal changes which alter the weight-regulating mechanism.

A dog's appetite increases during cold weather so in winter is often prudent to increase the overall bulk of the diet while reducing the calories if one's dog has a tendency to become overweight. Uncooked carrots are a good stand-by as a dog usually seems happy to crunch on these instead of biscuits, and apart from limiting the calorie intake, they are a good aid to the teeth cleaning process. They can be given in lieu of snacks, and can be then chopped up and mixed in with a meal to make it last that little bit longer and appear to be more substantial.

Top
A balanced diet in important to ensure a healthy-looking coat.

Left
Begging for food should not be encouraged as this will form a habit and lead to obesity.

Bottom
Raising a bowl for larger dogs will aid digestion.

Grooming and General Care

THE AMOUNT OF GROOMING your dog requires depends largely on the breed. Length and texture of coat play an important part, but however long or short a coat it will need to be maintained in good condition.

KEEPING A DOG CLEAN

SOME LONG-COATED dog breeds need a bath once every week or so to keep their coats free from mats, with daily grooming in between. Other dogs with short coats, such as Whippets, need bathing only occasionally but their dead hair still needs to be removed, followed by grooming

with a hound glove, finishing with a chamois leather and velvet to add the finishing touches.

SPECIAL CARE

SOME BREEDS NEED expert stripping, while dogs like the Bichon Frise, which are kept in show coat, need careful preparation. For particular coat care, practical advice must be taken from specialists within your chosen breed, and a breed-specific book should also provide helpful information. Even if you decide to have your dog professionally groomed you will still need to attend to your dog's coat between visits.

Areas which need checking daily are the eyes, and around the anus to see that there is no soiling. It is also important to inspect ears; there should be no build-up of wax inside the ear; this can often be detected by odour or inflammation.

Toenails also need attention, more or less frequently depending on whether your dog regularly walks on hard surfaces. Guillotine-style clippers are usually the easiest to use, taking care not to cut the quick of the nail, which causes pain and bleeding. An experienced friend or your vet will be able to

Top and Above
Applying eye ointment to
an injured eye, and apply-
ing ear ointment.

Right
Some grooming equipment,
although some items
are more useful for
particular breeds.

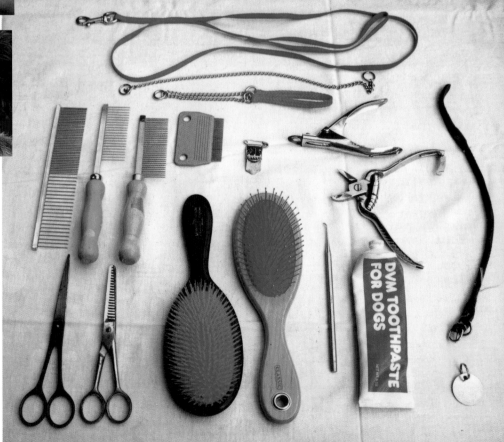

show you how best to deal with nails, and dew claws must never be forgotten as they do not wear down naturally. From an early age, teeth should be cleaned regularly using a toothbrush and special canine toothpaste.

A well-trained dog will always be easier to groom than one which is allowed to be unruly. This is especially important for long-coated breeds and those which require trimming. If a dog is not obedience-trained to lie down, and if the dog is reasonably small, one can lean one's body over the dog, to hold the front and back legs on the opposite side and ease it down. On the first occasions, stroke the dog and then gently introduce a brush in a soothing manner, all the while talking to the dog calmly. Soon enough the dog will treat this as a pleasurable experience and grooming will be an easier process for both parties.

When grooming, the coat should never be completely dry or this will cause the ends of the hair to break. Instead use a mild conditioning spray, although this should be one designed for dogs, not for humans. Most good pet stores have a variety of such sprays available so by reading the instructions carefully you will be able to decide which is the most suitable for your own dog, or better still take recommendation from a more experienced per owner or acquaintance who has the same breed. When grooming for the show ring, it is important to read the Kennel Club, rules as in some countries some types of coat preparations are forbidden. A dog should also be taught to stand on the grooming table so that one has the benefit of grooming from that angle too, and of course one will need to add the finishing touches when the dog is standing still. If a parting is necessary along the back of the coat this should be done from the neck backwards, carefully taking a comb through with its edge, in one smooth stroke.

Some breeds need to be clipped, trimmed or stripped and this is quite an art so obtain expert advice and instruction before spending large sums of money on expensive clippers which are initially difficult to get used to using. Purchasing unsuitable equipment can also be an expensive mistake.

BATHING

ALTHOUGH bathing a dog, especially a large one, can be a daunting thought at first, it should really not be a major problem. A dog trained from puppyhood can really enjoy a bath. It is important that the dog has a non-slip surface on which to stand and that the water is never too hot or too cold. Shampoo must be thoroughly rinsed out and then a conditioner is generally used, but again the products used will depend to a cer-

Left
Keeping a show Yorkshire Terrier's coat in top condition involves a lot of work.

Centre Left
All dogs need bathing regularly to keep their coats clean.

Below
Some breeds, such as spaniels, will need clipping.

tain extent on the breed. When bathing a dog, always stroke the shampoo and conditioner into the coat rather than rubbing it in because the action of the latter will only serve to create knots and tangles in the dog's coat, which will be painful to extract.

After a very thorough rinsing, it is useful to use a highly absorbent cloth to squeeze out excess water from the coat before wrapping the dog in a towel, ideally a warm one, and then lifting it out of the bath. The dog will invariably wish to shake himself immediately, so this should preferably be encouraged in the bath rather than on the table.

Drying can then take place with a hairdryer, although it should be put on a warm setting rather than hot, and in most breeds, grooming should continue throughout the drying process to obtain the best end result.

Health and Breeding

IMMEDIATELY AFTER BUYING a dog it is wise for it to have a veterinary health check so that no problems go undetected from the outset. However, even healthy dogs can be affected by illness and, although it is not possible to detail all the things which may befall your dog, here are a few common ailments.

Abscess: An abscess is very painful and in long-coated breeds may go undetected until it has reached an advanced stage. The abscess should be gently bathed in a solution of hot salt water. This will bring it to a head so that it bursts and the pus content is released and drained. Bathing must continue after the abscess has burst because it must drain completely before the skin heals over. If the abscess does not burst or if more than one abscess appears a vet must be consulted and a course of antibiotics may be prescribed.

Anal glands: Situated on either side of the anus, these cause discomfort when full, as often observed when the dog scrapes its bottom along the ground. These glands can easily be emptied by your vet, who can show you how to do this yourself for future occasions.

Constipation: Usually caused by diet, constipation can frequently be rectified by altering the feeding programme. Offer soaked biscuits rather than totally dry food, and also lightly cooked green vegetables. A teaspoonful of oil can also help to clear out any blockage.

Dandruff: This may indicate that more fat is needed in the diet. Try adding a little vegetable oil to each meal or give canine oil capsules.

Diarrhoea: Often caused by a change of diet or a slight chill, diarrhoea can usually be rectified by starving a dog for 24 hours, allowing the stomach to empty and settle. Fresh drinking water must always be available. Feed a light diet for the next few days. If there is blood in the diarrhoea, or it is coupled with vomiting or other symptoms, veterinary advice must be sought at once.

Ear infections: Build-up of wax and ear mites can give rise to canker. A dog may scratch at the ear, shake the head or hold it on one side, and often there is foul-smelling discharge. Special ear drops will usually rectify the problem but hot, red ears need immediate veterinary attention.

Eye problems: These are many and varied and some breeds have

Top
A happy, healthy Basset.

Top Right
Always look after your dog's teeth. They need to be cleaned regularly.

Right
A dog's nails should be cut regularly to prevent discomfort in your pet when walking and running.

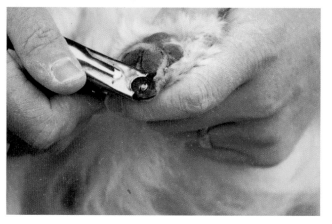

hereditary problems so must be tested accordingly. At any sign of ulceration or bluish colour in the eye seek veterinary advice without delay to avoid irreparable damage.

Heart problems: Although it is fairly rare to find a dog dying from a heart attack as we know it in humans, dogs can suffer from heart disease, especially when there is a either a gradual or sudden obstruction to the flow of blood to the brain causing them to collapse, becoming limp and unconscious. Frequently they recover within a matter of seconds, at which point they should be given fresh air. In coronary cases, which are caused by a poor blood supply to the heart muscle, the type of collapse is different – the limbs usually remain stiff and the dog does not lose consciousness. In either case veterinary attention for the dog must be sought without delay.

Hay fever: Dogs can have an allergy to pollens just as humans do and this is displayed by excessive watering of the eyes and sneezing due to inflammation of the mucous membranes within the nose. Finding the best form of relief is rarely easy but a vet or homeopath, often by trial and error, can discover some way of easing the problem.

Heat-stroke: A dog should always have access to shade and must never be left in a car, especially in warm or hot weather, even with the windows open. Heat builds up exceptionally quickly and death soon results as body temperature rises. Symptoms of heat stroke include vomiting, diarrhoea and collapse. To reduce body temperature, submerge the dog up to the neck in cool water, even a stream. If water is restricted, pour over whatever is available. Emergency veterinary help must be sought.

Inguinal hernia: Inguinal hernias, though not common, can be found in dogs or bitches and can be in one groin or in both. Sometimes they do not become apparent until a dog is well into adulthood. Veterinary advice should be sought upon first noticing such swelling in order to determine whether or not surgical intervention is necessary.

Intolerance to dairy products: A few breeds seem to have a particular intolerance to

a surfeit of dairy products which can cause a rash on the tummy or under the legs, either in patches or spots. If dairy products are fed, it is best to reduce or eliminate these to ascertain whether this is the cause of the rash.

Left
Puppy teeth are sore when they are developing.

Bottom
Dogs can suffer from hay fever, but like in humans, this can be treated.

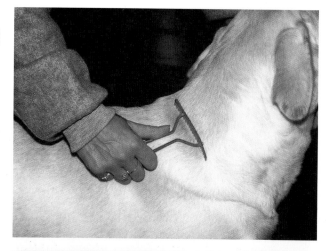

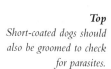

Top
Short-coated dogs should also be groomed to check for parasites.

Centre
It is sometimes easier to apply medicine with a syringe.

Right
It is necessary that hair between the pads are clipped to avoid knots from forming.

Kennel cough: Vaccinations are available to prevent kennel cough, which is highly contagious. In the early stages a dog attempts to clear the throat, later developing a hoarse cough. If this happens, your dog must be isolated and veterinary attention sought. Usually the problem is rectified with medication but young puppies and elderly or infirm dogs risk long term damage and even death.

Kidney failure: Frequent passing of water may indicate a kidney problem, especially if this is coupled with accelerated breathing and premature ageing. Veterinary advice is needed.

Liver diseases: All liver problems are serious so a vet must be contacted at the very first sign of any disorder. A noticeable symptom is jaundiced yellowing of the white of the eye, and of the membranes lining the eye and mouth. You may also notice a yellowing on the underside of the ear flap, less easy to detect in artificial light than in daylight. Other symptoms include sickness, loss of appetite, constipation and infrequent passing of highly coloured urine.

Pyometra: This is a serious problem caused by a bitch's uterus filling with pus, often initially noticed by high temperature and increased thirst. There are two forms of pyometra, one with vaginal discharge and one without, but both are life threatening and your vet must be consulted at once.

Spinal disorders: Especially in the low-legged, long-backed breeds one must be on the alert for back problems. Certain care should be taken, particularly with older dogs, when they are jumping on and off furniture. At any sign of spinal injury, a vet must be consulted at once. Sometimes a dog can recover, seemingly completely, but in other cases at least partial paralysis is a result. On veterinary advice only, swimming can be a useful means of exercise following injury. Some people have also used chiropractors on their dogs to good effect.

Travel sickness: Some dogs never suffer from travel sickness at all, others do so as puppies but outgrow this upon reaching adulthood. Take your vet's advice as to which travel sickness tablets to use if those easily available at pet shop counters do not have the desired effect. Always read the instructions very carefully.

Umbilical hernias: Breeding lines within some breeds of dog seem prone to umbilical hernias, appearing as a lump on the umbilicus. If present, this will be evident when a puppy is purchased. Such hernias vary in size and are usually soft. Veterinary examination is important for if they become hard they can strangulate, requiring urgent surgery.

Undescended testicles: Male dogs should have both testicles fully descended into the scrotum, usually clearly evident before the age of four or five months. If neither or only one appears, veterinary consultation is important because if testicles are present but have been retained there is risk of a tumour forming.

PARASITES

Internal parasites: In Britain, the two main internal parasites to infest dogs are roundworm and tapeworm. It is vitally important that a thorough worming programme is commenced while puppies are still with the breeder and that this is continued afterwards. In adulthood, dogs are usually wormed about once every six months. Always purchase your worming agent from a vet rather than a retail outlet and weigh your dog carefully so that you can administer the correct dosage.

Because the flea is an intermediate host to the tapeworm, be sure that the worming programme is up-to-date if your dog has fleas.

External parasites: If your dog begins to scratch the reason must be investigated immediately. A light rash on the stomach may be caused by an

allergic reaction to something but it is likely that the scratching is caused by irritation from a parasite, indeed a dog can even have an allergic reaction to fleas.

Fleas are small reddish-brown insects which thrive on blood and are not easy to see. They move quickly through the coat and can jump great distances. The presence of flea dirt which looks like small black grains of sand is a sure sign that your dog has fleas. A wide

variety of insecticidal agents is available but they should not be mixed, so take your vet's advice in this regard.

Lice are also biting insects but they move more slowly and do not jump, so are easier to discover and eradicate. They tend to accumulate on the animal's ears and neck.

Harvest mites, which can be cleared by using an appropriate shampoo bought from the vet, look like tiny grains of orange sand which form clusters between the dog's toes and sometimes also collect above the eyes.

Lastly there are *ticks*, blood-sucking insects which attach themselves to the skin, usually found in sheep and deer country. Careful removal of these is necessary, making sure that the head, too, is removed. Smothering in oil to prevent the tick breathing is one of several methods of removal.

Top
Dogs should be wormed while puppies and then every six months in adulthood to avoid getting internal parasites.

Centre
Dogs can pick up ticks from the long grass, especially in the summer months.

Emergency First Aid

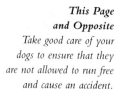

ANY ACCIDENT TO A DOG is greatly distressing, but perhaps road accidents rank among the worst and most dreaded. Through fear or because of pain, even a usually docile dog may be dangerous to handle, thereby exacerbating the problem, especially if the dog has been trapped in the accident.

ACTING QUICKLY

OBVIOUSLY A VET needs to be telephoned at once, although if possible it is quickest to take the dog to the surgery as a vet is unlikely to have all the equipment needed at the roadside. Telephone ahead to warn the vet and let him prepare for your arrival, giving as much information as possible as to the condition of the dog and what has occurred. During the telephone call tell your vet as much as possible about heartbeat, breathing, gasping, major haemorrhage, pale gums, inability to stand and any obvious fractures.

This Page and Opposite
Take good care of your dogs to ensure that they are not allowed to run free and cause an accident.

Do not panic. Approach the dog cautiously but reassuringly and restrained with a lead. If necessary, and for longer-nosed breeds only, a muzzle can be improvised, perhaps from a scarf or the like, tied around the muzzle and then around the back of the head. However, it is important that a muzzle is not applied if there is any sign of chest injury or if there is difficulty in breathing. A muzzled dog must not be left alone.

The dog must be moved extremely carefully, with you watching out for him going blue or having difficulty with breathing.

The dog can be transferred to a blanket which can be used as a stretcher, ideally aided by three people so that head, back and pelvis can be supported. In cases when help is not available, the dog should be moved onto the blanket slowly and carefully.

Thankfully, not all injuries are serious and the following information may help to alleviate some less serious problems which may be encountered:

Bites: Initially clean the wound by bathing it in warm water. If the skin's surface is broken, it needs examination by a vet in case antibiotic treatment or stitches are necessary.

Bleeding: Small cuts usually stop bleeding after a few minutes. Immediate professional help is needed if bleeding continues or pumps out from an artery. In an emergency, make a compress from clean material soaked in cold water, applied with enough pressure to arrest the bleeding.

Burns: Initially apply plenty of cold water to the burned area. Minor burns can be treated with a proprietary burns ointment but serious burns need veterinary attention as they are always accompanied by shock.

Collapse: Urgent veterinary attention is imperative. In the meantime, create an airway by clearing mucus from the throat and pulling the tongue forwards. If necessary, stimulate the dog's respiratory system with firm compressions to the chest wall every 10 seconds.

Foreign bodies lodged in the mouth: A dog which has difficulty in closing its mouth, is constantly pawing at its mouth or is salivating profusely may have something wedged between its teeth, or even across the roof of the mouth between the upper molars. If you are not able to dislodge this yourself with relative ease, a vet must be consulted without delay, because apart from the obvious discomfort to the dog, inflammation will almost certainly result.

Fur balls: In long- or heavily coated breeds, fur balls may sometimes be vomited without any sign of illness or discomfort. But they should never be regarded lightly as they can cause a dog to choke.

Poisoning: Although the causes of poisoning are varied, initial signs may include vomiting, muscular spasm and bleeding from an exit point such as the gums. If possible, tell your vet what poison may have been taken as the antidote will vary accordingly. When you are telephoning the vet, ask for advice as to whether or not vomiting should be induced; it may not be appropriate. Keep your dog warm and quiet with access to plenty of fresh air.

Stings: Dogs are apt to snap at flying insects and this must be discouraged as stings inside mouth and throat are dangerous, requiring immediate veterinary attention with anti-histamine injections. Keep your dog cool and pull the tongue forward, leaving the airway clear. Less serious are stings in the pad. Antiseptic lotions bring relief, and vinegar is good for wasp stings. Remove bee stings with tweezers and apply bicarbonate of soda.

Bottom
Long-haired dogs, such as Afghans, can cough up fur balls. It is important to ensure that these do not choke the animal.

Grass seeds: These can penetrate any part of a dog, their long barbs causing them to move further in to the coat. This can cause sudden irritation, infection or abscess and removal of the seed by a vet is often necessary.

Lameness: Lameness can arise for many reasons but if it occurs suddenly, the most likely cause is damage or discomfort to the pad of the foot. If there is a cut this will be noticed easily and veterinary help should be sought. However, sometimes it is not easy to find the reason for sudden limping. There could have been a bite, which may be seen by swelling, or the dog may have trodden on something sharp, such as a thorn, which has embedded itself. If the hair between the pads in long-coated breeds has not been kept short, a knot may have formed; this can be very painful and will need to be cut out with great care. Even a small stone may have lodged between the pads and, if so, can be removed with relative ease. Lameness which does not rectify itself quickly should always be investigated by a vet.

Caring for an Aged Dog

WITHOUT DOUBT, those who really care for their canine companions will wish them to have every comfort they deserve in their closing years. Different breeds mature at different rates and some live longer than others. As a general rule smaller breeds tend to live longer than larger ones, for example a breed such as a Lhasa Apso is likely to live for at least 14 years, whereas a Great Dane will have done well to reach double figures. Of course there are always exceptions, and good or bad general heath plays an important role.

MATURING RATES

THE DIFFERENCE in maturing rate means that breeds do not age at the same pace; in addition heavy dogs suffer from different age-related illness to lightweight breeds.

TEETH

IF YOU HAVE taken care of your dog's teeth throughout its life, there is a good chance in many breeds that your dog will keep all or most of its teeth into old age, although especially in the Toy breeds, and others in which teeth are shallow rooted, a dog is more likely to lose teeth, even at a fairly young age. If a number of back teeth have been lost, your dog will appreciate rather softer food to aid mastication. If an older dog is not used to having its teeth cleaned regularly it is unlikely to take well to this as a new procedure late in life. There are, however, palatable chews which can be useful as a cleaning agent.

WEIGHT

MAINTAINING A SENSIBLE weight is an important factor in retaining good health into old age as a dog which is obese will put more strain on tendons and ligaments and is therefore likely to develop problems with mobility in later life. Obesity puts additional strain on the heart and other organs and can cause respiratory problems. It should also be recognised that older dogs are more prone to weight gain than younger ones, especially if they have been spayed or castrated.

If a dog has habitually been fed only one meal daily, in old age it will appreciate the same amount being split into two separate meals. This not only aids digestion but adds another 'highlight' to the day. Some older dogs, according to their medical condition, thrive on a high-quality, low-protein diet and advice can be taken from the vet in this regard.

WORMS AND WORMING

ALTHOUGH A COUGH can be a sign of a heart problem, it can also indicate worm infestation, so a routine worming programme should have been carried out throughout the dog's life. If a dog is seriously ill, worming can weaken the system still further and veterinary advice must be sought before administration of worming tablets, so careful attention should always be paid to this aspect of canine husbandry.

Above

Looking after your dog's teeth throughout its lifetime will ensure a healthy mouth in old age.

Centre Right

Reduced mobility in old age can lead to weight gain.

Right

An elderly Lhasa Apso is an extremely amiable pet.

SIGHT

SOME DOGS ARE fortunate to retain their sight until their dying day, but in others, fading eyesight regrettably takes its toll. Providing an old dog has not gone suddenly blind it can usually cope very well – so well indeed that sometimes an owner has no idea that there is little or no sight left. If a dog's eyesight is failing, it is important that furniture in the house is not moved around unnecessarily and obviously the dog should be kept under close supervision in the garden or in any public place so that accidents do not occur.

TOILET

AN AGEING DOG CAN sometimes have problems controlling the 'water-works'. This can be for a variety of reasons so one's vet should be consulted to determine the underlying cause. Giving a reprimand for any accidents will have no positive effect and, after all, a dog which has been clean all its life will not take pleasure in causing soiling. An old dog should be given frequent opportunities to go outside, thereby reducing the chance of accidents.

INTRODUCING A PUPPY

ALTHOUGH THE INTRODUCTION of a youngster in to the household can in some cases put a sparkle back into the life of an old dog, introduction of a newcomer in the very last stages of a dog's life is not generally a good idea. It is of ultimate importance that an old dog is allowed to retain its position of importance in the home and only an owner will truly know how best that can be done. Undoubtedly, if a youngster is introduced, the two should only be left together under supervision as the older dog will need its rest and a little privacy.

TIME TO PART

SOONER OR LATER the dreaded time comes. If you are lucky, your aged dog will die peacefully in its sleep, without pain, and this will spare you the anguish of having to decide whether to make that important decision to have your dog put kindly to sleep. If a dog is showing signs of distress and pain, you may feel it is better to stop the suffering. In this sad case, you may feel it kindest to ask your vet to visit you and your dog at home, and remember that, in Britain at least, if your dog is put to sleep in the surgery you will not be able to take it home for burial in your garden.

Cremation services can be arranged, and although substantial cost is involved, they ensure that you have control over what happens to your dog when it moves to its happy hunting ground.

Left
This veteran Lhasa Apso is likely to live for at least 14 years.

Centre Left
At 13 years old this Lhasa Apso is still able to scale a fence.

Bottom
Older dogs will still enjoy being outside even if they are not as active as once they were.

Breeding Dogs

MAKING THE DECISION to play a part in producing a litter of puppies is not something to be taken lightly. Both sire and dam must be high-quality, healthy, strong and typical specimens of the breed which complement each other. If one parent has an anatomical fault which needs improvement then the other should be free from that fault in an attempt to eradicate it. Pedigrees must also be studied: not just of one generation of dog but several.

The long-standing idea that a bitch should be allowed to have a litter for her own good is pure myth. She can just as easily live a full and happy life without ever having produced puppies so owners who are planning to breed for this reason alone should rethink their plans.

Routine worming for the bitch is advisable before she comes into season. She will only be ready for mating for a few days while on heat – usually three to five. Before and after that time she will not be receptive to a dog's advances and her vulva is unlikely to be large enough to permit comfortable penetration. When a suitable stud dog has been selected and his owner has agreed to a mating, contact should be made again on the very first day of the season to give notice of an approximate date of mating. Mating should always take place at the stud dog owner's home and frequently two matings are given, with a day's gap in between. Any contractual arrangements should be agreed by both parties in writing. Often a stud dog owner will agree to a mating at a subsequent season if no puppies are produced.

PLANNING TO BREED

Right
Both bitch and dog should be archetypes of their breed for pedigree puppies.

AGE IS A consideration which is partly dependent upon the breed. No bitch should have a litter below the age of 18 months and as a general rule it is wise to have a first litter by the age of four. The upper limit for breeding from a bitch is usually seven years in Britain.

Bottom
This excellent whelping box allows sufficient space for the bitch and her three puppies.

THE MATING

DOGS DIFFER in their approaches to a visiting bitch, and the bitches in question can vary too. In an ideal mating, the two will show an interest in one another and frolic around a little before the male mounts the bitch. However, it is not always so easy as this might appear, especially in the case of either a maiden dog or a bitch, which is one of the reasons why it is inadvisable for two inexperienced dogs to be put together for a mating. At a successful mating, after penetration the dog and bitch will usually be tied together for some minutes, usually about 15, but this can be as long as an hour. The union should be supervised at all times

and the bitch not permitted to attempt to pull away for fear of injury to the dog. Eventually the bitch's muscles will relax to release the dog and they are often left together for just a few moments afterwards before being separated.

It is very important to realise that if a bitch is mated by more than one dog, there is very strong likelihood that some puppies will have one sire and some another, so it is imperative that a bitch is not allowed to come into contact with any other males.

THE PREGNANT BITCH

FOLLOWING A MATING, a bitch's size and behaviour changes little for the first five weeks, at which time some abdominal enlargement may become noticeable. Until then her food intake will be fairly normal, but it must be of high quality throughout her pregnancy. She should also be allowed to have her usual amount of exercise to keep her in good form.

Around the seventh week, her mammary glands begin to enlarge and she will already have been eating increasing amounts of food for a couple of weeks. Meals must be smaller but more frequent.

She will need access to a quiet place to rest and should be introduced to her whelping quarters no later than the eighth week as the gestation period is 63 days, although puppies can be produced a few days earlier or later. An ideal whelping box allows the bitch ample space to turn around without stepping on her puppies. A guard rail is essential around the sides of the box so that she cannot inadvertently crush the whelps. These rails can be removed as the puppies grow larger and are better able to fend for themselves. Placed in a warm place and raised slightly from the ground to prevent draughts, the box should allow the bitch to get in and out of it easily, and at the same time it must be sufficiently high to prevent the puppies' escape. An adjustable and detachable front to the box is useful so that when the puppies do get up on their feet,

they can have access to a small additional play area in front of the box.

CONDITION

THE BITCH'S COAT should be kept in good condition in pregnancy, though she should not be subjected to long grooming sessions. During the final couple of weeks she will take less exercise and must be discouraged from jumping. During the last 24 hours of her pregnancy she may refuse all food, her temperature will drop and she will become restless, scratching up her bedding. All this indicates that whelping time is close; notify your vet in case a house call becomes necessary due to complications in the birth process.

Top
A Shih Tzu puppy.

Above Left
A bitch on heat wearing sanitary knickers.

Above
A boxer bitch in whelp.

THE WHELPING

THE EASE WITH WHICH a bitch is likely to whelp depends to a large extent on her construction; breeds with larger heads or other over-exaggerated features being more likely to encounter problems than others. At some births assistance is needed, while in other cases a bitch is best allowed to do all the work herself, but one must be on hand to supervise and assist if necessary. Some breeds have a greater incidence of caesarean sections than do others, again depending on construction.

New mothers can be thrown into confusion until the first puppy has been born and is suckling, and in certain breeds it is usual for the owner to break the sac which surrounds the puppy and to cut the umbilical cord. In other breeds this may not be necessary. Advice must therefore be taken

Above
At a few days old with eyes closed, a Shih Tzu puppy.

Top Right
Shih Tzu puppies with their eyes open.

from established breeders as to what sort of whelping problems one is or is not likely to encounter. Obviously all those breeding litters with due forethought will have read extensively and taken breed specialist advice. Breeding courses are also available and well worthwhile.

THE NEWBORN PUPPIES

PUPPIES NEED TO SUCKLE from their dam as soon as possible and should be carefully observed, without too much interference, to see that all are suckling successfully and thriving. It is sensible to check for cleft palate at birth. A gap in the upper palate would be felt with the little finger and although a young whelp may be able to suckle, it is unlikely to cope with solid food. Some breeders weigh each puppy at birth and monitor weight gain over the first two or three weeks.

For the first couple of weeks at least, a dam should be allowed to enjoy her puppies without intrusion from a stream of inquisitive visiting neighbours and friends. There will be plenty of opportunity to show them off when they are a little older and when the dam will not be so possessive about them.

Almost all – around 90 per cent – of the newborn puppy's life will be spent sleeping and while asleep there will be a good deal of muscle twitching. This is normal and is essential in the development of muscles. Puppies' nails are very sharp and should be cut regularly with nail scissors to avoid discomfort to the bitch. They are always born with their eyes closed but these generally start to open between the ninth and eleventh day, though to begin with they will not focus properly. At birth the ears are sealed but these are usually open between the thirteenth and seventeenth days; from then on they will be responsive to sound and the world will slowly start to come alive to them.

WEANING

WEANING USUALLY COMMENCES during the third or fourth week, firstly with milk-based meals and then with the gradual introduction of meat meals on an alternate basis. Four meals per day will eventually be decreased in number and the puppies should no longer be dependent on their dam for food by the age of about seven weeks.

DEW CLAWS AND TAILS

FOR PEOPLE BREEDING DOGS to close specification, veterinary advice must be taken regarding removal of dew claws and tail docking. People breeding dogs purely as family pets may not consider this relevant, but in some breeds, removal of dew claws is a requirement of the breed standard. In others they must remain, while in most the choice is left with the breeder. If the decision has been taken to remove them, this must be done on the third day, certainly not later than the fourth. If you do not ask the vet to visit your home, puppies may be taken to the vet's surgery but the dam will

need to go along too because she will be distressed if they are taken away from her for any length of time. Under no circumstances, however, must she be with or within earshot of the puppies whilst the claws are being taken off for she will be unnecessarily distressed by their cries. Puppies miraculously stop crying within a matter of seconds so she will soon find herself back with them again.

Because laws and opinions vary regarding tail docking, specialist advice taken from within the breed is important. Also, because in some countries legislation has changed recently, advice regarding tail docking needs verbal clarification because that read in a book may already be rather out of date.

CARE OF THE DAM

A BITCH RAISING a litter of puppies will need all the care and attention due to her. Her meals must be of high quality and offered fairly frequently, in small portions. Liquid must be available, ideally

containing powdered glucose. A raw egg yolk (the white should not be given) seems always to be appreciated and will benefit her. To guard against eclampsia, most breeders also like to give calcium. The author personally gives calcium in liquid form from the day of whelping and finds this is lapped up easily if mixed in with the egg yolk.

There are medical problems, such as eclampsia, metritis and mastitis, which can occur in unfortunate cases, so your vet should have the opportunity of checking the bitch soon after birth, following which you should always be alert to changes in behaviour which may signal trouble.

Below
A young Lhasa Apso puppy nervously explores the garden.

Centre
Puppies find everything an adventure, not knowing what is safe or not.

Bottom
A Shetland Sheepdog puppy.

The History of Dogs

ANCESTORS OF THE DOG evolved because of changes in climate and habitat. As time went on they developed the social relationships needed to hunt successfully in packs, enabling them to bring down and kill animals larger in size and body-weight.

Right
The jackal may have contributed to the genes of the domestic dog.

Far Right
The dog evolved from the wolf, gradually becoming more domesticated.

Bottom
The dog's pack instinct meant that it could be trained to hunt.

RELATIONS OF THE DOG

THERE ARE TEN genera of *Canidae*, among which the dog belongs to the genus *canis* which also incorporates jackals, coyotes and wolves; these are the dog's closest relations. All share the same number of chromosomes and are capable of breeding with each other.

OTHER RELATIONS

MORE DISTANTLY related are the animals in the other nine generations, of which the fox is one, and of which there are 21 different species. Others include the African Wild Dog, also called the Cape Hunting Dog and African Hunting Dog, which lives in packs ranging between six and 25; India's Dhole, which has the widest range of habitat amongst all wild canids, and the Maned Wolf which differs from true wolves and lives in some South American countries. The Racoon Dog reputedly has no bark but has other behavioural characteristics in common with members of the dog family, while South America's Bush Dog communicates

by whining and is notably different from the dog's other distant relations.

Although it is likely that the coyote and jackal have contributed in a small way to the genes of the domestic dog, they do not share the social behaviour of the wolf which is now known to be dog's closest ancestor. The wolf is a social predator which, until the human hand intervened, was found throughout Europe, Asia and North America. As a scavenger, the wolf has long been associated with human settlements and has followed in man's footsteps at least since the beginning of *Homo sapiens*, a recent theory being that the connection goes back still further, around 100,000 years. There have been many different sub-

species of wolf, ranging from the Kenai Wolf, which finally became extinct in 1915, and the North American Wolf, which is the largest member of the family still existing today, to the Japanese Wolf, which is possibly the smallest member of the family that survived into the twentieth century; the last one was killed in 1905.

As a wolf cub grows up it develops attachment behaviour, as do puppies, and like the dog the wolf adopts dominant and submissive postures. The Asiatic or Arab Wolf, a particularly adaptable and sociable animal, inhabited areas from which dogs are known to have emerged and is likely to have its blood running through the veins of many of the European and Asian domestic dogs today.

EVOLUTION OF THE DOMESTIC DOG

THE WAY IN WHICH THE DOG developed from the wolf in the early stages probably occurred through natural selection. Wolves were attracted to human settlements because of their nature as scavengers and it is likely that some wolf cubs were brought up by humans, taken into the settlements to be raised and cared for. From these semi-domesticated animals, dogs would have evolved; these acted as guards and assisted in hunting, cleaned up campsites by way of scavenging and indeed may well themselves have provided food when meat was scarce.

DOG AND MAN

AS THE YEARS WORE ON, dogs developed to suit their association with man, yet still retaining behavioural stages of the wolf's development and many physical attributes of this ancestor. One has only to look at the Aboriginal Australians' associations with the dingo to realise how easily the dog could be accepted into the lives of such communities, each benefiting from the other.

The Aboriginals have reared young dingoes, caring for them like children and when fully grown they have been used successfully to flush game, reward enough for the kindness shown to them.

Eventually man played his part in adapting the dog to best suit his own environment and needs, selectively breeding for certain traits, both temperamental and physical. Sizes increased and decreased according to requirement and taste. A loud bark was required for dogs which were used to warn of danger and this, coupled with imposing size, could put fear into an intruder. Long legs and powerful muscles were needed in dogs used in the chase, while those hunting by scent needed an improved sense of smell.

NATURAL PACK MEMBERS

DOGS WERE USED TO behaving as pack animals and found themselves willing to become members of human packs, able to work with man or with other dogs as the need arose and capable of protecting other animals belonging to man when required to do so. Hunting methods were developed, and the dog's natural ability to track and to retrieve game was recognised and developed further, later becoming a leisure activity, not merely a necessity.

Dogs worked for their rewards and also became companions. Perhaps they provided warmth, and their affection and devotion was doubtless appreciated, but later the dog's appearance was refined to suit aesthetic taste and personal whim.

> **DOG FACT:**
> The Greyhound is the fastest dog in the world and the 18th fastest land mammal.

Top
Selective breeding enabled man to adapt the characteristics of the dog to suit pursuits such as hunting.

Left
The pariah dog is semi-domesticated and survives by scavenging.

Bottom
For hundreds of years dogs were expected to work in return for food and shelter, but in modern times they are more valued for their companionship.

> **DOG FACT:**
> Born in 1926, 'Mick the Miller' won the Derby twice, followed by 19 consecutive races.

Dogs in the Ancient Past

FROM EARLY PICTURE-WRITING we are able to learn something about dogs of Ancient Egypt and other great cultures. On the tombs of ancient people of rank are portrayals of dogs that had been their companions in life. In Egypt the oldest is the 'Khufu Dog', appearing on the tomb of King Khufu (also known as Cheops) who lived around 3730 BC and was responsible for the building of the Great Pyramid. His personal house dog was called Akbaru, always depicted tied close to his master's chair and wearing a fashionable collar tied four times around his neck.

Top Right
Greyhounds appear on the 2,500 BC tomb of Ptahhetep Sakkara.

Right
Mummified dogs indicate that the Ancient Egyptians deeply valued their companionship.

Bottom
Some cultures viewed dogs as sacred. They were depicted as companions of the gods or even worshiped as gods.

BAHAKAA

MANY ANCIENT EGYPTIAN DOGS were kept as household pets but others were for hunting and, on the tomb of Amten, some 200 years later than Khufu, dogs were clearly depicted attacking deer. Around the same time, dogs' names were recorded in temples. The tomb of Antefa II in 3000 BC represents four dogs at the king's feet, one wearing a narrow collar, tied with a bow at the front. Called Bahakaa, this dog was white with hanging ears, although most dogs of that time were shown with pricked ears.

Later, there were long-bodied Dachshund-like dogs with mottled black and tan markings, indeed the shape and colour of fashionable dogs seemed to depend largely upon the tastes of the ruling monarch at the time. There is conjecture about whether the Egyptians actually dyed their dogs' hair but certainly some were depicted in blue, red and green.

When their pets died, people went into deep mourning and anyone finding a dead dog was duty bound to send it back to its home town so that it could have a proper burial. From this it must be assumed that some means of identification was used.

SACRED BEINGS

IN SOME AREAS DOGS were considered divine beings, such as in Cynopolis, a town which took its name from a dog. Here, people were obliged to provide specified amounts of food for the dogs to eat. On one occasion there was even a war with a neighbouring town because one of its inhabitants had eaten a dog from Cynopolis. Although the bull and ibis were held in still higher esteem, the sacred character of the dog was acknowledged by many. Upon a dog's death people shaved their heads and mourned loudly. They also fasted and sometimes destroyed all food in the house. Carefully embalmed, the dog was placed in a tomb specifically allotted to dogs and at the graveside the master gave an account of all the good things the dog had done in his life whilst mourners beat themselves with grief. Each town had a burial ground just for dogs and often these were so full that they had to be enlarged. Many dogs' bodies recovered in later years were found to have been buried in their leather collars.

THE DOG STAR

DOG WORSHIP ORIGINATED in part from Sirius, the Dog Star, which marked the greatest day in the Egyptians' year, for when the star rose over the horizon it was a sign that the Nile would overflow, and on this flood their lives depended. The Dog Star, however, also rose at the hottest time of the year and people believed this made the dogs bad-tempered and prone to hydrophobia.

Another reason for worship of the dog revolved around the story of Isis, who was assisted by a dog in her search for the body of Osiris. The jackal-headed Anubis, also gave cause for reverence surrounding the dog because he played a part in the process of embalming bodies and saw to it that the beam of the balance used to weigh the heart was in the correct position. He also appeared before dead bodies to protect them from the Eater of the Dead.

Around 625 BC, many dogs of the Mastiff type were used to hunt lion and wild ass; some of these dogs had such imaginative names as The Biter-of-His-Foes, The Seizer-of-His-Enemies and He-Ran-and-Barked. One hundred years later an Egyptian king had large bands of fierce dogs trained to attack in formation.

ROLE IN OTHER LANDS

IN PERSIA IT was a crime to kill a dog, and in Babylon four towns were exempted from all taxes in return for which the people were trained to breed Mastiffs for the armies. In Ancient Greece, the dog was used by herdsmen and also in the chase, which was a favourite sport – it was through the chase that the Greeks trained themselves for war. Some of the larger dog breeds in Greece were used at war to fight alongside the army in squadrons, and it is believed that Corinth was saved by the watchdogs on duty on the ramparts while their masters slept.

In Japan, the dog was venerated because of its connection with the god Omisoto. Curiously, dogs in Japan were buried standing up with their heads left above the ground, so that for several days after they died, people came up to lay food beside them.

Top
Assyrian troops used dogs to fight in wars.

Bottom
The dog-headed Egyptian god, Anubis.

Popular Dogs

AS THEIR MANY ATTRIBUTES were soon recognised by man, it is not surprising that dogs became popular not only as hunting and working animals but also as pets. Portrayed in art forms for many a long year, they also played an important part in folklore and religion.

Eventually, these so-called sports became crimes, but dog-fighting became increasingly popular, taking over from the baiting sports to a certain extent. Money was won and lost and many a prized dog lost its life; ironic reward for having lined the pockets of its owner in previous fights.

Many a terrier has a reputation for being a good ratter but dogs not only killed rats as an efficient method of ridding neighbourhoods of vermin, there were also rat pits. Wagers were made based upon how many rats a dog could be expected to kill in a given period of time, one of repute having killed 100 large ones in five and a half minutes.

DOGS AND HUNTING

TODAY THERE IS MUCH contro-versy over the hunting sports, but dogs have been used to hunt in one form or another since time immemorial. Many of the old hunting parties were spectacular events, and boar hunting was frequently described vividly in old manuscripts. The dog has assisted both in the hunt and in the retrieval of animals and birds. The Irish Wolfhound and Borzoi were used very successfully against the wolf, the latter famously employed in the great hunts of Russia's Archduke Nicolai Nikolajawitsch, often involving as many as 32 couples – in that time a couple com-prised three, not two dogs as today – whilst in Scotland landed gentry used the Deerhound for stalking deer. Although now illegal, dogs have long been used against the badger and other animals. Bloodhounds have been used to track people down.

Dogs of many kinds have been used by the police, security and other services, their important work respected throughout the world. The compe-tence of sniffer dogs is also well-regarded and there are many impressive stories to be told.

IN THE SERVICE OF MAN

ANOTHER FORM OF HUNTING, of sorts, was truffle hunting, a skill known to only a few. Truffles were

Top and Bottom
Dogs have played an important role in the life from Ancient Egypt to modern day.

ANCIENT ROLES

IN ANCIENT EGYPT, dogs were mummified after their death and Anubis, the Egyptian deity who accompanied souls of the dead to their final judge-ment, was depicted with a jackal's head and human body. Even in the Christian church St Christopher has been portrayed with the head of a dog. Dogs were used in baiting sports and some were even put into cages with lions. Bull-running was another variation on a theme, with crowds of people running through the streets with dogs in pursuit of a bull, causing both delight and fear.

how difficult life has been for those living in regions where sled dogs were simply a way of life, undoubtedly an invaluable aid to owners who were otherwise completely cut off from the outside world.

Dogs were used extensively during the war years, for moving guns and wounded soldiers, and transporting supplies. Some even conveyed injured war dogs, a sort of canine carting ambulance service. During the war, dogs were also used to help lay mines and to convey messages to the troops stationed behind the lines, sometimes wearing gas masks.

Left
Dogs were an essential part of badger-hunting and were valued for their courage and tenacity.

Below
Baiting sports were a popular pastime and dogs were matched against a variety of creatures including lions.

cleverly found by the dogs whose powers of scent were greater than those of the pig or wild sow which had been formerly been used. Another dog, useful to the kitchen staff at least, was the Turnspit, a long, low-bodied dog who toiled away in the wheel by the fire to turn the roasting spit.

Draught dogs were frequently used to pull carts, especially in Europe where they were used by small traders as well as by coal merchants and others involved in industry and agriculture. Historically, there has been much conflict of opinion as to whether or not it was 'right' to allow dogs to be used as draught animals, but the pulling of sleds seems to have been less of a shock to people's sensibilities. Maybe it is relatively easy to visualise

MAN'S HELPERS

THE FIRST RECORDED attempt to train dogs for guide work was in the eighteenth century, when a Paris hospital provided blind patients with dogs in order to lead them through the streets. Since then there have been many blind and partially sighted people who have benefited enormously from the service provided by guide dogs; they undergo strenuous training and are judged on their performance before being accepted as guide dogs. Comparative services are performed by Hearing Dogs for the Deaf, and Dogs for the Disabled. PAT Dogs provide comfort to the infirm.

Bottom
Dogs have often been used as draught animals in the past but, with the exception of huskies, this no longer meets with approval in Western countries.

The Baiting Sports

BAITING SPORTS WERE undoubtedly abhorrent pastimes but none the less they are part of canine history and as such it is prudent to look back on how life was lived, and one cannot do that without remembering that such unsavoury sports were very much a part of everyday life. Looking at the subject from another viewpoint, perhaps we owe it to the many poor animals who suffered in this way to remember their plight and pledge to do better.

THE ROMAN EMPIRE

WHILE THE BAITING OF ANIMALS may be traced back to early records, it reached its heyday during the Roman Empire, when various wild animals were pitted against each other, or against criminals or professional hunters. It was realised that even the bull could provide a similar spectacle, so various animals which were better known in a domestic environment came to be used as well as wild animals such as lions.

BULL BAITING

IN ENGLAND, BULL BAITING became extremely popular during the Middle Ages. In the reign of Henry II (1154–89), in the forenoon of every holiday during the winter season, the youth of London amused itself with spectacles of boars matched against each other, and bears being baited by dogs. The first bear garden in London was known as the Paris Gardens and in such venues as this bulls and bears were fastened from behind and then worried by 'great English bull dogs'. This, however, was not without risk to the dogs which were sometimes killed on the spot. Fresh ones were immediately on hand to replace those badly wounded or killed.

When bull baiting was popular, municipal authorities not only gave public approval to these displays but actually enforced them. It was the duty of mayors to see that plenty of animals were provided for the purpose and records of Leicester's town books show an order was made that no butcher was allowed to kill a bull for sale within the town unless it had been baited. At Chesterfield in Derbyshire, a fine of three shillings and four pence was payable if a bull was killed without first being baited in the market-place.

Above
Contests between exotic wild animals were a favourite Roman pastime.

Right
Animal baiting took many forms. The entertainment always ended with the bloody death of all the animals.

DOG FACT:
In 1944 a litter of 23 was produced by an American Foxhound in Pennsylvania, USA.

A CRUEL 'SPORT'

SAMUEL PEPYS VIEWED THE MATTER with some compassion for in 1666 he described baiting as a 'very rude and nasty pleasure' and wrote of bulls tossing dogs, one of which went into the very boxes. In 1670, John Evelyn tells of bulls tossing a dog into a lady's lap as she sat in the boxes at some considerable height from the arena. He, too, was both weary of and saddened by the pastime. There are vivid pictures of several butchers and other men standing around a tethered bull, holding their dogs by their ears until the sport began. The bull was severely bitten by the dogs, while several dogs were killed having been tossed high into the air by the bull.

Bull-baiting had a particularly strong hold in the Midlands and men went to extreme lengths to obtain their bulls, many a bull being stolen from a neighbouring town. Men of Coventry once pawned their church bell and purchased a bull with the money they gained from the bell, but the unholy act met with judgement for the very same bull was stolen by men from Nuneaton who subsequently baited it.

In Warwickshire the owners of a bull usually charged eight pence for each dog to run at the bull, allowing four or five minutes for the baiting. Much depended on the skill, training and also the breeding of the dogs used. Too plucky a bull dog, lacking discretion, would rush at the bull's face and in consequence was tossed high for his pains. A more accomplished dog would approach from the rear, charging between the animal's legs and pinning him by the nose and lips, retaining his hold with strength and tenacity.

Berkshire was one of the last counties in England where bull-baiting was practised and Bracknell was particularly famous for it. Every town had its common, where at least once a year much blood of both bulls and dogs was shed. The favourite day of the year for this gruesome sport was Good Friday.

BAITING IS BANNED

TOWARDS THE end of the eighteenth century, growing sentiment led to protests against the so-called 'sport', but while some municipalities tried their best to stop baiting, other local authorities held with the old traditions of encouraging it.

Preston seems to have been one of the earliest communities to fight against the sport for, on 11 November 1726, a resolution was passed that no more bulls for baiting were to be purchased with public money. In 1801 Joseph Strutt wrote: 'Bull and bear baiting is not encouraged by persons of rank and opulence in the present day, and when practised, which rarely happens, it is attended only by the lowest and most despicable of the people.' Slowly opinion had begun to change.

Top
Although the baited bear was handicapped by being securely fastened to the wall it was still able to kill incautious dogs.

Centre
Bull baiting was a dangerous sport for the dogs, who could be gored or tossed. Much depended on the dog's training and skills.

Bottom
Towards the end of the eighteenth century public opinion began to turn against baiting. However, traditions die hard and, despite being illegal, baiting still takes place.

Carting Dogs

THE SOUND OF BUTCHERS' carts' iron wheels rattling along the cobbled streets of London in the early hours of the morning was a regular occurrence in medieval times. Meat was taken from Smithfield Market to shops all over the city and the carts were frequently drawn by dogs. These caused considerable disturbance as dawn broke because drivers were in the habit of racing each other, their dogs barking furiously with excitement. It was not unusual to see children arriving in carts similar to small goat carts, pulled by one or two substantial dogs, such as Newfoundlands. In Newfoundland itself dogs were used for the very same purpose, as well as for pulling wood from the forests to the houses.

THE DOG CART

Top Right
Dog carts were used by traders such as this Belgian milk-seller.

Right
Dog carts became illegal in Britain in the nineteenth century.

Bottom
Disabled John Gregory found that a dog cart enabled him to travel.

COSTERMONGERS USED CARTS on weekdays to sell fruit and vegetables and the very same ones doubled up at weekends as a means of conveying their sweethearts on leisurely outings. The dog cart was certainly used for many varied purposes. A woodcut of 1837 depicts the cats' meat man, with the vendor sitting on the back of the cart proffering meat on a skewer to any passer by that may have shown an interest. Beneath the woodcut is the following poem:

> They call me 'Paunch the Cats' meat Swell'
> In Peter's Street I dwells, Sir
> I keeps my whittlin hoffice there
> And mousers' grub I sell, Sir

Carts were also used for personal travel, not only for trade. John Gregory, born in Scotland in 1799, had lost both his legs whilst still young due to a coal mine explosion in the north of England. In order to get about as easily as possible, Gregory used a dog cart and this poem explains his reasons for doing so:

> The reason why I keeps a dog
> And drives about and begs,
> Is not because my betters does,
> But 'cause I've lost my legs.

CONTINENTAL DOG CARTS

IN BELGIUM AND HOLLAND during the twentieth century, dogs and their carts rendered such precious service to small traders and those in agriculture that no public authority dared suppress their use. There would have been an outcry had the cart been prohibited and the consequences disastrous, with many relatively affluent households finding themselves penniless.

In compromise, a club for the improvement of the draught dog was established to include encouragement of breeding dogs most suitable for the purpose. It aimed to improve the harnessing of dogs, they were to be better led and their carts better balanced and better moving. Drivers were offered advice and given opportunities to win prizes, ranging from diplomas and medals to cash.

In the 1930s, Belgium's markets were still busy with numerous small dog carts drawn by happy, barking dogs, most seeming well-pleased with their strenuous work. However, the carts were not only used by market gardeners, but also by milkmen and milkmaids, butchers, bakers and even coal merchants. In most cases only one or two dogs were harnessed, but sometimes there were as many as five. The cost of purchasing such a dog was in the region of £4 and they were usually fed on horse flesh which seemed to suit them well.

The laws relating to draught dogs in Holland were not very strictly employed but carts were also used in Switzerland, Austria and Czechoslovakia where their use was regulated by municipal councils. Dogs too old, too young, in whelp or still suckling a litter could not be used, and the minimum height of a draught dog was 61 cm (24 in). Dogs could not be left harnessed to their carts in the sun and some carts were adapted so that dogs had the chance to lie down under the cart while deliveries were made. No child under the age of 14 years was allowed to supervise dogs with carts.

ATTACHING THE DOG

HARNESSES HAD TO BE PADDED on those parts which came into contact with the dog, and vehicles with fewer than four wheels had either to have a support, or shafts curling outward so they did not hinder the dog if it wished to lie down. A third shaft was fitted to prevent the load pressing on the neck of the dog. Carts had to be on springs, axles greased and there were weight restrictions and instructions regarding dogs being covered in inclement weather.

CARTS BECOME ILLEGAL

IN BRITAIN THE DOG CART was officially made illegal in the nineteenth century, brought about largely by the coaching companies who were in competition with the dog-drawn carts, in particular for the delivery of parcels. Most of those who used carts were considered low social class and, with society as it was then, there was no difficulty in getting the Act passed.

> **DOG FACT:**
> Frequently, for amusement, dogs and drivers raced against each other with their carts for distances of up to 4.8 km (3 miles).

Above
In Newfoundland, dog carts were used for a variety of purposes from transporting the family to gathering fire wood.

Left
Dogs were widely employed to pull carts in many European countries. Regulations varied, but most countries attempted to protect dogs' welfare.

Carriage Dogs

I N DALMATIA, on the eastern Adriatic coast, the Dalmatian was trained to run alongside horse-men in the field, a dog well suited to this difficult task and one with excellent stamina. By the eighteenth century the breed's original purpose had fallen into disuse but later that century it arrived in Britain. Here, it came into use as a coach or carriage dog, although it was then common practice to cut down the ears, supposedly in order to increase the beauty of the breed. In some cases the entire flap was removed, exposing the ear cavity, but this increased exposure to infection and by about 1880 the practice had completely died out.

GUARD DOGS

DURING THE HEYDAY of the coaching era the Dalmatian was used as a guard for horses, coaches, carriages and their contents and could frequently be seen running alongside such means of conveyance throughout Victorian times. It is said that even as late as the 1950s they could still, very occasionally, be seen running between the wheels of a carriage.

THE COACH DOG

THROUGHOUT the nineteenth century, especially during the early years, the Dalmatian was better known by the name of Coach Dog or Carriage Dog. The Great Dane also accompanied

carriages and this, too, was often called Coach Dog. To differentiate between the two, sometimes the Dalmatian had to make do with the name 'Common Coach Dog'. Another name it often shared with the Great Dane was 'Plum Pudding Dog', whilst in France it was known as the 'Little Dane', to distinguish it from the Great Dane.

Due to the breed's spotting, the Dalmatian could be seen more easily at night so was particularly useful when running alongside carriages in the country-side. For many years the breed was thought to be lacking in intelligence, incapable of being employed in any other manner than with a carriage or accompanying its master's horse at exercise. Thankfully, with the progression of time, it became recognised that this supposition was far from the truth.

It was highly fashionable to have a dog attending a carriage and horses during their journey, an essential part of the entourage of smart people around town. However, fashion was rather tempered with the passage of time and the Dalmatian soon found itself under the axle of the carriage. The dog took up various places in terms of where it actually ran with the carriage. For the sake of ornament it often ran behind, galloped ahead of the carriage or ran by its side, but whatever the position, its powers of endurance were remarkable.

> **DOG FACT**
> Barry Manilow had his Beagle psychoanalysed.

Top Right
Dalmatians tend to inspire enthusiasm, but not many would go to the lengths of donning this fancy-dress ball outfit.

Right
Originally viewed as working dogs, dalmatians were transformed into fashion icons by Disney's 101 Dalmatians.

DANGEROUS JOURNEYS

A DALMATIAN DID not tire easily of hard road work and could travel an average of 24–32 km (15–20 miles) a day, this being a usual distance for private conveyances. When on the move the dog kept close to the horse and carriage, but when the carriage stopped the Dalmatian acted just like any other dog.

Running with a carriage put a dog in constant danger: a dog which regularly followed what, in 1851, was the only coach travelling the London to Brighton route via Dorking, Horsham and Henfield was tragically killed while jumping from the coach to take up his position under the high wheels. Sometimes this dog had actually ridden, but most of the time he could be seen trotting along beside the coach and was known to have followed this route of some 115.9 km (72 miles) on as many as eight consecutive days. After his death the dog's body was stuffed and placed in a glass case in a public house on London's Edgware Road.

DECLINE OF THE COACH DOG

AS THE NINETEENTH CENTURY drew to its close it appears that the sight of Dalmatians running with coaches had become quite rare. There is an account of a driving tour in the late nineteenth century on which the children present were all delighted after an unexpected encounter with a Dalmatian.

The Dalmatian was essentially a stable dog and rarely went into the house, but there were differences of opinion as to whether the breed's love of horses was inherent or merely the outcome of life's circumstances. Certainly, many strong friendships have been built up between dogs and horses and Dalmatians were said never to be happier than when bedded down in a horse's stable.

OLD SAM

AROUND THE TURN of the nineteenth century, a well-known dog was one called Old Sam who followed his owner's pony and cart. Old Sam and his canine companions got to know many principal hotels and 'put-up houses' and would regularly trot off on their own up to 32.2km (20 miles) to places where they had been hospitably entertained. They were brought home late so often that their owner attached collars to each, inscribed, 'To Restaurant Proprietors – Please do not detain this dog.'

Top

Dalmatians were used to guard coaches and carriages and were trained to run alongside them during journeys.

Left

When the Dalmatian lost its role as a coach dog, it took on a new lease of life as a fashionable pet.

DOG FACT

Arriving in Coventry in 1895, the Dalmatian, Lady Godiva, had her collar removed so that she could run through the streets dressed like her namesake.

Dogs and the Church

VERY OCCASIONALLY PETS have been allowed to be buried in the shadow of the church, but frequently legal battles have been fought regarding the rights of owners to have pets lying with them at death. Dogs, though, have a long association with the church, although the attitude towards them has not always been one of righteousness.

DOG FACT:
In AD 585 priests were forbidden from keeping dogs. This was due to dog's overt expressions of sexual interest, their noise and the risk of rabies.

Right
Dogs were depicted in religious paintings or included in effigies on tombs, but many churches refused permission for dogs to be buried with their owners.

Bottom
Dog tongs were used to haul unwanted dogs out of churches, often causing injury.

DOGS REMAIN OUTSIDE

NOBLEMEN WERE REPROACHED for attending divine service with their greyhounds, so their reaction was to listen to Mass from outside the church doors. As a result, doors to churches began to be left open and priests actually went into the square in front of the churches to bless this important section of their congregation, eventually leading to the custom of giving a church door blessing to all animals.

Soon after, and until comparatively recent times, it was not considered irreverent to take dogs into church as many worshippers had to walk some distance to church and may have needed canine protection. If one looks carefully, evidence of this can be found in several old churches which still have their original pews. A Lincolnshire church has a pew especially for the squire's dogs, which were kept there while the service was in progress.

From time to time fights broke out amongst these church-going dogs, such as the one in Durham which took its place amongst the choir boys, bringing the entire service to a halt. Despite many attempts, a fight in a church in Scotland could not be halted – eventually the vicar was heard to say he would put his money on the yellow one, whereupon the entire congregation settled down to watch.

KEEPING DOGS OUT

AS THE CENTURIES PROGRESSED dogs presented an increasing problem for church authorities. It is generally believed that altar rails, designed to keep dogs out, were invented by Archbishop Laud (1573–1645) but the rails he ordered were so widely spaced that they are unlikely to have served this purpose well. It is therefore possible that rails were used before that time. In 1636, Bishop Wren, uncle of the famous architect Sir Christopher, ordered a rail to be made in front of the communion table, with the pillars so close that dogs could not squeeze in.

DOG-WHIPPERS

BY THE seventeenth century, dogs had again become unwelcome in church and 'Dogdrivers,' or dog-whippers, were employed to keep the animals away. Payment was minimal, indeed sometimes they received no more than a gift of tobacco.

In 1659, a gentleman who died left the sum of eight shillings a year for a poor man to be paid for keeping the dogs out of Claverley Church. In 1725 money was left to Trysull Church in Staffordshire, but in this case the dog-whipper was expected not only to whip the dogs out, but also keep the congregation awake during sermons. This two-fold task was not unusual. Such people often carried a long staff with a

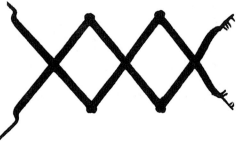

fox's brush on one end to tickle the faces of sleeping women, while on the other end of the staff was a knob, used to rap the heads of the menfolk. In Prestwick, 13 shillings was paid for the three-fold task of 'wakening sleepers in ye church, whipping out dogs, and keeping the pulpit walls clean'.

London's St Paul's Cathedral used to be home to dogs for six and a half days each week and, as a result, was often in a dreadful mess when people arrived for worship. Half an hour before the service was due to begin on Sunday mornings the dog-whipper arrived to drive out the dogs. It was said that blind and lame dogs fell out of the cathedral onto the streets, as did whole litters of puppies.

At church services it was not unusual for dogs to slip in, unnoticed, but the dog-whipper would soon dive in among people's legs to haul them out. It was situations like these which brought about the introduction of the dog tongs. These resembled old-fashioned sugar tongs, but with the appalling sight of a number of bent nails at the end. It was not unknown for

dogs to be gripped so tightly with the tongs that their skulls were fractured.

In some churches, however, the clergy were thankfully more kindly disposed towards our canine friends. Sometimes, especially in Wales and Cornwall, 'dog-doors' were cut into the larger entrance doors so that dogs might leave the church to relieve themselves when necessary, and in rural areas it was quite usual for sheepdogs to be present during services.

> **DOG FACT:**
> A Sunday service is recorded as having taken place without bread because a dog had dashed up to the altar and stolen the loaf.

Top Left and Right
Until comparatively recent times dogs were tolerated in churches; pews and doors were adapted for their convenience.

Left
Because it was so difficult for dog-owners to obtain permission for their pets to be buried in church grounds, private pet cemeteries began to appear — often with elaborate tombs.

Collecting Dogs

P UT YOUR HAND into your pocket,
Pour it out;
Give your gold or even a locket,
If the cash is rather short
For the business we're about –
Bringing Britain into port.
From 'Tommy's Little Dog' by F Harald Williams
(1900)

PARADING FOR CHARITY

DOGS HAVE LONG BEEN USEFUL and
indeed talented at collecting money for
good causes. On a snowy January day in
1900 the Ladies' Kennel Association
arranged a parade of 400 dogs to collect
in aid of the Soldiers' Widow and
Orphan Fund, between them raising
the commendable sum of £3,000.

It was a highly organised affair.
Many wore costume of a patriotic
nature and the dogs were divided into 'companies', each under the direction of a 'divisional
officer', the British Bulldogs were led by one
called Simple Simon. Sergeant Locker's dog of
Cheltenham looked a wonderful sight in his
little red breeches and scarlet coat, with a
miniature gun and flags crossed over his back.
On the day the place of honour and silver cup
were awarded to a young girl with her
'wee Jap', which she carried under a
cloak, also managing to carry a flag
of which she refused to be relieved.

GYP

THAT SPECIAL parade marked a
very important day for dogs and
owners but many dogs collected
money on an individual basis
throughout the year, year in and
year out. Gyp was an intelligent
Rough Terrier who came into the
hands of his new master in 1898, when

Top
*Zulu was a regular
fixture on the Hastings
sea front and was much
commended for his ability
to raise money for charity.*

Bottom
*Absent-Minded
Beggar lived up
to his name
when he
tipped the
coins out of
his mug.*

his original owner was found levelling his gun at
the dog, for whom he had no further use. Lucky
timing allowed Gyp to be taken into a more
appreciative home and from then on he collected
for numerous charities, including the Transvaal War
Fund, for which he raised £9. Gyp was said to
have a miser's perfect greed for money, the jingling
of coins attracting him like a magnet. Once he had
secured a coin between his teeth he held it with
the tenacity of a pair of pincers. He would sit on
his haunches to beg and with remarkable accuracy
could catch a coin in his mouth when one was
flung in his direction.

BHUTAN, THE LHASA APSO

ANOTHER DOG WHO SAT UP to beg was Bhutan,
a Lhasa Apso imported from the Himalayas and
registered with the English Kennel Club in 1896.
Bhutan begged at shows, sitting for hours in that
position; indeed on one occasion Princess
Alexandra, a frequent visitor to these events, was
heard to remark, 'That little dog is begging to leave
the show'. Unfortunately, while begging for the
Hospital Fund, Bhutan contracted distemper and,
said his owner, 'He fell at his post, so to speak.' The

determined little dog kept sinking down into a lying position but, after a short rest, would once again resume his usual pose. 'He kept his end up to the last,' said his owner, 'and then went home to die'.

ABSENT-MINDED BEGGAR

A FLUFFY, WHITE DOG with a strong-minded aversion to the police and an equal dislike of newspaper boys, was Absent-Minded Beggar. But his unsociable manners were overlooked because of the good work he did collecting money for patriotic causes. One Saturday he was standing in the market place collecting money as usual but that day, for some reason, the rattling of coins in the tin mug at his neck seemed to puzzle him. Beggar took it into his head to tip out the coins onto the pavement, to the delight of the urchins who made off hastily with the money.

Another famed collecting dog was Zulu, a Curly-coated Retriever, who collected on the sea

> **DOG FACT:**
> Dadles habitually waited for hotel guests with his head cocked at an angle of 45 degrees.

> **DOG FACT:**
> Collecting boxes used included tobacco boxes, toy post office pillar boxes, satin bags, money boxes and leather pouches of every description.

front at Hastings on England's south coast. He usually collected where the band played, decked in red, white and blue ribbons and a khaki cap. In 1900 Zulu paid over £20 to the *Hastings Observer* and was acknowledged in the newspaper for his valuable work.

DADLES

DADLES COLLECTED in Cirencester for the Cottage Hospital, amongst other charities. He had a natural affinity with strangers who enjoyed being entertained by Dadles' abilities. Regulars, though, tended to ignore him and one can perhaps understand why. He waited amongst the carriages at the far end of the yard outside a hotel; setting his targets on someone approaching, he would meet them at the hotel entrance and accompany them to the smoking room. Once comfortably seated, he would commence his irresistibly funny programme involving a series of pantomimic illustrations of canine life, at the end of which he would 'sicken' and 'die'. After what he considered to be a decent interval he was miraculously 'resurrected' and went around to make his collection, using every available means open to him and all his guile until a coin was deposited in the box.

Above, Top and Top Left
Gyp collected for numerous charities, while other dogs collected for the blind.

Left
The Ladies' Kennel Association parade of 1900 was a gatherings of over 400 dogs. Between them, they collected £3,000.

Travel with Dogs

TOWARDS THE BEGINNING of the twentieth century, very few people had cars and so transporting dogs from one place to another was by no means as easy as it is today. Many of the dog-showing fraternity, however, were people of substantial means and when advertising in canine press of the day, were proud to portray themselves and their dogs sitting in the luxury of a four-wheeled vehicle, or even a large motorbike and sidecar. Most dogs travelled by rail.

RAILWAYS

FOR MOST, THOUGH, transport was restricted to travelling by rail and often dogs travelled to shows and to other destinations on their own. In the late nineteenth century it was generally thought that facilities for conveyance of valuable animals were wholly inadequate and in 1883 the public considered it quite unfair that a parcel could be transported from London to Plymouth for nine pence, whilst it cost five shillings for a dog to travel the same distance. Both took up about the same amount of space and both stood just as much chance of being crushed in the luggage van. Large dogs were required to travel in the luggage compartment but smaller ones could, if their owners wished, go in little lockers under the carriage seats, although these were considered 'miserable contrivances for the comfort of highly sensitive animals'.

The public claimed they would not have minded paying more to transport their dogs had the accommodation been more comfortable and safe, but many mistakes occurred, although the railway claimed this was often due to the fussiness or carelessness of the dogs' owners. In many instances some of the most valuable dogs in the country were transported in rotten old hampers from which dogs could all too easily escape. Often, the bottom had completely fallen out and the dog was effectively carrying the hamper, rather than the hamper carrying the dog. Another problem was that often the most flimsy of collars and chains were used. Worst of all, some dogs were not even in crates, but merely sent loose.

Top and Right

At the beginning of the twentieth century, car ownership was restricted to the wealthy, who enjoyed taking their dogs for a drive.

Bottom

Most dogs and their owners had to travel by train. Dogs were often sent unaccompanied.

Conversely, some owners were far too pedantic in their requirements, giving precise instructions that were unlikely to be attended to by overworked, busy officials. Some owners who travelled with their dogs insisted that the approximate space of a second-class carriage should be devoted to them and woe-betide anyone who dared to object to such an arrangement.

STATION KENNELS

AT SEVERAL RAILWAY STATIONS in London there was kennelling for dogs and it would have been a mistake to think that the railway companies did not provide some comfort for canine travellers. Some of the porters at stations were equally as good as kennelmen and looked after their charges well. A particular porter at Euston station was considered the very best and many of the dogs in his care acted as if they had known him all their lives.

At Kings Cross, the accommodation for dogs was also good. To the left of the arrival platform were comfortable little 'cribs' let in from the wall and these were both warm and clean. Officials on the Great Northern Line were also very careful and even dogs which had been left on the station for a week were said to look very well.

The worst accommodation for dogs was at Paddington station, where there were just two or three dingy-looking boxes for the dogs at the end of the platforms. Sometimes, dogs left at Paddington were housed in a nearby mews with access from a lane, so it was easy for someone to simply walk in from the street and steal any of the dogs.

At Liverpool Street, the kennels were safer for they were let in from the station wall. Although small, they had plenty of air and stout doors with locks. The porter there, too, was highly recommended and people with valuable dogs thought him quite capable of taking care of their canine companions overnight.

Waterloo and St Pancras were also reputed to be good, but not as good as Euston, Kings Cross and Liverpool Street. Although the railway companies did not actually profess to lodge dogs, it was highly creditable that such accommodation was available when needed by travellers.

THE RISING COST OF DOG TRAVEL

THE COMPLAINTS about the cost of canine travel in 1883 were probably valid, for in 1931 the cost of conveying a dog via London and North East Railway was six pence for up to 15 miles, three shillings and sixpence for 76–100 miles and 10 shillings for any distance over 300 miles, with various prices in between. These were single fares but on certain days the same prices were charged for return journeys if dogs accompanied their owners .

In 1934, it cost three pence for a dog to travel in the guard's van for up to 10 miles but it was stipulated that such dogs had to be muzzled, although the guards did not always exercise this railway rule.

VALUABLE LIVE PUPPY

Above
Unaccompanied dogs were transported in the luggage van of the train, while other dogs travelled in style in their owners' car.

Performing Dogs

I T'S NICE TO KNOW I am admired,
But, frankly, I am getting tired.
I've sat up, begged, I've worn a hat,
I've 'died for England' on the mat,
Until I feel inclined to drop, So kindly note I'm
going to stop!
From 'Mercenary Montmorency' by Joe Walker
(1930)

These dogs were 'dressed in motley and short waisted jackets'. There were also serious reports of dogs which had been trained to speak, one in the eighteenth century reputedly knowing 30 words of German as a result of three years' training.

THEATRICAL PERFORMERS

DOGS ALSO PLAYED ROLES in theatrical performances, especially during the early nineteenth century when 'dog dramas' were in vogue. *Le Chien de Montargis, ou, La Fôret de Bondy* (The Dog of Montargis or the Forest of Bondy) opened at the Gaite Theatre in Paris in 1814 and was so popular that it was translated into Dutch, German, Italian, Polish, Russian, Spanish and English. In Britain the play ran for over 1,100 performances.

In the nineteenth century, there was a curious performance by dogs on stage at Sadler's Wells. The dogs stormed a fort amid the firing of guns and fumes of gunpowder, a 'deserter' was shot dead for the offence and carried off by his companions. At the same time other dogs demonstrated symptoms of extreme pain from which they gradually recovered, displaying every possible means of joy as a result.

ENTERTAINING DOGS

Top
Showmen taught dogs to play dominoes to the delight of the crowd, who could not detect trickery.

Right
Dogs in fancy dress have always provided popular entertainment, particularly if they act the part.

DURING THE MIDDLE AGES the dog frequently served a triple function, that of body guard, companion and the working partner of travelling entertainers. Elizabethan clowns, known as 'tumblers', also appeared alongside performing dogs and at this time we can read of dogs belonging to what were described as 'vagabundical masters', dancing to music and 'showing many pretty tricks by gestures of their bodies – as to stand bolt upright, to lye flat upon the grounde, to turn rounde as a ringe holding their tails in their teeth'.

In William Harrison's *Description of England*, published in 1586, we read of dogs being trained to beg for meat and to take a man's cap from his head.

DOG FACT:
The royal puppeteer usually used mongrels for the part of Toby as he found they responded better to training.

TRICKSTERS AND SHOWMEN

SHOWMEN'S DOGS WERE tutored to play games of dominoes in front of crowds of onlookers. Such games were played in a most orderly manner, each playing one piece after the other, the dog taking his selected dominoes to the master to place down. Close observers could not detect any signs given to the dogs, though there may have been clues in the short chuckling sounds made by their masters as the dogs walked round to select each piece.

FANCY DRESS PERFORMERS

THE WRITER, General W. N. Hutchinson, reported some fascinating sights in Paris where six dogs were yoked in pairs to a light carriage. On top sat a fantastically dressed terrier who managed to stand on his hind legs even when the coach was in motion. Inside the carriage were other dogs, two of greyhound type and a 'Russian poodle'. These dogs performed numerous tricks. One, dressed in a petticoat and smart cap, danced a minuet and one of the Greyhounds leapt through a hoop held by a boy, high above his head. After jumping, the dog trotted off feigning lameness on each of his legs in turn.

As the scene wore on the circle was enlarged by the carriage being driven round in increasing circles. Then the dogs' master spread out 10 cards on the four sides of an old cloth. Each card bore a number and spectators were invited to call out any figure, provided that it did not exceed four digits. The dogs were released at random and duly collected up numbers totalling the various figures requested, taking them diligently to their master. There were various attempts to discover if this had been done by trickery, but it seemed not to be the case.

PERFORMING POODLES

PARIS WAS CERTAINLY FAMOUS for its entertaining dogs and was classed as the home of performing Poodles. Those at Pont Neuf were well known for being trained to soil the boots of passers-by, in order that they would be obliged to employ the services of a 'boot black' to get them clean again.

In the streets of London, Punch and Judy were a familiar sight, with the dog, Toby, wearing a ruff with bells in order to frighten away the devil from his master. This famous piece of 'theatre' was first performed in Covent Garden in 1662 and Toby was only a stuffed figure until the 1820s when a dog was trained to take the part. The show became known as 'Punch and Toby' before being re-named 'Punch and Judy'. Even royal puppeteer staged performances of Punch and Judy for the children of both Queen Victoria and Edward VII.

Top
The dog can serve as a guard, a companion or an entertainer.

Above
Dogs can be trained to perform any number of entertaining acts and to accept being dressed in human clothing.

Left
Poodles adapted easily to performing and were particularly renowned in Paris.

> **DOG FACT:**
> The dog, Toby, was taught to sing and to smoke a pipe, as well as to shake hands and to seize Punch firmly by the nose.

Sled Dogs

THE ANCIENT RECORDS of the Inuits, crudely inscribed on rock or bone, prove that dogs were used to pull sledges from very early times. In the sixteenth century, travellers to Greenland in search of gold, and navigators on the Arctic seas took interest in the practical uses to which these wolf-like dogs were put.

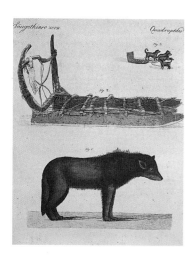

TRAVELLING IN THE ARCTIC

IN THE SEVENTEENTH and eighteenth centuries, Russians undertook extensive journeys from the borders of Europe to the Bering Strait, taking with them large numbers of dogs. European travellers took fewer but an American explorer, Lieutenant Peary, saw the advantage of using large numbers and was known to have 100 or more.

From the works of Taplin, a nineteenth-century writer, dogs living in these arctic conditions were known to excavate their own beds in the snow, leaving little more than their noses visible. They swam admirably and hunted both in packs and individually. They were used to hunt the Arctic fox, seal and polar bear and had the reputation of being fiercely aggressive with any domestic animals they encountered. Among themselves they would often fight to the death.

Above and Right
Early sled-dogs looked very different from the modern huskies.

Bottom
In the summer dogs could be used to pull boats but were more apt to be pack animals.

SIBERIAN SLED DOGS

THE KAMTSCHATKA DOGS were strong and active, little different in size from the Russian Boor-dogs and they were held to be the most long-winded runners in Siberia. Dogs there fetched high prices in the early nineteenth century, around the equivalent of £10. Money was also spent liberally on the elegance of the dogs' trappings. Seats were covered with furs or bear skins and each sledge had a cross-bar to which the harness was joined. On this hung iron links or small bells: the noise reputedly encouraged the

DOG FACT:
'Nipper' rescued 300 sheep in a fire and, despite his paws being burned, returned for the cows.

dogs on their way. Sledges seldom carried more than one person at a time but behind the driver were bundles of provisions. Such sledges were usually pulled by a team of four dogs, but some used five.

DOGS AND THEIR DRIVER

THE DOGS RESPONDED PRIMARILY to voice commands but the driver also used a crooked stick for striking at the snow to regulate speed. Perhaps the most difficult manoeuvre for a driver was when he threw the stick at the dogs to chastise them and then picked it up again while on the move, requiring remarkable dexterity.

Even though owners of these dogs were heavily dependent on them, they were not renowned for their kindness. Usually the dogs were left to fend for themselves, eating mussels, berries and whatever else they could find. Occasionally, if there had been a large capture of seals, the dogs would be given the blood and other unused portions of the kill. Some dogs were actually used as food and fattened for the purpose, but nothing was wasted. The dogs' skins were used for coverlets and clothing, as well as for borders and seams of their owners' icy homes. The dogs' intestines were used to make sewing thread.

ENDURANCE TEST

IN GREENLAND AS MANY as 10 dogs were used in a team when pulling a sledge carrying five or six heavy seals as far as 60 miles in a day. By the mid-nineteenth century sometimes even 12 dogs were used, attached to the sledge by a single trace and without reins. Each dog was reported to be capable of transporting 54.6 kg (120 lb) over the snow at a rate of 11–13 km/h (7–8 mph). In the summer dogs were used as pack animals, carrying goods up to a third of their own weight fastened securely to their backs. At this time of year the dogs fared better for they could feed on the remains of whales and sea-calves. Towards the end of the century there were reports of teams of four dogs carrying as much as 136.5–182 kg (300–400 lb) for up to 56 km (45 miles) a day over a good track.

There were smaller but similar breeds in Lapland and Iceland but often the general name,

Esquimaux Dog, was used to describe them all. Many wolf-like traits could be observed, such as that these dogs were not habitual barkers but tended to howl. They also had the ability to pick flesh from a fish just as cleanly as if it had been scraped. A dog used in Canada around the beginning of the twentieth century was a cross between the Eskimo Dog and one

which in Canada was called the Staghound. For speed, strength and stamina these dogs were reputed to be second to none. The Samoyed was also used with the sleigh in winter but was better known for its use in shepherding reindeer and acting as a household guard.

The dogs used as sled dogs in cold climates varied considerably.

This Page
Sledge dogs were valued for speed, strength and stamina. They were usually left to find their own food and shelter.

James Spratt

IN THE CANINE WORLD James Spratt was a household name who had achieved fame by making dog biscuits. Spratt, a great traveller who lived in America for many years, had not begun his career in the world of dogs; he was an electrician specialising in lightning conductors.

PROVIDING FOR THE DOG'S EVERY NEED

HIS BUSINESS AS A manufacturer of dog foods and other items began in a fairly small way in Holborn, London. Charles Cruft was one of his very first employees and proved to be of great assistance in developing the company. As the company's products increased in popularity the business moved to larger premises, but Spratt was concerned that imitations of his own company's goods were beginning to find their way onto the market. In consequence Spratt felt it important that he had a trademark, as well as a show card, as a result, he bought up an entire issue of engravings by Sir Edwin Landseer so that these could be used on his cards.

The well-known 'X', used as Spratt's trademark, was the distinguishing mark made by the young Charles Cruft when he wished to differentiate between trade and private customers in his work for the company as a ledger clerk. Later Cruft was to work his way up in the company, becoming Manager.

James Spratt was always rather secretive about the meat used in the manufacture of his dog biscuits and after selling the company he retained the contract for supplying the meat, something he is believed to have retained until his death in 1880.

> **DOG FACT:**
> The first living creatures to return from space alive were the dogs Belka and Strelka.

Top

Spratt's dog foods and other canine supplies were renowned throughout the dog world

Right

James Spratt was an electrician and ardent traveller before he founded his dog-food business.

THE COMPANY EXPANDS

THE BUSINESS DEVELOPED in many ways and soon had thousands of agents spread over five continents selling goods which catered not only for show dogs, but also for sporting dogs and domestic pets. The business even became successful in the game and poultry field.

Apart from foodstuffs, the company also sold portable kennels described as 'palatial' or like 'a drawing room cot', clearly designed to suit the most fastidious and valuable of toy dogs. There were travelling boxes, chains, collars and canine clothing as well as numerous kennel accessories and appliances, indeed the company had grown immensely from its small beginnings, especially since it also sold various products used in the treatment of ailments.

PROVIDING AND INFORMING

JAMES SPRATT WAS ANXIOUS that his clients should understand more about the goods sold by his company and so regularly put out informative little booklets offering practical advice to readers. Some of the booklets even described the way in which the biscuits were made. Grain, flour and other ingredients were conveyed to the factory in ships and barges from Limehouse

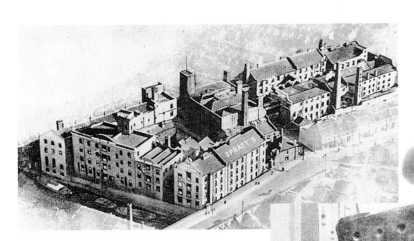

Basin, where for storage they were hoisted to the fifth floor of the great building. When the flour had been blended with Meat Fibrine it was conveyed automatically into a huge receptacle called a dough drum where it was mechanically kneaded, eight and a half hundredweight at a time. The dough was then drawn onto a machine to be rolled out to the required thickness; by now it was forming a huge dough blanket. It was then carried forward to the cutting machines where it was stamped out at a rate of almost 50,000 biscuits every hour.

Now carrying the famous 'X', the biscuits went into cavernous ovens and emerged as 'row upon row of brown, health fellows, each and every one of them done to a turn'. The biscuits then went into drying bins and after 48 hours were taken out and packed ready for the canine world, eagerly awaiting their arrival.

BISCUITS, BISCUITS AND MORE BISCUITS

THE NUMBER OF BISCUITS produced by the company has been extremely well documented. During the First World War, the total weight of biscuits supplied to army dogs was 70,144 tons, amounting to the incredible number of 1,256,976,708 biscuits. Had these same biscuits been laid flat, side to side and end to end they would have covered 2,554 acres, 3 roods, 36 poles, 10 square yards, 2 square feet and 120 square inches. As an alternative measurement, had they been placed end to end they would have measured more than three times the distance round the earth's equator. Placed on top of each other they would have extended upwards to the magnificent height of 15,955km (9,910 miles and 7 furlongs).

The Spratt's booklets also gave valuable advice concerning the treatment of minor canine ailments, as the company also sold various pills and potions which might have relieved these. There were things like Purging Pills, used for opening the bowels, Cure For Jaundice, Stimulating Liniment and Tonic Condition Pills. There were also remarkable treatments for parasites, such as Spratt's Dog Soap which was 'absolutely free from poison' and Spratt's claimed that even a man might swallow this soap without injury. There were various worming agents on offer and, if diarrhoea ensued, Spratt's had an answer to that as well.

Above
Spratt's London factory produced almost 50,000 of his famous 'X' marked biscuits per hour.

Bottom
In addition to dog biscuits, Spratt's also sold pills and potions.

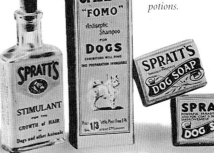

War Dogs

DURING THE FIRST WORLD WAR, dogs were an invaluable asset to European armies. Guidance given for training of war dogs was just as punctilious as that given out for the loading of rifles and guns, as it was recognised that much depended on these dogs and of course the consumate skill of their trainers.

> **DOG FACT:**
> A white Bull Terrier which was presented to the Territorial Army in 1949 was ranked as Sergeant.

Top and Bottom
Dogs were parachuted behind enemy lines and used to deliver rations in the First World War.

'DOGS OF WAR'

THE BREEDS MOST USUALLY associated with carrying out duties during the war years were the German Shepherd Dog (Alsatian), Airedale, Rottweiler and Giant Schnauzer, although many other breeds were used because, apart from the skill of the trainer, success depended on a dog's intelligence and endurance. France appears to have been the first country to employ the dog in infantry manoeuvres, but the experiment was rather short lived as there was some criticism that credits had not

been entered regularly in the Ministry of War budget. The dog was used extensively in Germany and also in Russia where at every dog show there was a special section reserved for 'Dogs of War'.

Dogs called 'kettle-drum dogs', or simply 'drum dogs' were used in the Austrian army for drawing the large drum of the regimental band. The drum was pulled along on a small carriage but eventually the dogs which had pulled the carriage were replaced by ponies. The dog carried out a variety of valuable services during wartime – some took the place of night watchmen, while others did sterling work conveying the injured, both human and canine, with a special canine ambulance service for transporting injured dogs. It was recognised that a good dog was well worth effort in nursing it back to health and when fully recovered many were sent back to the front. Dogs were also highly useful in pulling carriages which conveyed supplies and light artillery.

DOG RECRUITS

DURING THE EARLY YEARS of the First World War, dogs were not always appreciated as much as was

their due and messenger dogs were not frequently used. However, it quickly became apparent that dogs could accomplish great things and they earned high respect. Like the dogs used for conveying artillery, many different breeds of dogs were used as messengers although the Airedale, Sheepdog, Lurcher and

could usually be expected to reach 'home' within half an hour.

ACCLIMATISING TO WARFARE

DURING TRAINING, DOGS became accustomed to all the sounds of war, including battery shells screaming overhead and lorries passing by. It was imperative that they got used to the sound of gunfire so that when carrying messages it would be no deterrent. They coped with explosions of hand grenades in their immediate vicinity. Punishment was not resorted to during training and most of the dogs seemed to enjoy the training.

Top
A dog carrying a basket containing a messenger pigeon across a river.

Left
Dogs had to be trained to become used to gunfire and other loud noises such as exploding grenades and shells.

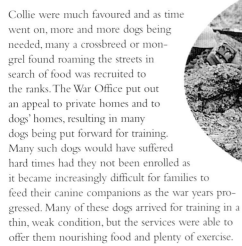

Collie were much favoured and as time went on, more and more dogs being needed, many a crossbreed or mongrel found roaming the streets in search of food was recruited to the ranks. The War Office put out an appeal to private homes and to dogs' homes, resulting in many dogs being put forward for training. Many such dogs would have suffered hard times had they not been enrolled as it became increasingly difficult for families to feed their canine companions as the war years progressed. Many of these dogs arrived for training in a thin, weak condition, but the services were able to offer them nourishing food and plenty of exercise.

Dogs in action helped to keep the army's communication lines unbroken by getting safely through under shellfire, carrying urgent messages to and from headquarters. Frequently messenger dogs could get through when there was virtually no chance of a human runner surviving the journey. They could more easily negotiate treacherous ground and could cover 3.2--4.8 km (2–3 miles) in a few minutes.

When attack was expected, the dogs were taken to the front-line trenches where they were sheltered in a dug-out during bombardment. Then, when an urgent message needed to be sent, it was enclosed in a small leather pouch and attached to a dog's neck, indicating the time of release. If successful, a dog

As messengers, dogs had advantages over other means of communication and when they knew their destination they tried hard to get there. Pigeons could not be sent in fog or in the dark, but some dogs conveyed messenger pigeons in crates on their backs. Mustard gas did affect the dogs but not as much as the soldiers. During service, dogs were not allowed to be petted in case it detached their minds from their keepers, but all were well fed before going to the front and they were never kept there for more than 12 hours at a time.

Left and Bottom
Dogs were able to carry urgent messages or to lay signal lines successfully, whereas soldiers would have been killed.

Early Dog Care

Bottom

The Christian world was slow to take an active interest in dogs. When it did, health care became an important issue.

ARABS GAVE MEDICAL ASSISTANCE to their ill and wounded dogs, and even performed operations on those which had been wounded or disembowelled, but in the Christian world, until the eighth century, dogs were scorned and the only ones to have been treated with really great care were the hounds of princes. Slowly, however, dogs became objects of interest and affection and people began to take concern over their health.

INEFFECTIVE CARE

VETERINARY IGNORANCE MEANT that many 'cures' were of little real use. Eleventh-century treatment for a rabid dog was to take the worm out from under its tongue, cut it into sections and bury it in a fig. The 'worm' was the stringy tissue running from the tongue to the lower part of the mouth. This practice continued until the nineteenth century.

DEVELOPMENT OF CARE

BY THE FOURTEENTH CENTURY some wonderfully illustrated books had been published to aid huntsmen, teaching how best to employ dogs and also ways of caring for them. Kennels were to be situated in a sunny place, cleaned each day and provided with fresh straw and, following a hunt, dogs needed to be rested in a heated room with a fireplace and chimney. One must consider that at that time heating in peoples' homes was most unusual, except for cooking fires. Usually, a kennel boy slept in a loft above the kennels so that he was on hand to prevent the hounds fighting at night.

Recommendation for diet was meat and bread, and after walking each dog was to be rubbed down thoroughly with straw. Some manuscripts recommended that dogs were to be bathed each evening, doubtless a time-consuming business for the kennel boys who were also expected to spin the dogs' leashes, used to couple hounds when on a hunt. By the sixteenth century some people even allowed their dogs to sleep in their bedrooms, indeed the dog was working its way into people's affections, even in the Christian world.

THE PAMPERED POOCH

IN THE DAYS OF France's Louis XIV (1638–1715) small dogs were pampered to excess, their coats crimped, cropped and styled to the fashion of the day. The money spent on hunting kennels had grown to sums of ridiculous proportion. The Italian Greyhound was the subject of particular pampering in the eighteenth century, considered too delicate for Britain and only suitable for 'the comforts of the tea table, the fireside carpet, the luxurious indulgences of the sofa, and the warm lap of the mistress'. Those taken out in winter were wrapped in warm clothing before setting out from the house.

In rural areas, the sheepdog, a firm favourite both as pet and working dog, was carefully nursed back to health when injured. An old tinder-box was used to light the fire to boil water, and the wounds wrapped in bandages made from old flannels.

VETERINARIAN CARE IMPROVES

VETERINARY METHODS, at first more an art than a science, changed slowly as the centuries progressed. Dogs run to exhaustion were bled to aid their recovery, but it is likely that it was the rest which aided their recovery more than the procedure of bleeding. Owners also realised it was prudent to remove parasites such as ticks, which they did by rubbing the dogs skin over with oil to stop up the ticks' breathing pores.

rubbed with powdered root of white hellebore and hogslard but, if they failed to heal, butter was boiled and mixed with gunpowder. This was applied to the wound at night and washed off with vinegar the following morning. Usually three such applications would suffice. Ear canker was another troublesome problem in dogs and was eased as much as possible with shag tobacco boiled in water. The dog's ears were dipped into the hot mixture until it was two inches above the cankered part and the poor dog had to suffer this on three consecutive days. This so-called 'cure' caused the hair to fall out but this was usually restored by use of burned 'old

DOG FACT:
Goose-grease was used to dry up a bitch's milk, the grease having been mixed with rum.

Above
This nineteenth-century drinking fountain shows the vast change in people's attitudes towards dogs. No longer scorned, dogs are now pampered pets.

Top Left
Veterinary care slowly improved with the advent of folk remedies such as milk and water washes and hogslard ointments.

Left
This delightful illustration on dog care comes from a fourteenth-century French hunting book.

CURATIVE REMEDIES

MILK AND WATER WERE USED for washing deep wounds and a poultice made of bread and milk was laid on. Washed again, the wound was wiped dry with lint before being lightly covered with burned alum and wrapped in bandages for 10 days; clean linen was applied daily. Sore patches could be

shoe' mixed with hogslard. Hogslard was a useful commodity used also to rub the feet of pointers and setters following bathing in salt-water after work. Warm beer and butter was an alternative. Melted goose-grease, strained through a sieve, and mixed with spirits of wine and turpentine could be used as a dressing for shot wounds.

Early Canine Equipment

COLLARS USED IN THE PAST were much more elaborate than those today. Large dogs which accompanied their owners primarily for the sake of ornament usually wore brass ones, attached to which was a neat padlock carrying the name of the owner, engraved on an inserted plate of silver or steel. Spiked collars were used for quite a different purpose, to save the dog if engaged in a fight. These were made of thick brass or leather and studded with metal spikes. They were frequently used by owners of dogs who wished to induce a fight, knowing that their own dog had an advantage over its opponent

Right

Collars vary immensely from a simple leather band to decorative brass. Over the years they have become less decorative and more functional.

Bottom

Travelling baskets often looked like miniature kennels and could be quite elaborate.

COLLAR VARIETIES

THE CURB-CHAIN COLLAR was another variation. This was an imitation of the curb chain used to secure a horse's bit, and was usually made of steel. It was kept polished and fastened by a bolt lock with a key. Most curb-chain collars had a brass or steel plate on which the owner's name and address was engraved. The majority of collars were made of leather, some lined with flannel or chamois leather. Broad collars were used for heavy dogs but unfortunately many owners buckled these collars over-tightly to enhance the appearance of loose skin and wrinkles in the bull breeds.

BEDDING

BECAUSE DOGS WERE USUALLY bedded down on straw and their exercise area was most probably covered in ash, dogs often wore coats before visiting a show, for it was realised that a well-presented coat went a long way toward achieving success in the showring. Indoors, materials such as a plain white calico was used in the summer months and in colder weather, fawn-coloured horse clothing. Mackintosh sheets could be used in rain. The most popular style of coat was that which buckled in front and to which a breast cloth could be added in cold weather, of particular use in attempting to avoid draughts while at shows.

Little importance was paid to creating whelping boxes when litters were imminent, instead a bitch was far more likely to have a warm place allocated to her in the kitchen, perhaps next to the stove.

FOOD PREPARATION

LARGER KENNELS HAD their own special 'food-boiler' which required great attention to keep food at the boil without allowing it to burn. But with the advent of Parish's Steam Cooker, preparation became easier, for this could be maintained at a temperature which never rose beyond 210°F, thereby allowing bits of meat, gristle and other odds and

ends to be stewed without leaving any waste. These cookers were available in sizes ranging from two to 32 gallons, so could be used by many kennels, whatever their size.

KENNELS

SMALL HOUSE PETS HAD beautifully made baskets in which to sleep, and some looked like little houses, miniatures of larger outdoor kennels. These were somewhat impractical as the dogs could so easily damage the basketwork, so they usually had a mat or rug placed inside to prevent the animal scratching the floor. More practical for indoor use were 'toy kennels', raised on castors.

Some of the outdoor kennels were very well made and there was even a folding, portable kennel which was made of wood, a convenience for those who wished to travel with their dogs. When travelling to shows, some exhibitors accompanied their dogs on trains, but often they were sent on alone. Travelling baskets or 'hampers' were needed as containers for the dogs. In the early years these were crudely constructed and were barely large enough to contain the dog inside. Unfortunately, little thought appears to have been given to the matter of ventilation in the hampers, and many cases of suffocation were reported.

MODERN EQUIPMENT

THANKFULLY, OWNERS BECAME more aware of their pets' needs and ventilation became an essential feature of any travelling basket. A particularly popular one was the 'Cottage-top Ventilated Hamper', available in numerous sizes to suit all dog types. The roof space could be used for stowing away items which exhibitors needed to take to a show, while the dog occupied the space beneath.

Spratts Patent brought out another clever piece of travelling equipment, a 'Combination Travelling-Box and Kennel'. This had a moveable tray for carrying show equipment and a wire guard and door which covered the kennel's entrance when the dog was being transported. Powerful dogs, however, needed a secure travelling box rather than a basket, so these were provided with a lock and key and two strong handles. An important feature of any such equipment was a label which was clearly displayed on the outside, indicating the train's time and date of departure, in an endeavour to prevent the precious cargo from being left on the station platform as was sometimes the case.

Top
The elaborate collar of this lapdog has been chosen to match its owner's outfit.

Top Left
A miniature four-poster bed.

Bottom
A favourite couch!

Kennel Staff and Nursing

ONCE LIFE HAD BEGUN to settle down again following the First World War, dog ownership grew in popularity, leading to an increase in breeding and boarding kennels and a consequent increase in demand for staff. There were plenty of applicants for such positions, often young ladies who were well-educated and had some means of their own, believing this to be a healthy, pleasant and interesting way of occupying themselves before settling down to married life. Other applicants were in a less fortunate financial position and badly in need of the meagre remuneration, somewhere between 10 and 50 shillings a week plus board and lodging.

KENNEL STAFF

SOME ASSISTANTS WERE inefficient and lax, causing endless trouble within a kennel, but others were more than good value for the rates paid. Ladies were reputed to have more sympathy both with sick and healthy animals than men and many who boarded their dogs preferred them to be in the hands of kennelmaids rather than kennelboys or men.

KENNEL OWNERS

TRAINING KENNELS VARIED, some specialising in just one or two breeds, others catering for a wider range. Some kennels owned by prominent exhibitors even offered training for paying pupils or 'working guests'. Such exhibitors frequently kept a kennel of between 50 and 100 dogs so the trainee had plenty of opportunity to learn, providing services in return for board and tuition. After training, kennel staff were sometimes offered an opportunity to work for money. They had studied pedigrees, selective mating, whelping and rearing of puppies, as well as general kennel and office duties, standing them in good stead if they eventually decided to set up a kennel of their own. Frequently, they started on the very bottom rung of the ladder, but some worked their way up methodically, ending up as kennel manageresses.

KENNEL STAFF UNIFORM

IN LARGE KENNELS there was often some uniformity of dress, often light riding breeches, golf stockings and shoes, with a shirt or blouse and tie. Sometimes,

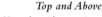

Top and Above
Kennel maids sometimes went on to train as canine nurses, although there was no recognised diploma.

Right
Kennel maids worked long hours for low pay, but it was a popular choice of occupation for many young women after the First World War.

men's khaki or dark blue dungarees were worn but many ladies thought them too masculine in appearance, so pale blue dungarees were an alternative. No member of a kennel's staff was to be untidy or dirty as this reflected badly not only on their work but also on the kennel.

DUTIES OF A KENNEL MAID

STAFF WERE OFTEN EXPECTED to rise at 6 a.m. so that all the kennels could have been cleaned out by breakfast time, allowing the remainder of the morning free for trimming, stripping and exercising the dogs. Afternoons were usually spent washing out food and water vessels and getting ready for the evening feed – remember that no facility foods were available then so a fair amount of preparation was involved. Besides breaks for many of them did not. Apart from obvious kennel tasks, their work also involved knowing how to detect ill health and the signs of oestrus, how to handle vicious dogs and how to groom dogs, as well as to bath and dry them. It was also important to learn how to administer medicines and to know how to disinfect kennels and clothing thoroughly.

Top
Kennel maids were expected to look clean and tidy, so many adopted a uniform dress, such as breeches or dungarees.

Left
Kennel maids were expected to keep the dogs clean, fed and exercised. They also had to learn how to bath and groom them, administer medicines and handle difficult or vicious dogs.

CANINE NURSES

FOLLOWING KENNEL training, some chose to train as canine nurses, another area of canine husbandry which had increased in demand since the War and was deemed fashionable at the time. Not only was kennel work reputedly better suited to the ladies, so was the nursing aspect. It was possible to obtain a diploma in canine nursing, but there was no recognised teaching institute so many certificates issued were hardly worth the paper on which they were written. Practical training was not always given so unless the trainees also served a number of months in a veterinary surgery or hospital, there was little opportunity to gain those all-important, practical skills.

breakfast and lunch, with luck a kennel maid might have an hour's relaxation during the afternoon and could expect their work to be complete by 5.30 pm. Most girls worked for nine hours a day and a working week was six days.

Each girl was expected to keep her own quarters tidy, so it was recommended that before taking on such work or training she at least knew how to make her own bed, wash up and cook an egg, for

Those trained to work with dogs undertook a demanding and sometimes expensive career, but this was an area of employment considered suitable for young ladies, affording a pleasant career and an open-air life-style for those who loved dogs.

DOG FACT:
At well-staffed kennels there was sometimes a chance of a whole or half day off mid-week, while Sundays were generally arranged on a rota basis.

Early Veterinary Treatment

ALTHOUGH VETERINARY TREATMENT has developed greatly in recent decades, much pioneering work was also undertaken in the 1930s, a time at which the veterinary profession had much to be proud of. Numerous developments were made in technology following the First World War, and the care of animals took on greater importance, with many varied facilities and treatments having become available.

VETERINARIAN HOSPITALS

CANINE HOSPITALS WERE divided into several different classes, with those at the top of the range being well-equipped establishments such as those in use at veterinary colleges. Here, there was usually also a post-mortem department so that attempts could be made to trace the cause of death, for much valuable information could be obtained by following up fatal cases. Canine hospitals, as they were called, maintained by individual practitioners, were a great deal smaller and only a few had the range of expensive equipment of the veterinary colleges.

X-RAY REVOLUTION

WHEN THE X-RAY PROCEDURE was introduced in 1896, an exposure time of 20 minutes was required, making it of little use for veterinary science, but by the 1930s it had become widely used in canine work, particularly for diagnostic purposes. By then a good machine could take an x-ray of any part of a dog's body in as little as two seconds but portable machines were frequently used as practitioners simply could not afford to install their own equipment.

X-ray was of particular use in making correct diagnoses in leg and foot injuries to racing Greyhounds, after all, good dogs could be worth anything up to £300, some even as much as £1,000. The x-ray machine could also be used to assess bone abnormalities, such as the diseased condition of the jaw bone – a case of an Elkhound whose upper jaw was affected created much publicity, for without such advanced equipment, removal of teeth would have been necessary. Canine dentistry was then considered almost as

> **DOG FACT:**
> By the 1930s, small fractured bones could be wired together with silver, an indication of how far canine surgery had progressed.

Top
Canine dentistry was taken very seriously and included regular scaling and tooth-extraction.

Right
Diagnostic skills improved as technology became more advanced. By the 1930s, for example, many veterinaries were using x-rays to assist them.

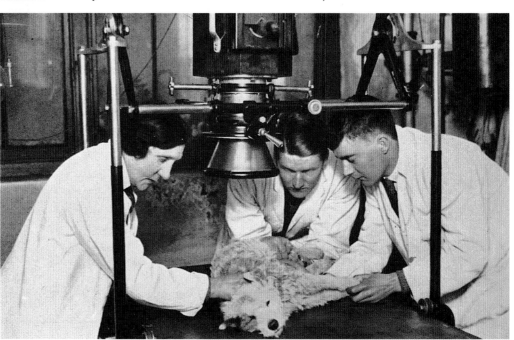

elaborate and efficient as that for humans. Scaling of teeth was frequently carried out by experts, and if teeth were already loose, as many as 10 could be removed without anaesthetic, provided the person carrying out the operation was sufficiently dextrous. For difficult cases and distressed patients, morphine could be administered an hour before the operation to calm the nerves and help relaxation.

In the most up-to-date surgeries, ultra-violet ray treatment was used, although results were certainly not 100 per cent effective and the dogs must surely have looked somewhat incongruous wearing

their protective goggles. Rickets and non-parasitic skin diseases could also be treated in this way, with fairly frequent success, and dogs suffering from eczema, ulcers, boils, abscesses, acne, alopecia and bruising sometimes also derived benefit.

SURGICAL PROCEDURES

CLEANLINESS HAD BECOME recognised as a necessity and delicate surgery was frequently undertaken. Many bitches were spayed and successful operations were often carried out on the bladder, although there was always a certain risk involved. In eye surgery, the skill of the surgeon played a large part in whether the operation was successful or otherwise.

Limbs could be amputated and false legs fitted, and, although more risky, operations which involved incision of the intestine to remove foreign bodies or tumours were also carried out. Despite hygiene rules, infections regularly set in, resulting in death shortly following the operations.

In the years between the two World Wars, a white coat, spotlessly clean premises and high fees were by no means any guarantee that a surgeon had

received training to qualify him as such. At that time there were many so-called quacks and charlatans about, and such people were readily able to hoodwink honest folk into believing that they had recognised qualifications.

ESTABLISHING LAWS

IN 1919 THE Animals' (Anaesthetics) Act was designed to prevent the infliction of pain, making it illegal for certain operations to be carried out without general anaesthetic. There were fixed financial penalties for first convictions and imprisonment for subsequent offences, but the stipulations were not all they might have been

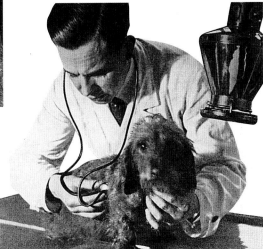

and revision was needed. One major loop-hole was that general anaesthesia was only called for if an animal was over the age of six months. In addition, only certain amputation operations were required to be done under anaesthetic, others were not. Local anaesthesia was required for tail docking and ear clipping or rounding, but only if the animal was over six months, and only a local anaesthetic was used for correction of umbilical hernias and incision into the urethra.

Although the veterinary profession had progressed a long way by the 1930s, it is interesting to compare the situation then with that of today. In so doing we can recognise how very much has been developed and improved upon in recent decades.

Top
Operations, such as amputation, were carried out successfully, provided infection did not set in.

Far Left
New technology included ultra-violet ray treatment for non-parasitic skin diseases.

Left
Standards of treatment varied considerably, from the top-quality veterinary colleges to quacks with no recognised qualifications.

DOG FACT:

When scaling a dog's teeth, canine dentists usually used a gag to protect them from being bitten.

Early Coat Presentation

AS THE DOG WORLD MOVED from the nineteenth to the twentieth century more and more attention was paid to the best methods of keeping dogs' coats clean, although there were still many who did not agree with bathing at all because they felt this caused the coat to hold in dirt, despite making it look temporarily clean. However, the strange preparations used for bathing a dog may have had some bearing on the reasons behind the opinions of those who disagreed with bathing.

The ideal bath tub for a dog was made of wood, with a hole at the bottom which was stopped up with a cork. The tub was placed over a gutter or drain so that it could be emptied easily.

Coming up to the beginning of the First World War cleansing options started to become available for those who favoured bathing, but the old-fashioned blue curd soap was still considered best of all. Another popular soap was Wright's Coal Tar, but this was not economical as a bar did not go far, especially when bathing one of the larger breeds. When there was any suspicion of skin trouble carbolic soap was a must. Unfortunately, though, the strong smell was always left behind in the coat, giving away the secret that the dog had a skin problem.

WELL-PRESENTED AND GROOMED

BY THE 1920S, PEOPLE generally accepted that their chances of success in the show ring were increased by better presentation of the coat and it was particularly beneficial to bath black and white dogs. Wire-haired dogs were rarely bathed for fear of making their coats too soft, but breeds with other coat types were often bathed as frequently as once a week. Dog grooming was becoming an art.

Many little 'additives' were used, such as a blue bag in the water to enhance the colour of white coats, or a few drops of Brilliantine for dogs which were required to have glossy coats. Dog baths had now been much improved because those made of galvanised iron had been introduced, available in various sizes and easier to handle. One of the main dangers in bathing a dog was scalding, but most people thought there was little harm in adding

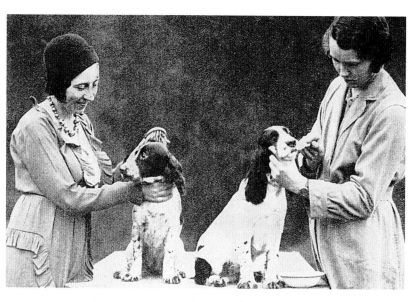

Above
By the 1920s show dogs were regularly bathed and groomed to improve their chances in the ring.

Top Right
Early bath tubs for dogs were made of wood. Galvanised iron tubs were much easier to use.

BATHING THE DOG

EGG YOLK WAS SMEARED into the coat and rubbed in well with water, thereby creating a lather. Unfortunately the yolk did not rinse out easily so copious ablutions were necessary. One of the main advantages of using egg yolk over soap was that it did not cause the eyes to smart or the skin to burn, nor did the dog sicken if the coat was licked. Another advantage was that if by chance the yolk had not been thoroughly washed out the dog could lick itself to remove any residue.

either a disinfectant or a few drops of ammonia to the water to remove grease.

DOGGY TOILETRIES

FLEAS AND OTHER PARASITES caused inevitable problems and when a dog was being bathed fleas had a nasty habit of escaping to the ears of the dog. A solution was to thoroughly soap the neck before applying water to the rest of the body and then leave this area well lathered until the rest had been rinsed off. The most convenient way of using soap was to cut each bar into several pieces so that they would each fit into the palm of the hand. Soft soap was not satisfactory because when applied liberally lumps of soap were often left in the coat. Many groomers made up their own preparations, mixing a pound of soft soap with powdered camphor and mercurial ointment. Others were quite happy to use a reputedly excellent new soap produced by Spratt's and called by the delightful name, 'Fomo'.

After bathing, a dog was taken into a warm room, one with a fire in winter. There the dog was placed in a box with clean straw. However, because the track to the house was often covered in cinder, small dogs had to be carried and large ones had to be on a short leash so they could not roll in the cinders as they were prone to do. It was exceedingly difficult to remove cinders from a

wet coat, indeed no less difficult than removing sand and earth.

For some of the larger breeds, instead of bathing, a swim followed by a good run was considered sufficient, while smooth-coated breeds needed to be kept in good condition by using a dandy-brush or hound glove. Although there were then no commercial tooth-pastes on the market, powdered charcoal with a toothbrush served its purpose very well.

Top
Drying dogs in front of the fire gradually gave way to hair-dryers in the 1930s.

Left
As owners took grooming more seriously, they made greater efforts to improve the condition of their dog's coat.

Bottom
Fleas were kept under control with grooming brushes dipped in a mixture of paraffin and sweet oil or in spirits of camphor.

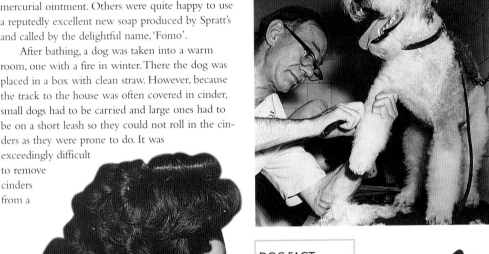

DOG FACT:
In Paraguay and Peru, human wet-nurses were employed specifically to look after orphaned puppies.

Some Canine Heroes

THROUGHOUT HISTORY, MANY dogs have received fame and recognition for services offered to mankind and stories of dogs such as Greyfriars Bobby are well known. Less well reported are the stories of those dogs who were awarded VC collars because they had put their lives at risk for the sake of humans. In the 1930s, a League of Kindness was inaugurated by the *Daily Mail*, resulting in the setting up of a Brave Dogs Roll of Honour. Hundreds of individual cases were investigated but only a few were selected to receive this prestigious award of a handsome collar, made of blue morocco leather, on which were silver mountings and a silver badge inscribed simply: 'For Bravery'.

CHARMING CHUM

ONE DOG SO HONOURED WAS CHUM, a charming Sealyham Terrier who was also a highly talented actress in her younger days, never tiring of performing to an appreciative audience. Chum was one of those dogs who simply delighted in any sort of trick or play-acting which put her in the limelight. As part of her medley of performances she could feign illness, write a letter, laugh at a joke, say her prayers and put her 'arm' round the waist of a cat, who would also allow itself to be used in a bathtime routine. Upon the completion of a performance Chum would sit up and clap her 'hands' together in applause, seemingly at her own cleverness.

In 1929 Chum performed another talented act and earned for herself a VC collar, but sadly it cost her the sight of one eye. She lived in Southsea with her owners, who had retired for the night, leaving Chum downstairs. They were awoken at about 1 a.m. by the sound of their four-legged friend scratching at the bedroom door. Rushing downstairs at the smell of burning, the master found the lower part of the house ablaze, the rooms filled by dense smoke. He headed for the street to call the fire brigade but due to the smoke his wife could not follow him, instead she turned back, climbed out of a window and crawled along a narrow ledge to the adjoining house.

Confusion ensued, with firemen, fire engines, hose pipes and onlookers. Although Chum was nowhere to be found she had been seen outside and it was therefore assumed she was safe. A while later when firemen reached the upper storey they found a rather grey-looking Sealyham sitting patiently beside her mistress's bed. It seems she had left the house but had dashed back through the flames to the bedroom again to look for her mistress. Finding the room empty she had sat down to await her return.

Chum was badly burned around the head and ears, losing the sight of one eye as a result but was fortunately restored to health thanks to long and careful nursing. From then on Chum's performances altered somewhat. Her photographs appeared in

Top Right
Nip received his VC collar at the expense of two broken legs.

Right
Chum was a highly intelligent Sealyham who delighted in performing tricks in front of an audience. Her bravery in saving her owners from fire left her badly burned and minus an eye.

DOG FACT:
In carrying out his brave deed, VC dog, Nip, jumped from a window and had to have his legs set in plaster of Paris.

what shy puppy, often confused by the fact that the family's parrot called out his name, bringing him rushing into the room, for no good reason. Probably partly because of this Bunty became terrified of unusual noises and would not allow any stranger to touch him. Four years later he changed owners and quickly established a close friendship with his new master whose housekeeper was subject to fits. On one occasion she fell across the open front of the kitchen range, the velvet folds of her dress quickly catching alight. Fortunately Bunty, his self-confidence recovered, was at hand. He tore away the burning portions of the girl's clothing by scratching and biting at them, burning his mouth and paws as he worked. Dragging at her skirt, he pulled her limp body away from the fireplace. The burns on both the housekeeper and Bunty took five weeks to heal. News of Bunty's bravery soon spread and he was presented with a silver-mounted collar and his VC, as well as many other medals donated by admiring animal lovers.

Chum and Bunty were just two of the carefully selected dogs who earned their collars, but there were many hundreds more who had performed great deeds but just didn't quite manage to make the grade.

numerous newspapers and she appeared with other Brave Dogs at dog shows held around the country, because at that time public interest in dogs which had performed such incredible feats was so great that a special section of the show was set aside so that members of the public could have the opportunity of meeting these canine heroes.

BRAVE BUNTY

ANOTHER DOG who received a VC collar as a result of a fire incident was Bunty, a male of mixed breeding but with a good deal of the Labrador Retriever about him. Bunty had thoughtful, dark brown eyes, but was a some-

> **DOG FACT:**
> In 1935 Britain had only 25 Guide Dogs for the Blind. Mona, a white Alsatian was one of them and considered a heroine.

Top
Bunty pulled his owner's unconscious housekeeper away from the kitchen range and then tore away her burning clothing.

Top Left
After Chum had fully recovered from her ordeal, she moved on to a second acting career, appearing at Brave Dog shows.

Left
Tess saved two-year-old Aaron from drowning when he fell into a rock pool.

Tail-Waggers' Club

the slogan for 1929 was 'On to the 100,000!' By August of that year membership had already exceeded the goal. Applications for membership numbered several thousands a day and during one 12-day period the club recruited 55,000 new members, both a joy and a veritable nightmare for the organisers.

The Tail-Waggers' Club was set up with great enthusiasm in 1928, its aim being to link up all thoughtful and considerate dog owners and their pets in one great organisation designed to promote canine welfare. Fifteen dogs were enrolled as members at the first meeting, after which applications simply poured in so that barely three months after the inaugural meeting membership had risen to 10,000, enabling a cheque for £1,000 to be donated to the Royal Veterinary College Canine Diseases Appeal Fund. Things were moving fast.

JOINING THE CLUB

THE MINIMUM MEMBERSHIP FEE, valid for the lifetime of the dog registered, was just two shillings. It was a simple procedure to apply, requiring only the name or pet name of the dog and details of the owner's name and address. In return the Club forwarded an oxidised silver collar medallion, depicting the emblem of two crossed tails and the motto: 'I Help My Pals'. On the reverse was the dog's membership number with details of the Club's headquarters.

Above
Each new member of the Tail-Waggers' Club received a collar medallion engraved with its membership number.

Right
On one day 810 kg (1,800 lb) of outgoing mail was despatched.

Among the Club's earliest members were dogs belonging to The Prince of Wales, Princess Mary, the Countess of Harewood and Queen Maud of Norway. Other royal personages soon took up their lead and membership continued to rise unbelievably fast. After five months there were 22,000 members and

DOG FACT:
Arthur Croxton Smith became a member of the Kennel Club in 1899, later becoming Vice-Chairman and was Chairman from 1937 to 1948.

TAIL WAGGERS' HANDBOOK

TO WRITE FOR ITS VARIOUS publications, the Tail-Waggers' Club was fortunate to have the support of Arthur Croxton Smith OBE who had specialised in writing about dogs since 1909. Messrs Spratt's Patent Limited also allowed much material from their own guides to be used by Tail-Waggers' and generously offered to pay for the printing and distribution of a handbook.

As was the fashion of the day, the club enjoyed circulating statistics. In a year 2 tons and 10 cwt of membership certificates were used, with about 360,000 sheets of letter-headed paper for correspondence. Incoming post weighed an average of 45 kg (100 lb) a day but the medallions and certificates posted out were around 171 kg (380 lb). On one day incoming mail weighed 281 kg (625 lb) and outgoing mail 810 kg (1,800 lb), while the club's records occupied over 19.6 cubic metres (700 cubic feet) of space.

MEMBERSHIP BENEFITS

THE 'LOST AND FOUND' service operated by Tail-Waggers' became one of the most appreciated of all the club's services, with the use of the collar medallion facilitating the retrieval of many lost dogs. As the club grew it found itself in the position of being able to make many charitable donations so was effective in both a practical and philanthropic way.

In poor districts dogs were turned out to fend for themselves simply because their owners could not afford

The "Tail-Waggers" Map of the World

through the Fiji Islands, Siam and New Zealand to Venezuela and Zanzibar. The dog with the distinction of being Tail-Wagger No 0 was Bobby, actually a bitch, owned by the originator of the club and regarded as the 'Mother of all Tail-Waggers'. There was even a Tail-Waggers' class at Cruft's. A particularly famous member of Tail-Waggers' was the Cocker Spaniel, Lucky Star of Ware, winner of Best in Show at Crufts in 1930. A competition somewhat different in nature was for photographs of member dogs. Called the 'Snaps'

Top and Left
Applications flooded in from all corners of the world from Albania to Zanzibar. Five months after the Club was set up it had 22,000 members.

Bottom
Lucky Star of Ware was the winner of Best of Show at Crufts in 1930.

to pay dog licence fees, so Tail-Waggers' set up its own Dog Licence Clubs. Through the club people of meagre circumstances could pay two pence a week, leaving the responsibility of paying the licence fee to Tail-Waggers'. This was an easier means by which people could pay, though in effect the total of 8s 8d paid left a surplus of 1s 2d, of which 6d was retained for working expenses and 6d donated to the local branch of an approved animal welfare society.

Competition, it enabled every member dog to join in the club's activities in some way. A number of leaflets provided practical advice.

Undoubtedly thanks to Tail-Waggers' many dogs received better treatment than they might otherwise have done. The one millionth member joined in 1958.

WORLDWIDE APPEAL

THE CLUB TRULY COVERED all corners of the earth with member countries ranging from Albania,

Myths and Magic

IN DIFFERING CULTURES and various periods dogs have suffered greatly, partly because they have been treated as ritual objects, with the tradition of the day involving ceremonies which inflicted pain and sometimes death.

Above
Dogs were often associated with witchcraft and feared accordingly.

Right
In some cultures, the blood of a dog was an integral part of the wedding ceremony as the couple swore fidelity.

> **DOG FACT:**
> Chinese dogs of more than one colour can be named Hua Tse, meaning 'flowery child'.

Right
Ceremonies and rituals involving dogs often meant pain or death.

CHINESE SUPERSTITIONS

MANY DOGS HAVE suffered in China, a nation in which it is widely recognised that dogs have been killed for many reasons, including for use in medicinal preparations. Once, large dogs such as the Tibetan Mastiff were killed in China because they were a symbol of loyalty and ferocity, and high prices were paid for them by women in love: in an endeavour to keep their menfolk true to them, Chinese women engaged a dog spirit which they instructed not to allow the man to visit another woman. Instead, the spirit was expected to guide him back to the lady who had engaged its services. Ladies apparently were more ready to part with their money for a small portion of a Tibetan Mastiff than an entire Pug or other small dog.

In due course of time, the custom was mercifully replaced by dogs' heads being drawn on paper as charms. These were both cheaper and more practical. The woman told the dog charm what was to be done, then burned the charm and secretly rubbed the ash on her lover, or mixed it in his tea. However, the tradition remained of displaying a dog's flesh or blood outside a house to frighten away disease, insect pests and intruders.

DOGS USED AS CURES

THE DOG WAS USED as a cure by many other cultures, not only the Chinese. Three doses of 'rubbed dog' was believed to cure a child of stomach ache and in Japan something known as the 'dog-box' was a charm, bringing good luck and ensuring an easy birth. This talisman also protected the child from fever spirits and were-animals. In the daytime the box was placed beside the baby and at night hung above the bed to keep the child's dreams free from evil spirits. During the eighth century the Chinese had a relatively harmless way of stopping a child from crying. A little hair was taken from beneath the throat of a dog, tied inside a red bag and put into the hands of the baby, whereupon the baby would reputedly stop crying.

As part of a religious ceremony, the Babylonians sent a white and a black dog out to sea; they also thought the bite of a dog could signify either good or evil, depending upon the dog's colour. At each side of the entrance to Babylonian houses a type of Mastiff was depicted as a magic guard.

In Hebrew literature, people were warned not to live where barking dogs could be heard, and if barking were heard on the way to a wedding it was better to call it off. However, in some cultures a dog was part of the wedding ceremony. The groom swore an oath by taking the blood of a dog which had been killed and the wife swore her fidelity by the dog.

The poor dog was also used to eliminate disease. Its tail was severed and, screaming in agony, the dog was taken around each room of the house and subsequently kicked violently out of the door. This ritual symbolised the spirits of disease running from corner to corner, eventually leaving home pursued by the dog. The farther the dog was kicked outside, the farther he chased the spirits away, thus lessening their chances of return.

THE WITCH AND HER DOG

WITCHES WERE SAID FREQUENTLY to turn themselves into dogs so that they could use the powers of revenge which they had received from the devil. In Goya's fascinating painting: *Le Transformation des Sorciers*, four witches are depicted in their hovel, making up charms while transforming themselves into dogs at the same time.

Dogs were often said to be the familiar spirits of a witch: it was said when a witch first made her pact with the devil he gave her a small animal to wait upon her. The familiar was allowed to suck the witch's blood in order to renew its strength and help form a close bond between the two. In these cases, instead of transforming themselves into dogs, the witches sent out their familiars. People were employed as witch finders and one, Matthew Hopkins, wrote a fascinating book explaining his methods of detection.

RELIGIOUS SYMBOLS

IN THE MOST ANCIENT representations of Western Christianity, Saint Christopher was depicted as a young man with the head of a dog. He was believed once to have been an exceptionally handsome Roman soldier, his good looks leading him to temptation by both men and women. For deliverance, he prayed he might be made ugly and grew the head of a dog. Another dog-headed being was in the imaginings of some eighteenth century explorers who believed they had met an animal which was part bird, part pig and part dog. It supposedly followed them, attacking any human or animal which approached, thereby aiding their safe passage through what must have been an incredibly strange new land.

Above

Cerberus, the three-headed dog, guarded the entrance to the Underworld.

Below

When a witch made her pact with the devil he gave her a dog to attend upon her.

Dogs and Royalty

JUST AS TODAY many members of Britain's royalty are closely associated with dogs, there have been many notable friendships and connections over the centuries. In the 15th century, King Edward IV presented five Mastiffs to the King of France, and two centuries later James I gave Mastiffs to the King of Spain. In cathedral monuments, pets frequently lie at the feet of those of royalty and rank, depicting loyalty to their master or mistress, even in death. At Canterbury Cathedral is the tomb of Edward, the Black Prince, and at his feet lies a French Bulldog.

Above and Top
The children of King Charles I kept spaniels; Queen Elizabeth II prefers her corgis.

Right
The Duke and Duchess of Windsor were devoted to their canine chums.

DOG FACT:
King George V ordered that no steel-toothed traps were to be used on royal estates.

HENRY VIII

THE COURT of King Henry VIII was overrun with dogs, to such an extent that he put out a decree that no dogs except small spaniels could be kept in court except by commandment of the King or Queen. One of the King's spaniels, Cut, must have been lost or stolen, for there is record in the King's privy purse of payments of five and 10 shillings for the return of the dog. Another royal dog, Cutie, was returned upon payment of four shillings and eight pence.

Henry made it known that dogs were to be kept 'sweet, wholesome and clean', but he did not to object to baiting sports, for it was under him that the office of 'Master of the Royal Game, of Bears and Mastiff Dogs' was created, and remained in existence until 1642. Records show that Henry sent 400 dogs to Charles V of Spain for use in his war against France.

KING CHARLES AND THE SPANIELS

SMALL SPANIELS continued to increase in popularity and importance, especially under the Tudors and Stuarts, and the court of Charles II (1660–85) was filled with them – the king was famous for playing with his spaniels all the while rather than looking after business matters. So closely was he associated with them that the King Charles Spaniel actually took his name.

VICTORIAN ERA

QUEEN VICTORIA PLAYED a very important part in the world of dogs and was such an ardent dog lover that, following her coronation ceremony, she hurried home to give her dog its usual bath. Often, her dogs were exhibited at shows and both she and the Princess of Wales were frequent exhibitors at Cruft's famous dog show.

Queen Victoria also supported sheepdog trials in Wales, attending personally in 1889 with other royal family members. Her Deerhounds at both Windsor and Sandringham did much to help kindle wide support for the breed. Among her many pets were three 'Turnspit Tykes', those curious, long-bodied dogs used in the wheel to turn the roasting spit, although in Queen Victoria's household they were kept purely as pets.

Landing in Newfoundland in 1860, the Prince of Wales was presented with a magnificent Newfoundland dog, wearing a heavy collar of silver. In 1875, the Prince became Patron of the Kennel Club and remained so following his accession to the throne as King Edward VII.

Queen Alexandra was much involved in the world of dogs, owning Borzois, Basset Hounds, Chow Chows, Skye Terriers, Japanese Spaniels and Pugs. She and her husband frequently visited shows, stopping to speak to many of the dogs and displaying an evident bond of sympathy, especially when they came across dogs from their own kennels. The royal kennels were as fine as the royal stables, admirably ventilated and fitted with hot water pipes. For exercise there was a choice of three paddocks in front of the kennels, or a yard paved with red and blue brick tiles. There was also a 'nursery', hospital and a kitchen for preparation of the dogs' food.

EDWARD VII

KING EDWARD VII HAD an aversion to hunting tame deer so abolished the pack of Royal Bloodhounds. He was also vociferous in his dislike of ear-cropping, a practice which became illegal in Britain. Perhaps the most famous of his canine companions was a terrier on whose collar were engraved the words, 'I am Caesar. I belong to the King.' Caesar travelled all over Europe with his master and, after the King's death on 6 May 1910, Caesar was inconsolable, whining pitifully outside the bedroom and refusing to eat. Queen Alexandra placed Caesar in the funeral procession behind the gun carriage and the sight of this famous little terrier with the solemn cortege touched the hearts of thousands lining the route.

King George V had inherited from his mother, Queen Alexandra, an appreciation of dogs and considered it of prime importance that a dog could do a good day's work. He became the first Royal President of the RSPCA in 1893 while he was still the Duke of York.

> DOG FACT:
> Many breeds interested King Edward VII, including the Tibet Sheepdog, but it was a Dandie Dinmont called Venus who was his inseparable companion.

Left
Queen Victoria at Balmoral in 1874 with one of her many pet dogs.

Below and Bottom
Edward VII with his dog Caesar, and Princess Alexandra with her pack of greyhounds.

Dogs in the Arts

THROUGHOUT HISTORY THE DOG has played a prominent part in literature. We know that the Greeks were fond of dogs, many of which have been mentioned by name in Greek writings, described almost always as being faithful to their masters. There is even rather an amusing section concerning the dog, Labes, who was thought to have stolen some cheese. A particularly strange reference to the dog, though, appears in the writings of Plutarch who tells of a dog with a luxurious tail. The dog's owner ordered that it be cut off so that people would speak of the owner as a mild eccentric.

DOGS IN ANCIENT HISTORY

IN ROMAN TIMES writers gave more of the impression that dogs were workers, primarily guardians of flock and home. Again we read of their faithfulness but fewer are mentioned by name than in the writings of the Greeks.

In the Old Testament, although the dog is mentioned it is almost always regarded with scorn and hatred by the Hebrews who clearly held the dog in low esteem. We read: 'Him that dieth of Jeroboam in the city shall the dogs eat' (1 *Kings* 14:11), and '... they are all dumb dogs' (*Isaiah* 56:10).

GELERT AND LLEWELLYN

BY THE END OF the twelfth century, the dog in literature re-emerged in a very different light. The fabled story of the hound, Gelert, has been told in many different ways down the centuries, but perhaps the poem which leaves the most indelible impression is that written by The Hon. William

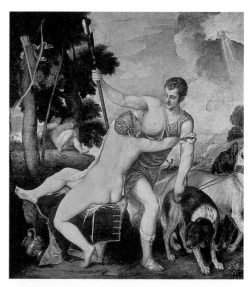

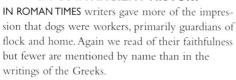

Above
Sir Percy Fitzpatrick's chronicle of the little runt who became renowned as Jock of the Bushveld became a literary classic.

Right and Above right
Dogs appear in Roman and Greek myths and legends, as well as in Biblical stories. However, they are not always viewed in a favourable light. These fifteenth century paintings give a contemporary view.

Robert Spencer (1770–1834). Prince Llewellyn's faithful hound, which had always gone with him to the chase, remained behind one day and, upon returning from the hunt, Llewellyn found the dog smeared in blood, sitting by his son's empty cradle:

He called his child – no voice replied;
He searched – with terror wild.
Blood! Blood! he found on every side,
But nowhere found the child!

Hell-hound! my child's by thee devoured!
The frantic father cried;
And, to the hilt, his vengeful sword
He plunged in Gelert's side!

His suppliant looks, as prone he fell,
No pity could impart;
But still his Gelert's dying yell
Passed heavy o'er his heart.

Aroused by Gelert's dying yell,
Some slumberer wakened nigh:
What words the parent's joy can tell,
To hear his infant cry?

Concealed beneath a tumbled heap,
His hurried search had missed,
All glowing from his rosy sleep,
The cherub boy he kissed.

Nor scathe had he, nor harm, nor dread –
But the same couch beneath
Lay a gaunt wolf, all torn and dead –
Tremendous still in death!

Ah, what was then Llewellyn's pain,
For now the truth was clear:
The gallant hound the wolf had slain,
To save Llewellyn's heir.

The poem ends with the description of Llewellyn's incredible remorse, claiming that a consecrated spot now holds the name of 'Gelert's Grave' in memorial to the dead dog. Indeed there does appear to be such a grave, in Snowdon in Wales, but in truth this was actually created by an innkeeper who wished to increase business in his public house. One can find many similar stories to the tale of Gelert by looking through literature of many other countries. Some legends substitute a serpent in place of the evil wolf.

THE EPITAPH

MANY A WRITER has written an epitaph to his dog so one can see how much the dog has been loved by man, not just now but through the centuries. Some refer to specific breeds, such as the Newfoundland belonging to Lord Byron, or the charming Dachshund, Islet, of which we read:

Our Islet out of Heligoland, dismissed
From his quaint tenement, quits hates and loves.
There lived with us a wagging humourist
In that hound's arch dwarf-legged on boxing gloves.

(George Meredith (1828-date unknown)

Many an epitaph brings a silent tear to the eye, and often the most moving are those which mention no specific breed, allowing even the most contemporary readers to associate freely with them and to use their imagination. Such a poem is 'Tory, A Puppy', written by Mortimer Collins (1827–76):

He lies in the soft earth under the grass,
Where they who love him often pass.
And his grave is under a tall young lime,
In whose boughs the pale green hop-flowers
  climb;
But his spirit – where does his spirit rest?
It was God who made him – God knows best.

Rudyard Kipling

BORN IN INDIA IN DECEMBER 1865, Joseph Rudyard Kipling, apart from being a novelist and poet, was a short story writer who had great respect for dogs, whatever their status. He had no compunction about writing about mongrels, or even dholes, Indian Wild Dogs.

DOG STORIES

KIPLING'S FATHER WAS a professor at the Bombay School of Art and also curator of the Lahore Museum, but in 1871 Rudyard and his younger sister were taken to England and placed in boarding school. Kipling was awarded the Nobel Prize for Literature in 1907, but it was not until 1930 that his story, 'Thy Servant A Dog', was published and in 1934 this was also included in *Collected Dog Stories*, which is a charming compilation of tales including a few touching poems. It was illustrated with delightfully simple drawings allowing the characters to shine through.

Top Right
'Beware
Of giving your heart to a
dog to tear.'

Bottom Right
Boots is the central
character in a number of
Kipling's dog stories.

Bottom
The engaging drawings of
the canine characters in
Collected Dog Stories
complement the text to
perfection.

BOOTS

'THY SERVANT A DOG' revolves around a terrier called Boots who has 'written' his story himself, using simple, down-to-earth language. When chatting with his canine chums, they make reference to their various gods and to people who are useful to them, such as Cookey and also Harry-with-Spade. Conversations occur in the text between the various animals and all sorts of exciting escapades take place, such as among the hens when they find a fish head, en route carefully avoiding someone they called 'pig-lady with pups'. Though simplistic, this is not an easy story to read, but

doubtless appealed to young minds of the day. Boots features again in 'The Great Play Hunt', which involves such antics as looking for rat holes in the Old Nursery and hunting a fox, albeit none too successfully! Boots is also the narrator in 'Toby Dog', about the terrier friend with whom he rabbited around borders in the garden for bones which they had hidden, 'in case of hungries'. Toby Dog was thought to be quite a 'dash', but was very much a terrier at heart and taught Boots a lot about ratting.

Other Rudyard Kipling stories and poems appeal to more general tastes, such as the well-known 'The Power of the Dog':

There is sorrow enough in the natural way
From men and women to fill our day;
And when we are certain of sorrow in store,
Why do we always arrange for more?
Brothers and sisters, I bid you beware
Of giving your heart to a dog to tear.

Buy a pup and your money will buy
Love unflinching that cannot lie –
Perfect passion and worship fed
By a kick in the ribs or a pat on
* the head.*
Nevertheless it is hardly fair
To risk your heart for a
* dog to tear.*
When the fourteen years
* which nature permits*
Are closing in asthma, or
* tumour, or fits,*

Left
'Our loves are not given, but only lent,' writes Kipling in his sentimental poem, 'The Power of the Dog.'

Below
The great writer Sir Rudyard Kipling was born in India in 1865, but moved to Britain as a child. He died in 1936, having written tales of many canine heroes.

And the vet's unspoken prescription runs
To lethal chambers or loaded guns,
Then you will find – it's your own affair, –
But … you've given your heart to a dog to tear.

When the body that lived at your single will,
With its whimper of welcome, is stilled (how still!),
When the spirit that answered your
*   every mood*
Is gone – wherever it goes –for good,
You will discover how much you care,
And will give your heart to a dog to tear!

We've sorrow enough in the natural way,
When it comes to burying Christian clay.
Our loves are not given, but only lent,
At compound interest of cent per cent,
Though it is not always the case, I believe,
That the longer we've kept 'em, the more do we
*   grieve;*
For when debts are payable, right or wrong,
A short-time loan is as bad as a long –
So why in Heaven (before we are there)
Should we give our hearts for a dog to tear?

QUIQUERN

KIPLING'S WELL-RESEARCHED story of 'Quiquern' is based around an Inuit teenager and opens with a vivid verbal picture of a young puppy kept in a sealskin pouch, hung above the warmth of a blubber lamp, while meat for the dogs hung from a kind of gallows made from a whale's jaw bones.

The dogs had to be extremely fit as they were used to pull sleds and travelled 32–48 km (20–30 miles) a day as the Inuit people went about their search for food. Sometimes they were able to travel with the humans in their big skin boats; the dogs

and babies alike lying amongst adults' feet, the women singing songs as they glided over the glassy, icy waters. This is a story in which Kipling is at his best, and from which one can learn about the lives of indigenous peoples, as well as take immense pleasure in the prose. The reader easily joins in the Inuit family's trials and tribulations, sharing both their happy times and their sorrows.

OTHER STORIES

THERE ARE OTHER STORIES of Kipling's, notably 'A Sea Dog', 'A Hostage' and 'The Dog Hervey', in which dogs play a central role. Hervey is a cute little rascal of a character, about whom a little girl commented when she saw him, 'I like the cast of his countenance.' So it was that Hervey was deemed to be adorable and found himself a new family and home. Having suffered distemper, Hervey was a sandy-pied, broken-haired terrier, with one ear upstanding and the other floppy, and two most hideous squints in his eyes. He was an absolute dream of a dog.

Rudyard Kipling died on 18 January 1936, but his works and many of the canine characters he portrayed are certain to live on in people's memories for centuries to come.

Above
Although Hervey was not a handsome dog, he was very well-loved and shared many adventures with his humans.

Right
The story of the Inuit teenager, Quiquern, his family and their dogs paints a vivid picture of the lives these wandering people led.

Other Writers

MANY WRITERS HAVE IMPARTED great character to their dogs. Dickens' works show a certain independence in his dogs' nature, such as Dora Spendlow's dog, Jip, in *David Copperfield*. Upon approaching him for the first time, Copperfield says: 'I approached him tenderly, for I loved even him; but he showed his whole set of teeth, got under a chair expressly to snarl, and wouldn't hear of the least familiarity.'

DICKENS'S DOG CHARACTERS

BULL'S-EYE, THE DOG which belonged to Bill Sykes, in *Oliver Twist*, came to an alarming end when, 'Missing his aim, he fell into the ditch, turning completely over as he went; and striking his head against a stone, dashed his brains out.'

On a lighter note, in *The Pickwick Papers*, Mr Jingle says, 'Ah! you should keep dogs – fine animals – sagacious creatures – dog of my own once – Pointer – surprising instinct – out shooting one day – entering inclosure – whistled – dog stopped – whistled again – Ponto – no go: stock still – called him – Ponto, Ponto – wouldn't move – dog transfixed – staring at board – looked up, saw an inscription – 'Gamekeeper has orders to shoot all dogs found in this inclosure' – wouldn't pass it – wonderful dog – valuable dog that – very.'

AND OTHERS

DOGS APPEAR in so many books throughout the ages that it is impossible to do justice to them all but one of the more famous must surely be Elizabeth Barrett Browning's Flush, who is written about in Virginia Woolf's biography of the poet. There are undoubted literary problems in writing an entire novel centred around an animal, but other authors, too, have succeeded in doing this, such as Sir Percy Fitzpatrick with his story of *Jock of the Bushfeld*, illustrated so well by E. Caldwell.

This is just one of the charming descriptions of Jock – here a tiny puppy, born small and weak, bullied and crowded out by the others in the litter. 'At that time he looked more like a big tock-tockie beetle than a dog. Besides the balloon-like tummy he had stick-out bandy legs, very like a beetle's too, and a neck so thin that it made the head look enormous, and you wondered how the neck ever held it up. But what made him so supremely ridiculous was that he evidently did not know he was ugly; he walked about as if he was always thinking of his dignity, and he had that puffed out and stuck-up air of importance that you only see in small people and bantam cocks who are always trying to appear an inch taller than they really are.'

Jock will undoubtedly live on in the memories of those who have read about him, as will so many wonderful canine characters with which we have become acquainted through the centuries.

Above
Bull's Eye and his master Bill Sykes make an unpleasant pair in Dickens's Oliver Twist.

Left
Writers often portrayed their own favourite dogs in their books, some in a supporting role, others as the central character.

Sir Walter Scott

I N 1812, WALTER SCOTT, his family and dogs, took up residence in what was to become their wonderful family home, Abbotsford, in Scotland's Melrose. The old farmhouse was demolished, the main block built, and in 1820 Scott became a baronet. Today the home is preserved much as it was in Sir Walter's day, housing a veritable wealth of interesting paintings and memorabilia.

DEVOTED MASTER

Top

The Scottish writer Sir Walter Scott lived for most of his adult life in Abbotsford, in the Borders region of southern Scotland.

Below

Walter Scott had a number of favourite dog companions, but Maida is undoubtedly the most famous of them. His statue still rests in the grounds of Abbotsford.

THROUGHOUT SCOTT'S LIFE, his dogs came next to his children. Camp, a large Bull Terrier, had died before the move to Abbotsford but this was a dog Scott always spoke to as if he were a man, considering him a wise old fellow. He was buried in the garden behind Scott's house in Castle Street, Edinburgh. The dogs had free access to Scott's study at all times, and his Greyhounds, called Douglas and Percy, were famous for leaping in and out of the study window. When Maida chose to leave the room, he signified his inclination by thumping against the door with his large paw as violently as would a fashionable footman of the day.

Maida was actually the product of a Glengarry Deerhound dam and a Pyrenean sire, the white in his coat possibly having a bearing in the small amount of white found in Deerhound coats to this day.

SIR WALTER SCOTT'S GREAT HOUND MAIDA.

Maida's gravity amused Scott who commented: 'I make no doubt when Maida is alone with these young dogs he throws gravity aside, and plays the boy as much as any of them, but he is ashamed to do so in our company ...'.

All animals seemed fond of Scott who, although he wrote at high speed and with profound concentration, was in the habit of talking to the animals while he worked. Now and then he stopped to pat the head of Maida, while a fat tom cat generally sat watching from the top step of a tall ladder used to reach the highest books.

Other dogs abounded not only in the library but also in the breakfast room at Abbotsford. There was a black Greyhound, Finnette; Lady Scott's Spaniel, Ourisque; a Highland Terrier and Dandie Dinmonts named after the cruet stand: Pepper, Mustard and Ketchup. On Sunday evenings Sir Walter always dined at home, sometimes with a few friends, the Dandies gambolling about his heels whilst Maida grinned and wagged his tail at the prospect of such a relaxed evening.

Maida remained active well into old age but towards the end Scott was parted from his faithful dog during the winter and was desperately concerned for Maida's welfare. He wrote to William Laidlaw: 'Dear Willie – I hope Maida will be taken

care of. He should have a bed in the kitchen, and always be called indoors after it is dark, for all the kind are savage at night. Please cause Swanson to knock him up a box, and fill it with straw from time to time. I enclose a cheque for £50 to pay accounts, etc. Yours W. S.'

MAIDA'S DEATH

SADLY, ON 22 OCTOBER, 1824, Maida died quietly in his straw, following a good supper. He was buried beneath a stone likeness carved by Scott's mason and placed at the gate of Abbotsford a year before Scott's death. The couplet on the epitaph reads: 'Beneath the sculptured form which late you wore, Sleep soundly, Maida, at your master's door'. Unfortunately there was an error in the Latin and this was circulated in the press causing a 'contemptible rumpus' which vexed Scott, though he subsequently wrote, 'So Maida died, but lives'.

FAVOURED PETS

THE MANY DOGS WHICH featured in the *Waverley* novels provided clues to the identity of the author, although Scott's publishers were not allowed to reveal his name. Bevis and Roswal are clearly meant to represent Maida, whilst Fangs, Wasp and Juno are the 'cruet' terriers.

His dogs were with Scott in the weeks before his death; 'his dogs had assembled about his chair – they began to fawn upon him and lick his hands, and alternately he sobbed and smiled over them,

until sleep oppressed him.' Today, life still goes on at Abbotsford and a very special atmosphere still permeates the place. Sleeping soundly in his rightful place at his master's door, Maida was not to know that, in 1992, Walter Scott's descendants, Patricia and Jean Maxwell-Scott, would open their home and the gardens to the Deerhound fraternity who took along 71 Deerhounds to pay homage to Maida and his master, Sir Walter Scott.

Very poignant is this extract from one of Scott's letters, written at Abbotsford on 24 April 1822: 'I have sometimes thought of the final cause of dogs having such short lives, and I am quite satisfied it is in compassion to the human race; for if we suffer so much in losing a dog after an acquaintance of ten or twelve years, what would it be if they were to live double that time?'

Top Left
The white found in Deerhound coats is attributed to Maida's Pyrenean sire.

Top
In 1992, 71 Deerhounds came to Abbotsford to celebrate the relationship between Scott and Maida.

Centre Left
The statue of Maida, under which lie his remains, still guards the door of Abbotsford.

Dogs in Art

EVEN EARLY ROCK PAINTINGS can be considered a form of art, as can carving found on the sides of ancient tombs, so it is difficult to know quite where and when in the history of art to commence this section. From art we are able to learn a great deal about the way dogs have developed, not least from Greek, Egyptian, Roman and Assyrian art well before the birth of Christ.

POTTERY AND SCULPTURE

THE BRITISH MUSEUM houses a splendid black-figure amphora, a Greek vase dating back to 520–500 BC and depicting Cerberus, guardian of the underworld, leading two magnificent dogs which appear to be of hound type and wearing collars. Perhaps one of the most famous dog sculptures of all time is that of two seated greyhounds, discovered in Italy in the eighteenth century and dating back to the second century AD. This is now housed in London's British Museum and it is fascinating to see how little this particular breed has changed over the centuries.

Above right
Stag hunting with hounds has been popular for hundreds of years, as this 15th century illustration of the chase shows

Below
Sir Edwin Landseer was one of Queen Victoria's favourite artists. Here, she is depicted reviewing the troops with the Duke of Wellington.

Pottery jars have been found carrying simple decorative patterns, several of which depict dogs which are clearly being used in the hunt, while many pottery watchdogs have been found in Chinese graves of the Han dynasty.

MANUSCRIPTS, TAPESTRIES AND HERALDRY

EARLY MANUSCRIPTS AND tapestries have frequently depicted dogs. Of especial interest is Gaston Phoebus' *Le Livre de Chase* which is a treatise on hunting originally written in 1382. From this, readers and observers today can learn an enormous amount about the way dogs were treated at that time, how they were used and even what collars they wore.

The dog has also been used as an heraldic emblem, giving the identity of the bearer in pictorial language. Often the dogs were portrayed in stylised form, but some looked natural. Several breeds of dogs have been included in heraldry; the Greyhound was most popular, and then the Talbot Hound, which was used as the coat of arms for the families of Talbot, Earl of Shrewsbury.

ITALY, SPAIN AND FRANCE

THE FAMOUS PAINTING, *The Vision of St Eustace* by Antonio Pisano (c.1395–c.1455), clearly shows dogs of greyhound-type with other more substantial dogs, not so tall and with longer coats. Pisano, known as Pisanello, surely had an excellent knowledge of canine anatomy and used this to portray dogs in a thoroughly lifelike way. Italian animal art was to an extent influenced by St Francis of Assisi, who was known for his great love of animals, so it is not surprising to find so many Italian paintings depicting dogs. Paolo Caliari (1528–88), better known as Veronese, painted several breeds of dog, among which were about 30 paintings of Salukis.

In Spain, the paintings of Velázquez (1599–1660) are well known for the dogs they include. The artist often used large dogs to contrast with the children portrayed in his works.

French seventeenth century artists often portrayed Dwarf Spaniels, now generally known as Papillons, in their works, while on a completely different theme some are famous for their portrayal of Diana the Huntress with her Greyhounds.

Two of the most famous animal painters in the world are undoubtedly Alexandre-François Desportes (1661–1743) and Jean Baptiste Oudry (1686–1755). Oudry was idolised by Louis XV, who asked him to paint several dogs in the Louvre, working in sumptuous rooms set up for the artist. Not only did Oudry produce hundreds of paintings of dogs, he was also much involved as director of tapestries, designing the series entitled *The Hunts of Louis XV* which portrayed hunts at Fontainbleu, Rambouillet and Chantilly. Moving into the eighteenth century, dogs continue to play an important role in paintings, a breed similar to those now called Cavalier King Charles Spaniels were often included, sometimes merely as colourful companions to the main subject.

THE LOW COUNTRIES
IN THE LOW COUNTRIES many artists included the dog in their paintings, but most portrayed people's daily home lives rather than themes based on mythology or religion. Jan van Eyck (c.1385–1441) included a now famous Rough-coated Terrier in one of his paintings, while Hieronymus Bosch (1450–1516) included a white Greyhound in his painting of *The Adoration of the Magi* and in *The Garden of Earthly Delights*, there are many dogs among other bizarre animals and grotesque humans.

Peter Paul Rubens (1577–1640) clearly seems to have been fond of dogs because those in his paintings seem to have been painted with joy and flamboyancy. Among his other paintings was a series of hunting scenes of which *Wolf and Dog* shows several large dogs attacking a wolf.

BRITAIN
THERE ARE A NUMBER of famous British artists who have included dogs in their paintings, Sir Joshua Reynolds (1723–92) and Thomas Gainsborough (1727–88) being two which spring readily to mind.

Reynolds painted what is believed to be the first portrayal of a black Cocker Spaniel on canvas, as well as the first known British painting of a Maltese. Often he included children in his paintings and successfully managed to impart a warmth between the sitters and their canine friends.

GEORGE STUBBS
GEORGE STUBBS (1724–1806), although better known for his excellent portrayals of horses, also painted dogs, among which are many studies of Fino, a black and white Spitz which was owned by the then Prince of Wales, later to become George IV. Philip Reingale (1749–1833) also became involved with dogs with his introduction to the painting of sporting subjects, several of which are well known and include Setters, Greyhounds and Italian Greyhounds. Perhaps surprisingly, it was

Below
A typical nineteenth-century hunting scene. Riders, horses and hounds take some refreshment.

Reingale who was responsible for the 24 studies of dog breeds commissioned for inclusion in the book *The Sportsman's Cabinet*, published in 1803.

JOHN EMMS
ANOTHER BRITISH ARTIST reputed for his skillful painting of terriers and foxhounds was John Emms (1843–1912) who was also a recognised authority on dogs, and of especial significance to the dog showing fraternity is R. Marshall's intricate painting

HIS MASTER'S VOICE

TOWARDS THE END of the nineteenth century, Francis Barraud (1856–1924), who was a photographer turned painter, created the world-famous work entitled *His Master's Voice*. This was based on his dog, Nipper, who was partly Bull Terrier, and the painting was subsequently sold to a gramophone company as an advertising and promotional logo. The executives of the company later provided the artist with a small studio in which to paint replicas of the original picture of Nipper for their headquarters abroad. The original painting still hangs in EMI's boardroom and the little dog Nipper, who lived to the age of 11 and was buried at Kingston-upon-Thames, remains one of the most famous dogs in the world for that picture has created a lasting image in people's minds.

Above
Dogs are very much in evidence in this vivid portrayal of a picnic from the Livre de Chasse.

of *Jemmy Shaw's Canine Meeting*, dated 1855. The particular significance of this work, owned by the English Kennel Club, is that it is probably the earliest known painting of a dog show, which was held at the Queen's Head Tavern in Haymarket, London. At least nine different breeds are represented in this painting, and the beautifully executed 'paintings' which hang on the walls of the tavern show, amongst other sports, rat-killing contests.

GEORGE AND MAUD EARL

STILL APPROACHING the present day in the art world, we come to the familiar names of George and Maud Earl. George, who was Mary's father, was born in 1800 and came from a sporting family who were based in the west of England. With a practical interest in dogs besides his art, George Earl painted many different breeds and also drew their portraits on wood.

His daughter, Maud, was born in London's West End and soon she was also painting. Her works were praised highly during the early 1880s, leading to the granting of a royal commission by Queen Victoria, whose favourite Collie she painted. In addition, she executed work for both King Edward VII and Queen Alexandra.

ARTHUR J ELSLEY

ANOTHER ARTIST WHOSE WORK was of a sentimental nature was Arthur J Elsley (1860–1952). Elsley's paintings largely featured children and their pets and were reproduced many times over for use on posters. Indeed they are still immensely popular as greetings cards and calendars. Elsley was reputed to have thoroughly enjoyed his work and one can see this from the reality with which both dogs and children are portrayed. His work now fetches high prices at auction; some have made six-figure sums.

Another artist who lived and painted dogs in London was Arthur Wardle (1864–1949), who was a self-taught painter and a draughtsman. His dog paintings were often exhibited in various London galleries, spanning a period of 75 years.

There are of course many other talented artists throughout the world who really do not deserve to go without mention, among them relatively recent, much loved, artists such as the exceptionally talented Herbert Dicksee and, working in a totally different style, Cecil Aldin, Lucy Dawson and Vere Temple. Even the work of today's cartoonists comes under the umbrella of art so that most people can always find something which appeals to them.

TODAY'S ARTISTS

DEIRDRE ASHDOWN IS A SELF-TAUGHT artist whose distinctive work has achieved high acclaim in the world of dogs. Much admired for her perceptive portrayals of the canine race, she primarily carries out her work in pen and ink using a very fine, hard mapping pen nib and sometimes as many as 30 different coloured inks, always overlaid and never blended. This is a medium and style which suits the artist, although many of her works additionally use coloured pencils or even water colour to fill in small areas of colour when great subtlety is required.

EARLY INFLUENCES

DOG SHOWS WERE ALWAYS an absorbing passion for Deirdre Ashdown. She can scarcely remember a time when she was not drawing dogs, and as a child she recalls drawing pictures of dogs she especially liked, pressing them into owners' hands and then rushing off. At 14, she worked as a Saturday kennel girl for an important Boston Terrier breeder who became a lifelong friend. She learned to clip Poodles, learning more about the anatomy of dogs. The process of handling and examining dogs through the bathing and trimming process, feeling structure and musculature, training her eye, and being able to compensate for a dog's deficiencies and enhance their virtues was a great learning experience – something she put to good use in the years to come.

Deirdre Ashdown has always specialised in dog portraiture, but of show rather than pet dogs, and she considers a thorough understanding of the breed standards vital to her work. The art, she considers, is to portray the dog at its very finest hour, which means the artist has to know not only what the dogs actually looks like, but also what it should look like. Ideally she likes to see her subjects, watching them in their home environment and taking photographs her-self so that she can subsequently minimise any faults as far as possible, drawing attention to the dogs' positive features. Some faults, such as flat, splayed feet, can be remedied in a painting by illustrating the dog up on its toes, looking alert and inquisitive. Other faults cannot be rectified, except by falsifying the dog, so instead of that she minimises the fault by drawing attention to other, favourable, aspects of the sitter.

Top
Pugs in the Guise of Angels *by Deidre Ashdown.*

Centre
Shar Pei with Hummingbird.

Bottom
Papillons.

Edwin Landseer

S IR EDWIN LANDSEER (1802–73) can probably be distinguished as the most well-known animal painter of all time. His works are familiar to most canine enthusiasts. This most important of artists became a particular favourite of Queen Victoria and Prince Albert, and he painted many of their lovely dogs, amongst them Eos, the splendid Greyhound that was such a favourite of the Prince Consort. He also indulged the Queen's newly-found passion for Scotland by paintings and sketching sentimental scenes in the Highland for her. However, although the great majority of Landseer's work is well-known to most people today, as so often happens when the work of an artist becomes valuable many of his studies and sketches have been bought and housed in private collections or were sold over a century ago by public auction, and so sadly have not reached the public gaze.

EARLY TALENT

ALTHOUGH IT HAS BEEN REPORTED that Landseer began drawing dogs when he was five, the earliest canine drawing the author has come across was done at the age of about 10, as it is dated 1812. Entitled *Among the Turnips*, it depicts a setter which appears to have scented some turnips in a parsnip field. With his nose pointed forward and his tail uplifted, the setter attracts the attention of the sportsman to their presence.

At the age of 14 Landseer drew *The Dustman's Dog*, a simple reminder of the days when the approach of the dustman in the city's streets was announced by the loud ringing of a bell. Sketched in pencil, the artist's immaturity in terms of age is

Top
This pensive lithograph is entitled Cora.

Right
Dogs at Bay *is a lively pencil sketch in which two dogs tease a hedgehog.*

Above
Alpine Mastiffs *is
sketched in chalk.
Despite the title, only
one dog can be seen*

evident from the writing below the picture. The dustman's dog waits patiently on a mat, keeping guard over his master's bell and it is not difficult to imagine the master away emptying the dustbin of some local house.

EVOCATIVE IMAGES

ANOTHER EARLY SKETCH in pen and ink is called *The Braggart*, exhibited in 1819. However, in the final picture which may be more familiar, the dogs are just as seen in the sketch but to the right is a beautifully painted landscape. *The Rescue* is the forerunner of the better-known work *Highland Shepherd's Dog in the Snow*. In the former a sheep dog can be seen vigorously scratching away the snow from a stranded ewe, the artist clearly wishing to depict that the dog is doing all in its power to give the sheep a chance of recovery before alerting the master.

Another study, this one entitled *Highland Maiden*, led to *The Highland Whisky-still*, although in this case the final work differs somewhat. In the preparatory sketch, the maiden seems vulnerable and in need of some form of protection. Her dog, so simply and yet admirably portrayed, is held on a cord indicating that it would need to be restrained if there were an intruder.

SENTIMENTAL SUBJECTS

Just a few brush strokes are enough to portray both boy and dog on the beach at Hastings in *The Fisherman's Dog*. They lie in wonderfully relaxed attitudes and yet the sketch appears full of life, so real are they that they might awake at any moment to resume their toils.

The dog Cora found herself the subject of a lithograph in 1824, an engraving of which was subsequently published under another title, giving the dog something of a masculine image. First she was sketched keeping watch over some luggage left by a passenger coach. In the background we can see that the coach has stopped to change horses

and thus one can easily conjure up images of the passengers having dinner at the roadside inn, as was then the custom. Indeed how easy it is to become absorbed in this simple sketch and to relive the activities of days gone by, appreciating of course the merits of the worthy Cora whose memory surely deserves to live on.

MANY BREEDS PORTRAYED

ALPINE MASTIFFS was sketched in chalk on blue-grey paper in 1820, but although the title of the sketch was plural, only one dog could actually be seen properly. The other animal was depicted by nothing more than an out-line, still then a figment of the artist's imagination. The monastery of Mount St Bernard could just be seen in the upper right corner of the sketch and it seems certain that this was the original work that inspired the better-known painting, *Alpine Mastiffs Re-animating a*

Right
Highland Maiden *followed the Victorian trend for all things Scottish.*

Below
The Braggart *is an early pen and ink sketch, which was exhibited in 1819.*

Traveller, which was engraved in 1830 by John Landseer, Sir Edwin's father.

Quite different in style is a realistic and rather elaborate head study of a Newfoundland dog called Caesar. Little is known about this dog but it was clearly trained to the gun, and Landseer's caption underneath reads 'Newfoundland dog of Wales'.

Jocko with a Hedgehog is the original subject for the better-known *Dogs at Bay*. Two dogs are seen attacking a hedgehog, as fiercely as they can, but dog owners know that the prickles of a hedgehog are formidable and it is therefore likely that the hedgehog escaped unscathed. Worked in pencil on buff paper with chalk used for the highlights, this is an amusing little piece.

Above
The oil painting King Charles's Spaniels.

Left
Detail of the greyhound from Landseer's Queen Victoria and the Duke of Wellington.

Dogs in Film and Theatre

SINCE TIME IMMEMORIAL dogs have been entertainers of various sorts, though some of the so called 'entertainments' were by no means in the best interest of the dogs. Although dogs played some parts in early Commedia dell'Arte, perhaps the formal debut of the dog in the literary world was in Shakespeare's *Two Gentlemen of Verona* when, in Act 2, Scene 2, Launce enters 'leading a dog'. Although there was no script written for the dog, it is highly likely that the dog stole the scene, as indeed dogs so often do when in the limelight.

DOGS AS PERFORMERS

IT WAS LONG AFTER the days of Shakespeare that dogs really came into their own in theatrical performances. Philip Astley presented equestrian dramas in the amphitheatre in London's Westminster Bridge Road in 1770, and found that the highly successful performances of the horses somewhat overshadowed those of the human artists involved in the show. Astley went on to open theatres in Dublin and in Paris and, delighted by the success of the horses he employed, advertised 'an amazing exhibition of dancing dogs from France and Italy and other Genteel parts of the Globe'.

Top
Canine stars Blair and Rin-Tin-Tin.

Above
Renee Adoree and chum in Man and Maid.

Right
Charlie Chaplin and dog in The Champion.

In the early years of the nineteenth century, dog dramas came into vogue, sweeping Europe and America. In 1810 the heroic dog, Carlos, starred in a short 'afterpiece' at Drury Lane, his act being to rescue someone from a tank of water. The use of a live dog and real water on stage really captured the enthusiasm of audiences.

First performed in Paris on 18 June 1814, was *Le Chien de Montargis ou La Forêt de Bondy,* which included a canine star and its success is described in an earlier chapter. As the nineteenth century progressed, more and more dogs were cast in spectacular melodramas, which were popular in America.

In drama, dogs were frequently portrayed with human characteristics and sentiments, and the cinema was well suited as a medium to exploit this further to satisfy demand. Using trick photography and clever editing, surprising illusions could be produced and although there may have been many unused shots, producers could just utilise those of dogs in the exact situations required. Then, like now, the animal artists were tempted with some tasty delicacy of food, while dextrous use of the camera made it appear to the audience that the dog was carrying out some talented or heroic deed. This technique is still used in film-making today, as has been seen in the highly successful film of the 1990s, *Babe*, in which a multi-talented pig works with canine chums to great effect.

EARLY CINEMA

IN THE VERY EARLY DAYS of cinema at the close of the nineteenth century, dogs' roles were primarily of a 'walk-on' nature, but in Cecil Hepworth's film, *Rescued by Rover*, released in 1905, the dog's true potential was recognised. The drama lasted seven minutes, during which time a Collie dog rescued a baby from kidnappers, and almost unbelievably the film was made for the cost of under £8. Hundreds of copies of the film were sold at about £10 each and were in such in demand that it had to be re-made twice, because in those days the negatives simply fell to pieces through overuse.

This successful short film led to several sequels, but the Collie died in 1910. Upon his death Hepworth wrote, 'Even his name was only an assumed one for theatrical purposes. His real name was Blair in commemoration of his Scottish origin. He was a true friend and a great companion, but my most persistent memory of him was the way every morning in life he jumped up on a washing basket by my dressing table and waited and longed for a dab on the nose from my shaving brush. Then with every expression of ineffable happiness, he licked off every trace of soap and waited for more.'

RIN-TIN-TIN, THE FIRST CANINE STAR

UNDOUBTEDLY ONE OF the greatest and most well-known canine stars was Rin-Tin-Tin, an Alsatian. Found in a German dugout by an American Air Force man, he was adopted and taken to the USA, where he was trained as a police dog. To begin with Rin-Tin-Tin built up an impressive war record carrying out

important dispatch, sentry and general duties for the Red Cross. In 1923 he appeared in the film *Where the North Begins*, directed by Chester Franklin. It was this film, the success of which was immediate, that served to put Warner Brothers back on its feet following a financial setback. The popularity of Rin-Tin-Tin rivalled great names like Charlie Chaplain and the Gish Sisters, and in 1925 he was voted the most popular star in America according to one poll.

Rin-Tin-Tin appeared in over 40 films and by 1927 was said to have been earning the US equivalent of £400 per week. This sum enabled the canine star to maintain his own bank account and run a car, apart from the luxury of eating two fresh steaks a day. This remarkable dog shared pages with human stars in gossip columns and fan magazines, and universal concern was apparent when the notice was

put out that he was to leave Hollywood in order to visit England and other European countries. Rin-Tin-Tin was never able to enjoy retirement as he died in 1932 while on location, but he had certainly lived a remarkable life and was even the cause of his

Above
Lassie, one of the most famous canine stars of all time, was really a male Collie called Pal.

trainer's divorce; his wife having felt that the dog had alienated her husband's affections. The court supported her claim without any hesitation whatsoever.

Rin-Tin-Tin sired several litters of puppies, of which one, Rin-Tin-Tin Junior, also went into films. However, no individual dog, before or since, has achieved quite the notoriety of the original Rin-Tin-Tin.

LASSIE

THE FAMOUS Rough Collie, Lassie, was actually a male dog called Pal and was remarkably born the runt of his litter. His trainer, Rudd Weatherall, used verbal commands to induce Lassie to show fear, exhaustion and resolution. The actor Roddie MacDowell had nothing to do with the dog off the set, except for during the shooting the famous homecoming scene when he spent a week with the dog, which was isolated the day before the shoot. MacDowell was the first person that Lassie saw on his release and his joyful emotions were exaggerated by licking the ice cream which had been smeared on Roddie's face.

Right
Charlie Chaplin became very fond of Scraps, the mongrel who starred with him in A Dog's Life.

Below
Dogs are not always shown as friendly companions; some films portray them as savage killers.

OTHER DOG STARS

MANY OTHER DOGS have reached stardom, often in the company of great theatrical names. Charlie Chaplin occasionally had dogs as his comedy partners, one of which was described as 'a splendidly thoroughbred mongrel' and who took part in *A Dog's Life* in 1918. The dog, called Scraps, was even smuggled into a dancehall inside Chaplin's trousers where he caused great commotion to the undoubted enjoyment of Charlie Chaplin's dedicated

audiences. Scraps was reputed to have continued his friendship with the actor long after their working relationship was complete – he was apparently always at the gate to meet Chaplin upon his arrival for work each morning.

Dogs have played many roles in films, usually as important support artists, often to notable actors and actresses. A small terrier who played in *The Thin Man* with William Powell was paid £700 a week by MGM. The same dog earned £5,000 for his role in *Piccadilly Circus* with Gracie Fields. During the making of this film, the terrier was accommodated in a luxury suite on board the Queen Mary, where he apparently dined off Irish stew and ice cream. Canine film stars made their mark in other countries too, one of the earlier ones being in an adaptation of Chekhov's *The Lady With the Little Dog*, made in the former Soviet Union.

THE CANINE CARTOON HERO

MANY A MEMORABLE DOG has played a part in Walt Disney productions, originally as clever cartoon characters, but more recently real dogs have been included. The making of *One Hundred and One Dalmatians* caused a great deal of controversy in the canine world, as not only was concern expressed about the training of the dogs, there was also understandable fear for the resultant commercial value of the Dalmatian breed. Undoubtedly there is always a genuine danger of high profile breeds causing dogs to be bred for entirely wrong reasons, often commercial, or frequently merely for prestige.

In the film, several adult Dalmatians were used, with their spots carefully adapted to look the same, and in addition there were lots of puppies used, because as every batch of youngsters grew in size, it was replaced by another batch of younger dogs for consistency. All the dogs were kept in pristine condition, and were well cared-for by the film company.

DOGS ON THE SMALL SCREEN

IN TELEVISION, DOGS were a little slower to achieve great fame than on the silver screen. When the film *Lassie* was made into a television series, it immediately captured the love and admiration of television viewers. Dogs were also introduced in children's television shows such as *Blue Peter*, in which the dogs Petra, a German Shepherd, and Shep, a Sheepdog, took an active part in in the programme every week. When Petra had developed into a co-operative adult dog, it was agreed that the programme would become involved in supporting Guide Dogs for the Blind. Programmes such as these provided a great service to our friends of the canine race, bringing them in to people's homes and to their attention via the television screen. In recent decades, an increasing number of programmes have incorporated dogs or matters of interest to the dog-owning and dog-loving public.

With the recent surge in television's 'fly on the wall' approach, there have been many successful programmes peering into the lives of veterinary surgeons, police dog trainers and animal welfare workers. Documentaries have also been made about dog refuges, in particular the world-famous Battersea Dogs' Home in London.

Above
The star of The Thin Man *was paid £700 per week.*

Left
Dogs played an essential part in the 1935 film The Call of the Wild.

Above
Television personalities on a 'dog jog' to raise money for charity.

Dogs in the Human World

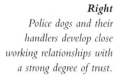

SINCE DOG FIRST became acquainted with man, a working association and close friendship has developed, with both man and dog deriving benefit from the other. Climates, times and customs have changed but the relationship between these two species has remained strong and dogs have been developed, as the years have progressed, to fit in with man's needs today.

MAN AND DOG

Right
Police dogs and their handlers develop close working relationships with a strong degree of trust.

IT IS OFTEN DIFFICULT to trace any friendship to its root and it is equally difficult to know just when dog and man formed their great partnership, but we do know that it has stood the test of at least 5,000 years and probably very much longer.

today travellers in the desert may still see dogs following the caravans and wandering with Bedouin tribes, one of so many important relationships which are to be found in the symbiotic world of dogs and mankind.

Because of an increased awareness of the transmission of *toxocara canis* (rabies) to children, and media attention in the few cases of dogs biting children, much adverse publicity surrounds our canine friends nowadays. However, the rapport which has always been evident between children and dogs can surely not have gone unnoticed for there are so many stories which have lasted through time, displaying all too clearly the devotion of one to the other.

According to legend, among the ruins of Pompeii a skeleton of a huge dog was found entwined around the bones of a young boy. On the dog's collar was an inscription which brought home the dog's courage and its devotion to its master. The inscription told that twice the dog had saved the life of the boy, once from attack by marauders and once from drowning. Sadly, the third time both lost their lives, but one can imagine what comfort each gave to the other in their last moments together.

Above and Opposite
No matter what your age, nationality or lifestyle, a dog will always provide enjoyment and companionship.

MAN'S BEST FRIEND

ONE OF THE OLDEST DOGS to be found on monuments of Egypt is the Khufu dog, which dates from the reign of Cheops, builder of the great pyramid in 3733 BC. Later, in 3000 BC, Antefa II is represented with four dogs at his feet. Even

CHILD'S BEST FRIEND

THERE ARE MANY INSTANCES in which it can be clearly perceived that a dog is attached to a child, possibly because a dog recognises that such young beings need their protection. Those of us who observe dogs carefully will perceive faithfulness, devotion, instinctive guarding and sometimes even self-sacrifice for their owners.

A very interesting survey was carried out in the USA in the 1930s, disclosing that only one per cent of men with prison records had owned a dog as a child. This was an incredibly low percentage and although it is, of course, not possible to draw conclusions from this, these statistics cannot but imply that children who have owned or had contact with dogs while young, may grow up to be more stable adults.

NATURAL DOG-LOVERS

THOSE PEOPLE TODAY WHO truly love dogs may have been born with a close affinity with the canine species. Even observing a small child, one

can often see clearly which children are likely to grow up as dog lovers and which are not. However, environment and upbringing also play a great part. A child whose parents are afraid of dogs or whose culture teaches that dogs are unclean, or

animals to be feared, are less likely to form a bond with dogs, partly due to lack of contact.

On the other hand, parents who teach their children to respect animals and be gentle with them, even though they may not be dog owners themselves, are far more likely to instill an interest in dogs, thereby leaving children's horizons open to decide whether or not they will choose to share their lives with this popular animal companion.

It goes without saying that people of all ages can strike up intimate relationships with dogs, and in many cases each is devoted to the other. Dogs provide a listening ear and, if treated kindly, do not sit in judgement. A dog can love a poor person just as much as a rich one, and really does not care one jot about the clothes one wears, whether a person is tall or short, fat or thin, nor indeed about any other physical aspect. What matters is the communication and warmth conveyed between the dog and the human. A dog can play an integral part in

family life and for many of those who live alone, the company of a dog is incredibly important. A dog is affectionate, loyal and willing to please as well as providing release from the stresses and strains of today's hectic lifestyle, in particular when taking it for daily walks in peaceful surroundings.

DOG FACT:

Despite her important, high-profile lifestyle, Her Majesty Queen Elizabeth II regularly takes time to spend in the company of her canine companions

The Behaviour of Dogs

AS THEY ARE NATURAL pack animals, dogs have an instinct to share their lives with others, a mentality inherited from the wolf. A social animal, from birth a puppy is part of its own small 'pack' made up of siblings and the dam, leader of the pack. It is she who provides food, warmth, security and is the provider of discipline within the unit.

LEARNING FROM PUPPYHOOD

AS THE PUPPIES' EYES OPEN and they begin to move about on their feet they learn to play, both with each other and their dam who teaches them how to behave socially, something which will stand them in good stead in later life as much of a dog's strength depends upon a capacity to react to and communicate with other dogs. These early weeks are highly important because at this stage the puppy is still very impressionable.

If transferred to a new environment while still at this receptive age, it should be easy to look upon the human family as the new pack of which the puppy is an integral part, after all a dog is capable of communicating and socialising not only with other animals but also with humans. One of the humans in the family will become a natural leader, most usually the person who provides meals and exercise and who takes the place of the dam in teaching the rules of life.

Top Right
Dogs in the same household can become devoted companions and will pine in the absence of their friend.

Right
Puppies learn to play with their siblings. If they transfer to a new environment when young they will continue to play with their new owners.

THE PACK INSTINCT

GROWING INTO adulthood, given the opportunity and if of suitable mentality, the dog may take over as the leader – the reason why human control and firm discipline is vital during those formative months. When more than one dog lives in the same household they will decide between themselves which is to be 'top dog'. The hierarchy may change with circumstances as time goes on.

Whatever the ranking within the pack, it is in a dog's nature to guard the pack and its territory, expressed by barking at strangers to warn of potential danger to other pack members and to the home. It is also natural that a dog should wish to protect people, items of furniture, toys and even other family pets, to which the dog is greatly attached, just another reason why discipline is important so that situations do not get out of hand. An untrained dog which is protecting what it sees as its own property can be troublesome and, at worst, dangerous so sensible canine management is important in any home.

Within packs dogs form their own small packs, something which can frequently be observed in feral and pariah dogs which group together to form small bands, heading off on their own each day to explore their local environs.

Sometimes these small packs will begin to form their own hunting groups and then eventually leave the main pack to form a new pack of their own. This is because, in the canine world, dogs only allow each pack to reach a certain size, beyond which it splits up so that the population is diluted over a much wider area, thus enhancing the ability of each group to survive.

THE CANINE COMMUNITY

BOTH CO-OPERATIVE and competitive social behaviour is needed in any balanced canine community. Most dogs, if living naturally or together with others in a home environment, spend most of their time in close proximity to one another. They also often do things at the same time, observed by one dog setting up a howl and the others joining in, making veritable music to the ears of a hound lover. Likewise when one dog barks, others will very probably also join in the commotion. That is not to say that some dogs do not choose to keep themselves somewhat apart from others, either because they prefer to do so, or because they are relatively new members in the pack and have not yet accepted their pack ranking.

When hunting in a pack, behaviour of the various individual members reaps rewards by its complementary nature, some chasing after prey, others surrounding the animal to cut off its retreat, thus making for an efficient hunt. This ability to hunt in a complementary manner is especially important when prey is larger or stronger than each individual pack member.

IMPORTANCE OF COMPANIONSHIP

COMPANIONSHIP IS IMPORTANT in a dog's life as a puppy, but this need continues into adulthood and some dogs show noticeable distress when parted from other canine company. This can easily be noticed when a dog is separated from its pack, so that if a kennelled dog is taken into a home situation it is usually happier if it has other canine companionship. Another distressing time, at which loneliness becomes apparent, is when an elderly canine partner dies and the surviving dog clearly suffers greatly from the loss – it is usually prudent to introduce another dog into the household for companionship.

Above and Below
Dogs are pack animals and therefore are usually happier if they can share their environment with at least one other dog.

Partnerships with Mankind

BESIDES INTERACTING WITH other dogs and with humans, dogs are also adept at striking up some remarkable relationships with other animals. Clearly caution needs to be exercised when introducing any new animal into an environment where others are already ensconced, as they will already have established their own hierarchy and may look upon the newcomer as an intruder. Although there are exceptions such as two male dogs (especially if both used at stud), given time and sensible introduction and management on the part of the owner, life soon enough settles down to a normal pattern and new friendships are made among the dog community.

A DOG'S BEST FRIEND

Right

Dogs often form close relationships with other animals, ranging from chicks to lambs.

Below

Buddy, a German Shepherd Dog, guided his blind companion through the Boston streets in addition to collecting the daily paper for his owner.

THERE ARE MANY INSTANCES of firm associations being made between dogs, other animals and things, often in the most unlikely combination. Cats and dogs, although arch enemies by repute, often get on extremely well together, although frequently a dog which will tolerate the family cat would chase and probably kill any intruding feline. While many dogs would chase and catch a rabbit given half a chance, others are more kindly disposed to them, indeed in childhood the author had a Rough Collie who regularly rounded up her pet rabbit from the nether regions of the garden to herd it back to the house when the Collie decided it was bedtime. The dog was happy in the sitting room of the house with the resident mynah bird and rabbit, all hopping around the room.

LOOKING OUT FOR EACH OTHER

PERHAPS STORIES OF FRIENDSHIPS between dogs and other animals are now rather taken for granted, but earlier this century many were well documented. In Washington, a German Shepherd dog became a familiar sight guiding his half-blind canine friend through the streets. Another German Shepherd took a paternal interest in a Scottish Terrier which he regularly took for a walk on a lead. In wartime a dog was witnessed scratching for 16 hours at the rubble of a bombed house, eventually releasing his Fox Terrier friend, who was dragged out to safety.

Another remarkable story is of a Collie attached to its kennel on a very short chain outside a farmhouse. One bitterly cold night, with hail beating down, the dog was found lying outside the kennel while comfortably installed inside was a strange bitch with a litter of five new-born puppies.

DOGS AND LAMBS

DUKE WAS A DOG OF no distinct pedigree but was reputed to be exceptionally clever in many ways and was in the habit of leading his mistress's horse by the rein to a nearby field and there exercising it on the grass. A Border Collie was remarkably trained to feed lambs with a bottle at lambing time, of invaluable assistance at the very time of year when a farmer has virtually no time to spare. The dog learned to hold the lamb in position with its paw and, as those who have bottle-fed lambs will know, a young lamb soon learns to trust the hand that feeds it. In a

Cincinnati Cat's Home a dog was trained to bottle-feed ailing cats, serving a useful purpose which the dog seemed to thoroughly enjoy.

There have been many cases of dogs fostering the puppies of another dog, frequently of another breed, something which can sometimes prove to be successful in the event of a bitch dying in whelp or if a dam has a particularly large litter, or insufficient milk. More remarkably, there have also been cases of dogs fostering litters of other animal,s such as a bitch which obligingly suckled six piglets.

DOGS AND MUSIC

DOG'S RELATIONSHIP WITH MAN is well-known but there are a few interesting examples of other strong attachments which are worthy of mention. Although it is commonly believed that the majority of dogs dislike music, this is a theory which has been disproved many times. In Japan a dog had a penchant for singing to the accompaniment of a mouth-organ, while elsewhere a Boxer dog which reputedly 'played the piano' became irritable and moody when separated from this instrument. This became a particular problem when travelling any distance, but he eventually found consolation in a mouth-organ which could be taken along with him.

On the subject of music, a Poodle named Bobo enjoyed musical evenings with his owners and became absorbed when listening to Sibelius, but would fall asleep to the sounds of Bach.

The organist of Hereford Cathedral, who was a friend of Sir Edward Elgar, had a Bulldog named Dan. The dog attended chorus rehearsals in the cathedral and growled when people sang out of tune. Elgar was particularly fond of Dan, and in a note on No XI of

'Enigma Variations' he explained that the first few bars were suggested by the dog. Bar one of the music represented Dan falling down a bank of the River Wye, while bars two and three had him paddling upstream to find a landing place and the second half of bar five was his happy bark upon landing.

Above and Below
Many dogs respond favourably to music; some provide vocal accompaniment, while a few have even learnt to 'play' an instrument, such as a piano or a mouth-organ.

Dogs as Pets and Helpers

DOGS ARE WONDERFUL companions and, if well treated, are thoroughly loyal to their owners. They are unaware of the barriers of class and many a listening canine ear hears stories the owner is unable to share with another of the human kind. The dog may not have understood the meaning, but will have listened intently and the owner will probably have been relieved of a heavy burden. Touching a dog also gives great pleasure, and gentle stroking is a thoroughly rewarding experience for both parties concerned and known to reduce blood pressure and slow down heart rate.

FAITHFUL COMPANIONS

Right

Dog owners who belong to PAT Dogs share their pets with elderly people in hospitals and long-term residential homes.

Right and Opposite

A dog can not only be a companion but can provide practical help to the elderly, the blind and the disabled owner.

THOSE WHO LIVE SOLITARY LIVES, either by choice or through force of circumstance, often derive great pleasure from the company of a dog. It is much more pleasurable to watch a television programme or read a book with a dog by one's side or at one's feet than when completely alone. Having a dog around the house gives a lonely owner a reason to do things, and through a dog it is frequently easier to come into contact with other people and make new friendships. Many people end up in conversation because of their dogs; people who would otherwise never have had reason even to pass the time of day with one another.

Exercising a dog is another important feature of canine ownership. Playing, even around the home, gives both dog and owner enormous pleasure, and walking is for most people a much more enjoyable experience when accompanied by a dog. The pleasure experienced by a dog on a long or interesting walk is clearly visible and of course the health and muscle tone of both dog and owner are improved as a result.

GUIDE DOGS

BECAUSE DOGS ARE SUCH wonderful companions, coupled with the fact that they are intuitive and easily taught, they have found themselves helping mankind in many ways through the centuries. No one can help but be aware of the invaluable service they have been to the blind, Guide Dogs for the Blind having been formed in Great Britain as long ago as 1934. This Association has expanded enormously over the years and centres have been set up throughout the country. Puppies are housed, socialised and walked by others until they are ready to perform the task for which they have been

destined and to enter into what will, in most case, become a lifetime bond between dog and sightless or partially sighted owner. A guide dog undoubtedly makes life much easier and more enjoyable for those who do not enjoy good sight and, importantly, such dogs also seem to enjoy their roles, thus making the relationship a doubly rewarding one. There are many guide dog centres, associations and movements throughout the world, from the USA to the Far East, with organisations in both northern and southern hemispheres. All carry out work which is greatly appreciated, not only by those who have guide dogs of their own, but also by those who recognise what valuable partnerships have been built up.

More recently in operation, although now well-established, are Hearing Dogs for Deaf People and Dogs for the Disabled. Dogs are trained to

assist their owners in the most practical ways. In the case of a deaf person, they learn to signal when the telephone rings, while in the case of someone physically disabled the dog will learn to pick up the telephone receiver and take it to the owner. There are many other sounds around the house which dogs can bring to the attention of their owners, such as the doorbell, or an alarm ringing, or even a baby crying. To alert the owner, a dog will perform a pre-agreed act to draw attention, perhaps tugging at a trouser leg and then leading the person to the sound.

HELPING THE DISABLED

A SOCIETY called Dogs for the Disabled helps people in many-faceted ways according to their disability, and like guide dogs and hearing dogs for the deaf, dogs are trained and allocated to each individual. The dog will learn to live with the individual's own lifestyle and carry out the most useful of tasks.

> **DOG FACT:**
> Some Dogs for the Disabled load and unload washing machines, something readily taken for granted by most of us but an impossible feat for many people.

At dog shows, it is wonderful to see people with physical disabilities showing their dogs with just as much skill and expertise as able-bodied handlers, another important bond between dog and owner for those who wish to take part in yet another aspect of dogdom.

Dogs which are involved with the organisation known as PAT Dogs are those owned by people who feel that lives can be enhanced by others sharing the company of their own dogs. After suitable assessment for temperament, dogs are taken along to hospitals and homes for the elderly where they are introduced to patients and residents. Many visits are to long-term patients, thereby allowing permanent friendships to build up through regular contact.

Dogs as Workers

SINCE DOGS FIRST shared their lives with man they have played an important role in the human world. These roles have undoubtedly changed with man's lifestyle, but many uses today are much the same as they have always been, merely adapted to suit modern circumstances. Even now, many farmers consider their dogs of just as great assistance as they did decades ago and rely on their canine workers to assist them in tending their flocks and herds.

A VARIETY OF ROLES

WE KNOW THAT THE DOG has long been used as a guard and today little is different, but the role has been developed a stage further as dogs are not just used in security work but also in police work, some trained as sniffer dogs because their scenting abilities can be put to good use in detecting drugs and other illicit goods. A fine opportunity to observe dogs displaying their many talents is to visit Crufts where every year a wide variety of skills are demonstrated in the main rings. Besides the displays of Guide Dogs for the Blind and Hearing Dogs for the Deaf there are remarkable Gundog displays showing off the skills of dogs which have been trained by their handlers to search out and retrieve game in the testing environment of the field. Perhaps surprisingly there is even a regular display of Duck Herding when one can enjoy watching the dog using his wits against the vagaries of duck behaviour.

Top Right
Dogs play a valuable role in much police and security work.

Above
Dogs have been used for hunting from earliest times. This vivid portrayal of a hare hunt comes from the fifteenth-century Livre de Chasse.

At Crufts there is also a Terrier display where one can watch terriers of various kinds chasing a lure at incredible speeds, true terrier character shining through all the while. The excellent Police Dog displays demonstrate very well the rapport between dogs and handlers and reconstruct some of the operations encountered in police work, including working amidst gunfire.

JOBS FOR DOGS

GERMANY WAS THE FIRST COUNTRY to use dogs in wartime but Britain followed some years later. Our canine friends were of enormous value in relaying messages across enemy lines and helped to transport ammunition and casualties, both canine and human, by pulling especially designed carts. The use of dog-carts has long since been abolished in Britain, but transport by this means is still within the living memory of some and was used extensively, especially on the European mainland.

In frozen climes, dogs have provided valuable service in pulling sleds and many a human life has been saved when dog meat has, of necessity, been eaten in arctic conditions. The dog's reputation as a rescuer is also put to good use today in search and rescue work so once again it is dogs we have to thank for saving more human lives.

the lion and wolf. Although wolf hunting was taken to extremes, leading to the decimation of the wolf population, there were undoubtedly many instances in which dogs used for this purpose were put to legitimate use.

VERMIN HUNTERS

DOGS HAVE ALSO been used to hunt vermin which would otherwise have caused considerably more damage than was the case. Most terriers are renowned for their ability to catch rats, something which is less of a problem now than it used to be, largely thanks to modern science. However, there are intriguing stories of old buildings being demolished and rats emerging in their hundreds, bringing into perspective how very important it was, and still is, to keep down the rat population.

In the Americas, dogs were employed to hunt the raccoon, something which had to be done at night because raccoons are nocturnal animals, and the 'coon dogs had to enlist centuries of training to match the wits of their prey. Wild boar, mink and many other animals have of course also been hunted by dogs and it is understandably difficult to draw a strict line between what, through the years, has been true work and what has been effectively sport. Sadly, one cannot help but reason that what was once valuable work performed for highly legitimate purposes has been turned into sport, hence causing the decimation or serious decline of various species of wild animal. None the less, in a dog's mind I doubt that any 'work' was born of malice, the dog has merely carried out the work required of it, in many cases work which it has been trained to do and which has become instinctive over time.

THE HUNTING INSTINCT

HUNTING PACKS ARE COVERED in a later section but there are many dogs of different kinds which hunt alone. Although this is an activity very much frowned upon by many, hunting dogs have, over the centuries, been legitimately used to provide food and sustenance for their owners, often where life is lived under difficult conditions, such as in the Australian outback where the Kangaroo Hound has been usefully employed. Some breeds have also been effectively used against dangerous predators such as

Top and Above
Good hunting dogs are valued in every society and every age. The Bayeux Tapestry shows Harold's men taking their best dogs with them to Normandy, while a successful lion hunter poses proudly with his two dogs.

Left
Fox terriers make excellent ratters and were widely used to rid agricultural land and buildings of vermi .

Search and Rescue Dogs

DOGS WHICH PERHAPS conjure up the most vivid pictures in people's minds are those which have gained a reputation for rescuing people when disaster has struck. As time has moved on their duties have become more and more varied and an increasing number of breeds have been used for rescue work. All are deserving of merit.

Below and Right
St Bernards are the best-known breed of rescue dog.and are always shown carrying a small barrel containing food and a stimulant.

THE ST BERNARD

THE HOSPICE OF ST BERNARD was founded in AD 962 and was served by monks of the order of St Augustine. It was the duty of these particular monks to give assistance to travellers in distress because at that time travellers between Switzerland and Italy were obliged to go on foot through the Great St Bernard Pass. The monks found that their dogs aided them in their search for lost travellers, as the dogs were able to detect victims buried beneath deep snow drifts. Some dogs actually carried out their toils alone and if they came across an exhausted traveller in the desolate mountain passes they would lie across him to impart warmth, barking and howling until assistance came.

The dogs of the Hospice in the early years were different from those we now associate with it today; they were short-haired, with an exceptionally broad chest and massive head. In the early years of the nineteenth century, the monks realised their stock was beginning to decline and so introduced new blood by cross-breeding with long-haired Newfoundland bitches.

From early puppyhood, St Bernards were trained by means of dummy figures used to instruct them in first aid. The dogs wore spiked collars to protect them against wolves and carried around their necks a small container holding food and stimulant. Many monks have believed that the St Bernard is endowed with the power to foresee danger and there are many records of occasions when the dogs have prevented the monks from returning to the monastery by the normal route, only to find later that, had they done so, they would have been overwhelmed by an avalanche.

MOUNTAIN RESCUE DOGS

EVEN TODAY many mountain rescue organisations employ dogs to help them with their work because dogs can travel over terrain which is difficult for man, and certainly they can negotiate land over which it would be impossible for vehicles to travel. Added to this, the dogs' keen sense of smell is most useful in mountain rescue work and an ability to dig in snow is another great advantage.

THE NEWFOUNDLAND

ANOTHER BREED NOTED for its courageous work is the Newfoundland, a breed around which many touching stories revolve. Like the St Bernard, the Newfoundland seems to have a sense of impending danger and, because of the breed's stubborn perseverance, rarely relinquishes a task in hand.

Left
Korean rescue dog and handler practicing searching through wreckage for signs of a buried human.

This dog has always appeared to take a natural delight in saving humans from water and, on several occasions, the Newfoundland has been instrumental in saving entire crews of ships: establishing a lifeline between a sinking ship and rescuers ashore. This has been in situations which have been so dangerous that no lifeboat could set out. But Newfoundlands have not only saved humans, they have saved other lives too, including a touching story of a canary which was a great favourite with sailors on exercise in the Mediterranean. Seeing the tiny bird escape from its cage, a Newfoundland jumped into the sea, seized the bird in its mouth and swam back to the ship. The bird was scared but unharmed, just proving how delicately such a large dog can hold a small thing, even when swimming.

POLICE AND SECURITY WORK

SEARCH AND RESCUE IS NOW an important area of police and security services throughout the world and, as the benefits of such work have spread, so has the training and dissemination of information. In the last few years English trainers have been sent as far afield as South Korea so that both dogs and people can be trained in the best methods of putting dogs to good use when rescuing people from various places, including mountainous terrain.

Often such dogs work in a twofold manner, also being trained to search out drugs, arms, ammunition and explosives, so the employment of rescue dogs now encompasses a very much wider area than before. Hence rescue work has extended into other fields and sniffer dogs, as they are often called, are employed by army, navy and air forces in many countries, as well as by customs and excise departments, so they are frequently used at air and sea ports.

Many different breeds have been of service in this way so it seems perhaps unfair to single out just a few, but commonly used in recent years have been German Shepherd Dogs, Labrador Retrievers and other of the gundog breeds such as English Springer Spaniels, Flat-coated and Golden Retrievers, Irish Water Spaniels and German Short-haired Pointers. These and others have proved to be of invaluable service in their many ways.

> **DOG FACT:**
> Despite its large size and heavy coat, the Newfoundland is able to swim exceptionally well because of the breed's particularly well-adapted webbed feet.

Above
Despite their massive size St Bernards are intelligent, gentle dogs that make ideal rescuers.

Left
St Bernards are trained for rescue work from early puppyhood.

Tracking Dogs

MANY A TALE WAS TOLD of feudal castles and forays across border lands with dogs in pursuit of man, but the use of dogs as man-trackers was born of grim necessity. They were used in Ireland and against the Clansmen in Scotland, as well as in the border country. Here raiders worked in bands, seizing anything upon which they could lay their hands.

BLOODHOUNDS – THE FIRST TRACKERS

TWO FAMOUS BLACK St Hubert Hounds, 'unmatched for courage, breath and speed', were brought by pilgrims from the Holy Land. Other dogs of the same name were larger and pure white, while another similar dog was a greyish red. Most probably, Bloodhounds of the present century carry the blood of many or all of these varieties. St Hubert was the patron saint of hunters and his own dogs are believed to have come to England during the Norman Conquest, the dark dogs becoming known as Bloodhounds and the white, as Talbot Hounds. However, it is possible that the ancestry of the Bloodhound goes back further than the Norman period because, even before Christian times, Sleuth Hounds were imported from 'Britain' into Gaul, although 'Britain' may in fact have been Brittany.

Henry VIII used Bloodhounds in wars against the French, while during the reign of Queen Elizabeth I, 800 Bloodhounds apparently assisted in suppressing the Irish Rebellion. In later times Bloodhounds created terror in the minds of deer and cattle stealers, as well as poachers, since they were kept on large, important estates to track trespassers down.

BLOODHOUNDS IN THE SERVICE OF MAN

IN 1805, AN ASSOCIATION for the prevention of felons in Northamptonshire provided and trained a Bloodhound for the detection of sheep stealers. In order to demonstrate the capabilities of the dog, a day was appointed for a public trial and a great crowd assembled, the criminal among them. Eventually the dog was slipped and ran up to a tree in which the man had taken refuge, this some 24.15 km (15 miles) from the starting place of the test.

The Cuban Bloodhound, more akin to the Mastiff and Bulldog than to the Bloodhound, was employed to track down runaway slaves in Jamaica and on the slave-holding estates of America. It was likened to the Mastiff in bulk, the Bulldog in its courage, the Bloodhound in scent and yet again, the Greyhound in agility, gaining a reputation both for sagacity and ferocity.

Use in the pursuit of poachers and criminals has caused the Bloodhound to suffer prejudice. In a Sussex village, around the turn of the twentieth century, local people believed that Bloodhounds would attack and were likely to devour any children with whom they came into contact so Bloodhound owners had constantly to be on the lookout for poisoned meat. In country districts

Right
This alert-looking team has the scent in their nostrils and are just waiting for their handler to give them the word.

Bottom
The Bloodhound boasts an ancient ancestry, possibly predating the Norman Conquest.

public sentiment was certainly against the idea of the police using such hounds.

CRIME-BUSTING DOGS

BEFORE THE FIRST WORLD WAR, Lieut. Col. E. H. Richardson, who was a renowned dog trainer, kept a number of Bloodhounds. He was sometimes called upon for the service of his hounds for tracking work by the police. At least one murderer was apprehended in this way, the dog tracing the complicated tracks to a railway station where the murderer had boarded a train.

Richardson found Bloodhounds especially useful in tracking poultry stealers, rick burners and poachers, as the hounds would trace the culprits to their homes. A Bloodhound which went to the owner of a large property tracked a gang of poachers for 14.4 km (9 miles) across country, helped by the keeper who set the dog on the trail before the sun and wind had obliterated the scent. Dawn and the evening hours were the usual time for working the dogs as this was when the scent laid best, the trail usually being across open country or woodland.

FEARSOME TRACKERS

DOGS THUS USED WERE CONCERNED only with tracking and were rarely savage, displaying no evil intent towards their quarry, but the very name, Bloodhound, carried with it dread and superstition, a powerful deterrent. The deep, bloodcurdling bay of the hound would put fear into the person being pursued, though it was music to the handler, an indication that the dog had discovered a sure scent.

Occasionally Bloodhounds were dangerous. These dogs appear to have had ancestry going back to the Cuban Bloodhound with crosses having been deliberately been made among savage strains to track runaway slaves on the plantations. In the early twentieth century slightly lighter but very similar hounds were still used in America for tracking escaped prisoners.

Bloodhounds may have been associated with tracking more than any other breed but several other dogs are also used both in work and in sport for tracking of various kinds.

Left and Below Left

Bloodhounds are frequently employed to track down criminals and poachers. Their stamina and persistence ensure a high degree of success.

> DOG FACT:
>
> Trained Bloodhounds are not easily diverted from the trail and try their utmost to regain a lost trail, even taking up the scent after crossing water.

Bottom

The Bloodhound makes an affectionate, intelligent companion but it is not easy to obedience train.

Police Dogs

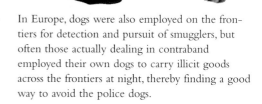

BY THE BEGINNING of the twentieth century, various countries had begun to pay considerable attention to the training of dogs to assist the police, Belgium being especially notable. Most renowned were those of Collie type and a number of Belgian Collies were introduced to America to form the nucleus of a working team to assist the police there, whilst others were exported to China and Japan.

SWIMMING DOGS

IN 1900, *CHIENS PLONGEUR,* or swimming dogs, were attached to the river police and used on the banks of the river Seine in Paris. Making the riverside safe for pedestrians during the hours of darkness, these dogs were trained not only to track down criminals but also save those whom had fallen or deliberately thrown themselves in to the river. The dogs used were mainly of Retriever type or cross-ed Newfoundland and Leonberg type, and were kept in special quarters in the police station of the Quai de Tournelle.

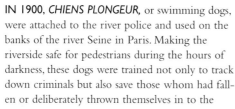

Top
The modern police force use dogs for a wide variety of duties from criminal to rescue and protection work.

Centre and Right
Dogs have to be trained to tackle all kinds of situations, from stopping a burglar in his tracks to continuing the pursuit despite being faced with a gun.

In Europe, dogs were also employed on the frontiers for detection and pursuit of smugglers, but often those actually dealing in contraband employed their own dogs to carry illicit goods across the frontiers at night, thereby finding a good way to avoid the police dogs.

THE FIRST POLICE DOGS

IN THE EARLY twentieth century, the British Police Force used dogs for detection and defence. Highly alert, sagacious and self-controlled, although they needed to be capable of assisting their masters, it was important that there was no ferocity in their nature. In the early days, many people were against the introduction of what was known as the Alsatian, a German breed used with success in its homeland. This was partly because of its country of origin, and in part because it was somewhat misunderstood, not helped by the misnomer 'Alsatian Wolf Dog'. The German police preferred a dog that was capable of serious attack, because laws there did not pre-suppose innocence until proven guilty, as is the case in Britain. Indeed, in Germany, one often saw dogs attacking people in a manner that would not have been tolerated in Britain.

In Britain dogs were useful for patrolling country lanes and suburban neighbourhoods, on the lookout for burglars and petty pilferers.

Airedales, Retrievers, Border Collies and crosses involving these breeds were commonly used in this work. They required no elaborate training and had a natural aptitude for work.

TRAINING A POLICE DOG

THERE WAS A CERTAIN DIFFERENCE in the training procedure for dogs expected to work in a city as opposed to those destined for the country. In towns, they were employed to clear public parks at night and to attract the attention of the police to any untoward happenings, such as thieves behind closed shutters in a jeweller's shop, or suspicious characters lurking inside streets. The dog was trained to walk ahead of the handler to the next turning and to return to him if he saw anything suspicious ahead. Dogs were also trained to retrieve, including potentially dangerous items such as guns, daggers, knives and glass objects. This was a step towards discrimination exercises, which involved picking out certain items belonging to a particular person.

Training involved learning a multitude of skills, such as scaling heights so that the dog would be capable of overcoming gates and following nose work, or tracking courses. In this the dog was taught to follow specific scents, following perhaps that of a footprint or an item of clothing. Then there was the man-work course in which a dog was taught never to bite a stationery person, but to hold up and prevent escape. Full training took a year of intensive and highly specialised work, although those undertaking just the obedience

section could expect to complete the course in three months. Several training societies were set up for the purpose of obedience training and these were often attended by amateurs who simply wanted to train there own dog for personal interest or use. It was, however, important that such societies did not allow amateurs to go beyond obedience and nosework courses, as it would not have been wise to train fully a dog unless it was going to be used in Police Dog Trials when it would need to be kept in constant training.

As the decades moved on, dogs used in police work have become an increasingly familiar sight as their value has come to be highly recognised, and with careful training, dogs rarely act in uncertain ways. Many of the skills they were taught in the earlier years of this century have been modified to cope with today's lifestyle. The types of crime dogs are expected to deal with covers a wider compass than before and of course the dog is used also for protection and rescue work, all this coming within the realm of police work and associated services.

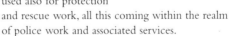

Top and Bottom
Training might include attacking a suspected criminal without causing them any injury or learning to accept the presence of fire. Training has to be very intensive and will take a very long time.

Herding Dogs

DOGS HAVE LONG BEEN of assistance to cattle drovers and shepherds, but only those adapted physically to the work required of them would have survived. They needed to be capable of living in a bleak climate and therefore a coat capable of resisting wet and cold was indispensable. The author regularly travels to Himalayan regions, marvelling at the way dogs bring down sheep and goats from high altitude to locate grazing on lower pastures.

Below
Shepherds in all parts of the world use dogs to help them manage their flocks. They are invariably tough, intelligent animals.

CONTINENTAL HERDING DOGS

SHEEP FARMS WERE VERY WELL managed in Belgium where there were many kinds of dog to work the sheep. All of them were prick eared and, according to early writers, bore some suggestion of the wolf in their general appearance, believing that the wolf had played a part in contributing to litters of bitches who tended sheep on outlying pastures. Although the sheepdogs in Holland closely resembled their Belgian cousins, they were reputed to have been less carefully bred although again divided into types according to coat, one variety having dropped ears. In France the early sheepdogs were the breeds we now know as the Briard and Beauceron, while in Italy the Maremma Sheepdog has been important for guarding flocks.

In Germany the best pastoral dogs were those still showing traces of wolf blood. These were bred with extreme care, not only for work among sheep, but also for competition in shows. Many sheepdogs in Germany were vaguely of spitz type, an aspect which became more marked in the working dogs further north in Denmark, Norway and Sweden where there was difficulty in actually distinguishing sheepdogs from breeds such as the Elkhound and Samoyed.

Right
An Hungarian shepherd with his dogs in the 1930s – they needed to be able to survive rough conditions and an extreme climate.

The largest of all European shepherd dogs were to be found in Russia, standing as high as 79 cm (31 in). These were the South Russian Ovtcharkas, strong in proportion to their size as they had to guard flocks against predatory wolves.

AUSTRALIAN KELPIES

AUSTRALIA, WITH ITS VAST FLOCKS of sheep developed the Kelpie which, in appearance, resembled a cross between the Collie and Dingo but was more likely to have descended from dogs imported from Scotland. This breed has always been renowned for its great intelligence and if ever such a dog were taken away from its work would reputedly fret and pine away. With a good Kelpie, in a day a stockman could muster sheep running on thousands of acres, a task which would have taken four or five men a week or more. Today it is still fairly common to see Kelpies walking over the backs of penned sheep before cutting out a small group. This is deservedly a highly prized breed, and one which often works entirely on its own.

SHEEPDOGS IN BRITAIN

IN BRITAIN, THE SHEEPDOGS are generally smaller and less aggressive than dogs which perform similar duties in the rest of Europe, largely because they have not needed to contend with wolves and other equally dangerous predators. Individual breeds have been rather slow to develop because dogs have been crossed and mated together in order to produce the best dog for the task required, rather than for any aesthetic reason.

The Border Collie is the sheepdog currently best known in Britain although, like all dogs bred to work with livestock, strict and careful training is needed. The dogs must be given plenty of work to keep them occupied because bored animals can turn into sheep-chasers. Sheepdog trials have gained increasing popularity in Britain since their introduction in 1873. These are practical working tests for both dogs and shepherds, not just competition for amusement.

The Old English Sheepdog was developed primarily as a large driving and herding dog, one which was both hardy and tractable. Although larger than Britain's other shepherding breeds, the Old English can lope for long distances and can explore the countryside with frequent easy turns, although now this breed is more closely associated with the showring or with the lifestyle of a household pet.

Of course throughout the world there are many different breeds used as herding dogs, not all of which can be mentioned in this section, but will be found under their respective breeds elsewhere in this book. Sometimes overlooked as herders by those who are not familiar with the breeds are the Cardigan and Pembroke Welsh Corgis. These long, low dogs are both tough and agile and over the years have proved excellent for the purposes of driving cattle in Wales, nipping at the heels of the cattle in order to keep them moving. The Corgi is also capable of quickly dropping down to avoid any backward kicks meted out by the cows.

Left

Sheepdog trials are a popular entertainment in Britain, but they are, first and foremost, a practical working test for the farmer and his dogs.

Below

An Australian Kelpie walking over sheep in order to reach the ones required by the farmer.

Gundogs

BEFORE THE PUBLICATION of Scott's *Antiquary* in 1816, there were few books dealing with the subject of shooting, but one writer in 1789 said there were only three dog breeds capable of receiving instruction and being trained as gundogs: the smooth pointer, the spaniel and the rough pointer, which was qualified as being a dog with long, curled hair, a mixed breed of with blood of the Water-dog and Spaniel.

Top Right and Bottom Dogs are essential when out shooting as they are needed to hunt, point and retrieve. Retrieving is particularly important when shooting near water or in thick cover.

OTHER GUNDOGS

THIS IS A STATEMENT which may surprise readers today, but the truth is that gundogs have taken a long while to be divided up into specific breeds, partly because the names used were frequently inconsistent, added to which dogs were bred for their purpose and abilities, rather than to conform to the standard of a breed which went under a specific name. Today, thankfully, our use of names is more exact than of old but, in the early nineteenth century, pointers, setters and retrievers were all known as spaniels.

ADAPTING TO THE CONDITIONS

IN THE LOW COUNTRY OF SCOTLAND and in England breeds changed with the methods of farming. Cornfields used to be cut with sickles but by the twentieth century the reaping machine was commonly used, leaving stubble just inches high, rather than long straws which were often laid and bent. As a result, it had become essential to drive partridge, because a day's shooting required a dog that could find birds which had dropped in thick cover or had run out of sight, whereas before the dog merely had to pick up birds which had fallen dead in the open.

Change, though, from pointer to setter was slow as it appears that there was little realisation that conditions in the field were changing. The change was probably best summed up at the turn of the twentieth century by Sir Ralph Payne Gallwey who wrote: 'A perfect retriever is rarely, very rarely seen working for his master – usually it is for a keeper, and it may be pretty safely asserted that in the British Islands there are not a score of perfectly broken retrievers that work only for and with their masters out shooting.'

THE RETRIEVER

THE RETRIEVER WAS CONSIDERED 'the king of all sporting dogs ... without the heaviness of the pointer or the fawning adulation for a master shown by the setter or spaniel.' The thoughtful sagacity of a well-broken retriever rarely failed him, though it was difficult then to say actually what a retriever should be: 'without doubt, a modern invention necessitated by the increase of game, by its wildness, which causes it to be oftener wounded, as well as by the decadence (from their comparative uselessness in shooting nowadays) of pointers and setters.' Doubtless owners of pointers and setters would not then have agreed, nor do they now.

Pointers certainly fell out of favour at that time, but there were still those who recognised the beauty of shape and poise of a pointer at work, '... coming up the field with the wind in her favour on reaching the centre, pulled up as in a cloud of dust, and stood like a statue, attitudinising like a stage dancer, her toes hardly touching the earth, her whole form quivering.' Indeed to see Pointers quartering under a good handler is considered one of the best sights on moor or field.

THE SETTER

THE NAME 'SETTER' was an old English alternative for the word 'sitter' and such dogs were frequently referred to as spaniels. They were generally divided into two sizes: the larger dog to sit while the net was drawn over the covey of partridges, the smaller dog to find and spring game. Only in recent decades have setters and spaniels been divided into different breeds by name.

GUNDOGS AT WORK

TODAY THERE IS STILL a certain mystery surrounding gundogs and their work. There are still old-style shoots supported by landed gentry, but many small farmers and farm workers also own gundogs and use such dogs to work with the gun, albeit in somewhat less grandiose style.

There are three main stages of gun work: finding the quarry and showing its position to the gunman, flushing out the game and thirdly its retrieval once the game has been shot. Although there are now breeds which hunt, point and retrieve (HPR breeds), pointers and setters which are quiet dogs and will not disturb the game are traditionally employed in the first stage, usually in open country, because if the dogs were to flush the game the guns may be out of shooting range.

Sturdier, lower-set dogs are needed to hunt game in heavy cover, a task usually associated with spaniels but one carried out by many other breeds, Retrievers, German Pointers, Weimeraners and Vizslas among them. Although spaniels and other gundogs also retrieve, this is traditionally the domain of the retriever breeds which are adept at carrying out this work with the required speed, accuracy and gentleness.

Top
Springer Spaniel retrieving a pheasant. It is important for a dog to have a soft mouth, so that the bird is not damaged.

Above Left
The English Setter is no longer used as a gundog in Britain, despite its keen scenting abilities.

Above Right
The Gordon Setter is the only native Scottish gundog. It is particularly good at hunting game birds.

> **DOG FACT:**
> Gundogs are reputed to inherit their ability from their parents, so youngsters from good working stock usually have a head start over others.

Hound Packs

WHETHER OR NOT ONE AGREES with sport involving packs of hounds, there can be no denying that hunting with hound packs is something which is part of canine history and it would be wrong to exclude this aspect entirely from this comprehensive book. At the UK's Hound Show dogs from various packs are all allowed to mingle together and none shows any animosity, even when the public is invited to join them for a friendly word.

STAG HUNTING WITH HOUNDS

HUNTING WAS KNOWN as the sport of kings and stag hunting was particularly associated with memories of medieval courts. In many of the French forests it was considered heresy to kill a deer other than with hounds, and French hounds were especially bred to the sport. The stag's range was restricted to the forests of the north and north-east of France and certain parts of Burgundy. In other areas, the hounds' quarry was roe deer, boar, fox and hare. By the turn of this century, France's remaining deer forests, once royal domains, had become the property of the state and were leased on nine-year terms to the highest bidder. It was packs belonging to the Duc de Lorge, one of which was considered the finest in France, which hunted at Fontainbleu, hunting red and roe deer alternately. The French tradition clung to line hunting, drawing and perseverance; pace and speed were not considered an important asset and were therefore not encouraged as characteristics in their hounds.

FRENCH AND GERMAN HOUND BREEDS

THE NUMBER OF FRENCH HOUND breeds is great. Some are large, such as the Norman Hound, introduced to the country during the reign of Louis XIV, while others are relatively small. Some are rough-coated and some smooth – the variety is enormous and each breed has carried out its own special task. The Griffon Vendeen has by nature been meant for the chase, often working in waterways and tracking deer and boar whilst the Griffon Nivernais, similar to the Vendeen, has for a long while been useful for rough work in the forest.

In the neighbourhood of Hanover in Germany, the Hanoverian Schweiss-hund was used to track wounded deer and marvellous stories were told concerning this breed's powers of scent. With

Above
Stag hunting with hounds has been popular for hundreds of years, as this 15th century illustration of the chase shows.

Right
A typical nineteenth-century hunting scene. Riders, horses and hounds take some refreshment.

its muscular quarters, elastic action and energetic expression the best of the race were considered admirable representatives of the Continental sporting hound.

RUSSIAN HOUNDS

IN RUSSIA, THE CZAR and Grand Dukes kept huge packs of Russian Hounds, called the Gontschaga Sobaka, an exclusive and aristocratic strain. It was said that from a distance these dogs resembled wolves with their hind quarters being much lower than their forequarters, though this is not always depicted in old pictures of the breed. The head, too, was considered wolf-like, broad between the ears and tapering to a fine muzzle. Colour was undoubtedly also a contributing factor in drawing a comparison with the wolf, for it was either grizzle or black, with tan markings, frequently with a white collar or tail tip.

Another Russian dog, more massive than the former, was the Medelan or Bear-hound. The bear provided sport not only in Russia but also in Norway where, during the latter half of the nineteenth century, the number of bears greatly diminished in the Scandinavian forests. Despite this the Norwegian Bear-hound still existed as a well-trained and intelligent hunter, possessing magnificent scenting powers. When employed in the chase such dogs were usually fitted with a light leather harness, with a leash attached. A well-trained dog, of the spitz type, was capable of leading the hunter surely and silently up to his game. The varieties of

Bearhound differed primarily in size and prominent amongst them was the Elkhound, sometimes referred to as the Scandinavian Pointer as this was used not only for hunting both elk and bear, but also as a gundog for black-cock. The Elkhound was prized not only for intelligence, courage and endurance but also for scenting, with the ability to scent an elk or a bear from as much as three miles distant.

BRITISH HOUNDS

BETTER KNOWN IN BRITAIN than elsewhere, and albeit now under threat of decline, are packs of Foxhounds which observe a strict hunting season and were probably introduced from France by the Normans and used at that time for deer hunting. During the season, such packs have historically

hunted two or three times a week, with 15 to 20 couples selected from the pack each time.

The Beagle is still used in Britain and Europe for tracking the hare, whilst in the USA it is used to track the cottontail rabbit. With the exception of part of the seventeenth and eighteenth centuries when fox-hunting took preference, beagling has been popular for hundreds of years. Impressive packs of Otterhounds are also still to be found, dogs renowned both for their special scenting abilities and their 'music'.

Left
The Otter Hound, as its name suggests, was originally used to hunt otters. Its thick, insulating undercoat meant that it was impervious to icy cold water. It is now used for more general outdoor pursuits.

DOG FACT:
The most famous packs of French Staghounds met in the environs of Paris, such as in the forests of Rambouillet, Chantilly and Fontainbleu.

Above
Each local hunt has a large pack of Foxhounds. About 15-20 couples are are selected for each hunt.

Left
The Otterhound does not make a good pet because, once on a scent, it becomes totally absorbed and will not listen to any commands.

Showing Dogs

EVENTS WHICH CAN LOOSELY be described as dog shows have taken place for thousands of years, but in essence these were merely shows which involved dogs as some sore of side attraction. They did not in any way resemble modern shows. However, by the eighteenth century, there were some shows that might have been remotely familiar to us today.

EARLY DOG SHOWS

Right

Early dog shows had their origins in public houses, so it was hardly surprising that they were all-male affairs.

Below

By 1862, dog shows were so popular that the Islington Show attracted 803 entrants.

THE FIRST OF THE Hound shows took place in 1776, and these were held in the summer months mainly as a way of fellow huntsmen keeping together out of season. Later that century some of the agricultural shows had dog sections too and, by then, dogs were also becoming popular with townsfolk. It was believed that as many as 25 per cent of households owned a dog and there was an increasing change in attitude toward some of the more brutal sports involving dogs.

In 1834 a show was held for '9 lb spaniels', and the prize for the winner was a silver cream jug, so the more delicate side of the dog game was beginning to show its face. This show was in a public house because it was in places like this that dog showing began in earnest. Such shows were a natural progression from events which had taken place around the dog-pit so, although the sport had changed, the venue had not.

Dog clubs were formed and there was sometimes a rule that anyone attending must take along a dog either for show or for sale, thereby ensuring a good 'show night'. Participants were always men but they had now begun to represent different classes of society.

SHOWS INCREASE IN POPULARITY

DOG SHOWS TOOK PLACE in public houses both in urban and rural areas, but until the advent of the railway, people were unable to travel any distance to shows. A famous early dog show, often mis-reported as being the very first, was held at Newcastle-upon-Tyne's New Corn Exchange on 28 and 29 June 1859. Incredibly, one of the judges had travelled from as far away as London.

Held as part of a well-established poultry show, breed competition was restricted to Pointers and Setters, although other breeds of dog were also exhibited. There was much praise for the organisation of the show, the dogs being chained and protected by barriers so that they could neither injure nor alarm visitors. The 26 pointers and 36 setters competed for the major prize of one of Pape's celebrated double-barrelled shotguns, worth between £15 and £20. Such an important competition caused exhibitors to travel good distances, from Manchester, Huddersfield and Lancaster.

Mr J H Walsh, editor of *The Field*, was one of the show's judges and became one of the organisers of the next show which took place in Birmingham later that year. This show led to the formation of the Birmingham Dog Show Society. Birmingham was a great stronghold of the dog fancy, so great that it was doubted that any other town in the entire world could match its record of consistency, as by 1902 an annual show had been held there for 43 years.

LADY COMPETITORS

AS DOG SHOWING MOVED into the nineteenth century the numbers of exhibits at shows increased so that by 1862 a show in Islington attracted an entry of 803. It was in that same year that two lady exhibitors actually appeared amongst the prize winners. Times were indeed moving on. It was in 1867 that the custom of women exhibiting at shows really began to meet with approval as the Princess of Wales, later to become Queen Alexandra, exhibited at a show, thus setting an example to others. Although the Princess's Mastiff obtained only a second place it was described as 'the best ever exhibited'. Ladies had now most certainly become noticed at shows and just three years later there was a special prize awarded to the best dog owned by a lady.

'FIRST GREAT INTERNATIONAL DOG SHOW'

A SHOW GRANDLY ENTITLED the 'First Great International Dog Show' was supported with an entry of 1,678 in 1863, though it was believed there may have been 2,000 dogs in the hall. That same year a smaller show was held in Chelsea but the organiser was sadly described as 'overwhelmed by the difficulties of the task he had undertaken'. He had believed it would be a simple task to collect together a number of dogs to be viewed by a mass of spectators, but had overlooked many important points. Water was not available for the dogs which were in the most dreadfully overcrowded conditions, with no proper divisions between them, just an open wire fence, and although the hall was officially able to accommodate 600 dogs there were actually 1,214. Toys and pet dogs were exhibited in a new wing which had a glass roof, making the temperature inside either too hot or too cold and, on the first day of the show, it was said to be hot enough to cause dehydration, especially with the absence of water.

Top
By the mid-nineteenth century women were beginning to appear at shows, but were still very much in the minority.

Top Left
As shows became more popular, standards began to improve and benches were introduced.

Left and Bottom
It wasn't until the formation of the Kennel Club in 1873 that proper categorisation took place.

The Kennel Club and Crufts

FINDING DOGS for shows was a problem as the dogs entered in the catalogue were either absent. Confusion reigned supreme among the foreign dogs, some of which had no numbers at all. Contrary to rules today, each dog had the name and address of the owner displayed on a label attached to the collar, leaving the judge in no doubt as to which dogs belonged to whom.

finances presented a problem. Someone who had been involved in the organisation of some shows and recognised the problem was Mr Shirley, who had started to exhibit dogs himself in 1870. He decided to set himself the task of forming a permanent body which was to become the Kennel Club. In April of 1873 a small group of people met in a three-roomed flat and this meeting led later that year to the Kennel Club's first show at Crystal Palace with an entry of 975.

THE BEGINNING OF THE KENNEL CLUB

THE FIRST GENERAL MEETING of the Kennel Club took place in Birmingham's Great Western Hotel in December 1874, the same year as the Club published its first Stud Book containing the pedigrees of 4,027 dogs divided into 40 different breeds and varieties. The Kennel Club was still a young club, but it took bold steps as by 1880 it had put out an edict that all dogs entered at shows held under its rules had to be registered with the Kennel Club, something which was well received by many. In this way the Kennel Club established itself as a governing body which levied taxes on dogs for exhibition, and since then Britain's dog showing world has not looked back.

There were objections from some quarters, especially the Birmingham Dog Show Society, whose committee was in itself very influential. By 1885 two delegates of the Society were allowed to sit on the Kennel Club's committee and an amicable agreement was reached, albeit after a hard fought battle.

The Kennel Club had popularised the sport of dog showing and had elevated it from venues such as bars and public houses to fashionable locations including Crystal Palace, Ranelagh and the Botanical Gardens. Through the Kennel Club people could

Above
By the beginning of the twentieth century, women were involved in dog shows.

Right
In 1874 the Kennel Club published its first Stud Book with 40 different breeds on record.

CATEGORISING ENTRANTS

ALTHOUGH THERE were many high-quality specimens shown at shows in the 1860s, by the close of the decade it was recognised that many undesirable practices still took place and various local clubs attempted to apply some reform, but they lacked harmony in their policies and

obtain pedigrees for their dogs and were happy for their dogs to be included on permanent registers. The Club also acted as a court of appeal so that wrongs could be set right, and dishonesty was made both difficult and dangerous. It was said that the Kennel Club had done for dogs what the Jockey Club had done for racing - praise indeed.

PEOPLE AT DOG SHOWS

ONLY TOWARD THE END of the nineteenth century and with the intervention of the Kennel Club was a certain respectability brought to the dog-showing world - until then the majority of 'dog fanciers' were by no means the elite of society. As the decades moved on, more and more eminent people began to take part and to lend their support to shows - even Queen Victoria became an exhibitor. An active breeder and occasional exhibitor, the Prince of Wales, later to become King Edward VII, was made the Kennel Club's Patron in 1875. His wife, Queen Alexandra, was much involved with Borzois, Basset Hounds, Chow Chows, Skye Terriers, Japanese Spaniels and Pugs, and together the couple regularly visited shows, attending not merely in a formal capacity, but because they enjoyed seeing good dogs.

Her Grace the Duchess of Newcastle did much to raise the tone of dog shows by her personal patronage and the Countess of Aberdeen, someone greatly involved with Skye Terriers, was Patroness of the Ladies Kennel Association. Dog

shows had certainly brought together all classes of society and many a judge commented that he often had dogs from distinguished kennels competing alongside those belonging to members of the working classes. However, one cannot

help but think that sometimes the privileged classes were shown certain favour, such as the time when Queen Victoria wished to exhibit three Pomeranians of a colour not usually shown in England. This resulted in a special classes being provided for them and two were jointly awarded first prize. However, over the last century or so, dog showing has become a great leveller, and to this day members of the royal family still visit Crufts each year and chat enthusiastically to excited exhibitors and judges.

Above
Gradually, dog shows moved away from their working-class origins and were given the royal stamp of approval.

Below
The Deerhound class is scrutinised by a judge.

CRUFTS IS ESTABLISHED

AT THE TENDER AGE OF 14 Charles Cruft was already growing weary of academic studies and knew that he had no desire to join his father's jewellery business, so he applied to work for Mr James Spratt, the dog biscuit manufacturer. Cruft joined as an assistant in Spratt's shop and soon became one of the first commercial travellers, a job which brought him into close contact with

Above
Charles Cruft had the forethought to see that if dog shows were better organised they would improve the quality of pedigree stock.

Right
Cruft worked closely with the Kennel Club and classes and numbers of entries rose steadily both at Kennel Club Shows and at Crufts Dog Show.

dog owners both in the UK and abroad. Before too long, Cruft had become Spratt's right hand man and had built up strong connections with owners of shoots and with head gamekeepers. He became manager of the company's show department, as by now Spratt's had grown enormously, becoming a limited company.

CRUFT LEAVES SPRATTS

CRUFT REALISED THAT IF DOG shows were properly organised they would improve the quality of pedigree stock, as well as encouraging people to keep better-bred pets. He also recognised that the

level of show management was still lacking in many quarters and that this would need to be improved. Charles Cruft had already become well known in the world of dogs and in 1878 he was placed in charge of the great Paris Exhibition. His early experience of Continental dog shows was to stand him in good stead, as foreign dogs were later exhibited at his own shows and foreign judges secured. Although he moved on from Spratt's, Cruft never forget his debt of gratitude to the company and always retained cordial relations, indeed frequently dogs at Cruft's shows were both fed and benched by Messrs Spratt's.

CRUFT'S FIRST SHOW

IN 1886 CRUFT announced the First Great Terrier Show, held in the Victorian music hall called the Royal Aquarium at Westminster. With 57 classes, the show attracted 600 entries, most of which were registered with the Kennel Club. Public attention was drawn to the show, helped by full coverage in The Times. Cruft was also involved as secretary of various other shows, but the next year his chief interest lay again in a show of Terriers, this time held in Westminster's St Stephen's Hall. Sir Humphrey Trafford, himself a keen exhibitor, was appointed as President, and and the Cruft's veterinary surgeon was also surgeon to the Kennel Club. Consistency and efficiency of those working at the show contributed greatly to its success. The second show saw 75 classes, though rather fewer dogs entered this one.

Although the railway services were not then highly regarded, London and North Western Railway announced special arrangements to convey dogs to this show as Charles Cruft had realised that, however good the show, dogs needed to be transported easily, so he liaised regularly with the railway's representatives.

The first of the two Terrier shows that were held in 1888 is notable for the fact that various labels had been attached to the wrong dogs, causing a great muddle and prompting a change to the numbering system.

Classes and numbers of entries rose steadily to 164 classes at the final show to be held at the Royal Aquarium in 1889. The special prizes on

offer had also increased considerably, and the most valuable cup, worth 50 guineas, was offered for the best Dandie Dinmont. Two other cups were valued at 25 guineas each. Cruft's was fast gathering momentum so that by the following year entries were in excess of 1,500 and the prizes were worth around £1,500. Although the show was still officially known as the Great Terrier Show, it had become increasingly clear that this was, in reality, Cruft's own show.

PRIZES AND CLASSES GALORE

SPLENDID PRIZES WERE on the increase, such as the solid brass dog kennel of the Queen Anne period offered for the best Yorkshire Terrier, while winners of the valuable cups presented in the Team classes each took home a gold medal to commemorate the win. But despite the prestige of this annual event, following the show of 1890 more than one critic commented that the quantity of dogs was more remarkable than the quality. There were indeed some very strange classes scheduled,

perhaps the strangest being that for 'Stuffed dogs, or dogs made of Wood, China etc.' Entries in this unusual class included two terracotta Pugs, a marble statuette of a Toy Spaniel and two cases of stuffed dogs.

AN ANNUAL EVENT

BY 1891 THE SHOW was advertised as Cruft's Greatest Dog Show, the first at which all breeds were invited to compete, with around 2,000 dogs making almost 2,500 entries. The judges numbered 20 and they had 12 rings in which to officiate. Entries from Queen Victoria and Prince Albert added prestige to the show. The Royal Agricultural Hall remained its home until 1939, excepting the years 1918--20. By the close of the nineteenth century entries had risen to well over 3,000 and royal patronage continued, not just from British royals but also from great names abroad, such as Prince Constantine of Oldenburg, Grand Duke Nicholas of Russia and even the Czar himself who sent many Russian Wolfhounds from his own kennels.

Above
The 1891 Cruft's Greatest Dog Show was open to all breeds and attracted over 2,000 dogs.

Left
Cruft began his dog show career with Terriers and they remained a strong interest as the categories increased in number.

Although the show came to a temporary end in 1917 it was once again back on the canine lovers' calendar for 1921 with encouraging entries and continued royal support.

By 1922 the Papillon had created something of a novelty at the show and the Afghan Hound attracted a great deal of attention. In 1925 Miss Hardingham became assistant to Charles Cruft and it was she who was to take over as secretary upon Cruft's death 17 years later.

THE JUBILEE SHOW

AS THE SHOW APPROACHED its golden jubilee year in 1936 entries rose higher and higher and the number of scheduled breeds totalled 80. There was increased support for foreign dogs and overseas judges frequently found themselves taking the centre of the ring. Entries for that jubilee show amounted to the phenomenal number of 10,650, made up from 4,388 dogs. There were 898 Labrador Retrievers, 766 Cocker Spaniels and 226 Golden Retrievers, with Cairns heading the Terrier Group with 296. Already Alsatians (now known as GSDs) had become popular with 255 entries, but winning over them all that year was the Chow Chow Ch Choonam Hung Kwong who took the prestigious Best in Show award.

KENNEL CLUB TAKES OVER

FOR MANY A YEAR THE NAME 'Cruft' had been synonymous with dog shows and Cruft's shows were financially a great success at a time when it was possible to make a personal profit from shows, something no longer allowed by the English Kennel Club. Charles Cruft died in 1939 and three years later his wife decided that she no longer wished to run this famous show, although she wanted the name to be perpetuated, so asked the Kennel Club to take over the organisation. The Second World War intervened, but in October 1948, the first Cruft's Show organised by the Kennel Club took place at London's Olympia, with all 92 breeds scheduled. This proved to be an immediate success with exhibitors and public alike, and the show has undoubtedly gone on from strength to strength ever since.

Since 1891 the show's catalogue had included brief descriptive details of each breed with a photograph or engraving, a tradition which continues today and is invaluable for visitors to the show wishing to distinguish the various breeds. By 1959 the show's running costs caused entry fees to be

CRUFT'S IN THE TWENTIETH CENTURY

IN THE TWENTIETH CENTURY the administration of Cruft's show became very well organised and Charles Cruft himself became Secretary and Director. Until the 1930s regulations changed little, excepting for opening the show to dogs from any part of the world. Challenge trophies and special prizes, though, could only be competed for by members of Cruft's International Dog Show Society, involving a subscription fee of one guinea.

AFTER THE FIRST WORLD WAR

Top
In the 1930s, the exhibition of canine appliances became a regular feature of Cruft's.

Above
An early 20th-century prize card from Cruft's – something for the proud owner to cherish forever.

EACH DOG WAS FED and attended to without additional charge and the exhibition of canine appliances became a regular feature of the shows. This was the beginning of the many trade stands seen at Crufts today and was a popular feature with carriages, dog kennels, bedding, clothing and other useful items.

During the years of the First World War, Cruft was aware that he needed to preserve public interest and in 1915 held an exhibition of canine heroes. There were also army and navy classes in which exhibits were owned by those who served.

increased, much to the dismay of some, but still there was a new world record entry of 13,211. By now the Kennel Club had banned monorchids and cryptorchids from the show, after an earlier survey revealed that about 10 per cent of exhibits had been cryptorchids. Other than this no restriction had ever been placed on entries to a show in Britain but in 1965 the committee decided to restrict the size of the show, initially by not allowing puppies under the age of eight months to be shown. However, this only produced very limited control over entry sizes, so qualification by dint of winning a prize at a championship show during the previous year came into effect. Since then, the qualifications for Cruft's have become more stringent as the years have progressed.

A NEW VENUE

OLYMPIA WAS increasingly considered a venue with cramped and dreary conditions for this prestigious show but despite adverse comment the show remained there for a few more years. In 1974 the show's red and yellow colours used by Charles Cruft

were changed to the more restrained light and dark green shades and the apostrophe in the word Cruft's was dropped, changing the name of the show to Crufts.

In 1979 Crufts moved to London's Earl's Court and changes were made to the big ring to create more drama and glamour. There was also an increased number of trade stands, seemingly an ever growing aspect of Crufts show.

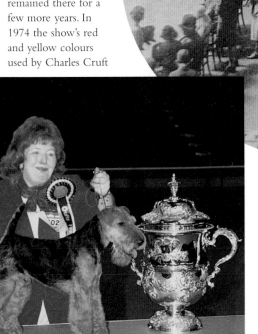

The show remained at Earl's Court until 1990 and from its centenary show the following year moved to Birmingham's National Exhibition Centre. This venue offered much increased floor space and good access by road, rail and plane although a high proportion of exhibitors and visitors, especially from abroad, had reservations regarding the choice of venue. Now the show has extended to four days and more and more halls have accommodated this enormous show so, although there is still a pang of sadness about the move out of London, the majority now agree that it was well worthwhile.

Top
A Chow Chow won Best in Show in 1936 – Cruft's jubilee year.

Centre
The first Cruft's Show organised by the Kennel Club took place at Olympia.

Left
The Best in Show winner of 1998 was an Airedale Terrier.

Dog Shows Today

MOST DOG SHOWS IN BRITAIN are held under the auspices of the Kennel Club with various levels of show at which a dog can compete. At the highest level are Championship shows which may have separate classes for the majority of breeds or may be breed-specific, usually organised by a breed club which runs perhaps a couple of shows each year, one of which, with the Kennel Club's permission, is probably a Championship event. Other shows are for one Group only and while the all-breed shows are held over two, three or four consecutive days, a Group show lasts just one. Crufts is of course also a Championship show but for this dogs must have qualified by winning certain awards at Championship level.

HIGH LEVEL OF COMPETITION

AT CHAMPIONSHIP LEVEL competition is extremely strong and dogs which win regularly are of high quality indeed. Championship shows provide opportunities to qualify for Crufts and for entry in the Kennel Club's Stud Book. Challenge Certificates are also on offer for many breeds at these shows, counting towards the title of Champion. Another important award for which points can be scored at these shows is a Junior Warrant.

Above and Right
Competition at Championship shows is always fierce, so winning Best in Show is always the cause of great excitement and much jubilation.

Fees for entry at such shows are relatively high and exhibitors regularly travel all over the country, so the cost of actively campaigning a dog in Championship competition is considerable.

To become a Champion a dog has to have won three Challenge Certificates under different judges.

This is more difficult in Britain than anywhere else in the world as in many cases it is necessary to beat several champions to gain this title. At conformation shows Gundogs compete for the title of Show Champion, because only if they have won a championship title in the field are they eligible to hold that of a full Champion. Border Collies, too, can only compete for Show Championship titles at such shows.

CHALLENGE CERTIFICATES

NOT ALL BREEDS at Championship shows have Challenge Certificates (CCs) allocated to them, this depending upon the numerical strength of the breed and often upon geographical location of the show. It is the Kennel Club which decides which breeds can have such status and at which shows, and in many cases the allocation varies from year to year. Other breeds which can compete at championship shows but are not eligible for CCs are those still on the Rare Breeds or Import Registers, because a breed must have attained a certain status in this country before being allowed to compete for the title of Champion.

Judges who award CCs at Championship shows have to be approved by the Kennel Club, and breed clubs are also asked to offer their opinion on new judges for consideration by the ruling body. This means that judges who officiate at this, the highest level, are usually those with the greatest experience. Some judges officiate only for their own breed; others choose, over a period of time, move on to award Challenge Certificates in several. Official training of judges is something which is still in its infancy in Britain although in other countries such schemes, or similar ones, have been in operation for years.

OTHER SHOWS

RATHER LESS FORMAL, and with much cheaper entry fees, are Open shows where overall entries at each show are considerably fewer, perhaps 1,000–2,000 exhibits, as opposed to 10,000–20,000 at a Championship event. For these shows exhibitors

Left
This Rotterdam show is typical of the more relaxed attitude on the Continent.

Below Left
A judge making notes in the show ring, while the handlers exchange anxious glances.

tend to travel less, perhaps within a radius of about 80 km (50 miles), for there are numerous Open shows throughout the year. They are an especially good training ground for puppies over the minimum permitted age of six months. To attain a Junior Warrant, something competed for up to the age of 18 months, it is now a rule that some points must have been won at Open shows.

From 1999 the Kennel Club has brought in a new rule that any judge officiating for more than three classes in any breed (more than four in the case of highly popular breeds) must be approved to judge at this level by a relevant breed society. Open shows are valuable training grounds for newer judges, and indeed for experienced judges wishing to widen their experience of other breeds, but it must be recognised that exhibitors pay for a judge's opinion and so every effort must be made to ensure that the opinions given by judges are well founded.

Above
An American Cocker Spaniel wins Best of Show in Rotterdam.

Judging Shows Today

AT BOTH CHAMPIONSHIP and Open shows, entries have to be pre-booked, and indeed there are also smaller shows which now operate on the same basis. However, Exemption show entries are made on the day. These are organised in aid of charity, but should still be held under Kennel Club licence.

ELIGIBILITY OF DOGS

CHAMPIONS AND OTHER DOGS which have won very highly at more formal shows are ineligible for entry. Exemption shows provide an enjoyable day out for the less serious exhibitor, with a limited number of mixed pedigree classes and several fun classes such as 'Waggiest Tail' and 'Most Appealing Expression', as well as some in which owners join in the fun, such as 'Best Set of Six Legs' and 'Fancy Dress'. Despite the small charge for entry there are often substantial sponsored prizes to be won, these generally having been donated in the hope that they will attract higher entries at the show and bring in additional revenue for the charity for which funds are being raised.

The experience of judges at these events is varied. Sometimes the judge has limited experience in the dog world, while occasionally well-known names take to the ring because the show is being organised for a good cause. In consequence, the standard of judging is varied, but some serious exhibitors use these shows as a training ground for their youngsters. When taking puppies to Exemption shows, remember that the minimum age for entry is six months and that not all dogs at the show are well-trained, or, occasionally, not well supervised, so one must take care not to allow one's young 'hopeful' to be put off the show situation through lack of caution on the part of the owner.

RINGCRAFT CLASSES AND SHOW TRAINING

MANY HIGHLY SUCCESSFUL exhibitors never take their dogs to ringcraft classes but, especially for novice exhibitors, such classes provide an ideal opportunity for both exhibitor and dog to learn how to show well. A ringcraft class must not be

confused with an obedience class, as the former is specifically aimed at training dogs for the show ring, while in obedience a dog learns to sit, stay, walk to heel and such like. A dog must be trained to stand.

Some ringcraft classes are good, others less so, so it is important to seek out a relatively local class which is well-run by dedicated enthusiasts who ideally have substantial experience in showing dogs themselves. Meetings usually take place on one evening each week, perhaps in a village hall, and on first visit it is wise to just sit by the ringside as an observer, thereby assessing

Top Right
Exemption shows are intended for the less serious exhibitor. Novelty classes include Fancy Dress – the winners of the First Prize and their happy owner.

Right
Exemption shows include some mixed pedigree classes, but are much more informal than the Championship shows.

whether or not the circumstances seem suitable and, in the case of a young puppy, allowing your dog to get used to a new environment.

Most ringcraft clubs operate on a non-profit making basis and many are registered with the Kennel Club, but this does not apply to all. Usually there is a nominal membership fee and then a small sum payable per visit so, except for the sake of practice, it is not essential to attend every week.

At a ringcraft class, exhibitor and dog will learn the basics of what is expected of them in the showring. A small breed of dog can learn to stand on a table in order to be assessed by a judge, because it is important that a dog stands still and shows off its merits to its best advantage. Larger dogs are trained to stand still on the floor, and on the whole, the way of showing off a dog in the ring will depend to a great extent on the individual breed. Most dogs are shown in profile when standing, but some breeds, such as Bulldogs, are shown with their head on to the judge. In some breeds, the tail needs to be held up or out at a certain angle, perhaps outward in line with the back, as in some of the Gundog breeds.

In the majority of breeds, the teeth will be inspected by a judge, usually to check their number and placement. In a few breeds, the colour of the tongue, gums, lips, flews and roof of the mouth are also assessed. It is essential that a dog tolerates such close inspection and that its temperament is steady because ill-tempered dogs may be asked to leave the ring and can be disqualified from showing.

This Page
The informality of Exemption shows encourages people to show their dogs and then perhaps to consider taking shows more seriously.

JUDGING AT A RINGCRAFT CLASS

FREQUENTLY RINGCRAFT CLASSES are held in small venues so there is not sufficient space to lay out a ring as it would be in a real show situation. However, there will still be an opportunity to move one's dog, hopefully at the correct pace according to the breed. It is important to learn to move at a speed which is right for the dog so that the judge sees it moving at its best. A structural fault will often show up even more evidently on the move, but this may be lessened by moving at the correct pace.

In the showring a judge will normally ask exhibitors to move around the ring with their dogs together in order to obtain a general impression and, especially in the case of younger exhibits, to give them a chance to get the feel of the ring. Then each dog will be assessed individually, either on the table or the floor according to the breed. After such assessment a dog will usually be asked to move in a triangle, with the dog on the left-hand side of the handler, then possibly once again up and down the centre of the ring or, as is used frequently on the Continent, move in an

Above
Ringcraft classes give owners valuable tips, such as wearing red to show off a white dog more effectively.

Right
Big shows like this can be intimidating if you and your dog have not spent time learning ringcraft and then gaining confidence in smaller venues.

arc back to the dog's original place along the side of the ring. When the ring is small the judge may ask that the dog is moved up and down the centre of the ring twice. On the first occasion the judge will assess movement coming and going and will then move to another position to assess profile movement. An important rule is that as an exhibitor one should never position oneself between dog and judge so it may be necessary in this instance to move one's dog on the right-hand side, again a technique which can be practised in ringcraft classes.

THE WINNER

WHEN ALL DOGS HAVE been assessed individually, the judge will make a final selection, in a particularly large class possibly selecting just a few before making final placings. Then the winners of each class will compete against each other in order that the judge can select the best. In shows held on a Group basis the best of each breed in its Group will compete against the others, then the ultimate Best in Show winner will be selected from the Group winners.

Whether one has won or lost, good sportsmanship is important, after all the judge is entitled to his or her opinion and on another day, under another judge, the results may be quite different. As is so often said at shows: 'one always takes the best dog home' at the end of the day, whether or not one has won as highly as one would have liked.

SHOWRING JARGON

THOSE ATTENDING DOG SHOWS on their first few occasions, as either exhibitors or visitors, are likely to be completely confounded by some of the colloquialisms used by the judges and other experts. It is relatively easy to become acquainted with general show terminology but some of the jargon used needs a little explanation:

Big Green One: Challenge Certificate, usually referred to as a CC.

Bridesmaid: Used to describe a dog which is frequently placed second but rarely wins. This can also refer to a dog which regularly wins Reserve CCs but insufficient CCs to gain the title of champion.

Can't get past: Implying that it is difficult to beat a certain dog.

Down the line: Placed lower than first or second, usually referring to Reserve (4th) or VHC (5th) placings.

Facey/face judging: A judge appearing to give high awards to well-known exhibitors (although one must always appreciate that those who are well-known probably have very good dogs).

Gained his/her crown or title: The dog became a champion.

Go Over: Assessing a dog with one's hands to feel construction.

Good doer: A dog which eats and thrives well.

In the cards: Awarded one of the class prizes.

In good company: Implying that although a dog was unplaced there were others of merit in the class which also unsuccessful.

Judging the other end of the lead: Judging the handler rather than the dog.

Knocked: Placed lower than expected.

Laying on of hands: Said of a judge who goes through the motions without feeling sufficiently well to assess structure.

Looking for his third: Hoping to win a third CC, hence becoming a Champion.

Made up: Made a Champion.

New dog: An exhibit not yet assessed by the judge of the current class.

Pulled out: Selected amongst the final few in a class. Often it is said that a dog was 'pulled out' but not placed.

Put through: Generally denoting a dog which has been declared Best of Breed and has therefore been selected to represent that breed in the Group.

Put up: Placed first, or may be used to denote the Challenge Certificate winner.

Reserve Ticket: Reserve Challenge Certificate.

Seen dog: An exhibit which has already been assessed by the same judge at that show.

Set up/Stack: To present a dog in standing position for the judge.

Table dog: A dog to be examined by a judge on the table, rather than on the floor.

Thrown out: Unplaced.

Ticket: Challenge Certificate.

Top
Both dog and owner have to be fit to take part in agility events.

Left
Obedience competitions are rewarding to enter and provide an impressive show for spectators.

Bottom
Dogs enjoy training for agility events and it is a good opportunity to develop the partnership between owner and dog

FREQUENT ABBREVIATIONS

CC: Challenge Certificate

RCC: Reserve Challenge Certificate

DCC/BCC: Dog/Bitch Challenge Certificate

BOB: Best of Breed

RBOB: Reserve Best of Breed

BOS: Best of Sex

BP: Best Puppy

BPIB: Best Puppy in Breed

BPIS: Best Puppy in Show

BIS: Best in Show

RBIS: Reserve Best in Show

BIG: Best in Group

OTHER EVENTS

THERE ARE MANY competitive events which can be enjoyed if one is a dog owner. For some, one needs to be almost as fit as one's dog but that is not always the case, indeed some disabled exhibitors derive much pleasure from competing at dog shows.

Many canine events can be watched at Crufts where participants must have qualified to compete, so the standards are extremely high. As well as activities in the main ring at Crufts, in recent years there has also been a Special Events ring in which demonstrations and competitive events take place all day for each of the four days of the show.

JUNIOR COMPETITIVE EVENTS

ALTHOUGH CHILDREN and teenagers are of course at liberty to enter dog shows just as adults do, there are other competitive opportunities open to them, such as Junior Handling classes.

For youngsters aged between six and 18 there are classes held at shows which are based on handling ability rather than on the quality of the dog. Divided into two age categories, even Juniors can have great fun and a serious challenge in these competitive events. Each year those who have qualified attend semi-finals and finals, the overall winner going on to compete against young winners from other countries.

Competition is high, and one hopes that Junior Handling standards will not be taken to extremes. But there are many dedicated, excellent and well-mannered young handlers who have moved gracefully into the adult show world. Their expert handling skills stand them in very good stead to show their dogs to best advantage; some are already on their way to becoming professional handlers.

KENNEL CLUB JUNIOR ORGANISATION

SET UP BY THE KENNEL CLUB in 1985, the Kennel Club Junior Organisation is known usually as the KCJO. The aim of the organisation is to encourage young people to be interested in the care and training of dogs, promoting courtesy, sportsmanship and discipline. Many events are held each year covering

all aspects of the canine world, with useful talks, practical demonstrations and regional visits to various interesting establishments which are involved with dogs. There are also quizzes and the ever popular KCJO Stakes classes, held at shows throughout the year.

AGILITY

AGILITY EVENTS are highly entertaining both for dogs and human participants, as well as for onlookers. This is a competitive activity which has become highly popular in recent years but both dogs and owners need to be physically fit. Handlers have to run around the course with their dogs which jump over hurdles, through hoops and negotiate their way through tunnels, over see-saws and the like. Penalty faults are awarded for any errors made, such as an erroneous route or a dog jumping down from a table before the given time, and each circuit of the course is also timed. Even small dogs can now compete in Mini-

Top
Junior Handling classes enable young people between six and 18 to take part in dog shows.

Above
This Tibetan Terrier is obviously enjoying taking part in an Agility event.

Right
"Heelwork to Music" requires great concentration from both dog and handler. It is an extension of obedience work and can only be achieved if there is a close understanding between the participants.

Agility which effectively means negotiating a scaled down version of much the same obstacles.

Agility training is fun in every respect - the dogs love it and so do their owners. Competition at the top level is extremely high, but along the way much fun can be had in good company with both dogs and humans.

FLYBALL

ANOTHER VERY RECENTLY introduced competitive sport - Flyball - is another in which dogs and owners show their energy and enthusiasm. Working in teams, dogs race each other, cleverly releasing and catching a ball en route. The atmosphere is electrifying and this, too, is a great spectator sport, one particularly enjoyed by Crufts' audiences who watch the competition played at the highest level.

OBEDIENCE

THERE IS PLENTY OF OPPORTUNITY for Obedience competition at various levels throughout the country. Some dogs shows, Exemption events included, host Obedience as well as Show classes. Such dogs have been trained to do things such as walk, sit, lie down, wait and retrieve at various competitive levels of ability. Even if one has no intention of progressing far in competitive Obedience, basic obedience classes are especially useful for owners who wish to have well behaved, well trained pets rather than show dogs.

HEELWORK TO MUSIC

ADAPTED FROM NORMAL obedience work is the increasingly popular 'Heelwork to Music', where dogs perform obedience, timed to synchronise with music, the speed of movements being altered accordingly. The skill of the handlers and dogs is really something which needs to be seen to be believed, and obviously an understanding of the amount of work involved in obedience work helps one to appreciate the time and effort which has gone into training for this, the newest competitive event with dogs, one which also makes for thoroughly enjoyable demonstrations.

Top and Above
Obedience training requires time and patience. It can be done for its own sake or taken further – training Dogs for the Blind, for example.

Left
There are a number of training aids available. This one is designed for retrieving.

Classifying Dogs

IN DECADES PAST, there have been varying theories about which animals the dog is most closely related to, Indeed even well-respected writers have changed their views with the passage of time. Now it seems that there is conclusive evidence that our domestic canine friend owes its direct origins to the wolf.

WOLVES

Right
Some people believe that the dingo is descended from the Phu Quoc of eastern Asia.

Bottom
Pariah dogs are natural breeds rather than mongrels, but few are domesticated; instead they form packs and survive mainly by scavenging.

LIKE DOGS, WOLVES VARY greatly in size, the largest being the North American wolf which migrated from Eurasia where it evolved. The European grey wolf, although still existing in central and eastern Europe, on the Iberian peninsula and in Scandinavia, has now been eliminated by man in most of western Europe. Smaller sub-species include the Red wolf; small and lean, it weighs only 15–30 kg (33--66 lb) but even this is now thought possibly extinct in the wild, although its blood appears to run through the veins of other wolf-like animals which can still be found, including the coyote.

MEXICAN WOLF

THE SMALL MEXICAN WOLF still exists in the mountain regions of central Mexico and the Asiatic or Arab wolf, likely to be progenitor of many Asian and European dogs, is still found extensively throughout Asia. This adaptable and sociable animal has certainly inhabited areas of the world from which the dog has emerged.

OTHER WOLVES

THERE ARE OTHER FASCINATING sub-species of wolf which are now definitely extinct. The Kenai wolf of Alaska weighed in the region of 45 kg (100 lb) and was closely related to the Grey wolf, while the Newfoundland White wolf, again related to the Grey, was sadly driven to extinction near the beginning of the twentieth century, as was the small Japanese Wolf.

> **DOG FACT:**
> The largest dog show was Crufts' Centenary Show in 1991 with 22,993 dogs.

COYOTE

THE COYOTE IS ANOTHER closely related wild canid which, less sociable than the wolf, is a lone hunter although it does form packs with blood relatives in defence of territory or food. Now inhabiting Mexico and Alaska, and the Pacific coast to Central Canada and New England, the coyote moved both to the north and east as the wolf population in the United States was decimated by humans.

> **DOG FACT:**
> 672 dogs of 103 breeds were involved in the Great North Dog Walk in 1996.

The coyote, like the jackal, is capable of breeding with both the wolf and with domestic dogs, but although somewhat similar in appearance to the dog we know as a domestic pet, the habits of both animals are further removed from the domestic dog than are those of the wolf.

THE FOX FAMILY

THROUGHOUT THE world there are many other wild dogs which are more distantly related to today's fireside companion than wolf, coyote and jackal. The fox family falls among these, as does the maned wolf, dhole and African wild dog. The latter has an unusual coat pattern and is renowned for its hunting abilities.

DINGOS

ACCORDING TO SOME theories, dingoes may have descended from the Phu Quoc dogs of eastern Asia, having been taken to Australia by seafarers. Although the men did not survive, the dogs did, and certainly many dingoes have been reared by Aboriginal families. Dingoes, though, developed a taste for killing and they prey on small marsupials, sheep, chickens and other domestic livestock. Indeed there are many who believe that this tantalising, and often vilified, canid is largely responsible for the extinction of the Tasmanian wolf.

While some consider that the dingo may have arrived in Australia as long as 9,000 years ago, another theory is that it was once a domestic pet and has since turned wild although those who have tried to train the dingo have maintained that this could never have been so, for it is so difficult to train. None the less, there is no doubt that the relationship between the dingo and the Australian Aboriginal has been a close one, which has undoubtedly been highly successful for both.

It cannot be denied that there are people who train and live alongside both dingoes and wolves without encountering major problems. Having said that it is of extreme importance that anyone taking part in such a programme is utterly aware that,

although there are similarities, these animals have many different behaviour patterns from those we take for granted in the domestic dog, and that some individuals are more well disposed to human beings than others.

PARIAH DOGS

ALTHOUGH NOT RECOGNISED as completely wild, the Pariah dogs which scatter the world do not fall into any other category within this book and so are deserving of mention here. Pariahs, also called Pi dogs, are found widely in Asia and North Africa, primarily living as scavengers, forming packs and keeping strictly within the bounds of their own quarter; they are a well-defined group of natural breeds which have remained relatively pure-bred. Not all ownerless street dogs in these parts of the world are Pariahs, but the true Pariah is certainly not just a mongrel as many would say. However, some have been tamed by people and live more closely in the community, and after two or three generations are born relatively tame.

Top
The dingo is unpopular with many farmers because it may kill stock. However, the Australian Aboriginals have often formed a close relationship with it to their mutual benefit.

DOG FACT:
It is now thought that dingoes descended from the Phu Quoc dog.

Pedigrees and Crossbreeds

A DOG IS KNOWN AS being a pedigree if both the parents are pure-bred and have been known for a number of generations. Unless the parentage of the dog can be proven, it cannot officially be registered with the Kennel Club in Great Britain.

Right
Each breed has its own official standard drawn up by the breed club and ratified by the ruling body.

Bottom
The Basset Hound originated in France but is now popular in Britain and the United States.

THE KENNEL CLUB

SET UP AS A RULING BODY in 1873, an early task of the Kennel Club was to compile a *Stud Book* containing important documentary information and published annually.

Another important publication is the *Breed Records Supplements* which, published quarterly, contain all litters registered, transfers of ownership and show titles attained, as well as certificates issued under the KC/BVA health scheme.

Well in excess of four million dogs have now been registered with the English Kennel Club and it currently recognises 189 individual breeds, each of which has its own breed standard, officially published by the ruling body but drawn up with the help of breed clubs.

Standards are regularly reviewed and occasionally amended, especially important for breeds which have been newly introduced to Britain and of which, initially, only a limited number of dogs have been seen.

FOREIGN BREED ORGANISATIONS

SIMILAR SYSTEMS ARE IN OPERATION in other countries, although rules vary quite considerably and breeds and individual dogs recognised in one country are not automatically accepted for registration in another. The English Kennel Club has a reciprocal agreement with many different countries which helps canine enthusiasts to work together throughout the world.

There are several major organisations which have control over pedigree dogs, among them the English Kennel Club, Federation Cynologique International, known universally as FCI, and the American Kennel Club. In Australia there is the Australian National Kennel Council and, in addition, there are various other Canine and Kennel Control councils for different areas of this enormous country.

CONTROLLING BREED STANDARDS

AS IS THE CASE IN MOST countries, registration with a Kennel Club does not guarantee the quality of the dog, but the responsibility must rest with breeders to ensure that the pedigree dogs they bring into this world are as healthy as possible. This responsibility of course rests also with breeders of any dog, whether they be pedigree, crossbreed or mongrel. Dogs are all living creatures and as such deserve to have been brought into this world with due care and attention, and every litter, whatever its parentage or monetary value, should be given the best possible start in life.

Pedigree dogs, like others, come in all shapes and sizes. There are enormous heavyweights and tiny Toy breeds, those with long coats needing a great deal of attention, others with short ones which take little more than a quick rub over with a clean cloth. Some, like the Mexican Hairless and Chinese Crested Dogs, are hairless breeds, though in such cases their skin usually needs attention to ensure that it does not become too dry. One of the major benefits of buying a pedigree dog is that one knows more or less what to expect, although undoubtedly there are many differences, even within a breed, depending on the bloodlines involved and of course on the care taken in planning and breeding.

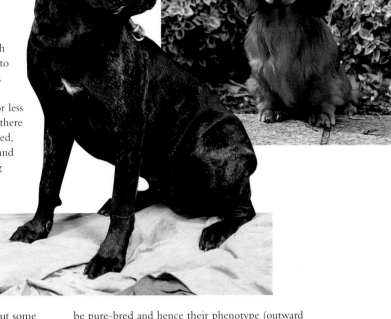

CROSSBREEDS

CROSSBREEDS ARE DOGS of which one parent is of one breed and the other something different, but again both sire and dam are pure-bred dogs. Occasionally mistakes simply happen and a crossbreed is produced, but some people decide to crossbreed by design. This may simply be because a certain combination appeals, but unfortunately it can also be used merely as a vehicle for cashing in on puppy sales.

SELECTIVE BREEDING

OCCASIONALLY IT happens that when selectively bred a cross-breed eventually gains official registration in its own country. The USA's Kyi Leo is one such example, a new breed which originally came about due to the accidental mating between a Lhasa Apso and a Maltese, but then became widespread and popular in its own right.

In taking on a cross-bred dog there should at least be some indication of what the puppies will grow up to be in adulthood, for both parents will be pure-bred and hence their phenotype (outward appearance) will be known. However if, for example, one breeds a Lhasa Apso which is long-coated to a Poodle which has a curly coat, the chances are that some of the offspring will resemble their sire and some their dam, while some will be a complete mixture of the two. It should go without saying that none of the puppies can be classified as pure-bred, even though it is possible that some may look like a fair representation of one of the two breeds. This is because genetically each puppy will carry genes of both sire and dam so that if they go on to produce puppies of their own their offspring may not resemble them, possibly looking more like the grandsire or grand-dam.

Top

There are six breeds of Dachshund: a miniature and standard variety of Smooth-haired, Long-haired and Wire-haired.

Top Left

This crossbreed comes from a cross between an English Mastiff and a Neopolitan Mastiff.

Left

A Lhasa Apso has been crossed with a Poodle to create an appealing crossbreed with characteristics of each original breed.

Non-Pedigree Dogs

DOGS WHICH ARE of completely mixed parentage are called mongrels; they can make lovely pets. Although one hears numerous stories of mongrels being abandoned and left to roam, there are many others which are well cared for and much loved pets, providing just as much pleasure and companionship as a pedigree dog, some indeed bred together from a sire and dam selected for their attributes.

TAKING ON A MONGREL PUPPY

Right

Although mongrels cannot be entered in regular shows, the Novelty classes, such as Fancy Dress, at Exemption shows allow owners to indulge in some fun and socialising.

ONE OF THE MAJOR PROBLEMS in obtaining a mongrel puppy is not really knowing how it may turn out in adulthood. A small, fluffy youngster can grow into a large, strong animal, probably much larger than anticipated and not suitable for one's home or lifestyle. For those considering taking on a mongrel from puppyhood, a fair guideline is the size of its feet; big, heavy dogs usually have large feet as youngsters.

Without knowing its parentage and breeding further back, temperament is another difficult thing to assess in a young dog, although obviously if the sire and dam are known this is an indicator of the sort of temperament one might expect. It is, however, necessary to bear in mind that characteristics, both good and bad, can crop up unexpectedly several generations on.

RESCUE DOGS

TAKING ON ANY DOG, mongrel or purebred, from a rescue society brings with it a certain amount of anxiety and risk. All good rescue societies try to find out as much as possible about a dog's background history and the circumstances which have led to the necessity of re-homing, but this is not always possible. Added to this, owners wishing to part with their pets are not always fully honest about the reason why. (Of course this applies also to pedigree dogs seeking new homes.) For these reasons it is important to find out as much as possible about any known background and the type of environment in which the dog has lived previously. Much as new owners would sometimes like to make contact with the previous owner, in the majority of cases rescue societies have a rule that no contact addresses can be passed on.

A mongrel dog needs just as much love and attention as any other and will need quality food and sufficient exercise for that particular dog's build. Although not eligible for competition in most shows, the

DOG FACT:

An indication of a heavy adult coat is when the coat on the tummy of young puppies is dense.

Lurchers are the result of an intentional cross between what is termed a Longdog, one of the sighthounds or similar, and usually a herding dog of some kind. They might also be the result of a mating by parents which had been bred in this way. Opinions differ as to exactly which crosses constitute a true Lurcher, but a collie/greyhound cross is usually well thought of. Likewise opinions vary somewhat as to the meaning of the term 'Longdog', some thinking it to be restricted to a cross between two kinds of coursing dog, while others include also pure-bred coursing hounds. In these circumstances, one can fully understand why, although bred with some care, such dogs cannot possibly be registered breeds with the Kennel Club.

Lurchers and Longdogs, like many representatives of pedigree sighthound breeds, are used both for coursing and, more recently, lure coursing, the latter an enjoyable exercise for dogs and owners without causing death and injury to live prey.

Although not officially recognised for exhibition purposes, white and long-coated German Shepherd Dogs also have a reasonably strong following. They have their own club, although not recognised by the Kennel Club, and are just as able to take part in obedience and agility events and such like as are their more familiarly coloured close relations. The Lucas Terrier, again unrecognised by the Kennel Club, also has enthusiasts and was created by Sir Jocelyn Lucas who bred Sealyham bitches with Norfolk Terrier dogs in the 1950s.

> **DOG FACT:**
> Sick people were treated by the licking of dogs; in successful treatments offerings were made.

Novelty classes at Exemption shows can provide great fun, combined with an opportunity to meet like-minded people who also love their pet mongrels. Other activities in which mongrels can take part are those of obedience, agility, flyball and now also heelwork to music.

UNRECOGNISED 'BREEDS'

THERE IS A HANDFUL of 'breeds', or varieties of breeds, some of them very popular, which are not recognised by the English Kennel Club. The Jack Russell Terrier, though recognised in some countries and therefore described in more detail elsewhere in this book, is one such dog, a great character and with a strong following. Generally small and fairly low to the ground, its size and construction does vary somewhat but often Jack Russells are bred with considerable care and forethought and make good working terriers and excellent, gentle and fun companions.

The Lurcher is another type of dog bred by design, indeed these dogs even have their own shows which are well supported by enthusiasts.

Top
Despite being a very popular breed, the Jack Russell Terrier is not recognised by the English Kennel Club.

Top Left
The Lurcher is the result of crossbreeding but, because the results are not standardised, it is not recognised as an official breed.

Left
A mongrel may be just as appealing as a pedigree dog and can have as much, if not more, character.

Old Dog Breeds

SEARCHING THROUGH recorded histories of the canine race, one can find many breeds that are no longer familiar, although their blood undoubtedly still runs through the veins of many others dogs that are with us today.

REVIVING BREEDS

SOMETIMES BREEDS THOUGHT to have become extinct, or on the verge of extinction, have been revived by one or more people who have felt that the breed should be saved by whatever means possible. Invariably this has involved incorporating other selected breeds in a carefully planned programme and it has, understandably, taken many generations before breeders felt they had even begun to achieve their aim. In some cases their long term efforts have proved successful, in others they have been less so, and the breed which has emerged seems not quite to faithfully represent the original.

Right
This young Alco puppy may have been used as a lapdog.

Bottom
The Hare Indian Dog lived in North America and hunted by sight like a gaze hound.

ALCO

IN 1840 THE ALCO was described as 'still to be fully made out' and for a long while was known only from a drawing by Fernandez who gave it the name *Michua canens* and, to add further confusion, the Alco was also called *Yzicinte potzotli*.

Viewed by some as a race of shepherd dog, it had a small head, short neck and a very bulky body. Its colour was said usually to be white and yellow, but according to Buffon's *Natural History* it was white and black, with rufous spots above the eyes. Certainly it was a lap dog kept by women-folk, but opinion was that it sometimes returned to its feral state.

One specimen of the breed was brought to the UK from Mexico and upon its death it was stuffed and shown in an exhibition of Mexican curiosities in London. Although called one 'of the wild race', when it appeared in England many considered it to be a Newfoundland puppy, even though the connection between the two breeds is hard to imagine. This dog was 'small with rather a large head; elongated occiput; full muzzle; pendulous ears; having long soft hair on the body. In colour, it was entirely white, excepting a large black spot covering each ear, and a part of the forehead and cheek, with a fulvous mark above each eye, and another black spot on the rump; the tail was rather long, well fringed, and white.'

CARRIER DOG OF THE INDIANS

THE CARRIER DOG of the Indians, also known as the Techici of Mexico, was a long-backed, heavy-looking animal with 'a terrier's mouth, tail and colours'. The hair was smoother than that of most terriers, short but not woolly. The ears were cropped and in comparison with the body length the legs were reasonably short, but not bent.

DOG OF THE NORTH AMERICAN INDIANS

ANOTHER DOG FOUND in North America was called the Dog of the North American Indians. Classified as a watchdog, it was an indigenous breed but may have been more wild, or at least feral, rather than truly domesticated. Those pictured here in 1840 were described as equal in size to 'a spaniel' and of 'unmixed blood', although 'hostile to the white man'. A distinctive feature was

The Hare-Indian Dog. (Youatt.)

the head which formed an equilateral triangle when measured from the nose tip to the tip of each ear. The coat colour was similar to that of the wolf, and though the dog reputedly looked savage, it was said never to utter a howl or a bark.

HARE INDIAN DOG

THE HARE INDIAN DOG inhabited areas near the Mackenzie River and the Great Lake of America, where it hunted moose and reindeer by sight, aided occasionally by its powers of scent. Although its general body shape gave the suggestion that it would today have been included in a Pastoral Group, its head shape, elongation and sharpness of muzzle caused the early canine authority, 'Stonehenge', to include it in the section relating to domestic dogs which hunted chiefly by sight and killed their game for use by man.

Depth of chest, tucked-up flank and muscular quarters marked this as a dog of speed. Although light in frame and not designed to hold any animal of considerable bulk, its length of toe and the width of web between each allowed it to bound over the snow without sinking. Easily able to overtake its quarry, it held this at bay until hunters arrived. Coat colour was white with patches of greyish-black or brown, and the erect ears were wide at their base and pointed at the tip, giving an appearance of great vivacity and sprit.

The dog featured here was one of three Hare Indian Dogs housed in London's Zoological Gardens. They were gentle and confident but none survived for long due to lack of exercise. In their homeland these dogs were good tempered and manageable, and were valuable to the Indians, who lived almost entirely off the produce of the chase. They never barked but howled and whined, although the youngest of the three at the Zoological Gardens, born a few days after its parents' arrival, barked like the dogs housed close by.

Top
The Carrier Dog of the Indians had short legs and a terrier's mouth.

Bottom
Always at least partly feral, the Dog of the North American Indians may have been used as a guard dog.

was so woolly, dense and fine that it was described as fleece or fur. When shorn off, the coat was described as being 'sufficiently inter-woven to lift the whole pro-duce of one animal by grasping a single handful'. This dog's hair was spun, with other hair, into gar-ments and it was thought in the nineteenth century that this breed would have been especially useful if intro-duced to the peasantry of Norway and Scotland.

HOUNDS

THE TALBOT HOUND is known to us visually today for it is pictured from time to time on signs outside public houses. The Talbot was much like the Bloodhound and differed only slightly from what were called the Southern and Northern Hounds. All were deep-mouthed and heavy, the Northern having a more slender head, longer foreface and more shallow flews than the Southern, which was found in the south of England, in Devon and in Wales.

Just before the middle of the nineteenth cen-tury several Southern Hounds were kept in the village of Aveton Gifford in Devon, where several wealthy farmers each kept two or three hounds. They had an excellent sense of smell and could trail a scent for longer and get in to places fox-hunting hounds could not reach.

The Talbot is variously described by different early authors, but seems to have been a breed mid-way between a Northern and Southern Hound. It had a large head, very broad nose and pendulous ears, with a rather rough coat. Its colour was usually pure white, but there are other reports of it having been pied, although it appears that hounds showing white were preferred to other colours. In early manuscript illuminations the Talbot was not portrayed as being particularly large, but according to most accounts it

Right
Hounds were used in early times to hunt deer and wild boar.

Bottom
The Talbot Hound appears to have been a cross between Northern and Southern Hounds.

ASIATIC NOOTKA DOG

MOVING NORTHWARDS, in the early part of the nineteenth century there is reference to the Asiatic Nootka Dog, seemingly an ancestor of the Eskimo Dog and Newfoundland breeds. A large dog, the Nootka was docile, with pointed, upright ears. Found in white, brown and black, the breed's chief value was its immense amount of coat which

did attain considerable stature. There is also indication that it was kept more for 'show' than for use.

The ancient house of Shrewsbury had very strong connections with the Talbot, a breed used on the family's coat of arms, and the head of this breed also formed the crest of several old princely families in Germany. The St Hubert Hound, too, was either the same as the Talbot or closely allied. In 1867 there were still several packs of very heavy, slow hounds in Devon, Yorkshire, Sussex and South Wales, but there was then doubt that these were truly representative of the original stock. In 1931 an eminent canine author, Edward Ash, said that at one time keepers in the New Forest were required to keep a couple of 'Bloodhounds' on their walk. He also says that these particular 'Bloodhounds' were known as Talbots. One of the keepers claimed that Talbots had been in his family for over 300 years. Certainly there is every likelihood that the Talbot Hound was the oldest scenting hound in Britain but is sadly no longer in our midst.

TURNSPIT

BY 1861 THE industrious little Turnspit was considered almost extinct. It varied somewhat in type and was not really a 'breed' in the true sense of the word, but all had short legs and a relatively long body. They were bred in this manner so that they could fit into the wheels which turned the roasting spits in the kitchens of huge houses. In general, their legs were crooked, their ears pendant and tails curled. The dogs usually worked in pairs and were last seen in Wales and in Germany.

TRUFFLE DOG

THE TRUFFLE DOG seems first to have arrived in Britain in the mid-seventeenth century, brought by a Spaniard who made a great deal of money from the truffles located in his native country by his dog. Pigs were commonly used by farmers for

sniffing truffles out, but the Truffle Dog had a very sharp sense of smell. Never officially recognised by the English Kennel Club, it did nevertheless receive recognition in France and Scandinavia under the name Truffleur and was actually shown at London's Botanical Gardens. Truffles lay just under the surface of the ground and a good

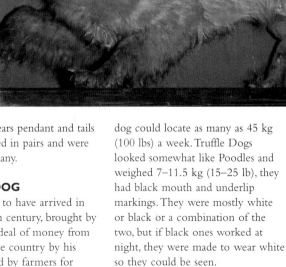

dog could locate as many as 45 kg (100 lbs) a week. Truffle Dogs looked somewhat like Poodles and weighed 7–11.5 kg (15–25 lb), they had black mouth and underlip markings. They were mostly white or black or a combination of the two, but if black ones worked at night, they were made to wear white so they could be seen.

Left
The Southern Hound was pied in colour and were excellent scent followers.

Below Left
The odd little Turnspit dog is now sadly extinct.

Bottom
The Truffle Dog was introduced from Spain in the mid-17th century.

following descriptions, some with their accompanying originally coloured drawings, are taken specifically from the Naturalists Library, as to incorporate descriptions of breeds given by other authors would serve to complicate the issue.

SPANIELS AND WATER-DOGS

LITTLE WAS SAID ABOUT the King Charles Spaniel except that it was a beautiful breed, usually black and white and presumed to be the parent of the Cocker which was shorter in the back than the King Charles.

As far as Cockers were concerned, the colours of Blenheim, Marlborough and Pyrame were given in the book, but in black spaniels, the colour was meant to be relieved by the presence of 'fire spots' above the eyes, with the same sort of marking on the chest and feet.

SETTERS AND WATER-DOGS

THE SETTER WAS NOTED for its long, silky hair and was usually thought of as a large breed of spaniel which originated from the Spanish peninsula. It was believed that the head of this breed showed a remarkable development of the brain. The intelligence of the Setter, its affection and docility, were said to have been unequalled by any other kind of dog. High prices were paid for Setters in Ireland where the more ancient colours were recognised as deep chestnut and white, or red. However, in England, they were mostly white with either black or brown marks.

The Springer as described in 1840 was quite different from the breed we know by that name today. Described as smaller than the Setter it was 'of elegant form and gay aspect'. Despite the accompanying illustrative material which shows a predominantly red coat, it was usually white with red spots, and a black nose and palate.

DOGS AS THEY WERE

IN THE EARLY NINETEENTH century, several decades prior to the formation of England's Kennel Club, a great many dogs were classified as individual breeds. In some cases the names are obscure and it has not always possible even to locate a drawing which fits the written description but fortunately W. H. Lizars' *Naturalist's Library*, published in 1840, gives a wonderful insight into examples of breeds as they were at that time. Many of these are breeds still familiar to us today, but some have been developed and divided into several different breeds. Others, in their appearance, only vaguely resemble breeds with which we are familiar now.

Classification has changed substantially over time, as dogs in what was described as the 'Hound' section include breeds called the King Charles, Setter, Spaniel, Springer, Cocker, Pointer and the Water-dog or Poodle. It would therefore appear that at that time the term 'Hound' could be interpreted as 'Sporting Dog' as, to add to the complexity, although some true hound breeds were included, many sighthounds were also classified separately as 'Greyhounds'.

Of course there were other notable writers on the subject of dogs whose works were published in the nineteenth century (most of them later), but so as to give readers as clear as possible an indication of views in the first half of that century the

Top Right
Foxhounds were classified as a distinct dog breed by 1840.

Bottom Right
Springer Spaniels were popular game and gun dogs.

During this period the Water-dog was also referred to as the Barbet of the Continent, and occasionally they were also known as the Poodle. Even though the Setter was described as having remarkable brain development for a dog, the Water-dog was said to have had a cerebral space more developed than any other canine. This breed was intelligent and attached to its master, and renowned for its perseverance in finding lost property. In one instance a gold coin had inadvertently been dropped by the owner, and the dog insisted on watching the coin so carefully that it refused all food until the coin had been recovered.

The legs of the Water-dog or Poodle were short and this breed's long, curly hair was black, white or sometimes rufous. Height was 18–20 inches (46–51 cm). The breed is mentioned as being found in Germany, France, Spain and the Netherlands and apparently a 'coarser, crisped-haired' Water-dog had long been known to England's middle classes. Such a dog was also familiar to fishermen and professional waterfowl shooters. Occasionally the Water-dog was found in and around London, but was mainly used in the countryside for the brutal sport of hunting and worrying to death domestic ducks which were placed on a pond for that very purpose.

THE SPRINGER.

WOLF DOGS

THE ALPINE or Great St Bernard was classified as a Wolf Dog, along with others such as the Esquimaux Dog, Newfoundland and Shepherd's Dog. The St Bernard, which was not found in great numbers, was said to have a head and ears like those of a water spaniel. Its colour was principally white, with black or fulvous spots, but some were marked with grey, liver colouring and 'black clouds'; these had close, short hair and although they carried out the same duties in mountainous regions, they were thought to carry either blood of the French Matin or of Danish Dogs.

Right
The Poodle had short legs and was also known as a Water-dog; Bulldogs were of moderate size and were noted for its strength.

Bottom
The Great St Bernard did not much resemble today's breed; the coat was shorter and contained more white.

St Bernards were trained to carry baskets of food and wine, sallying forth from the Hospice of Saint Bernard in search of travellers who had lost their way. Bass, though, was employed by the local postman to carry a letter bag from house to house. On one occasion when the postman was taken ill, another took his place, and did not allow Bass to take charge of the bag because he did not know of the normal working relationship between the usual pair. The story goes that eventually the dog put one of his great paws on each shoulder and laid the new postman flat on his back in the road then, quietly picking up the bag, Bass continued on his usual route, bag in mouth.

The Newfoundland was another large and powerful breed, considered a handsome dog and by then relatively common in Britain. However there were claims that it had been partially crossed with other dogs and so differed somewhat from the indigenous breed of America. Generally the Newfoundland was white, spotted with black, and some were of immense size. One was especially trained to show his great size by placing his forefeet against the lintel of any room door upon command. In 1840 it was generally thought that the original stock was smaller than the very large dogs of this breed found in England at that time.

Stories abounded concerning the Newfoundland's ability and prowess in water, and the breed's kindly disposition made training easy when this dog was used in the field. It was estimated that in the 1830s there were 2,000 or more such dogs in

Newfoundland. These were largely left to their own devices throughout the fishing season, after which time they were primarily used to pull wood, fish and other merchandise to the market from remote country areas. A good dog was considered quite capable of maintaining its master during the winter months.

In the early nineteenth century, several Esquimaux Dogs arrived in England, having been brought back from an Arctic expedition. Many of these were black and white or dingy white, although those found on the Labrador coast were frequently brown and white. The drawing shown here is of a dog owned by a gentleman who lived in Princes Street Gardens in Edinburgh. It was in that very street that the dog was described as having shown exceptional faithfulness when his master slipped and fell down a steep bank. The dog immediately seized him by the coat and helped to pick him up. This particular Esquimaux Dog was thought to resemble the fox by way of cunning, as he would strew his meat around him to induce fowl and rats to come within reach while he lay in wait, possibly pretending to be asleep. As the hens and rats crept forwards, the dog would pounce on them, always with success.

In terms of intellect the Shepherd's Dog or Sheep Dog was thought scarcely inferior to the Newfoundland, indeed it was considered superior to that bred in its acceptance of lengthy training sessions. In Scotland its coat colours were more mixed than those in England, but in both countries the coat was rather long, and rough. Seldom did the Shepherd's Dog reach 61 cm (24 in) in height but it was muscular in construction and had a long, rather pointed nose.

THE BULL-DOG BREEDS

THE *NATURALIST'S LIBRARY* gives a somewhat uncomplimentary description of Bull breeds as described by the Romans, their 'lips sordid and hanging loose, looking like monsters'. The writer of 1840 acknowledged that what he described as

the Bull-Dog known then was smaller than similar breeds described centuries earlier, but still they proved more than a match for a caged lion. Of moderate size, the Bull-Dog was moulded for

strength and elasticity. With its lower jaw projecting beyond the upper and frequent redness about the eyes, the breed produced a most forbidding aspect. A Bull-Dog had been witnessed pinning down an American bison, although the outcome was that the dog came off worse in the end.

Left
A powerful breed, the original Newfoundland dog was black, not white, in contrast to its European counterpart.

Below Left
Esquimax dogs were brought to England from the Arctic in the early 19th century.

GREYHOUNDS

EVEN IN 1840 the British Greyhound was a very well-known breed and so little was written about it, except to say that was 'unrivalled in the open country for speed, beauty and spirit, untied with docility' – surely praise indeed.

The breed called the Scottish Greyhound, now familiar to us as the Deerhound, was thought to

Top
A very fast hound with a gentle disposition, the British Greyhound was a firm favourite as a hunting dog.

Right
The Isle of Skye Terrier was pale in colour, and sometimes even white.

have higher intellectual abilities than the Russian Hounds, in part because it had been at some time crossed with the Stag Hound. The Irish Greyhound, now known as the Wolfhound, was thought to have originally been the same as the Scottish hound. According to some opinions it was not found in Ireland in the form known then until the Danes arrived on Irish coasts, even though no such breed was known in Scandinavian countries.

The earliest colour of the breed was thought to be buff or pale ochre and it was considered that the ancient race, similar to the Scottish, was crossed with the Danish Dog by 'Northmen', thereby increasing its great stature. In 1840 no two specimens of the Irish Greyhound were said to be alike in structure or colour so mastiff, stag-hound or blood-hounds may have crossed with early dogs to produce those then known. The dog was believed to be the largest in western Europe and the decline in wolves in Ireland was due, at least in part, to this breed's work.

TERRIERS

CONSIDERED INDIGENOUS to Britain, no dog carried its head so high nor so boldly as did the Terrier, which expressed a lively energy. There were, however, two evident varieties, though it seemed uncertain whether these had emerged by design or by accident.

The first variety was smooth, rounded and rather elegant, usually black in colour with tan spots over the eyes and the same colour on the belly and other extremities. Sometimes these terriers were also white. Their muzzle was sharp, their eyes bright and lively, the ears pointed or slightly turned down, while the tail was carried high and was rather bowed.

The second variety was considered a 'more genuine' breed, usually called the wire-haired or Scottish terrier, although they were also sometimes known as the Isle of Skye Terrier. The muzzle was shorter and fuller, the limbs more stout and the coat hard and shaggy. In colour the Scottish terrier was a pale sandy or ochre, sometimes white.

The legs of neither type of terrier, however, were as crooked as those of the Turnspit, nor were their backs so long. In Germany there was a large rough terrier employed to rouse even the fiercest beasts of the forest from their lairs in the thickest underwood. Such terriers worked with audacity and noisy clamour, never failing to achieve their purpose. These were usually a wolfish grey-brown, with some white around the neck and chest and a well-fringed tail curled over the back.

In England it could easily be seen that terriers had been crossed with working sheep and cattle dogs and most notable among these was the Bull-Terrier, so called because of its make-up. This was disparagingly described as 'the most determined and savage race known'. It was used in general 'for purposes little honourable to human nature, and most disgraceful to the lower orders of England, where, for the sake of betting, the true wild game qualities of the animals [were] exhibited in mutual combats, in which neither will give up while life remains, and the last struggle is borne without a groan!'.

DALMATIANS AND BOAR-HOUNDS

THE REASON GIVEN FOR including the Dalmatian or Coach Dog in the section on hounds was because of this breed's general structure. Although accepted as being a very handsome dog and not inferior in any way to the true hound breeds in elegance of form and beauty of marking, none-the-less it lacked scenting ability and sagacity of most hounds. As a result, it was invariably entrusted to the stables where it kept company with horses. Apart from a drawing of a dog of the 1840s, the *Naturalist's Library* also showed a dog which had

MASTIFF OF TIBET.

been taken to Britain from India, described as having 'small half dejected ears, and a grey-hound-like form'. It was believed possible that the breed known in Britain in the 1840s was descended from that dog.

The Suliot Dog, which was also known as the German Boar-Hound, was one of the largest breeds known in the 1840s, thought likely to be the true Molosser of antiquity. It was full in mouth, fierce, coarse in aspect and rugged in coat. None had been seen without ears which were cropped and the tail was always rough, with straggling hair. In colour they were tan, with brown or black on the back, shoulders and about the ears, although these colours described do not tie in at all with those portrayed in the accompanying drawing.

In the wars between Austria and the Turks, Moslem soldiers employed many such dogs to guard their outposts, and in the course of campaigns many were captured and secured by officers as their private property, or even adopted by the

Imperial Forces as regimental pets. One such dog was presented to the King of Naples and was reported to have been the biggest dog in the world – 122 cm (4 ft) high at the shoulder. The few that had been seen were described as being little smaller than Shetland ponies. The head of the dog resembled that of the large Danish Dog (now known as the Great Dane), than that of the Mastiff of today.

Dogs popular in Britain in the early nineteenth century were undoubtedly extremely varied and even at that time there were dogs to appeal to all tastes, just as there are today.

Top
Terriers were traditionally used as ratting dogs.

Left
Tibetan Mastiffs were brought in to Europe by the 1840s.

Below Left
It was thought that German Boar Hounds were the biggest dogs in the world when they were first seen in Europe.

Bottom
A Scotch Terrier worries a badger.

British Dog Breeds

Above
A German
Short-haired
Pointer in action
in the field.

THE ENGLISH KENNEL CLUB is the ruling body that approves or turns down British dog breeds and as such is responsible for registering pedigree dogs, provided that owners choose for this to be done.

KENNEL CLUB RULES

THERE IS SOME misunderstanding between what constitutes a pedigree dog and one which is Kennel Club registered. In effect, provided that ancestry can be proven, any dog can hold a pedigree. Usually it is taken as read that all dogs in that pedigree are of the same breed but in fact there are times when,

Above and
Right
The Griffon
Bruxellois and
an elegant
Afghan Hound.

often for good reason, another breed has been introduced with the aim of improving another. This can indeed cause controversy at the time, especially if it is not sanctioned by the guardians of the breed in question, but with time, and if very carefully monitored, the result can sometimes be beneficial.

However, when another breed has been introduced to a pedigree no full Kennel Club registration can be obtained until the fourth filial generation, as this is intended for pure breeds only.

Under certain circumstances, dogs of breeds which are fully recognised and yet whose breeding is impure (as above) or unverified can obtain registration, but they either has to have been bred under authority granted in advance or, in the case of importation, granted prior to import.

Another condition of Kennel Club registration is that both sire and dam are registered also. In the case of an imported dog registration abroad is acceptable, provided that the English Kennel Club has a reciprocal agreement with that country.

Pure bred imported dogs of breeds not previously recognised by this Kennel Club can apply to

Top
The Rhodesian
Ridgeback was origi-
nally used for in the
hunting of lions.

Above
The Pyrenean
Mountain Dog
has a white coat.

Left
A leading gundog in
Germany, the
Rottweiler is a popu-
lar dog worldwide.

be included on the Imported Breed Register. This is also applicable in cases when a breed has previously been recognised but for which there has been no active registration for ten years. When at least ten specimens of the breed have been accepted an interim breed standard is formulated. Those breeds with Imported Breed Register status may subsequently apply to be transferred to the Breed Register, subject to published guidelines. Dogs on the Imported Register and those still classified as Rare Breeds are not eligible for Championship status. A third register is The Obedience and Working Trials Register, for dogs ineligible for registration on any other register.

Apart from the Scottish and Welsh Kennel Clubs, there are other regional general canine societies in Britain, and numerous individual breed clubs, each of which has been set up for the benefit of the breeding and showing of pedigree dogs.

The Gundog Group

ALTHOUGH DOGS HAVE long been used in relation to hunting it was the advent of the sporting gun which caused gundog breeds to be developed. It was now necessary to locate game before being scared off by the hunter and, when found and brought down by the gun, it had to be collected.

Top
American Cocker Spaniel retrieving a game bird – the bird is almost the same size as this small spaniel.

Right
The Clumber Spaniel is a heavy, big-boned dog and, as a result, is much less popular than the faster breeds.

Below
The German Short-haired Pointer is a lean, athletic and responsive breed which is popular with leisure hunters.

LOCATING GAME

ALL DOGS WITHIN THIS GROUP were developed to help man with his gun, although some breeds are really all-purpose dogs, whilst others have particular duties in the field. Some locate the game, some put it up so that a sportsman can shoot at it, whilst others retrieve it later. Certain breeds are noted for being particularly adept in water.

It is primarily pointers and setters which locate game. They work in front of the guns, indicating exactly where it is to be found, the pointers standing rigidly, often in that familiar pose with one foot raised in mid-stride, carrying out their tails in a straight line. Setters tend to sink down when they have discovered game. Spaniels move the game, either putting birds up in the air or forcing ground game to run, as such they hunt vigorously in front of the guns, yet never causing the target to move out of range.

In general, the larger, stronger breeds are those which retrieve game once it has been killed. These dogs have excellent scenting powers and are able to mark fallen game, watching birds fall and fetching them with little help They can make their way quickly over rough ground and through difficult cover.

Some, as has been said, are capable of performing all functions whilst there also some specialists, such as the Irish Water Spaniel which was developed especially for use in lakes and estuaries, necessitating protection from wet and cold. Gundog people are highly enthusiastic about their breeds, all of which have benefited from generations of training to obey commands. They are also great companions for man.

The sight of the Irish Setter at work with the sun gleaming on its deep, red coat must surely be one of the delights of working in the field, as is the elegant pose of the pointer at work. Coats, their colour, length, texture and the amount of care they require varies substantially, but all gundogs are soft-mouthed breeds whose temperament should be thoroughly reliable. None within the group is exceptionally large, and none very small, with the

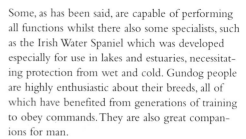

American Cocker Spaniel and Cocker Spaniels at the bottom end of the scale in overall size. However, some are very substantially built and work more slowly, while others are lithe and capable of good speed. Each dog within the group has a subtly different method of working, and today many are kept for work as well as for use in the show-ring. A large percentage of the dogs ate also kept purely for companionship. Of all breeds, in Britain the Labrador Retriever is the most popular, with numbers well in excess of the second most popular breed which is, incidentally, the German Shepherd Dog.

Bracco Italiano

HEIGHT 56-67 cm (22-26.5 in)

Gundog
GROUP **COAT CARE**
large
SIZE **FEEDING**

BREED INFORMATION

NAME	Bracco Italiano
OTHER NAMES	Italian Pointer
OFFICIAL RECOGNITION	Uk Gundog Group; FCI Group 7
COLOUR VARIATIONS	Orange/white; Orange roan; Chestnut/white; Chestnut roan

BREED FACT:
The attractive Bracco Italiano did not arrive in Britain until the last decade of the twentieth century.

A FASHIONABLE BREED in Renaissance Italy, and used for tracking, pointing and retrieving, the Bracco Italiano evolved in Piedmont and Lombardy, possibly the result of crossing the ancient Asiatic Mastiff with the Segugio. Others claim that the breed goes back to the St Hubert Hound. Undoubtedly, both hounds and gundogs are in the breed's ancestry for there was an old practice of mating these together to produce a dog capable of pointing, but with more stamina.

The Bracco Italiano is powerful, muscular and lean, the head long and angular with a pronounced occiput. The oval, intelligent eyes are in shades of amber. Jaunty in bearing, this is a gentle breed with a fine, dense, short, glossy coat. Weight ranges between 25–40 kg (55–88 lb).

Brittany

HEIGHT 47-50 cm (18-20 in)

Gundog
GROUP **COAT CARE**
medium
SIZE **FEEDING**

BREED INFORMATION

NAME	Brittany
OTHER NAMES	Épagneul Français, Brittany Spaniel
OFFICIAL RECOGNITION	Uk Gundog Group; FCI Group 7; AKC Sporting Group

BREED FACT:
The Brittany is used as a companion by many hunters in the USA and in Canada, and in France this is a highly popular breed.

FIRST SHOWN AT THE Paris Dog Show in 1900, the Brittany had already been known in Europe for centuries. Previously called a Brittany Spaniel, in Britain the breed is a relative newcomer, and one of the hunt, point and retrieve breeds. Although fairly light in weight, the breed is well capable of carrying hare or pheasant and is a strong runner, also at home in water. Although classified in some countries as a spaniel, the Brittany resembles a small setter and works rather like a setter or a pointer. The breed's ancestors almost certainly came from Spain.

Workmanlike, compact, lively and squarely built, the Brittany is energetic and intelligent, an affectionate breed, that is always eager to please. The brown or dark brown eyes harmonise in colour with the coat, which can be roan or any of the above colours. The ideal height for this breed is 47–50 cm (18–20 in) and weight 13–15 kg (28–33 lb).

Left
The most popular native breed in France, the Brittany Spaniel has only recently come to Britain.

Gundog

GROUP **COAT CARE**

large

SIZE **FEEDING**

English Setter

HEIGHT 61-68 cm (24-27 in)

○○○○○○○○○○○○○○○○○○○○○○○○○○
BREED INFORMATION

NAME	English Setter
OFFICIAL RECOGNITION	UK Gundog Group; FCI Group 7; AKC Sporting Group
COLOUR VARIATIONS	Black/white; Orange/white; Lemon/white; Liver/white; Tri-colour

BREED FACT:
The English Setter was shown at what many consider to have been the first real dog show, held at Newcastle in 1859.

Right
The English Setter is easy to train and is a responsive worker in the field.

ALTHOUGH THE HISTORY of the English Setter goes back some 500 years, modern representatives of the breed were greatly influenced by Edward Laverack who acquired two pure English Setters in 1825 and began his breeding programme. Later that century Laverack stock was bred with setter stock for hunting.

Standing 61–68 cm (24–27 in) and weighing in the region of 25–30 kg (55–66 lb), the English Setter is clean in outline and elegant both in appearance and in movement. Very active and with a keen game sense, this breed is intensely friendly and good-natured. The long, silky coat is found in a range of interesting colour combinations, black and white (known as 'blue belton'), orange and white (orange belton),

lemon and white (lemon belton), liver and white (liver belton) or tri-colour which is blue belton and tan or liver belton and tan.

Gundog

GROUP **COAT CARE**

large

SIZE **FEEDING**

German Long-haired Pointer

HEIGHT 60-66 cm (23.5-26 in)

○○○○○○○○○○○○○○○○○○○○○○○○○○
BREED INFORMATION

NAME	German Long-haired Pointer
OFFICIAL RECOGNITION	UK Gundog Group
COLOUR VARIATIONS	Brown; Brown/white; Brown/roan; Various roan colours

BREED FACT:
The original breed standard was set up in Germany in 1879, and updated in 1902.

THE GERMAN LONG-HAIRED Pointer was developed in the nineteenth century to produce a long-haired gundog with greater versatility. Principal breeds used in the make-up were Spanish Pointers, Irish and Gordon Setters, small Newfoundlands and French Spaniels. This is primarily a working dog, expected to hunt tirelessly all day, retrieving game from land or water. However, the breed also makes a good companion and watchdog.

Introduced to Britain in 1993, no breed standard has yet been issued by the English Kennel Club. By the close of 1998 there were 25 representatives of the breed in England and 11 in Ireland, several already proving their worth in the field. This strong, muscular dog stands 60–66 cm (23.5–26 in) high and weighs about 30 kg (66 lb). Giving an aristocratic appearance, the muzzle and skull are of equal length, the eyes as dark a brown as possible. Body hair is light, smooth or slightly wavy with good undercoat and the colours are brown, various roan colours and brown with white or roan.

BREED INFORMATION

NAME	German Short-haired Pointer
OTHER NAMES	Deutscher Kurzaariger Vorstehhund
OFFICIAL RECOGNITION	UK Gundog Group; FCI Group 7; AKC Sporting Group

German Short-haired Pointer

HEIGHT 53-64 cm (21-25 in)

Gundog
GROUP **COAT CARE**
large
SIZE **FEEDING**

BREED FACT:
The German Short-haired Pointer was the first hunt, point and retrieve breed to arrive in Britain.

WITH ORIGINS GOING BACK to the Spanish Pointer, a bird-dog which would point, retrieve, trail and also be a family companion was developed by seventeenth century German sportsmen. To achieve this, Bloodhound, Foxhound and later English Pointer blood were introduced to produce the German Short-haired Pointer, a name often abbreviated to GSP.

A noble, steady dog, showing power, endurance and speed, the GSP is alert and energetic with graceful outline. A dual purpose pointer/retriever, the breed has a keen nose coupled with perseverance in searching and initiative in game finding. Excellent in the field and a keen worker, this loyal, biddable dog stands 53–64 cm (21–25 in) and generally weighs 27–32 kg (60–70 lb). The coat, in various combinations of liver, white and black, with spotting and ticking, is short, flat and coarse to touch.

Left
The German Short-haired Pointer is equally good on land and in the water. It is also kind, affectionate and even-tempered.

BREED INFORMATION

NAME	German Wire-haired Pointer
OTHER NAMES	Deutscher Drahthaariger Vorstehhund
OFFICIAL RECOGNITION	UK Gundog Group; FCI Group 7; AKC Sporting Group
COLOUR VARIATIONS	Liver/white; Liver; Black/white

German Wire-haired Pointer

HEIGHT 62-66 cm (24.5-26 in)

Gundog
GROUP **COAT CARE**
large
SIZE **FEEDING**

BREED FACT:
The German Wire-haired Pointer was recognised by the English Kennel Club at Championship Shows from 1986.

BASED ON THE GERMAN Short-haired Pointer and a highly popular shooting dog in Germany, the German Wire-haired Pointer has evolved from what have been considered the best pointers, regardless of their type and size. Other breeds have been used to perfect the coat which is an important feature. The thick, outer coat is no longer than 3.8 cm (1.5 in) and there is a dense undercoat. Although the coat should not hide the body shape it should be sufficiently long to give good protection, this being a dog which excels in both field and water.

Standing 62–66 cm (24.5–26 in) and weighing 25.5–29.5 kg (56–65 lb), the German Wire-haired Pointer is a stylish dog with galloping lines; intelligent, able and dignified. Temperament is bold and outgoing, a breed of kindly, even disposition which is an all-round shooting dog.

Left
Recognised as a breed in 1870, the German Wire-haired Pointer is a hardy worker and a good family dog.

Gundog
GROUP COAT CARE
large
SIZE FEEDING

Gordon Setter

HEIGHT 62-66 cm (24.5-26 in)

○○○○○○○○○○○○○○○○○○○○○○○○○○
BREED INFORMATION

NAME	Gordon Setter
OFFICIAL RECOGNITION	UK Gundog Group; FCI Group 7; AKC Sporting Group
COLOUR VARIATIONS	Coal black with specified tan markings

BREED FACT:
There were black and tan setters in Britain earlier, but the Gordon Setter known today began its development in the eighteenth century

Right
The Gordon Setter used to be known as the Black and Tan Setter and dates back to at least 1726.

BRED ORIGINALLY AT Gordon Castle in Scotland, the Gordon Setter was the first officially recognised Scottish Gundog. The largest and heaviest of the setter family, the breed's ancestors include Bloodhound, Collie and other Setters, perhaps also including old Spaniel blood. This is both the heaviest and slowest of the setters but one which is built to work steadily all day. The British Gordon Setter Club was founded in 1927.

This outgoing, stylish breed is of even disposition, an intelligent dog, able and dignified. Symmetrical in conformation, the Gordon Setter has particularly good galloping qualities and loves a country environment. The shining coat is coal black in colour, without rustiness but with chestnut-red markings, its length and weight requiring time to dry. Height is 62–66 cm (24.5–26 in) and weight 25.5–29.5 kg (56–65 lb).

Gundog
GROUP COAT CARE
large
SIZE FEEDING

Hungarian Vizsla

HEIGHT 53-64 cm (21-25 in)

○○○○○○○○○○○○○○○○○○○○○○○○○○
BREED INFORMATION

NAME	Hungarian Vizsla
OTHER NAMES	Rövidszörü Magyar Vizsla
OFFICIAL RECOGNITION	UK Gundog Group; FCI Group 7; AKC Sporting Group
COLOUR VARIATIONS	Russet-gold

BREED FACT:
After the Russian occupation in 1945, many Hungarians fled to Austria, taking their native dogs.

THE HUNGARIAN VIZSLA is the national dog of Hungarian sportsmen, and a dog which has been identified as a Vizsla has been found in a fourteenth century Hungarian manuscript. The breed almost died out between the two world wars, but has survived thanks to a few dedicated supporters.

A breed of distinguished appearance with medium bone, the Hungarian Vizsla has graceful movement with a lively trot and a ground-covering gallop. Robust and medium boned, the breed stands 53–64 cm (21–25 in) high and weighs 20–30 kg (48.5–66 lb). Lively, intelligent, obedient, sensitive, very affectionate and easily trained, this dog was bred to hunt fur and feather, pointing and retrieving both from land and water. The striking, russet-gold coat is short, straight, dense, smooth and shiny, feeling greasy to the touch. Although small white spots on chest and feet are acceptable, they are undesirable.

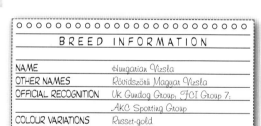

Hungarian Wire-haired Vizsla

HEIGHT 53-64 cm (21-25 in)

Gundog

GROUP   **COAT CARE**

large

SIZE   **FEEDING**

LESS WELL KNOWN than the smooth-coated Vizsla, the Hungarian Wire-haired Vizsla has been enjoying a great deal of popularity in Britain since the beginning of the 1990s. The Hungarian Wire-haired Vizsla differs from the other Vizsla primarily in coat and in the fact that weight is not specified in the breed standard; indeed this dog should be well-boned without losing its elegance. Height is again 53–64 cm (21–25 in).

Also russet-gold in colour, in the Wire-haired Vizsla small white feet on chest and feet should not be penalised. The coat is lustreless, the head hair short and harsh but longer on the muzzle, forming a beard. Eyebrows are pronounced and hair on the ears is longer and finer. Over the body the hair is longer, with short harsh hair on the forelimbs. This is a gentle-mannered, affectionate breed, fearless, and with a protective instinct.

BREED FACT:
The Hungarian Wire-haired Vizsla began to make a come-back in Britain in 1991 and has a small group of devoted followers.

Left
The Hungarian Wire-haired Vizla was developed in the 1930s. It has a good nose and fine tracking abilities.

Irish Red and White Setter

HEIGHT 57-66 cm (22.5-26 in)

Gundog

GROUP   **COAT CARE**

large

SIZE   **FEEDING**

ONE OF TWO BREEDS of Irish Setter, the Red and White is the older of the two, indeed early pictures of Setters show that many were nearly all white. Some believe that the two breeds of Irish Setter have always co-existed and

that the Red was more popular in the north of Ireland. With few exceptions, at early dog shows in Ireland the two breeds were shown together. Several specimens of the breed were kept in prominent seventeenth and eighteenth century kennels, including that of Lord Rossmore of Monaghan.

Athletic rather than racy, the Irish Red and White Setter is strong and powerful. No height or weight guides are given in the English breed standard, although in Ireland height ranges from 57–66 cm (22.5–26 in). Weight tends to be 27–32 kg (60–70 lb). This happy, good-natured dog is affectionate, biddable, highly intelligent and a good worker, deservedly increasing in popularity. The finely textured coat has good feathering.

BREED FACT:
By the end of the nineteenth century, the Red and White was believed possibly to be extinct.

Left
The Red and White Irish Setter came close to dying out, but is now becoming more widespread.

Gundog

GROUP   **COAT CARE**

large

SIZE   **FEEDING**

Irish Setter

HEIGHT 59-70 cm (23-27.5 in)

<table>
<tr><td colspan="2">BREED INFORMATION</td></tr>
<tr><td>NAME</td><td>Irish Setter</td></tr>
<tr><td>OTHER NAMES</td><td>Irish Red Setter</td></tr>
<tr><td>OFFICIAL RECOGNITION</td><td>UK Gundog Group; FCI Group 7;
AKC Sporting Group</td></tr>
<tr><td>COLOUR VARIATIONS</td><td>Rich chestnut</td></tr>
</table>

BREED FACT:

The frozen, bleached bones of an Irish Setter are said to have been found still in the sitting position.

PROBABLY THE MOST familiar of Irish dogs, the Irish Setter is generally thought to have descended from land spaniels used for taking game with the net. In the eighteenth century setters trained to find game for the gun became particularly popular in Ireland. Carefully planned breeding evolved the characteristic solid red colour.

Racy, balanced and full of quality, the Irish Setter looks a spectacular and handsome sight with rich chestnut coat of moderate length. The breed is tremendously active with untiring readiness to range and hunt under any conditions. Demonstrably affectionate, the Irish Setter loves fun and frolic and proper training is useful, plenty of exercise being essential. No height or weight clauses are given in the English breed standard but in Ireland height is 59–70 cm (23–27.5 in) and weight 29–39 kg (62–82 lb).

BREED INFORMATION

NAME	Italian Spinone
OTHER NAMES	Spinone Italiano
OFFICIAL RECOGNITION	UK Gundog Group; FCI Group 7;
	AKC Miscellaneous Class
COLOUR VARIATIONS	White; White/orange; White/brown

Italian Spinone

HEIGHT 59-70 cm (23-27.5 in)

Gundog
GROUP   COAT CARE

large
SIZE   FEEDING

ORIGINALLY FROM the Bresse area of France, the Italian Spinone is an old breed, established in Piedmont in Northern Italy. A popular all-purpose gundog, this is a hardy worker in the field, a hunt, point and retrieve breed, noted for good scenting abilities and a soft mouth. The Spinone works particularly well in marshland or rough woodland and is reputedly easy to train. Squarely built with strong bone, the Italian

Spinone is intrepid and untiring, a hardy dog, which is able to adapt to any terrain, including water. The dog's temperament is faithful, intelligent, patient and affectionate, and this is expressed in a kind and earnest expression. The tough, thick, slightly wiry coat is 3.8–6 cm (1.5–2.5 in) long with longer, stiffer hair on the eyebrows. Colours range through white, orange and brown, often with peppering and speckling. Height is 59–70 cm (23–27.5 in) and weight 29–39 kg (62–82 lb).

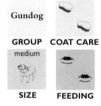

BREED FACT:
A breed which has become popular in Europe and America. In Britain the Italian Spinone achieved Championship status in 1994.

BREED INFORMATION

NAME	Kooikerhondje
OTHER NAMES	Small Dutch Waterfowl Dog
OFFICIAL RECOGNITION	UK Gundog Group; FCI Group 8
COLOUR VARIATIONS	White with clear orange-red patches

Kooikerhondje

HEIGHT 35-40 cm (14-16 in)

Gundog
GROUP   COAT CARE

medium
SIZE   FEEDING

BREED FACT:
Only 25 Kooikerhondjes were believed to have survived the Second World War so the genetic pool for this breed is understandably small.

FROM THE Netherlands comes the Kooikerhondje, the brightly coloured coat of clear orange-red colour on a white background used to attract swimming ducks, luring them into netting traps, although they were not used exclusively as decoy dogs. The breed fell into decline but was rescued from almost total obscurity in the 1940s, but was not introduced to Britain until 1985.

The breed has a high head carriage and the well feathered tail with its white plume is carried either level with the back or slightly above. A friendly breed, good natured and alert, the Kooikerhondje is both versatile and adaptable, making a good household pet. They usually love water and are excellent swimmers. Height is 35–40 cm (14–16 in) and weight generally 9–11 kg (20–24 lb). The medium-long, double coat is slightly waved or straight and a white blaze on the head is preferred.

Left
The Kooikerhondje love water and make excellent swimmers.

Gundog

GROUP **COAT CARE**

large

SIZE **FEEDING**

BREED FACT:
The Large Munsterlander was first registered with the English Kennel Club in 1971.

Large Munsterlander

HEIGHT 58-65 cm (23-25.5 in)

ALTHOUGH THE Large Munsterlander's ancestors are just as old as those of other German Gundogs, this is a relatively young pointing and retrieving breed. History tells us that the 23 black and white dogs entered at the first show organised by Munster's breed club in 1921 are the ancestors of modern Large Munsterlanders.

This multi-purpose Gundog is alert and energetic, with a strong, muscular body, ideal for the rough shooter. With an excellent nose and fine staying power, the Munsterlander works equally well on land and in water. This dog is a keen worker, easily taught. The long dense hair is not curly or coarse, lying short and smooth on the head. The head is solid

Right
Easily trained and hard working the Large Munsterlander makes an excellent gundog and obedient companion.

black with a white blaze, snip or star allowed. The body is white or blue roan with black patches, flecked, ticked or a combination of these. Height is 58–65 cm (23–25.5 in) and weight 25–29 kg

Gundog

GROUP **COAT CARE**

large

SIZE **FEEDING**

Nova Scotia Duck Tolling Retriever

HEIGHT 45-51 cm (18-20 in)

BREED FACT:
The Nova Scotia Duck Tolling Retriever has been selectively bred over generations for trainability and intelligence.

A NATIVE OF Canada, the Nova Scotia Duck Tolling Retriever did not arrive in Britain until 1988, since when this kind, confident and intelligent breed has made steady progress. The breed jumps and plays, using the tail to lure waterfowl within range of the gun. Then the Toller retrieves the fowl and, if in water, the dog is assisted by strongly webbed feet. A medium sized breed

Right
This Retriever seems oddly named but tolling comes from Old English tollen, meaning to entice.

standing 45–51 cm (18–20 in) high and weighing about 17–23 kg (37–51 lb), this is a compact, powerful and well-muscled dog which is easy to train. The medium sized, almond shaped eyes, brown to amber in colouring, have an alert expression. The straight, repellent, double coat is not difficult to groom and comes in all shades of red or orange, with lighter feathering under the tail. There are sometimes white marks on the tail-tip, feet, chest and possibly a blaze on the head.

BREED INFORMATION

NAME	Pointer
OTHER NAMES	English Pointer
OFFICIAL RECOGNITION	UK Gundog Group; FCI Group 7; AKC Sporting Group
COLOUR VARIATIONS	Many combinations

Pointer

HEIGHT 61-69 cm (24-27 in)

Gundog
GROUP **COAT CARE**

large

SIZE **FEEDING**

ALTHOUGH BELIEVED ORIGINALLY to have been Spanish, this dog is considered to have become an English breed over the last two or three centuries. The Spanish Pointer is thought to have been crossed with the French Hound and later the Foxhound, improving both stamina and conformation. The breed first came to Britain around 1650 and was used with Greyhounds for hare coursing: the Pointer finding the hare and the Greyhound chasing it.

Symmetrical and well built, the general outline of the Pointer is a series of graceful curves. This is an aristocratic dog, alert and with an appearance of both strength and speed. Of a kind and even disposition, this breed is an excellent working gundog, used to search out game ahead of the guns. The fine, short, hard coat is perfectly smooth and straight with a sheen and is found in a variety of colours. Height is 61–69 cm (24–27 in) and weight usually 20–30 kg (44–66 lb).

BREED FACT:
Pointers carry their heads high when testing the air and low in order to indicate quarry.

Left
The Pointer was often used for hare coursing in times gone by.

BREED INFORMATION

NAME	Chesapeake Bay Retriever
OFFICIAL RECOGNITION	UK Gundog Group; FCI Group 8; AKC Sporting Group
COLOUR VARIATIONS	Dead grass; Sedge; Brown

Chesapeake Bay Retriever

HEIGHT 53.3-66 cm (21-26 in)

Gundog
GROUP **COAT CARE**

large

SIZE **FEEDING**

Flat-coated Retrievers and Otterhounds. By 1885 this breed, which takes its name from the icy waters of Chesapeake Bay, had evolved and was used for retrieving wild duck.

An active worker with well-webbed bare feet, the distinctive coat is thick and reasonably short, not over 3.8 cm (1.5 in) long, with harsh, oily outercoat and dense, fine woolly undercoat. Because of working in all sorts of weather conditions, including ice and snow, coat texture is very important. The coat colour is that of dead grass (straw to bracken), sedge (red-gold), or any shade of brown. Standing 53.3–66 cm (21–26 in) and weighing around 25–34 kg (55–75 lb), the Chesapeake Bay Retriever has a strong, muscular appearance and with a bright, happy disposition coupled with independence and courage, makes a good guardian and companion.

OFF THE COAST OF MARYLAND in 1807 an English ship was wrecked. The two Newfoundland-type puppies on board were bred, then their descendants crossed with Curly and

BREED FACT:
The American Chesapeake Bay Retriever is reputed to be a breed which, for its size, particularly enjoys its food.

Left
Despite its rugged history the Chesapeake Bay Retriever makes an excellent family dog, and is especially good with children.

Gundog

GROUP **COAT CARE**

SIZE **FEEDING**

BREED FACT:
In 1889, Curly-coated Retrievers were exported to New Zealand in order to hunt birds there.

Right
The Curly-coated Retriever is a handsome dog with a thick mass of close-growing curls on the coat.

Curly-coated Retriever

HEIGHT 53.3-66 cm (21-26 in)

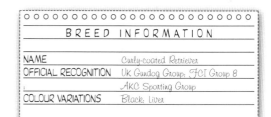

BREED INFORMATION

NAME	Curly-coated Retriever
OFFICIAL RECOGNITION	UK Gundog Group; FCI Group 8; AKC Sporting Group
COLOUR VARIATIONS	Black; Liver

OF THE RETRIEVING BREEDS, the Curly-coat is one of the oldest, derived from crossing the Irish Water Spaniel, Poodle and Labrador and possibly other retriever breeds and pointers. First shown at the Birmingham Show in 1860, the breed was at its most popular as a shooting dog late in the nineteenth century. Although a breed club was formed in 1896 it fell into decline and the present club was founded in 1933.

A strong, upstanding dog with a degree of elegance and distinctive black or liver coat, it has a thick mass of small, tight, crisp curls lying close to the skin. The Curly-coated Retriever may seem aloof but is bold, friendly, self-confident and independent, a dog which is intelligent, steady and reliable. Needing plenty of exercise, this breed stands

53.3–66 cm (21–26 in) high and weighs around 32–36 kg (70–80 lb). It has an ability to mark the fall of game and remember its location, and is reputed to be brilliant at retrieving wounded duck which lies hidden in rushes or in water.

Gundog

GROUP **COAT CARE**

SIZE **FEEDING**

BREED FACT:
Mr Shirley, Founder and former Chairman of the Kennel Club, helped stabilise breed type for the Flat-coated Retriever.

Flat-coated Retriever

HEIGHT 56.5-61.5 cm (22-24 in)

BREED INFORMATION

NAME	Flat-coated Retriever
OFFICIAL RECOGNITION	UK Gundog Group; FCI Group 8; AKC Sporting Group
COLOUR VARIATIONS	Black; Liver

BELIEVED TO HAVE evolved from the Newfoundland and Labrador, probably with Irish and Gordon Setter blood introduced, this was originally known as the Wavy-coated Retriever. Like the Curly-coat, the breed first appeared at the Birmingham Show in 1860. Also known as the gamekeeper's dog, this tireless worker and natural swimmer was used as a working dog on large shooting estates.

With a long, nicely moulded head, flat skull and intelligent, dark brown or hazel eyes, this is a bright and active dog. The Flat-coat stands 56.5–61.5 cm (22–24 in) with a preferred weight of between 25–36 kg (55–80 lb). The small ears are well set-on, close to the side of the head and the coat is dense, of fine to medium texture and as flat as possible. Generously endowed with natural gundog ability, the breed is full of optimism and friendliness, displayed in an enthusiastic tail.

Golden Retriever

HEIGHT 51-61 cm (20-24 in)

Gundog

GROUP **COAT CARE**

large

SIZE **FEEDING**

BREED INFORMATION

NAME	Golden Retriever
OFFICIAL RECOGNITION	UK Gundog Group; FCI Group 8; AKC Sporting Group
COLOUR VARIATIONS	Gold; Cream

DURING THE NINETEENTH century, a yellow Wavy-coated Retriever was mated to a Tweed Water Spaniel and from this union came four yellow puppies, acknowledged as the ancestors of all Golden Retrievers. It was Lord Tweedmouth who introduced Goldens as a definite breed, one which is used to retrieve game in the shooting field but is adaptable to many different roles including guide dog work, drug and explosive detection, tracking and obedience.

The flat or wavy coat has good feathering with a dense, water-resisting undercoat, the colour any shade of gold or cream but not red nor mahogany. An active, powerful breed, it stands some 51–61 cm (20–24 in) high and weighs from 27–36 kg (60–80 lb). The Golden Retriever is both biddable and intelligent, with natural working ability. This kind, friendly and confident dog is one of the most popular breeds in the world.

BREED FACT:

Originally known as Flat-coats and defined only by their 'yellow' colour, in 1920 the breed took the name, Golden Retriever.

Left
The Golden Retriever is one of the most popular dogs in Britain, as a gundog and family pet.

Gundog
GROUP

COAT CARE

large
SIZE

FEEDING

Labrador Retriever

HEIGHT 54-57 cm (21.5-22.5 in)

Right
The Labrador Retriever is not only rugged and hardworking, but also an affectionate and obedient companion.

BREED INFORMATION	
NAME	Labrador Retriever
OFFICIAL RECOGNITION	UK Gundog Group; FCI Group 8; AKC Sporting Group
COLOUR VARIATIONS	Black; Yellow; Liver/chocolate

THOUGHT TO HAVE originated in Newfoundland and off the coast of Greenland, the Labrador was used by fishermen to retrieve and drag the ends of fishing nets in to the shore. Employed for retrieving game and held in high regard as a guide dog and sniffer dog detecting drugs and explosives, this is an excellent water dog. It has a distinctive short, dense coat, hard to the touch and with a water-resistant undercoat.

Coat colour can be black, yellow or liver/chocolate, yellows ranging from light cream to red fox. Another characteristic feature is the breed's otter-like tail, very thick at the base and tapering towards the tip. Strongly built, short-coupled and broad, the ideal height is 54–57 cm (21.5–22.5 in) and weight is usually 25–34 kg (55–75 lb). Regular exercise and sensible feeding is important to prevent this breed carrying too much weight. The Labrador Retriever is good tempered and very agile, an adaptable and devoted companion who is intelligent, keen and biddable, with a very strong will to please.

Gundog
GROUP

COAT CARE

medium
SIZE

FEEDING

American Cocker Spaniel

HEIGHT 33.75-38.75 cm (13.5-15.5 in)

Right
The coat of the American Cocker Spaniel needs careful attention to keep it in good shape.

BREED INFORMATION	
NAME	American Cocker Spaniel
OTHER NAMES	Cocker Spaniel
OFFICIAL RECOGNITION	UK Gundog Group; FCI Group 8; AKC Sporting Group
COLOUR VARIATIONS	Various combinations

IN THE USA, the Cocker Spaniel developed along different lines from the breed we know as the English Cocker, the former being slightly smaller and having a shorter back and different head shape with a longer coat. Because of the increasing difference between them, the two breeds were divided in the 1940s.

The breed standard describes this breed as 'a serviceable-looking dog' with a refined, chiselled head and strong, well boned legs, overall compact and sturdy. Although, according to the breed standard the silky coat should not be excessive and not hide body lines nor impede movement, those appearing in today's show ring do have a great deal of coat which needs regular attention. Various colours are carefully detailed in the standard and the ideal height ranges from 33.75–38.75 cm (13.5–15.5 in). Weight is usually 11–15 kg (24–28 lb).

BREED INFORMATION

NAME	Clumber Spaniel
OFFICIAL RECOGNITION	UK Gundog Group; FCI Group 8; AKC Sporting Group
COLOUR VARIATIONS	White with lemon markings. Orange markings permissible

Clumber Spaniel

HEIGHT 48-51 cm (19-20 in)

Gundog
GROUP   COAT CARE
large
SIZE   FEEDING

RATHER DIFFERENT FROM other spaniels, the history of the Clumber Spaniel is somewhat unclear. It is likely that the breed came to England from Europe, developed by crossing the old Alpine Spaniel with St Hubert Hounds or Bassets. The Duke of Newcastle was given dogs by the Duc de Noailles and these were bred at Clumber Park, Nottingham.

The overall appearance of the Clumber denotes strength, the breed being heavily boned and well balanced. Stoical, great hearted and highly intelligent with a determined attitude, this is a silent worker with an excellent nose. Although rather more aloof than other spaniels there is no tendency toward aggression, and the breed's temperament is steady, reliable, kind and dignified. The abundant coat is silky and straight, and a plain white body is preferred with lemon markings, though orange is also permissible. A heavy breed, the weight for dogs is ideally 36 kg (80 lb) and for bitches 29.5 kg (65 kg).

BREED FACT:
Because in the eighteenth and nineteenth centuries there was an abundance of game, the slower Clumber became better appreciated.

Left
The thoughtful expression of the Clumber Spaniel mirrors its steady dignified nature.

BREED INFORMATION

NAME	Cocker Spaniel
OTHER NAMES	English Cocker Spaniel
OFFICIAL RECOGNITION	UK Gundog Group; FCI Group 8; AKC Sporting Group
COLOUR VARIATIONS	Various

Cocker Spaniel

HEIGHT 38-41 cm (15-16 in)

Gundog
GROUP   COAT CARE
medium
SIZE   FEEDING

THOUGHT TO HAVE originated in Spain in the fourteenth century, the Cocker is one of the oldest spaniel breeds. Used for hunting woodcock, quail and partridge, spaniels of this kind went by various names including 'Cocker' or 'Cocking Spaniel'. Accepted by the English Kennel Club in 1892, the Cocker Spaniel Club was formed in 1902.

The popular Cocker Spaniel has a gentle, affectionate temperament and yet is full of life and exuberance. Sturdy and compact, the breed has a merry nature with an ever-wagging tail. The full eyes express intelligence and gentleness but are wide awake, and the long, low-set ears are described as 'lobular'. Movement is typically bustling, especially when following scent and this dog has no fear of heavy cover. The flat, silky coat comes in various colours; the height is 38–41 cm (15–16 in) and the weight 12.75–14.5 kg (28–32 lb).

BREED FACT:
During the mid-1930s, Cocker Spaniels were the most popular dogs in Britain, a Cocker having won Cruft's Best in Show in 1930 and 1931.

Gundog
GROUP   **COAT CARE**

large
SIZE   **FEEDING**

English Springer Spaniel

HEIGHT 51 cm (20 in)

○○○○○○○○○○○○○○○○○○○○○○○○○○○○

BREED INFORMATION

NAME	English Springer Spaniel
OFFICIAL RECOGNITION	UK Gundog Group; FCI Group 8;
	AKC Sporting Group
COLOUR VARIATIONS	Liver/white; Black/white

BREED FACT:
This breed was known earlier as the Norfolk Spaniel, but the name English Springer Spaniel has been used since 1900.

Right

The English Springer Spaniel has a warm and friendly nature and makes a good working dog and an obedient companion.

A TRADITIONAL DOG for the rough-shooter, many consider that the English Springer Spaniel is the root from which all land spaniels, except Clumbers, have evolved. The breed standard clearly states that the breed is of ancient and pure origin and that this is the oldest of sporting gundogs.

An excellent all-round gundog, the breed's original purpose was finding and springing game for net, falcon or greyhound; now this dog is used to find, flush and retrieve game for the gun. Symmetrically built, merry, active and strong, the English Springer needs regular exercise to maintain fitness and prevent boredom.

The breed has a friendly, happy disposition and is amenable and biddable. The straight, weather-resistant coat with moderate feathering is liver and white, black and white, or either of these colours with tan markings. Height is approximately 51

Field Spaniel

HEIGHT 45.7 cm (18 in)

BREED INFORMATION

NAME	Field Spaniel
OFFICIAL RECOGNITION	Uk Gundog Group; FCI Group 8; AKC Sporting Group
COLOUR VARIATIONS	Black; Liver; Roan

Gundog

GROUP   **COAT CARE**

medium

SIZE   **FEEDING**

DEVELOPED IN THE LATE nineteenth century by sportsmen requiring a heavier Spaniel than the Cocker and yet lighter than the Sussex, the two were interbred. Initially the breed

became too low to the ground and too long in body, unsuitable for the work needed. Eventually breeding excesses were abandoned and in recent decades a much more workmanlike dog has been produced.

Built for activity and endurance, the Field Spaniel is ideal for rough shooting or as a companion for the country dweller, but not suited to city life. Its temperament is docile, sensitive and independent. The head and skull convey the impression of high breeding, character and nobility while the wide-open but almond shaped eyes have tight lids and show no haw, imparting a grave and gentle expression. The black, liver or roan coat is long, flat, glossy and silky in texture and the height is about 45.7 cm (18 in) with the weight from 18–25 kg (40–55 lb).

BREED FACT:
Originally Field Spaniels were sharply divided by colour; blacks were more important and called 'Black Spaniels'.

Left
The Field Spaniel had almost vanished by the end of the Second World War and is still not as popular as the Cocker.

Irish Water Spaniel

HEIGHT 51-58 cm (20-23 in)

BREED INFORMATION

NAME	Irish Water Spaniel
OFFICIAL RECOGNITION	Uk Gundog Group; FCI Group 8; AKC Sporting Group
COLOUR VARIATIONS	Rich, dark liver with purplish tint

Gundog

GROUP   **COAT CARE**

large

SIZE   **FEEDING**

THE EXACT ORIGINS of the Irish Water Spaniel remain obscure. It has been said that the breed was a manufactured one, the result of experiments in crossing Poodles, spaniels and Bloodhounds. However it is generally believed to have evolved from dogs which originated in Persia, finding their way to Ireland via Spain. An Irish reference to 'water dogs that pursue water fowl' dates from 1600.

The tallest member of the spaniel family at 51–58 cm (20–23 in), this is a smart, upstanding and strongly built animal, an enduring, versatile Gundog used for all types

of shooting, particularly wildfowling. Weight usually ranges from 20–30 kg (45–65 lb). Although initially aloof, the Irish Water Spaniel has an endearing sense of humour, a stable disposition and an affectionate temperament. The rich dark liver coat with its purplish tint is dense, with tight, crisp ringlets and a natural oiliness, so needs careful maintenance.

BREED FACT:
Numbers of this breed decreased before the First World War, but renewed popularity was enjoyed between the wars.

Left
The coat of the Irish Water Springer is naturally oily. The rings form a top-knot on the head.

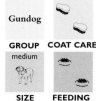

Gundog
GROUP

COAT CARE

medium

SIZE

FEEDING

Sussex Spaniel

HEIGHT 38-41 cm (15-16 in)

BREED FACT:
In show history, a Sussex Spaniel first competed at the Crystal Palace Show in London in 1862.

AT THE END OF THE EIGHTEENTH century the Sussex Spaniel was developed especially to work as a retriever in dense undergrowth on big sporting estates. Not as quick as some other types of spaniel, the breed has a tendency to give tongue or to bark on scent, a trait rather unusual amongst gundogs.

With a wide skull and frowning brows, the heavily and strongly built Sussex Spaniel has natural, albeit slightly slow, working ability. The breed is active and energetic with a characteristic rolling gait. The thick, fairly large, lobular ears are set just above eye level and the hazel-coloured eyes with their soft expression do not show much haw. Of kindly disposition, this is a very suitable family dog in a country household.

The rich, golden-liver coat is abundant and flat with an ample undercoat for weather resistance. The dog has a long, wide back, which is well muscled. Height is 38–41 cm (15–16 in) and weight approximately 23 kg (50 lb).

Spanish Water Dog

HEIGHT 38-50 cm (15-19.5 in)

Gundog
GROUP

COAT CARE

medium

SIZE

FEEDING

BREED FACT:
The name 'Water Dog' is common in Cantabria where the breed has plenty of opportunity to use its diving skills.

THE SPANISH WATER DOG is little known outside Spain, and in Britain, although it is recognised by the Kennel Club, no official breed standard has yet been approved. In Spain the breed is used mainly for herding sheep, goats and some cattle, but also to retrieve ducks and to retrieve fish from outside the net, diving under the water aided by webbed toes. References to an ancient Spanish Water Dog date back to the tenth century and its ancestry is believed to be Andalucian.

Size varies considerably, with height from 38–50 cm (15–19.5 in) and weight 12–20 kg (26.5–44 lb). The woolly coat is curly and does not shed but forms heavy cords when long. The coat may be clipped but should be the same length all over. Colours are black, brown, white or

Right
Although the Spanish Water Dog is obedient and has a pleasant temperament, it can get irritable with children.

parti-coloured with white, but never tricoloured. The Spanish Water Dog is faithful, obedient and has an even temperament.

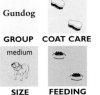

Gundog
GROUP **COAT CARE**
medium
SIZE **FEEDING**

BREED INFORMATION

NAME	Welsh Springer Spaniel
OFFICIAL RECOGNITION	Uk Gundog Group; FCI Group 8; AKC Sporting Group
COLOUR VARIATIONS	Rich red/white

Welsh Springer Spaniel

HEIGHT 46-48 cm (18-19 in)

ALTHOUGH NOT ACCEPTED by the English Kennel Club until 1902, the Welsh Springer Spaniel has been used in Wales as a working gundog for several hundred years and is considered a very ancient and distinct breed of pure origin. A faithful and persistent worker, the Welsh falls between the English and Cocker Spaniels in size, standing 46–48 cm (18–19 in) high and being slightly lighter in build than the English. Weight is usually 16–20 kg (35–45 lb).

Built for endurance and hard work, the breed is a quick and active mover, displaying plenty of push and drive. The well set-on tail should never be carried above the level of the back and is customarily docked. Strong, merry and very active, the Welsh Springer has a kindly disposition. The dense coat is straight or flat, and silky in texture. Its colour is a rich red and white only.

BREED FACT:

The ears of the Welsh Springer Spaniel are comparatively small, narrowing toward the tip and described as 'vine leaf-shaped'.

Left
The Welsh Springer Spaniel is a very active dog that requires an energetic and enthusiastic owner.

Gundog
GROUP **COAT CARE**
large
SIZE **FEEDING**

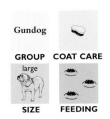

Weimeraner

HEIGHT 56-69 cm (22-27 in)

BREED INFORMATION

NAME	Weimeraner
OFFICIAL RECOGNITION	Uk Terrier Group; FCI Group 7; AKC Sporting Group
COLOUR VARIATIONS	Silver grey. Mouse or roe grey permissible

TAKING ITS NAME from the German court of Weimar, this breed is nick-named the 'grey ghost' because of its silvery coat colour. The Weimeraner was originally a large game dog, probably springing from the same stock as that which produced other German hunting breeds. As big game hunting declined in Germany, the breed was used on various game birds and as a water retriever. Although also a companion dog, this is primarily one of the hunt, point and retrieve breeds so hunting ability is of paramount importance. There are two varieties of coat, the most popular is short, smooth and sleek, the other is long, from 2.5–5 cm (1–2 in) on the body, longer on the neck, chest and belly with a feathered tail and backs of limbs. The eyes are in shades of amber or blue-grey. One of the tallest gundogs, its height is 56–69 cm (22–27 in) and although not specified in the British breed standard, weight is tends to be 32–39 kg (70.5–86 lb). The Weimeraner is fearless, friendly, protective, obedient and alert.

BREED FACT:

Although the Weimeraner is now well known in Britain, it did not reach the island until the 1950s.

Left
The Weimeraner is a triking dog with its unusual coat and eye coloration.

The Hound Group

AMONGST THE HOUND GROUP are some of the oldest breeds in the world. For thousands of years man has hunted animals for food and sport, originally using primitive trapping methods, bows and spears, but hound breeds evolved to aid man in his important pursuit of chasing game. Many of the dogs depicted on tombs of the pharaohs and in other Egyptian art clearly fall into this group.

CHASING GAME

ALTHOUGH THE BOW and arrow served its purpose well, in open country, game had to be chased down. This required both speed and stamina, something to which the Sight Hounds became well suited. All possess a lean, powerful body and long legs,. In addition, most have a deep chest.

Different types of hound were needed in densely forested areas, marshland and in jungle. To assist man in these areas other hounds were developed to follow scent over difficult ground. Within the two general categories of Sight Hounds and Scent Hounds, some have been developed to catch and kill their quarry, others to corner the game then bay loudly to attract the attention of the hunter, whilst smaller dogs go to ground where they hold the quarry until it is dug out.

The size, speed and strength of hounds is so varied that the quarry of some is the humble rabbit, whilst others have tackled large, ferocious animals including wolf, boar, elk and even the leopard and lion. Others, such as the Otterhound, can even follow scent in water and many is the tale of Bloodhounds successfully trailing a scent over a period of several days.

Hounds have long been kept for their hunting skills, both by scent and by sight, but some of the more glamourous among them have also been retained as something of a 'fashion accessory'. As this may well have been to their detriment, those days are hopefully now in the past. Now many are kept just as companion animals but owners should never forget that all hounds retain something of their ancestor's skills, and long may they continue to do so.

Of course, many of the breeds which fall within this group carry out their work as part of a large pack but fewer and fewer packs of hounds are now used for hunting. Many of the Sight Hounds take part in coursing and racing and all the hound breeds make a very splendid sight in the showring, several of them having changed but little over the centuries.

Dogs within the Hound Group make a spectacular sight with their varied coats, some as short as the Smooth-haired Dachshund, others as long as that of the Afghan Hound. Colours vary spectacularly too; in some breeds all colours are acceptable, others are restricted to specific colours or colour patterns, the tri-colour being especially striking.

Size and weight are also very varied. The Miniature Dachshund should weigh under 5 kg (11 lb) whilst the Basset, another breed low to the ground, is very much heavier. Of the longer legged breeds the Borzoi, Deerhound and Irish Wolfhound stand out as amongst the tallest of breeds, and each and every one has its own band of dedicated followers.

Above
Despite its size, the Irish Wolfhound has a gentle, patient nature.

Right
This Saluki originated in the Middle East, where it was highly prized as a hunting dog.

Below
The Smooth-haired Dachshund is an independent and intelligent breed, with an alert expression.

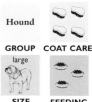

Hound		
GROUP	**COAT CARE**	

large		
SIZE	**FEEDING**	

BREED INFORMATION

NAME	Afghan Hound
OTHER NAMES	Tazi; Baluchi Hound
OFFICIAL RECOGNITION	UK Hound Group; FCI Group 10; AKC Hound Group
COLOUR VARIATIONS	All colours

Afghan Hound

HEIGHT 63-74 cm (25-29 in)

THE AFGHAN IS ONE of the most glamorous of the large breeds, standing 63–74 cm (25–29 in). This magnificent, long-coated dog comes from the mountainous and plains regions of Afghanistan. With an Oriental expression, its eyes look at and through you, conveying an aloof, dignified temperament. A typical Afghan also gives the impression of strength, combining speed with power and moving with a style of high order. Although a most glorious sight, the long coat needs much care and the breed's Eastern personality is often not easy to handle. Not always found, but highly typical of the breed, is a ring at the end of the tail.

Another interesting feature is the saddle of short, close hair from the shoulder backwards. Afghan racing is a enjoyable, competitive, sport followed by many.

BREED FACT:

A breed of dog considered more noble than the common dogs, this hound is prized by Afghan tribesmen as highly as horses and hawks.

Left
The Afghan is highly strung and difficult to train, but has always commanded great devotion from its fans.

BREED INFORMATION

NAME	Basenji
OTHER NAMES	Congo Dog
OFFICIAL RECOGNITION	UK Hound Group; FCI Group 5; AKC Hound Group
COLOUR VARIATIONS	Black/white; Red/white;

Basenji

HEIGHT 40-43 cm (16-17 in)

Hound		
GROUP	**COAT CARE**	

medium		
SIZE	**FEEDING**	

WITH ANCESTORS DEPICTED on ancient Egyptian tombs, the Basenji has a long lineage. In more recent times, it was used in the Congo as a pack dog to drive game into a net, and individual dogs were much prized. This breed has no bark but emits a characteristic noise which is a mixture of a chortle and a yodel.

A medium sized but lightly built dog of 40–43 cm (16–17 in) high, its wrinkled head gives a rather quizzical expression. The coat is short and sleek and the tail curls tightly over the back. Self-confident, friendly and very clean in its habits, the Basenji is odourless and an excellent household companion. Colours of the breed can be striking: pure black and white; red and white; black, tan and white with tan 'melon pips' and mask; black; or tan and white. The white is on the feet, chest and tail tip but there may also be white legs, blaze and collar.

BREED FACT:

The Basenji was first shown at Crufts in 1937 but was called an 'African Bush Dog' or 'Congo Terrier'.

Left
Unlike most breeds of dog, the Basenji only has one sex cycle instead of the usual two. In this respect it resembles the wolf.

Hound	
GROUP	**COAT CARE**
large	
SIZE	**FEEDING**

Basset Hound

HEIGHT 33-38 cm (13-15 in)

BREED FACT:
A Basset Hound can follow a scent trail which is hours old.

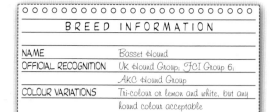

○ ○

BREED INFORMATION

NAME	Basset Hound
OFFICIAL RECOGNITION	UK Hound Group; FCI Group 6; AKC Hound Group
COLOUR VARIATIONS	Tri-colour or lemon and white, but any hound colour acceptable

Right
The word Basset *means dwarf in French, indicating its origins. However, it is very widespread.*

IMPORTED TO THE UK from France and renowned for a long body, loose skin and long, low-set ears, the Basset Hound stands only 33–38 cm (13–15 in) in height but is very substantially built, weighing around 18–27 kg (40–60 lb). The eyes are lozenge-shaped, neither prominent nor too deep set, the red of the lower eyelid showing, though not to excess. The breed is typified by its calm, serious expression. A hound of ancient lineage, the Basset hunts by scent in packs and is capable of great endurance.

Although they enjoy paddling through muddy fields, Bassets can easily be cleaned up again thanks to their smooth, short coats. The bark is deep and melodious and this is an affectionate, placid breed, never aggressive, though they can be wilful.

Hound	
GROUP	**COAT CARE**
medium	
SIZE	**FEEDING**

Basset Bleu de Gascogne

HEIGHT 34-42 cm (13-16 in)

BREED FACT:
The legs of the Basset Bleu de Gascogne have been dwarfed to slow down the breed's running speed.

○ ○

BREED INFORMATION

NAME	Basset Bleu de Gascogne
OTHER NAMES	Blue Gascony Basset
OFFICIAL RECOGNITION	UK Hound Group; FCI Group 6
COLOUR VARIATIONS	Black with white mottling and some tan

RE-CREATED FROM THE original French breed of the Middle Ages, the Basset Bleu de Gascogne does not yet have a breed standard drawn up by the English Kennel Club, but has been entered on the Import Breed Register. A grand voice and excellent nose enables this dog to hunt in virtually any conditions, even when there is a hard frost. These are clever hounds, though not fast, and have a tendency to dawdle, each one of them puzzling out the line of quarry.

The most reserved of the Basset breeds, their general appearance is large but not too heavy. Height is 34–42 cm (13–16 in) and weight ranges from 16–18 kg (35–40 lb). The rather sorrowful, dark brown eyes have a gentle expression and the low-set ears reach at least to the end of the muzzle. Colour is mottled, with or without a saddle, with specified tan markings.

Right
The Basset Bleu de Gascogne is not only an excellent hunter but also an obedient companion.

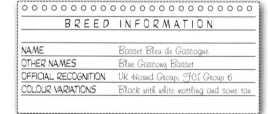

Basset Fauve de Bretagne

HEIGHT 32-38 cm (12.8-15.2 in)

BREED INFORMATION

NAME	Basset Fauve de Bretagne
OTHER NAMES	Fawn Brittany Basset
OFFICIAL RECOGNITION	Uk Hound Group; FCI Group 6
COLOUR VARIATIONS	Any recognised hound colour other than liver

Hound

GROUP **COAT CARE**

medium

SIZE **FEEDING**

INTRODUCED TO THE UK in 1983, the wire-coated Basset Fauve de Bretagne comes from France and is a lively, friendly breed, used for hunting small game. Traditionally the breed hunted

mainly in packs of four, but it is now used to hunt alone or in pairs. The harsh, dense, flat coat is always red-wheaten or fawn in colour and this dog stands 32–38 cm (12.8–15.2 in) high, and weighs some 16–18 kg (36–40 lb).

Not so low to the ground as the more

familiar Basset Hound, the Basset Fauve is nimble and always ready for exercise. Its scenting ability is good and this breed has plenty of courage, being lively, friendly and amenable. The long, low-set ears, reach nearly to the end of the nose when drawn out. Although the nose is preferably black a lighter colour is permissible in lighter coloured hounds.

BREED FACT:
The Basset Fauve de Bretagne is one of the smallest French hounds and is rarely seen outside France, except in Britain.

Left
The Basset Fauve de Bretagne thrives on lots of physical exercise and is good at working difficult terrain.

Bavarian Mountain Hound

HEIGHT 50.5-51.5 cm (20 in)

BREED INFORMATION

NAME	Bavarian Mountain Hound
OTHER NAMES	Bayrischer Gebirgsschweisshund; Bavarian Mountain Scenthound
OFFICIAL RECOGNITION	Uk Hound Group; FCI Group 6
COLOUR VARIATIONS	Fawn; Red; Red-or Black-brindle.

Hound

GROUP **COAT CARE**

large

SIZE **FEEDING**

STILL ON THE KENNEL Club's Imported Breeds Register as this book goes to press, there are only about 30 Bavarian Mountain Hounds in Britain and no breed standard has yet been approved in the UK. This hound resulted from crossing the Hanoverian and short-legged Bavarian hounds to create one which could track wounded deer. Kept primarily by professional foresters in Germany and in the Czech and Slovak Republics, the breed is often used to relocate a trail which has been lost by other hounds with less powerful scenting abilities.

The expressive face has a mask and the ears are long and drooping.

Colours of the short coat are fawn, red, red-brindle and black-brindle. Height is 50.5–51.5 cm (20 in) and weight 25–35 kg (55–77 lb).

BREED FACT:
The feet of the Bavarian Mountain Hound are broad and strong with extremely tough nails and very thick pads.

Left
The gentle expression of the Bavarian Mountain Hound gives no indication of its amazing scenting abilities.

Hound
GROUP

COAT CARE

 medium
SIZE

FEEDING

BREED FACT:
Queen Elizabeth I owned a pack of 'Pocket Beagles' which were reputed to be under 25 cm (10 in) in height.

Beagle
HEIGHT 35-40 cm (13-16 in)

Right
The nose of the Beagle is dark at birth, but usually turns brown-pink as the dog leaves puppyhood.

BREED INFORMATION

NAME	Beagle
OFFICIAL RECOGNITION	UK Hound Group; FCI Group 6; AKC Hound Group
COLOUR VARIATIONS	Any recognised hound colour, except liver

THE BEAGLE IS ESSENTIALLY a British breed and, although its history is somewhat vague, was bred down in size from Foxhounds to create a dog which could hunt with men on foot. Mentioned in Chaucer's fourteenth-century *Canterbury Tales* the breed was also popular with monarchs.

This sturdy, compact dog gives an impression of quality, a merry hound which follows scent to hunt primarily hare. The Beagle is active and bold, with both stamina and determination. With fairly large, dark brown or hazel eyes the breed is intelligent with an amiable, even temperament. Height is 33–40 cm (13–16 in) and the Beagle generally weighs 8–14 kg (18–30 lb). The short coat, which can be any of the recognised hound colours, is dense and weatherproof.

GROUP Hound

COAT CARE

 large
SIZE

FEEDING

Bloodhound
HEIGHT 58-69 cm (23-27 in)

BREED INFORMATION

NAME	Bloodhound
OTHER NAMES	Chien de Saint-Hubert
OFFICIAL RECOGNITION	UK Hound Group; FCI Group 6; AKC Hound Group
COLOUR VARIATIONS	Black/tan; Liver/tan (red/tan); Red

Right
Bloodhounds descend from an ancient breed of hound.

BREED FACT:
The Bloodhound probably came to England with the Normans in 1066. By the Second World War it was on the verge of extinction.

THE BLOODHOUND IS FAMOUS for detective work and can follow human scent over all types of ground for many hours. Despite an imposing appearance, the Bloodhound is a rather reserved, sensitive dog, affectionate and not at all quarrelsome. Its origins are generally believed to go back to the French St Hubert and the Talbot Hounds.

A very powerful hound standing some 58–69 cm (23–27 in) high, the Bloodhound weighs up to 50 kg (110 lb). Its skin is especially loose on the head, hanging in deep folds, and the thin ears, soft to the touch, are long and pendulous, giving the dog its characteristic appearance. The long, tapering tail is carried scimitar-fashion. This breed epitomises dignity, solemnity, wisdom and power and the sounds which emerge from this magnificent hound need to be heard to be believed.

BREED INFORMATION

NAME	Borzoi
OTHER NAMES	Russian Wolfhound; Barzaia
OFFICIAL RECOGNITION	UK Hound Group; FCI Group 10; AKC Hound Group
COLOUR VARIATIONS	Any colour

Borzoi
HEIGHT 68-74 cm (27-29 in)

BREED FACT:
The Borzoi used to be known as the Siberian Wolfhound; the Russian word *borzoi* is really a term to encompass all Sight Hounds.

BUILT FOR SPEED and grace, the Borzoi was originally used to hunt the wolf in Russia and is an aristocratic dog. First imported to the UK in the late nineteenth century, Princess Alexandra, later to become Queen, was especially fond of the breed and did much to increase its popularity in Britain.

A courageous, faithful coursing hound, the Borzoi's temperament is sensitive, alert and aloof. The silky coat, longer in dogs than in bitches, requires constant, careful attention to keep it in good condition. The minimum height is 68 cm (27 in) for bitches and 74 cm (29 in) for dogs; weight ranges upwards to around 48 kg (105 lb).

Typically the Borzoi's back is rather bony and rises in a graceful curve. This breed needs plenty of exercise both for fitness and for the sake of contentment.

Left
The Borzoi is no longer used for hunting and its breeding has made it a gentle and obedient companion.

BREED INFORMATION

NAME	Scottish Deerhound
OFFICIAL RECOGNITION	UK Hound Group; FCI Group 10; AKC Hound Group
COLOUR VARIATIONS	Dark blue-grey; Grey; Brindle; Yellow; Sandy-red; Red-fawn with black points

Deerhound
HEIGHT 71-76 cm (28-30 in)

BREED FACT:
Commoners were not allowed to own Deerhounds for fear of them poaching their lordships' deer.

FORMERLY KNOWN as the Scottish Deerhound, this is a breed of great antiquity, used for hunting the red deer in the highlands of Scotland. Fitting so beautifully into the scene of baronial halls it is easy to image this magnificent breed in the chase, built with sufficient speed, endurance and power to pull down a stag, though the breed has a gentle dignity.

Friendly in temperament, with a height range from 71–76 cm (28–30 in) and weight can be up to 45.5 kg (100 lb) – this is not a breed which fits comfortably into a small flat. The thick, close-lying coat is harsh to the touch but does not require a great amount of grooming. Although the breed standard lists a wide variety of colours for this breed, the majority are dark.

Left
The collapse of the clan system and the cutting of the forests led to the rapid decline of the Deerhound in Scotland.

Hound

GROUP **COAT CARE**

small

SIZE **FEEDING**

Dachshunds

HEIGHT 30-35 cm (12-14 in)

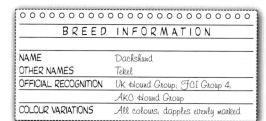

BREED INFORMATION	
NAME	Dachshund
OTHER NAMES	Tekel
OFFICIAL RECOGNITION	UK Hound Group; FCI Group 4; AKC Hound Group
COLOUR VARIATIONS	All colours; dapples evenly marked

THERE ARE SIX VARIETIES of Dachshund in the UK, falling into two sizes, Standard weighing 9–12 kg (20-26 lb) and Miniature which must not be over 5 kg (11 lb). The three coat types are Smooth-haired, Long-haired and Wire-haired. Although there are some minor differences between them, all should conform to the same Kennel Club Standard. The Miniature Wire-haired Dachshund was not recognised in Britain until 1959.

The breed name translates from German into badger dog and this may have been their original purpose. However, they will also go to ground after other

animals and were used above ground to track down wounded game and to flush game out of thick cover. Popular in the UK since the nineteenth century – Queen Victoria had several – they lost public interest during the two world wars because of anti-German feeling, although they rose highly in the popularity stakes in the 1950s.

Although long and low in stature, they have a well muscled body; their love of food should not be pandered to, otherwise they may put on weight. Their defiant carriage of head and intelligent expression indicates their courage, sometimes to the point of rashness. Firmness is necessary during early training as Dachshunds can be rather independent, but they should be obedient. All colours are acceptable but no white is allowed except for a small patch on the chest which, though permissible, is not desirable.

Hound

GROUP **COAT CARE**

large

SIZE **FEEDING**

Elkhound

HEIGHT 49-52 cm (19.5-20.5 in)

BREED INFORMATION	
NAME	Elkhound
OTHER NAMES	Norwegian Elkhound; Norsk Elghund Grå; Norwegian Elkhound grey
OFFICIAL RECOGNITION	UK Hound Group; FCI Group; AKC Hound Group

DEVELOPED BY HUNTSMEN in Norway, this handsome breed hunted the massive, well-antlered elk; often they worked over frozen, wooded ground. This is undoubtedly a hardy member of the spitz family, with a bold, energetic disposition. Stamina, agility and courage were, and still are, vital.

Compact in body and square in outline, their height is some 49–52 cm (19.5–20.5 in) with a weight of up to 23 kg (50 lb). Capable of putting on excess weight, the Elkhound must not be allowed to get too lazy but is content to live with any family, however hectic its lifestyle. This friendly, intelligent breed is excellent with children though it can, at times, be a little vocal. The close, abundant, weather-resistant, double coat is fairly easy to maintain and carries a rich ruff around the neck.

Finnish Spitz

HEIGHT 39-50 cm (15.5-20 in)

Hound
GROUP

COAT CARE

medium

SIZE

FEEDING

ANOTHER MEMBER of the spitz group, this breed is easily distinguishable by its bright red colour. This is a double-coated breed, and the undercoat is of a lighter colour which has the effect of making the whole coat glow. The Finnish Spitz is originally descended from Russia's Laika, although it was developed in Finland and used primarily for bird hunting. However, despite being only 39–50 cm (15.5–20 in) in height and weighing in the region of 14–16 kg (15–20 in) the Spitz has also been known to tackle larger game including bear and elk.

A lively, friendly, active companion, like all the spitz breeds the Finnish has well-developed vocal abilities and,

although happy in all weathers, this breed likes to be indoors. The undercoat is short, soft and dense, the outercoat on the shoulders is longer and coarse, particularly in males.

Left
The Finnish Spitz makes an excellent watchdog and has a tremendously loud bark, which is equally useful in the field.

Foxhound

HEIGHT 58-64 cm (23-25 in)

Hound
GROUP

COAT CARE

large

SIZE

FEEDING

THE HISTORY OF THE Foxhound is recorded in hunting records rather than those of the showring and, thanks to the Masters of the Hunt, the ancestry of modern Foxhounds can be traced far back.

A pack of Fox-hounds can spend the whole day in the field and must be capable of jumping, as well as crashing through thick undergrowth.

Now seen more frequently in small

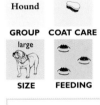

numbers in the showring, the Foxhound is a powerful, clean-cut dog with stamina, endurance and a natural ability to hunt. Its temperament is friendly and not aggressive and its expression is keen. The Foxhound height ranges from 58–64 cm (23–25 in) and weight roughly from 25–34 kg (55–77 lb). The short coat is weatherproof. The hazel or brown eyes are keen and alert. The pendant ears are set high and carried close to the head. The muzzle is square and straight.

Left
The Foxhound is primarily used for fox-hunting, but also makes an attentive, vocal guard dog.

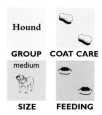

Hound

GROUP | **COAT CARE**

medium

SIZE | **FEEDING**

Grand Basset Griffon Vendéen

HEIGHT 39-43 cm (15.5-17 in)

BREED INFORMATION

NAME	Grand Basset Griffon Vendéen
OTHER NAMES	Large Basset Griffon Vendeen
OFFICIAL RECOGNITION	Uk Hound Group; FCI Group 6
COLOUR VARIATIONS	White with lemon, orange, tri-colour or grizzle markings

BREED FACT:
For around a century, the Desamy family have bred Grand Basset Griffon Vendéen at La Chaize-le-Vicomte.

Right
This breed had nearly disappeared by the end of the Second World War. Although revived, it is still rare.

THE GRAND Basset Griffon Vendéen is extremely popular in its homeland, France, and is one of the best represented hound breeds in that country. This good rabbit and hare hunter is taller than the other Bassets better known in Britain, standing some 39–43 cm (15.5–17 in) high. The breed has a strong will and can be a little obstinate but is a happy, out-going breed, thoughtful, not easily agitated and, though independent, is willing to please. It has been said that the Vendeen people are reputed to be stubborn, independent characters and that their human characteristics have been transmitted to their hounds.

An intelligent, noble-looking dog, the Grand Basset Griffon Vendéen has a rough, long coat but without exaggeration. It must always be flat, never silky or woolly, and there is a thick undercoat. Reaching at least to the end of the nose, the ears are also covered in long hair and they fold inwards.

Hound

GROUP | **COAT CARE**

large

SIZE | **FEEDING**

Grand Bleu de Gascogne

HEIGHT 60-70 cm (23.5-27.5 in)

BREED INFORMATION

NAME	Grand Bleu de Gascogne
OTHER NAMES	Large Blue Gascony Hound
OFFICIAL RECOGNITION	Uk Hound Group; FCI Group 6
COLOUR VARIATIONS	Black marked on white, with black mottling (appearing blue)

Right
Although not fast, the Grand Bleu de Gascoigne has great stamina when on the trail.

ONE OF THE LARGER French hunting hounds, the Grand Bleu de Gascogne is an ancient breed with origins thought to lie in racing breeds taken to France by Phoenician traders. Used as a scent-trailing, working dog, the breed has a highly developed sense of smell and a deep bay.

The Grand Bleu is gentle and kind, the large, long head giving a distinguished look with eyes which have a rather sad, trusting expression. The ears are low set and fine, hanging at least to the tip of the nose and they are curled inward. The coat is smooth and weather resistant and the colour interesting, always with tan spots above the eyes, giving a 'four-eyed' effect. Height ranges from 60–70 cm (23.5–27.5 in) and weight is generally 32–35 kg (71–77 lb).

BREED FACT:
Although Grand Bleu de Gascogne were shown in France 100 years ago, they were then predominantly black.

Greyhound

HEIGHT 68-76 cm (27-30 in)

Hound

GROUP   COAT CARE

large

SIZE   FEEDING

MENTIONED IN THE FOREST LAWS made by King Canute in 1016, the Greyhound is generally believed to have been brought to Britain by the Celts, though its origins are most probably in the Middle East as dogs resembling this type have been discovered carved on Ancient Egyptian tombs, which date back some 4,000 years. A gentle, affectionate, kindly breed, this is a sighthound closely connected with coursing, which means that it is sensible to exercise caution with cats and small dogs.

The breed is also used for track racing, which generally employs Greyhounds smaller than those seen in the show ring; the latter are 68–76 cm (27–30 in) in height and weigh on average 27–32 kg (60–70 lb). Easy to keep clean, the Greyhound makes a delightful companion, which is happy in the company of children.

BREED FACT:
The Waterloo cup for Greyhound racing was founded in 1836 and the breed can reach speeds up to 60 km/h (37 mph).

Left
The Greyhound requires less exercise than one might expect, although it obviously enjoys going for walks.

Hamiltonstövare

HEIGHT 53-57 cm (21-22.5 in)

Hound

GROUP   COAT CARE

large

SIZE   FEEDING

THE MOST POPULAR of the hound breeds in Sweden, the Hamiltonstövare was founded primarily on English Foxhounds and German hounds. This is a strong, striking, richly coloured dog with a black, brown and white coat, the proportion of colourings clearly specified in the breed standard. A hardy breed with good stamina, the ideal size is 57 cm (22.5 in) for dogs and 53 cm (21 in) for bitches, while weight usually ranges from 23–27 kg (50–60 lb).

More suited to the country than the town, because it is a hunting dog, the 'Hamilton' enjoys spending hours in the fields and is not always quick in returning. This is an even tempered hound, a happy companion and friend. The coat, though short and soft, is especially thick during winter and there is ample hair between the pads.

BREED FACT:
First shown in 1886, the breed is named after Count Hamilton, who was the founder of the Swedish Kennel Club.

Left
This is a handsome breed, which deserves to be known more widely outside its native Sweden.

Hound
GROUP

COAT CARE

large
SIZE

FEEDING

Ibizan Hound

HEIGHT 56-74 cm (22-29 in)

○○○○○○○○○○○○○○○○○○○○○○○○○○○○

BREED INFORMATION

NAME	Ibizan Hound
OTHER NAMES	Podenco Ibicenco
OFFICIAL RECOGNITION	Uk Hound Group; FCI Group 5; AKC Hound Group
COLOUR VARIATIONS	White; Chestnut; Lion; Any combination

DEPICTED ON ancient Egyptian tombs and pottery, the Ibizan Hound now takes the name of the Island of Ibiza which was invaded by Carthaginians in the sixth century BC. A century later they left behind their hunting dogs, forerunners of this breed. Despite the breed's name, this dog is also reputed to have been living on the island of Formentera for around 5,000 years.

Loyal companions to man, Ibizan Hounds have a tremendous ability to jump great heights and have a reputation of being great

escapologists, so they need sensible, considerate but firm handling.

Distinguished by large, erect and highly mobile ears this is a tall dog, varying from 56–74 cm (22–29 in) and weighing 19–25 kg (42–55 lb). There are two types of coat, rough and smooth. The Ibizan's ribcage is not so deep as in the majority of dog breeds and there should be a gap of 7–8 cm (2.5–3 in) between the base of the ribcage and the elbow.

BREED FACT:

Ibizan Hounds came to Britain in 1928 but took 30 years to become established because of problems with distemper.

Hound
GROUP

COAT CARE

large
SIZE

FEEDING

Irish Wolfhound

HEIGHT 81-86 cm (32-34 in)

○○○○○○○○○○○○○○○○○○○○○○○○○○○

BREED INFORMATION

NAME	Irish Wolfhound
OFFICIAL RECOGNITION	Uk Hound Group; FCI Group 10; AKC Hound Group
COLOUR VARIATIONS	Grey; Brindle; Pure white; Fawn; Wheaten; Steel grey

ADMIRED FROM THE TIME of the Roman invasion, the ancestors of the Irish Wolfhound we know today were used for centuries in Ireland to hunt wolf, boar and Irish elk. However, by the seventeenth century the breed was on the verge of extinction, but was revived by Captain Graham in the mid-nineteenth century.

Despite the breed's enormous size and strength the Wolfhound has a gentle, kind and friendly nature. Never appearing to hurry, this dog can quickly cover an enormous amount of ground for this is a breed with great power, activity, speed and courage. The desired average height ranges from 81–86 cm (32–34 in) and the weight can be as much as 55 kg (120 lb). For the huge frame to develop properly a high quality diet is essential and the Wolfhound also needs plenty of space and a reasonable amount of exercise.

BREED FACT:

The tail of the Irish Wolfhound is long, slightly curved, carried low and sweeps up at the end.

Norwegian Lundehund

HEIGHT 32-38 cm (12.5-15 in)

Hound	
GROUP	**COAT CARE**
medium	
SIZE	**FEEDING**

NOW PRIMARILY A COMPANION dog, the Norwegian Lundehund was once used in Norway to collect puffins from their precipitous cliff nests. This small, spitz type dog is rectangular in shape, lightly built and little known in Britain – it is considered the rarest breed in the world. Characteristic are the extra toe on each foot, an ear which can close for protection and double dew claws on the forefeet. The front legs are capable of 180 degree rotation and the neck is double-jointed.

Always an alert, energetic and lively dog, the Norwegian Lundehund is not nervous or aggressive.

The dense, rough outercoat lies flat against the body whilst the undercoat is soft. The breed's weight is roughly 6–7 kg (13–15.5 lb) and height 32–38 cm (12.5–15 in). Unfortunately, breeding in Britain has been curtailed due to an inherited genetic problem but, although rare, this unusual breed is still bred in its native Norway, where it is thriving.

BREED FACT:

The Norwegian Lundehund originated in northern Norway and although it had been used for centuries to hunt puffins, it was not recognised until 1943.

Left

The Norwegian Lundehund's physical adaptations enable it to scale cliff paths and cross rocky crevasses in search of puffin nests.

Otterhound

HEIGHT 60-67 cm (24-27 in)

Hound	
GROUP	**COAT CARE**
large	
SIZE	**FEEDING**

THE HISTORY OF OTTER hunting can be traced back to the reign of King Henry II (1154–89) but first mention of the Otterhound as a specific type of dog came in the fourteenth century when they were described as 'a rough sort of dog between a hound and a terrier'.

A big, strong hound, built for a long day's work in water, the breed must also be able to gallop on land. A rough, double coat and large feet are essential. This even tempered, amiable breed has a loud, baying call. Owners should ideally be energetic but not house-proud. Its height is 60–67 cm (24–27 in) and its weight varies greatly but can be anything from 30–55 kg (65–120 lb). Pigment should harmonise with coat colour and this is one of the few breeds in which a slight butterfly nose is permissible.

BREED FACT:

At the beginning of the twentieth century there were more than 20 otter hunting packs in England.

Left

The Otterhound's thick, insulated undercoat enables it to swim safely in the most icy of waters.

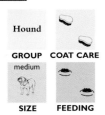
Hound

GROUP **COAT CARE**

medium

SIZE **FEEDING**

Petit Basset Griffon Vendéen

HEIGHT 33-38 cm (13-15 in)

BREED FACT:

The Petit Basset Griffon Vendéen, often known simply as the PBGV, prefers fresh, cool weather to oppressive heat.

FROM A RUGGED REGION of Western France comes the Petit Basset Griffon Vendéen, familiarly known by its initials, PBGV. Low to the ground and rough-coated, this is a strong, active hound, capable of a day's hunting and with a good voice which is freely used. The large, dark eyes impart a friendly, intelligent expression and the red of the lower eyelid does not show.

This happy, extrovert character is independent and yet willing to please. The long eyebrows give a slightly comical look while the beard and moustache pick up all sorts of debris as the nose sweeps the ground. Height ranges from

33–38 cm (13–15 in) and weight averages 14–18 kg (31–40 lb). This is a charming breed, a good choice for a fun-loving family.

Right

The most popular of the griffon venéens, the Petit Basset makes an alert, friendly pet.

Hound

GROUP **COAT CARE**

large

SIZE **FEEDING**

Pharaoh Hound

HEIGHT 53-56 cm (21-22 in)

Right

Phoenician traders took these dogs to Malta with them 2,000 years ago.

DOGS SIMILAR TO THE Pharaoh Hound are to be found in ancient Egyptian art, but it is thought that some 2,000 years ago Phoenician traders took the breed to Malta, now considered this dog's native home. First imported to Britain in the 1920s, the breed did not become established here until the 1970s.

A hunter using both scent and sight, the Pharaoh Hound is noted for erect ears, amber eyes and keen, intelligent expression. Always tan in colour, certain limited white markings are allowed and the nose must be flesh coloured to blend with the coat. In height, bitches are ideally 53 cm (21 in) and dogs 56 cm (22 in), and their weight is usually

in the region of 25 kg (45–55 lb). The Pharaoh Hound is a graceful yet powerful dog with fast, free movement so this friendly, playful hound needs not only affection but exercise too.

BREED FACT:

White sometimes found on the chest is called 'The Star'; toes can be white, and a white tail tip is highly desirable.

Rhodesian Ridgeback

HEIGHT 61-67 cm (24-27 in)

BREED INFORMATION

NAME	Rhodesian Ridgeback
OTHER NAMES	Ridgeback; Lion Dog
OFFICIAL RECOGNITION	Uk Hound Group; FCI Group 6; AKC Hound Group
COLOUR VARIATIONS	Light wheaten to red wheaten

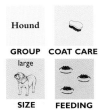

Hound

GROUP COAT CARE

large

SIZE FEEDING

DESCENDED FROM DOGS kept by the Hottentots since the fifteenth century at least, big game hunters used to call the Rhodesian Ridgeback the 'lion dog' because in Zimbabwe (formerly Rhodesia) this breed helped in the pursuit of quarry, often lions. The dog did not actually attack the lion but worried it until the hunter arrived. Now in Africa the Ridgeback is used as a guard and is regarded as South Africa's native dog.

Standing 61–67 cm (24–27 in) in height and weighing up to around 39 kg (85 lb), this is a handsome, strong, muscular and active dog, capable of great endurance with fair speed. An important distinguishing feature is a ridge of hair along the back, formed by hair growing in the opposite direction from the rest of the coat.

BREED FACT:
The breed standard of the Rhodesian Ridgeback was drawn up in South Africa in 1922, since when there have been only minor changes.

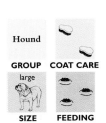

Left
The Rhodesian Ridgeback is a good family dog. It is very loyal but tolerates no threats from strangers.

Saluki

HEIGHT 58.4-71.1 cm (23-28 in)

BREED INFORMATION

NAME	Saluki
OTHER NAMES	Persian Greyhound, Gazelle Hound, Arabian Hound
OFFICIAL RECOGNITION	Uk Hound Group; FCI Group 10; AKC Hound Group

Hound

GROUP COAT CARE

large

SIZE FEEDING

THE SALUKI HAS BEEN called 'The oldest race of hunting dogs in the world', and has been known in its Arab homeland since 5,000 BC. Historically considered a prized possession, the Saluki has been looked upon quite differently from other dogs, largely because of the breed's hunting abilities and beauty. An honoured status assured purity of descent.

A sighthound, used with the hawk for coursing hare and gazelle, the Saluki has great speed and endurance. Combining

grace with symmetry, there is a dignified expression with far-seeing eyes. The coat is smooth and silky with feathering except in the smooth variety. The height of males is from 58.4–71.1 cm (23–28 in) with bitches rather smaller, and weight is in the region of 14–25 kg (31–55 lb). Although the Saluki should not be nervous or aggressive, this a very sensitive dog, reserved with strangers and not really suitable for any family which does not appreciate this rather special personality.

BREED FACT:
When exhibited at FCI shows, the Saluki is divided by coat: a) long-haired or fringed and b) short-haired.

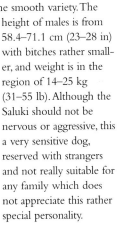

Left
As the Saluki's alternate name suggests, it was used by the Bedouin to hunt gazelle, often in conjunction with hawks.

Hound
GROUP   **COAT CARE**

large
SIZE   **FEEDING**

Segugio Italiano

HEIGHT 48-59 cm (19-23 in)

Right
*Although there are
still only a few
Segugio in Britain, it
is becoming more
popular outside Italy.*

BREED INFORMATION	
NAME	Segugio Italiano
OTHER NAMES	Italian Segugio, Segugio, Italian Hound
OFFICIAL RECOGNITION	UK Hound Group; FCI Group 6
COLOUR VARIATIONS	Black/tan; Deep red to wheaten

ANOTHER BREED WITH ANCESTRY going back to the coursing hounds of the early Egyptians, mastiff blood was introduced to the Segugio Italiano to give more bulk. With long legs, like those of a sighthound, and a head more like that of a scent hound, the beauty of the breed was highly regarded during the Italian Renaissance. This breed has an exceptional sense of smell and shows interest not only in the capture but also in the kill.

There are two coat varieties for this breed: coarse which is harsh, dense, wiry and close lying; and smooth which is thick and shiny.

This medium-sized breed, at 48–59 cm (19–23 in) varies somewhat in weight from 18–28 kg (40–62 lb). It is gentle, affectionate and even tempered . Equally good as a working dog and companion, the Segugio requires minimum grooming.

Hound
GROUP   **COAT CARE**

large
SIZE   **FEEDING**

Right
*The large rib cage of
the Sloughi indicates
its great lung capacity,
ideal for hunting
gazelle and hare.*

Sloughi

HEIGHT 60-70 cm (23.5-27.5 in)

BREED INFORMATION	
NAME	Sloughi
OTHER NAMES	Arabian Greyhound, Tuareg Sloughi
OFFICIAL RECOGNITION	UK Hound Group; FCI Group 10
COLOUR VARIATIONS	Shades of sable or fawn, with or without black mask. Some other colours

THE SLOUGHI HAILS from the deserts and mountains of North Africa and is thought to be depicted on the tomb of Tutankhamun. Suited to running down hare, gazelle and antelope this dog has a muscular, lean appearance. There are both desert and mountain varieties – the former is slender, light, graceful and elegant, while the mountain type is more compact with stronger bone.

The breed becomes attached to its owner and family at an early age and is usually reluctant to transfer loyalty if a change of home is necessary. The Sloughi is indifferent with strangers. The hair is tough and fine and there are various coat colours, with or without a black mask, although parti-colours are not permissible. The ideal height is 60–70 cm (23.5–27.5 in) and the breed usually weighs from 20–27 kg (45–60 lb).

```
○○○○○○○○○○○○○○○○○○○○○○○○○○
     B R E E D   I N F O R M A T I O N
NAME                  Whippet
OFFICIAL RECOGNITION  UK Hound Group; FCI Group 10;
                      AKC Hound Group
COLOUR VARIATIONS     Any colour or mixture of colours
```

Whippet

HEIGHT 44-51 cm (17-20 in)

Hound
GROUP **COAT CARE**
medium
SIZE **FEEDING**

THE SMALLEST OF the hounds commonly originally used for hare coursing, the Whippet that we know today originated from numerous crosses in the nineteenth century between Greyhounds selected for their speed and strength and some terriers, for the size and tenacity, although sporting hounds go back longer than that. In the North-East of England and the Midlands, the racing of Whippets became popular in the late nineteenth century, racing and coursing is still enjoyed by many.

Fairly small in size, 44–51 cm (17–20 in) and weighing from 12.5–14 kg (27–31 lb) on average, the Whippet is a balanced combination of muscular power and strength, coupled with great elegance and grace. This is a breed built for specifically for speed and work and should show no form of exaggeration. The fine, short coat requires little work and the gentle, affectionate, even disposition makes this breed an ideal companion. Whippets have very thin skin so feel the cold and scar easily.

BREED FACT:

Whippets became 'straight racers' because many had to race in the straight alleyways between rows of houses.

Below
Highly adaptable and easy to train, the Whippet suits both domestic and sporting purposes.

The Pastoral Group

THE PASTORAL GROUP officially came into being in Britain as recently as January of 1999, bringing the total number of groups here to seven. With the exception of the Leonberger, which was in the Utility Group, all the other breeds had previously been together under the Working Group which was excessively large in number. Now it is this newly formed group which has the highest number of breeds, currently totalling 30.

DOGS IN THE GROUP

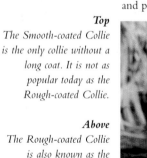

SIZES OF BREEDS VARY in this group but all have been used, at least in the past, for work on pastoral land. The low-set Welsh Corgis, along with some other breeds, are renowned for driving cattle by nipping at their heels, while larger breeds, like the Pyrenean Mountain Dog and Anatolian Shepherd Dog, have protected shepherds and their flocks from predators. Breeds in this group are used to herd and protect reindeer in northern climes, while the Malamute offers protection against bears and wolves. The Samoyed has doubled as both a sled dog and as a herder.

Several are sheepdogs, and among them are some of the most highly renowned in the world. Indeed many farmers, especially in Wales and Scotland, still say that a good working Border Collie is as valuable as several trained men, and on the vast expanses of land in Australia, dogs provide invaluable service. The German Shepherd Dog was one of the first breeds to be used in war and indeed is a prime example of the heights of training which can be reached by dogs within the Pastoral Group, and many are highly skilled in obedience work and, more recently, agility.

Because breeds such as these are worked in all weathers, a serviceable and protective coat is essential. Most have dense undercoats as protection against the elements and the Hungarian Puli and Komondor have distinctive coats which form cords, whereas that of the Bergamasco forms strands or loose mats and is greasy to the touch.

The smallest breed within this Group is the Shetland Sheepdog, familiarly known as the Sheltie, a glamorous, small breed with an abundant, luxurious coat which comes in a variety of colours. Even this breed's eyes can be different, one each of two different colours. The Bearded Collie is another breed with a long coat, although quite different from that of the Sheltie, while the Anatolian Shepherd Dog is a short-coated but very substantial and imposing breed which usually weighs well in excess of 45.5 kg (100 lb).

Personalities vary from breed to breed, and even within a breed, so it is important to ascertain this aspect, too, before selecting a new dog to share one's home. It is also wise to bear in mind that working dogs prefer to lead a busy life so need plenty to occupy their minds. Many of the breeds in this Pastoral Group are undoubtedly glamorous, indeed some have changed almost beyond recognition from those seen a hundred or so years ago, but all were bred originally to do a job of work and in an ideal world all should still be capable of doing that work.

Top
The Smooth-coated Collie is the only collie without a long coat. It is not as popular today as the Rough-coated Collie.

Above
The Rough-coated Collie is also known as the Lassie Collie because of its association with that famous canine film star.

Right
The Border Collie is prized for its ability to herd sheep, displaying great stamina and intelligence.

Anatolian Shepherd Dog

HEIGHT 71-81 cm (28-32 in)

BREED INFORMATION

NAME	Anatolian Shepherd Dog
OTHER NAMES	Coban Köpegi, Turkish Shepherd Guard Dog
OFFICIAL RECOGNITION	UK Working Group; FCI Group 2
COLOUR VARIATIONS	All whole colours

Pastoral
GROUP COAT CARE
large
SIZE FEEDING

DESCENDING FROM the ancient breeds of Mastiff and Middle Eastern flock-guarding dogs, the Anatolian Shepherd is also known as the Turkish Shepherd Guard Dog. This old breed goes back some 3,000 years and, because of its faithful work as a guardian of flocks, working in extremes of heat and cold, it is held in the highest regard by Turkish shepherds.

A large, upstanding and powerfully built dog, the Anatolian stands 71–81 cm (28–32 in) high and weighs 41–64 kg (90.5–141 lb). With size, stamina and speed, this is an active, hard-working breed with broad, heavy head and short, dense coat. All coat colours are acceptable, but they should be whole

colours, cream to fawn, with a black mask and ears. Although naturally independent, this is an intelligent breed, proud and confident, steady and bold.

BREED FACT:
The Anatolian Shepherd Dog first came to Britain in 1965, since when the breed has had a small, but dedicated following.

Left
The Anatolian Shepherd Dog makes an excellent guard, but is slightly unreliable as a companion unless it has been carefully trained and socialised.

Australian Cattle Dog

HEIGHT 43-51 cm (17-20 in)

BREED INFORMATION

NAME	Australian Cattle Dog
OTHER NAMES	Blue Heeler, Queensland Heeler, Australian Heeler, Hall's Heeler
OFFICIAL RECOGNITION	UK Working Group; FCI Group 1; AKC Herding Group

Pastoral
GROUP COAT CARE
medium
SIZE FEEDING

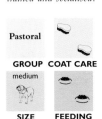

THIS BREED IS HIGHLY prized in Australia for controlling and moving cattle in all environments. The alternative name 'Heeler' came about because of the breed's method of dealing with cattle, crouching behind them and nipping the heels. By careful selection, the Australian Cattle Dog was developed by crossing breeds including the Dingo, Kelpie, Bull Terrier and Dalmatian.

A strong, compact, symmetrical dog, the breed has substance and power, in hard muscular condition conveying agility, strength and endurance. Apart from cattle work, the Australian Cattle Dog also guards the stockman and his property. This is an alert, intelligent and watchful breed, naturally suspicious of strangers but biddable and amenable to handling, a courageous, trustworthy dog, devoted to work. Its height is 43–51 cm (17–20 in) and weight generally 16–20 kg (35–45 lb). The double coat is smooth with a short, dense undercoat and the colour is basically blue, blue-mottled or speckled, or red speckled.

BREED FACT:
Various different breeds are ancestors of the Australian Cattle Dog but it has been pure-bred since the mid-1890s.

Pastoral	
GROUP	**COAT CARE**
large	
SIZE	**FEEDING**

Australian Shepherd

HEIGHT 46-58 cm (18-23 in)

```
○○○○○○○○○○○○○○○○○○○○○○○○○○○○○○
      BREED INFORMATION
NAME                  Australian Shepherd
OFFICIAL RECOGNITION  UK Working Group; AKC Herding
                      Group
COLOUR VARIATIONS     Blue; blue merle; Black; Red merle
```

BREED FACT:
The Australian Shepherd is actually an American breed and in the USA the first official registry was in the 1950s.

BASQUE SHEPHERDS from Spain emigrated to Australia towards the end of the nineteenth century taking their dogs with them, later moving on to the Americas and again taking their dogs. From these dogs in the USA the breed originated. Although the breed is a relatively recent arrival in Britain, it rapidly became popular and has a seemingly ever-increasing number of enthusiasts.

An intelligent dog with strong herding and guarding instincts, the Australian Shepherd has great

Right
The Australian Shepherd has adapted well to search and rescue work, as well as to family life

stamina, is loyal, attentive, animated, lithe and agile, able to alter both speed and direction instantly. It has an even disposition, and the breed may show initial reserve but should never be shy or aggressive. The medium length coat is straight to wavy with a weather resistant undercoat and the range of colours is quite spectacular: blue, blue merle, black and red merle all with or without tan points. White is only allowed in specific areas. The height is 46–58 cm (18–23·in) and weight varies considerably from 16–32 kg (35–70 lb).

Pastoral	
GROUP	**COAT CARE**
large	
SIZE	**FEEDING**

Bearded Collie

HEIGHT 51-56 cm (20-22 in)

```
○○○○○○○○○○○○○○○○○○○○○○○○○○○○○○
      BREED INFORMATION
NAME                  Bearded Collie
OFFICIAL RECOGNITION  UK Working Group; FCI Group 1;
                      AKC Herding Group
COLOUR VARIATIONS     Various, with or without white markings
```

Right
Lively, friendly and easily bored, the Bearded Collie is ideal for owners with time and energy

ONCE known as the Hairy Mountain Dog, later as the Scottish Bearded or Highland Collie, this breed is known to have herded cattle on the hills of Scotland for many a long year. Records appear to date back to around the sixteenth century. It is also said that Polish Lowland Sheepdogs were abandoned on the Scottish coast and that these bred with local herding dogs.

BREED FACT:
Familiarly known as the 'Beardie', the Bearded Collie virtually disappeared as a working dog, but was revived in 1944.

Belgian Shepherd Dog

HEIGHT 56-66 cm (22-26 in)

THERE ARE DIFFERENT varieties of Belgian Shepherd Dog: the Groenendale, Laekenois, Malinois and Tervuren, the four differing only in colour, length and texture of coat. Names are taken from the individual towns in Belgium from which each hails. The breed dates back to the Middle Ages but not until 1891 did a professor of the Belgian Veterinary School establish standards for the types, thereby separating them. In Britain they are now shown together as one breed.

All stand 56–66 cm (22–26 in) high and weigh from 27.5–28.5 kg (61–63 lb). They are intelligent and hardy, but not aggressive. The Belgian Shepherd is a guard as well as a sheepdog. Their arched toes are very close together, the soles thick and springy, the forefeet round and the hind feet oval.

BREED FACT:
Belgium originally recognised eight different standards for the Belgian Shepherd Dog and in Britain only in recent years have the four varieties been shown together.

Bergamasco

HEIGHT 54-62 cm (21-25 in)

FROM NORTHERN ITALY comes the Bergamasco, of which there are still very few in Britain. This medium sized sheepdog of ancient origin stands 54–62 cm (21–25 in) high and weighing 26–38 kg (56–84 lb). A vigilant guard with very strong protective instincts, this breed is intelligent, cautious and patient, consequently needing sensible handling and firm control. The Bergamasco prefers a countryside environment to city life.

Square in profile, a distinctive feature of the breed is the coat which is abundant and long, of harsh texture on the front of the body but softer on the head and limbs. The coat is greasy to the touch and tends to form into strands or loose mats from the top of the body. It should not form cords like those of the Hungarian Puli and Komondor. The colour is solid grey or with patches of all shades of grey through to black.

BREED FACT:
Roman writers described an ideal sheepdog which was agile and sufficiently fearless to repel the wolf. Many believe this to have been the Bergamasco.

Left
The Bergamasco can also be black, Isabella and light fawn in colour.

225

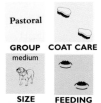

Pastoral

GROUP | **COAT CARE**

medium

SIZE | **FEEDING**

Border Collie

HEIGHT up to 53 cm (up to 21 in)

BREED INFORMATION	
NAME	Border Collie
OFFICIAL RECOGNITION	Uk Working Group; FCI Group 1; AKC Herding Group
COLOUR VARIATIONS	Various. White should never predominate

BREED FACT:
Renowned as one of the world's finest sheepdogs, the Border Collie has been used to herd sheep for centuries.

Right
The Border Collie is not suited to being a pet; it needs constant stimulation and firm training. It may become snappy if bored.

THE NAME BORDER COLLIE was not used until 1915 and the breed is better known as a working dog rather than a show dog. Sheepdog trials have been held since 1873 but the breed is a relative newcomer to shows. The breed's original function was to work sheep, primarily on England's borders with Wales and Scotland.

Keen, responsive, intelligent and alert, the Border Collie needs to work to be happy, requiring regular mental stimulation and physical exercise. The outline shows quality, gracefulness and perfect balance, combined with sufficient substance to give an impression of endurance. Ideal height for dogs is 53 cm (21 in) with bitches slightly less and weight varies between 14–22 kg (30–49 lb). There are two coat varieties, moderately long and smooth, both with dense topcoat and soft, dense weather resistant undercoat. Eyes are brown except in merles where one eye or both, or part of one or both, may be blue.

Pastoral

GROUP | **COAT CARE**

large

SIZE | **FEEDING**

Briard

HEIGHT 56-68 cm (23-27 in)

BREED INFORMATION		
NAME	Briard	
OTHER NAMES	Berger de Brie	
OFFICIAL RECOGNITION	Uk Working Group; FCI Group AKC Herding Group	
COLOUR VARIATIONS	Fawn; Brindle; Black; Slate grey	

Below
The long, wavy coat of the Briard needs regular care.

BELONGING TO AN ancient race of sheep-dogs and originating in the Brie district of France, the Briard's primary use was to herd and guard sheep and it has also been employed as a pack dog by armies.

Rugged in appearance, with suppleness and muscularity, this is a fearless breed, without timidity or aggression. Gay, lively and intelligent, the Briard is a good household dog. Its height is 56–68 cm (23–27 in) and its weight is generally 33.5–34.5 kg (74–76 lb). It is important that this breed has double dew claws set low on the hindlegs. The long coat, which understandably needs care, is slightly wavy and very dry, with a fine, dense undercoat. The head hair forms a moustache, beard and eyebrows. Coat colour is all black, or with white hairs scattered through the coat, various shades of fawn, of which the darker are preferred, or slate grey.

BREED FACT:
During the First World War, the Briard was used as a Red Cross dog and was later introduced to the USA by returning American soldiers.

Rough Collie

HEIGHT 51-61 cm (20-24 in)

Pastoral
GROUP **COAT CARE**

SIZE **FEEDING**

I T SEEMS THAT SEVERAL different breeds have been used in the formation of the Collie, and the difference between the Rough and Smooth Collies is only in coat. It is believed that they evolved from dogs taken to Scotland by the Romans around 50 BC, these having mated with local dogs. The Rough is now a rather refined version of the working Collie owned by shepherds in Scotland.

Of friendly disposition and impassive dignity, the Rough Collie is a dog of great beauty with physical structure on the lines of strength and activity, and no trace of coarseness. The coat is very dense with the outer coat straight and harsh to touch and a soft, furry undercoat. The three recognised colours are Sable and white, Tri-colour and Blue Merle. Height is 51–61 cm (20–24 in) and weight is from 18–30 kg (40–66 lb).

BREED FACT:
The Rough Collie today is longer in the leg than the early working breed of this name.

Left
The expression of the Rough Collie is of great importance and must be in proportion to the size of the dog.

Smooth Collie

HEIGHT 51-61 cm (20-24 in)

Pastoral
GROUP **COAT CARE**

SIZE **FEEDING**

L ESS POPULAR THAN the Rough, the Smooth Collie appears gifted with intelligence, alertness and activity, differing primarily in coat with a

similar gay, friendly disposition. In the past Rough and Smooth Collies have been classified as the same breed, but are now separate.

The head is of great importance and when viewed from the front or side it resembles a well-blunted, clean wedge, smooth in outline. The end of the muzzle is smooth, well-rounded and blunt, but never square. The moderately large ears are wider at their base, carried thrown back in repose but brought forward and semi-erect when on the alert. Coat colours are the same as those of the breed's cousin but there tend to be more blue merles in this breed. Height is generally 51–61 cm (20.5–24 in) and weight 18–29.5 kg (40–65 lb).

BREED FACT:
Although breed history can only be traced back to 1873, there is thought to be a trace of Greyhound in the Smooth Collie.

Left
The coat of the Smooth Collie is short and flat. The topcoat has a harsh texture and the undercoat is very dense.

Pastoral

GROUP | COAT CARE
large
SIZE | FEEDING

Estrela Mountain Dog

HEIGHT 62-72 cm (24.5-28.5 in)

Right

The Estrela Mountain Dog is extremely popular in Portugal but not widely known outside the country.

BREED INFORMATION

NAME	Estrela Mountain Dog
OTHER NAMES	Cão da Serra da Estrela
OFFICIAL RECOGNITION	UK Working Group; FCI Group 2
COLOUR VARIATIONS	Fawn; Brindle; Wolf grey

ONE OF THE OLDEST breeds of the Iberian Peninsula, the Estrela Mountain Dog is from central Portugal and related to the numerous other flock-guarding dogs found in many parts of the world.

This sturdy, well built dog of mastiff type, conveys an impression of strength and vigour and is active with considerable stamina. The Estrela is a hardy guard dog, loyal and affectionate to owners, but indifferent to others. Intelligent and alert, the breed is inclined to be

stubborn. There are two coat types, long and short. The long outer coat is thick and harsh, resembling goat hair, while the dense undercoat is normally lighter in colour; the short coat is thick, moderately harsh, again resembling goat's hair and also with a dense undercoat. Preferred height is 62–72 cm (24.5–28.5 in), although a tolerance of 4 cm (1.5 in) above is allowed, and weight can vary considerably between 30 and 50 kg (66–110 lb).

Pastoral

GROUP | COAT CARE
medium
SIZE | FEEDING

Finnish Lapphund

HEIGHT 41-52 cm (16-20.5 in)

BREED INFORMATION

NAME	Finnish Lapphund
OTHER NAMES	Lapland Dog Suomenlapinkoira, Lapinkoira,
OFFICIAL RECOGNITION	UK Working Group; FCI Group
5COLOUR VARIATIONS	All colours

FOUND THROUGHOUT northern Scandinavia and the Karelian district of Russia, the Finnish Lapphund is still used in the harsh climate of Finland to herd reindeer and to sort out sheep and cattle. This is one of the spitz-type dogs and it enjoys family activities, especially those of the

outdoor type. Strongly built, the Finnish Lapphund is an intelligent, brave, calm and faithful breed with a tendency to herd and it is suitable both as a companion and a watchdog. Standing 41–52 cm (16–20.5 in) high and weighing around 20–21 kg (44–47 lb), the breed has a profuse coat. The outercoat long and coarse, and the undercoat soft and thick. All colours are allowed but the main colour must dominate. Markings of a different colour can be found on the head, neck, chest, legs and tip of tail.

German Shepherd Dog

HEIGHT 57.5-62.5 cm (23-25 in)

BREED INFORMATION	
NAME	German Shepherd Dog
OTHER NAMES	Deutscher Schäferhund; Alsatian
OFFICIAL RECOGNITION	UK Working Group; FCI Group 1; AKC Herding Group
COLOUR VARIATIONS	Black/tan; Gold; Light grey; Sable

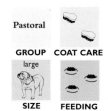

Pastoral
GROUP **COAT CARE**
large
SIZE **FEEDING**

NOW A PARTICULARLY well-known breed with staunch enthusiasts throughout the world, the German Shepherd Dog used to be known as the Alsatian. Developed in Germany and derived from old breeds of herding and farm dogs the breed provides a wide range of services to man. Used as war dogs, they later took part in police and security work, and are used as guide dogs and for guard, sniffer and rescue work. This dog is an excellent obedience worker, too.

Slightly long in comparison to its height, the German Shepherd Dog is ideally 57.5–62.5 cm (23–25 in) high, these proportions coupled with the position of the fore and hindquarters producing a far-reaching and enduring gait. The weight range is 34–43 kg (75–95 lb). Attentive, alert and resilient, the breed is steady of nerve, loyal, self-assured, courageous and tractable and should never be over-aggressive or shy. For exhibition the coat should be straight, hard and as close lying as possible, with a thick undercoat.

BREED FACT:
During the First World War, the incredible number of 48,000 German Shepherd Dogs were enlisted with the German army, many taken forcefully from their owners.

Left
When kept as a pet, the German Shepherd needs firm training and regular exercise.

Hovawart

HEIGHT 58-70 cm (23-27.5 in)

BREED INFORMATION	
NAME	Hovawart
OFFICIAL RECOGNITION	UK Working Group
COLOUR VARIATIONS	Black/gold; Black; Blonde

Pastoral
GROUP **COAT CARE**
large
SIZE **FEEDING**

KNOWN ORIGINALLY AS THE Hofwarth, the Hovawart was mentioned as a reliable watchdog in documents from the Middle Ages. German breeders effectively re-created the breed using farmers' dogs of the Hartz, the Black Forest and other mountain regions, and some of the old-type Hovawart are believed to have survived in rural and isolated farm areas.

With a breed height of 58–70 cm (23–27.5 in) and comparatively low weight of 25–40 kg (55–88 lb), the Hovawart is a hardy animal, capable of working in all weathers. The breed is watchful, agile, swift, dignified and self-assured. Devoted to the family, playful, alert and intelligent, this breed can be wilful and dominant toward other dogs. The coat is long, averaging 10–22.5 cm (4–9 in) and has longer feathering. Its colour includes black, black with gold, and blonde, with pigment suiting the colour of the dog.

BREED FACT:
Officially recognised by the German Kennel Club in the 1930s, the Hovawart only became known in Britain during the last quarter of the twentieth century.

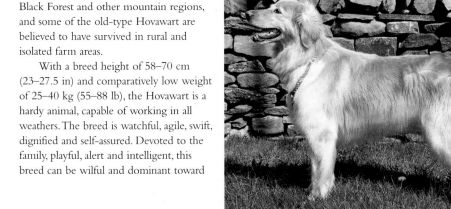

Left
The Hovawart is an agreeable but reserved pet, which is easy to train, but may bite if frightened.

Pastoral

GROUP **COAT CARE**

large

SIZE **FEEDING**

Hungarian Kuvasz

HEIGHT 66-75 cm (26-29 in)

BREED INFORMATION	
NAME	Hungarian Kuvasz
OTHER NAMES	Kuvasz
OFFICIAL RECOGNITION	UK Working Group; FCI Group 1; AKC Working Group
COLOUR VARIATIONS	Pure white

BREED FACT:

The Kuvasz was first mentioned as a breed in the seventeenth century but is believed to have arrived in Hungary five centuries earlier.

Right

The name of the Hungarian Kuvasz comes from the Turkish kavas, *meaning armed guard.*

THIS BREED IS AN ancient Sheepdog, taken to Hungary by nomadic Turkish shepherds in the Middle Ages. Used by herdsmen to protect flocks in the breed's homeland, the Hungarian Kuvasz has adapted as a guard for both people and property. This is a powerful dog, needing firm and

sensible treatment as the breed does not take kindly to unfair discipline.

Large and sturdily built, the Kuvasz stands 66–75 cm (26–29 in) high, weighing 66–114 lb), a well balanced dog of power and nobility. This is not a bulky dog, but a muscular one. Bold, courageous and fearless this breed is protective of its owners and though devoted, gentle and patient, is suspicious of strangers. The double coat is slightly wavy with a medium-coarse top coat and fine, woolly undercoat, the colour is pure white and the skin highly pigmented with patches of slate grey. The dark brown, almond-shaped eyes are slightly slanted, the eyerims and lips black and the roof of the mouth slate grey.

Pastoral

GROUP **COAT CARE**

medium

SIZE **FEEDING**

Hungarian Puli

HEIGHT 37-44 cm (14.5-17.5 in)

BREED INFORMATION	
NAME	Hungarian Puli
OTHER NAMES	Puli
OFFICIAL RECOGNITION	UK Working Group; FCI Group 1; AKC Herding Group
COLOUR VARIATIONS	Black; Rusty black; White; Grey;

BREED FACT:

The Puli's distinctively corded coat keeps out the rain and hair overshadows the eyes, rather like an umbrella.

BETTER KNOWN OUTSIDE Hungary than the country's other breeds, the Puli is believed to have arrived from Asia in the ninth century. Expected to withstand intense cold whilst working, this breed herds flocks of sheep. Sturdy and muscular

with fine bone structure, the overall outline is fairly square, rather like that of the Tibetan Terrier, to which the Puli is distantly related.

This lively, nimble dog is extremely intelligent and although wary of strangers is not nervous and does not display unprovoked aggression. Standing 37–44 cm (14.5–17.5 in) high and weighing 10–15 kg (22–33 lb), one of the most distinctive features of the Hungarian Puli is its coat. Top coat and undercoat in correct proportion cause the coat of the adult to form cords naturally, although the coat of a youngster looks quite different. Colours are black, rusty-black, white and various shades of grey and apricot.

○○○○○○○○○○○○○○○○○○○○○○○○○
BREED INFORMATION

NAME	Komondor
OTHER NAMES	Hungarian Sheepdog
OFFICIAL RECOGNITION	UK Working Group; FCI Group 1; AKC Working Group
COLOUR VARIATIONS	White

Komondor

HEIGHT 60-80 cm (23.5-31.5 in)

ANOTHER BREED FROM Hungary, though much larger than the Puli, is the Komondor which again descends from dogs coming from the East, when the nomadic Magyars moved westward taking with them their Owtcharka breeds. The Komondor is an excellent guard for flocks and herds on farms – indeed a strong, sharp guarding dog that should be treated with respect. A full understanding of the breed is essential before deciding to become an owner.

Wary of strangers and noted for imposing strength and courageous manner, the Komondor is none the less faithful and devoted. With plenty of bone and substance this dog stands 60–80 cm (23.5–31.5 in) on average, and its weight ranges between 36 and 61 kg (80–135 lb). The long, white, coarse outercoat has a softer undercoat, the hair clinging together like tassels, giving a corded appearance. The puppy coat is soft and fluffy and the cords may not be fully formed until the age of two.

Pastoral

GROUP | **COAT CARE**

large

SIZE | **FEEDING**

BREED FACT:
The Komondor has been known in Hungary for over a thousand years and was first mentioned by name in 1544.

Left
The hair of the Komondor requires regular attention to prevent it from becoming matted.

○○○○○○○○○○○○○○○○○○○○○○○○○
BREED INFORMATION

NAME	Lancashire Heeler
OFFICIAL RECOGNITION	UK Working Group
COLOUR VARIATIONS	Black/tan

Lancashire Heeler

HEIGHT 25-30 cm (10-12 in)

THE HISTORY OF THE Lancashire Heeler is somewhat obscure, but it is likely that the Welsh Corgis, which herded cattle from Wales to the Ormskirk area, there met the Manchester Terrier, and that this breed is the outcome of those chance meetings.

A low-set, strong and active worker, the breed works cattle but also has a terrier instinct when rabbiting and ratting. Happy and affectionate with its owners, the Heeler is eager to please and enjoys the company of children, always finding an excuse to join in fun and games. Despite its small stature, standing some 25–30 cm (10–12 in) high and weighing 3–6 kg (6–13 lb), the breed has great energy and needs to be kept occupied. Coat length varies slightly according to the time of year, a sleek, shiny short coat changing to a longer one, showing hair at the mane. The colour is black with rich tan markings.

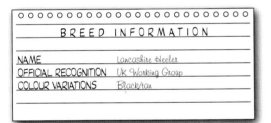

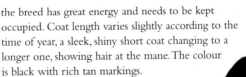

Pastoral

GROUP | **COAT CARE**

small

SIZE | **FEEDING**

BREED FACT:
Although dogs of this kind have been bred in the local area for generations, today's Lancashire Heeler was re-created in the 1960s.

Pastoral

GROUP | **COAT CARE**

large

SIZE | **FEEDING**

Maremma Sheepdog

HEIGHT 60-73 cm (23.5-28.5 in)

BREED INFORMATION	
NAME	Maremma
OTHER NAMES	Cane da pastore Maremmano-Abruzzese
OFFICIAL RECOGNITION	Uk Working Group; FCI Group 1
COLOUR VARIATIONS	White

THE MAREMMA IS NAMED after the grazing plains in southern Tuscany and was used to protect sheep from bears, wolves and also from thieves, as well as offering protection for property. Its origin is uncertain but this breed is thought to have descended from white working dogs of the Magyars.

A majestic dog standing some 60–73 cm (23.5–28.5 in) high and weighing between 30–45 kg (66–99 lb), the Maremma is lithe, sturdy and strongly built with an expression of aloof awareness. The head is conical in shape and appears large in proportion to the size of the body; the jaws are powerful and there is plenty of substance in the foreface. This distinguished dog is lively, intelligent and courageous but not aggressive. The coat is all white, although a little shading of ivory or pale fawn is permissible; it is long, plentiful and rather harsh.

Pastoral

GROUP | **COAT CARE**

medium

SIZE | **FEEDING**

Norwegian Buhund

HEIGHT 45 cm (17.75 in)

BREED INFORMATION	
NAME	Norwegian Buhund
OTHER NAMES	Norsk Buhund
OFFICIAL RECOGNITION	Uk Working Group; FCI Group 5
COLOUR VARIATIONS	Wheaten; Black; Red (not too dark); Wolf sable

Right
The Norwegian Buhund has a lean, wedg-shaped head that narrows towards the nose. The dark eyes have dark lids.

KEPT IN NORWAY for thousands of years, the Buhund has been used primarily as a farm dog. Buhund means dog found on the homestead, or on the farm, and indeed this is a breed which thrives on work; it is a sharp guard and an efficient herder.

A lightly built breed with erect, very mobile, pointed ears and tail carried over the back, the ideal height for a Norwegian Buhund male is 45 cm (17.75 in) and is somewhat less for bitches. Weight is usually 24–26 kg (53–58 lb). The coat colour is wheaten, black, wolf sable or red, but the red should not be too dark. Certain small symmetrical white or black markings are permissible. The outercoat is close and harsh, but smooth, while the undercoat is soft and woolly. The dark brown eyes have a fearless expression in keeping with this energetic, brave, fearless breed.

Old English Sheepdog

HEIGHT 56-61 cm (22-24 in)

Pastoral

GROUP   **COAT CARE**

large

SIZE   **FEEDING**

BREED INFORMATION

NAME	Old English Sheepdog
OTHER NAMES	Bobtail
OFFICIAL RECOGNITION	UK Working Group; FCI Group 1; AKC Herding Group
COLOUR VARIATIONS	Grey; Grizzle; Blue

THE OLD ENGLISH SHEEPDOG'S history seems only to have spanned a few centuries and although it is believed to have descended from European shepherd dogs it is now considered a native British breed, possibly developed in the West Country as a working sheepdog. Familiarly known as the 'Bobtail', the breed is one of great stamina with a typical roll when ambling or walking.

A strong, square-looking dog, this is a thick-set, muscular breed, able bodied and with an intelligent expression. This bold, faithful, trustworthy dog is biddable and of even disposition. The profuse coat has a good harsh texture, with an undercoat of

waterproof pile, and takes both time and patience in its preparation. The colour can be any shade of grey, grizzle or blue, with or without white socks. Height is upwards of 56 cm (22 in) for bitches and 61 cm (24 in) for males while weight is in the region of 29.5–30.5 kg (65–67 lb).

BREED FACT:

A familiar breed, the Old English Sheepdog was depicted by the artist, Gainsborough, in 1771 and today is well-known for its successful use in commercial advertising.

Left

Despite its size and strength, the Old English Sheepdog is very gentle, especially with children.

Polish Lowland Sheepdog

HEIGHT 40-52 cm (16-20 in)

Pastoral

GROUP   **COAT CARE**

medium

SIZE   **FEEDING**

BREED INFORMATION

NAME	Polish Lowland Sheepdog
OTHER NAMES	Polski Owczarek Nizinny
OFFICIAL RECOGNITION	Working Group; FCI Group 1
COLOUR VARIATIONS	All colours

THE POLISH LOWLAND Sheepdog is thought to have arrived in Britain some time in the sixteenth century, used for exchange when sailors from Gdansk arrived at Scottish ports. Known as a working dog since the sixteenth century, the breed is descended from the long-coated herding dogs of Poland and from the Hungarian Puli. In Britain, the Polish Lowland Sheepdog is rather a newcomer to shows, not exhibited until the 1980s.

Standing 40–52 cm (16–20 in) high and weighing around 14–16 kg (30–35 lb), this is a cobby dog, strong and muscular. Watchful, bright, clever and perceptive, the Polish Lowland is easy to train as a watchdog and with an alert, equable temperament, it is lively but self-controlled. The whole body is covered with a long, dense, shaggy coat of any colour. This is of harsh texture and has a soft undercoat. The medium sized head is proportionate to the body, with the profuse hair on forehead, cheeks and chin making it appear larger than it actually is.

BREED FACT:

During the Second World War, the Polish Lowland came close to extinction but its future is now assured.

Left

Seldom used for herding today, the Polish Lowland Sheepdog is a popular household pet in Poland.

Pastoral

GROUP | **COAT CARE**

large

SIZE | **FEEDING**

Pyrenean Mountain Dog

HEIGHT 65-70 cm (26-28 in)

BREED FACT:
The Pyrenean Mountain Dog has been known for centuries and in the Second World War, was used by the French to carry messages and packs.

Right
The imposing size of the Pyrenean Mountain Dog makes it unsuitable for urban environments.

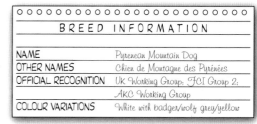

BREED INFORMATION	
NAME	Pyrenean Mountain Dog
OTHER NAMES	Chien de Montagne des Pyrénées
OFFICIAL RECOGNITION	UK Working Group; FCI Group 2; AKC Working Group
COLOUR VARIATIONS	White with badger/wolf grey/yellow

KNOWN IN THE PYRENEES as a natural guard and protector of shepherds and flocks against wolves and other predators, although dogs of this general type were known in France well before the birth of Christ. They are said to have been discovered by the French; indeed, Louis XIV called the Pyrenean Mountain Dog the Royal Dog of France.

With its great size, substance and power, the Pyrenean Mountain Dog looks immensely strong, with males standing a minimum of 70 cm (28 in) high and bitches 65 cm (26 in), although most considerably exceed these heights. The lowest weight of dogs of the minimum required height are 50 kg (110 lb) and 40 kg (90 lb) respectively. With its attractive, profuse coat and strong head without coarseness, the breed imparts a certain elegance. The coat can be all white or mainly white with patches of badger, wolf grey or pale yellow. Its temperament is quietly confident.

Pastoral

GROUP | **COAT CARE**

medium

SIZE | **FEEDING**

Pyrenean Sheepdog

HEIGHT 38-48 cm (15-19 in)

BREED FACT:
A breed developed amongst rural communities, the Pyrenean Sheepdog was not registered with the English Kennel Club until 1988

BREED INFORMATION	
NAME	Pyrenean Sheepdog
OTHER NAMES	Berger des Pyrénées
OFFICIAL RECOGNITION	UK Working Group; FCI Group 1
COLOUR VARIATIONS	Several

THIS ENERGETIC, SMALL SHEEPDOG was selected to herd large flocks of sheep in rural areas. With its strong herding instinct, the highly intelligent Pyrenean Sheepdog has tremendous energy and stamina for its size. Proper socialising is important during the early weeks of life in order for this alert, lively dog to adapt to household situations.

The coat of this breed comes in several different colours and can be various shades of fawn, light to dark grey (often with white), blue merle, slate blue, brindle, black or black and white. There are two coat types: 'long', which has long hair on the legs to cover the toes, or 'semi-long' which is short hair with fringing on the forelegs and short hair below hocks. The quality of the coat is harsh, dense and almost flat or slightly wavy. Height falls between 38–48 cm (15–19 in) and weight ranges between 8 and 15 kg (18–33 lb).

```
 o o o o o o o o o o o o o o o o o o o o o o
   BREED  INFORMATION

 NAME                 Samoyed
 OTHER NAMES          Samoiedskaïa Sabaka
 OFFICIAL RECOGNITION Uk Working Group; FCI Group
                      AKC Working Group
 COLOUR VARIATIONS    Pure white; White and biscuit/cream
```

Samoyed

HEIGHT 46-56 cm (18-22 in)

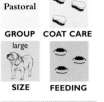

Pastoral
GROUP   **COAT CARE**
large
SIZE   **FEEDING**

BREED FACT:
The Samoyed took its name from a nomadic Siberian tribe, which went by that name. The dog had travelled with this tribe for centuries.

A MEMBER OF THE spitz family, the Samoyed is a striking animal which has worked for centuries as a sled and herding dog, coming to the West in 1889. Around 1900, the breed was introduced to Britain by fur traders, although there were then black dogs and white ones, both colours having been used in early Polar exploration.

Strong, active and graceful, the Samoyed is capable of great endurance and is universally affectionate. Intelligent, alert and full of action, the breed has a characteristic 'smiling' expression. The pure white coat, with occasional tones of biscuit or cream, and the silver-tipped outercoat, is thick and close and requires regular attention to maintain it in good order. Height is 46–56 cm (18–22 in) and in general weight is around 23–30 kg (50–66 lb).

Left
The Samoyed has a double coat – the top-coat is harsh and water-resistant and the undercoat is soft and very dense.

```
 o o o o o o o o o o o o o o o o o o o o o o o o
   BREED  INFORMATION

 NAME                 Shetland Sheepdog
 OFFICIAL RECOGNITION Uk Working Group; FCI Group 1;
                      AKC Herding Group
 COLOUR VARIATIONS    Sable; Tricolour; Blue merle;
                      Black/white; Black/tan
```

Shetland Sheepdog

HEIGHT 35.5-37 cm (14-14.5 in)

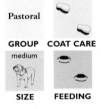

Pastoral
GROUP   **COAT CARE**
medium
SIZE   **FEEDING**

Left
Rarely used today as a herding animal, the Shetland Sheepdog has become a popular pet, particularly in Japan and Britain.

FROM THE SHETLAND ISLANDS off the north coast of Scotland comes the breed which carries the islands' name, originally known as the Shetland Collie. The name was changed in 1908 when the Shetland Sheepdog Club was formed in Lerwick.

One particular animal, Loggie, who would now be known as a Shetland Sheepdog, was entered at Cruft's in 1906, and was shown as a miniature Collie.

This small, long-haired working dog is one of great beauty, of symmetrical outline so that no part appears out of proportion to the whole. The coat is abundant, with a mane and frill, and the striking colours are pale gold to deep mahogany-sable, tricolour, blue merle, black and white, or black and tan. The ideal height is 35.5–37 cm (14–14.5 in) and weight is, perhaps surprisingly, 6–7 kg (14–16 lb). This is an alert, gentle and intelligent breed, affectionate and responsive to owners and reserved with strangers, but never nervous.

BREED FACT:
An early name for the Shetland Sheepdog was Dwarf Scotch Shepherd and now the breed is often referred to by the familiar name of 'Sheltie'.

Pastoral

GROUP | **COAT CARE**

medium

SIZE | **FEEDING**

Swedish Lapphund

HEIGHT 43-48 cm (17-19 in)

BREED INFORMATION	
NAME	Swedish Lapphund
OTHER NAMES	Svensk Lapphund
OFFICIAL RECOGNITION	UK Working Group; FCI Group 5
COLOUR VARIATIONS	Bear brown; Black; Brown; Black/brown

A LONG-ESTABLISHED BREED, the Swedish Lapphund was used as a guard and herd by the Sami people, protecting their reindeer

Right
Despite its many positive characteristics, the Swedish Lapphund is rarely seen outside Sweden.

from predators. In the 1960s, the Swedish Kennel Club undertook a special breeding programme with the aim of further improving the working capacity of this breed which is seen in only limited numbers outside Sweden.

A typical spitz dog of rectangular shape and medium size, height is ideally 43 cm (17 in) for bitches and 48 cm (19 in) for dogs, with weight roughly 19.5–20.5 kg (43–45 lb). Intelligent, quick to learn and patient, the Swedish Lapphund is a kind, friendly and devoted dog, which is also lively and alert. The hair of the weather-resistant coat stands straight out from the body and forms a ruff around the neck. Colours are bear brown, black, brown or a combination of black and brown. Solid colours are preferred but small white marks on chest, feet and tip of tail are acceptable.

Pastoral

GROUP | **COAT CARE**

medium

SIZE | **FEEDING**

Swedish Vallhund

HEIGHT 31-35 cm (12-13.5 in)

BREED INFORMATION	
NAME	Swedish Vallhund
OTHER NAMES	Vastgotaspets
OFFICIAL RECOGNITION	UK Working Group; FCI Group 5
COLOUR VARIATIONS	Several

ALSO KNOWN as the Swedish Cattle Dog, the breed has long been used in Sweden as a watch-dog and herder. The Swedish Vallhund may be distantly related to the Welsh Corgi which was taken to Scandinavia by the Vikings who had previously settled in Pembrokeshire.

This is a multi-purpose farm dog, excellent at guarding, droving and controlling rodents. Sturdily built, with a fairly long body, the Swedish Vallhund is 31–35 cm (12–13.5 in) high

and weighs 11.4–15.9 kg (25–35 lb). The medium length coat is harsh, close and tight, with an abundant, soft, woolly undercoat. Colours are steel grey, greyish brown, greyish yellow, reddish yellow or reddish brown, with darker guard hairs. This breed tends to be aloof and protective in temperament but has an lively, cheerful disposition. Its appearance and expression denote a watchful, alert and energetic dog.

Welsh Corgi (Cardigan)

HEIGHT 30 cm (12 in)

Pastoral

GROUP   COAT CARE

medium

SIZE   FEEDING

THOUGHT TO BE THE OLDER of the two varieties of Welsh Corgi, the Cardigan is one of Britain's oldest breeds, having been used for centuries by Welsh farmers to herd cattle. Incidentally, in Celtic the word *corgi* means dog.

Not until the 1930s were the two varieties of Corgi divided. The Cardigan has a tail and is allowed more coat colours, though white should not predominate. Long in proportion to its height, this is a sturdy, tough and mobile breed, capable of endurance. The tail, like a fox's brush, is moderately long and set in line with the body. An alert, active, intelligent and steady dog, the Cardigan Corgi is not shy or

aggressive and ideally stands 30 cm (12 in) at shoulder with a weight of about 11–17 kg (25–38 lb). The short or medium coat is of hard texture, weatherproof and with a good undercoat.

BREED FACT:

Opinions vary greatly regarding the history of the Cardigan Welsh Corgi, some believing it arrived in Britain 3,000 years ago, others around 1,000 years ago.

Left

The Cardigan Welsh Corgi is snappy and prone to nip heels. It is not good with children, but can make a good watchdog.

Welsh Corgi (Pembroke)

HEIGHT 25.5-30.5 cm (10-12 in)

Pastoral

GROUP   COAT CARE

medium

SIZE   FEEDING

COMING FROM PEMBROKESHIRE in Wales, this breed is believed to have been brought to Britain by Flemish weavers around the year 1100, though other sources claim arrival in 920. Pembrokes and Cardigans interbred until they were separated in 1934.

Possessed of sufficient stamina to be well-capable of a day's work on a farm, and nipping, as intended, at the heels of cattle, this is a highly practical dog, happy to live with all types of family. Low-set, strong and sturdily built, the Pembroke gives the impression of substance and stamina in a small space. Alert, active, bold in outlook and workmanlike, its temperament is friendly and outgoing. The head is foxy, the tail short, and the coat red, sable, fawn or black and tan, with or without white markings on the legs, brisket and neck. The medium length coat has a straight, dense undercoat. Height is around 25.5–30.5 cm (10–12 in) and weight 10–12 kg (20–26 lb).

BREED FACT:

The Pembroke Welsh Corgi is a great favourite of Her Majesty Queen Elizabeth II, who keeps several of them

Left

The Pembroke is less apt to nip than the Cardigan, but is still not an ideal pet for young children.

237

The Terrier Group

I N THE MAIN, BREEDS falling into the Terrier Group are vermin hunters, a high proportion of them having originated in Britain. As long ago as 1677 Nicholas Cox divided the terriers he then knew into two groups, those he called the short-haired and crook-legged type which would take to earth well, and the long-legged, shaggy sort which would hunt above ground but would also enter the earth with much fury. Suffice to say that some of the substantially taller of the terrier breeds today would certainly find it difficult to go to ground in the true sense of the term.

certain areas, such as in Ireland and on the islands off the coast of Scotland, as well as in very localised areas around the towns and cities.

Different breeds evolved for different reasons. Some were used by working men who created sport from hunting rats around industrial buildings, other terriers worked in conjunction with hound packs, their purpose being to drive the fox from his earth, or hold him there until huntsmen could dig him out. Still others have been used to assist in hunting otters. When badgers were still officially baited a stronger terrier was needed with more powerful jaws, and some were crossed with Bulldogs to create fighting dogs, a popular though decidedly unpleasant sport of the eighteenth century.

As laws have changed, some sports and pastimes have mercifully become illegal and yet the breeds originally involved in these have retained their popularity amongst enthusiasts. However, generally at shows the numbers of terriers participating are not as high as those of breeds in other groups, although there are indeed some very high-quality specimens amongst them.

The Airedale stands out clearly as the tallest representative of the Terrier Group, and the Soft Coated Wheaten Terrier is also somewhat different from others in terms of coat. Most in the Group are of small to medium size and the majority of them need considerable attention to their coats so the services of a professional are likely to be required if one does not decide to learn how to do this specialist task. Exceptions are the Bull and Staffordshire Bull Terriers which are smooth-coated. Like dogs in other groups, colours vary considerably, ranging through from white to black, with various colours and colour combinations in between.

Above
The Norfolk Terrier is one of the smallest terriers but is utterly fearless.

Right
Traditionally, the Soft Coated Wheaten Terrier is a farm dog.

Below
This Welsh Terrier was Best in Show winner at the 1998 Cruft's.

SELECTIVE BREEDING

THIS HAS SUCCEEDED in creating considerably different types, influenced to a certain extent by requirements for exhibition purposes. In several cases, because of the geography of Britain, ease of transport in the early days being far from what it is now, particular types of terrier evolved in

Terriers seem always to be full of character and self-confidence and although many will not actively look for a fight, most will retaliate if provoked, so owners should be well aware of this and handle their dogs sensibly.

BREED INFORMATION

NAME	Airedale Terrier
OTHER NAME	Waterside Terrier
OFFICIAL RECOGNITION	UK Terrier Group; FCI Group 3;
	AKC Terrier Group
COLOUR VARIATIONS	Black/tan

Airedale Terrier

HEIGHT 56-61 cm (22-24 in)

Terrier
GROUP **COAT CARE**

large.
SIZE **FEEDING**

HAILING FROM YORKSHIRE and the largest of all the terrier breeds is the Airedale, also sometimes called 'the King of Terriers'. A muscular, active dog, outgoing and friendly, this is a wonderful family dog, always ready to join in with children's games, a companion for town or country.

With its small, dark eyes, a keen expression and quickness of movement, the Airedale constantly appears to be expecting something exciting to happen, alert at all times, not aggressive, but fearless. The tail is set on high and carried gaily. Height is 56–61 cm (22–24 in) and weight roughly 20–23 kg (44–50 lb). The hard, dense, wiry coat is not so long as to appear ragged and is a double coat, which needs stripping. It is waterproof and sheds twice each year. In colour, the body saddle, the top of the neck and the surface of the tail are black, all other parts are tan.

BREED FACT:
The first Airedale breed classes were on offer at the Airedale Agricultural Society Show in Yorkshire in 1879.

Left
The breed's alternate name of Waterside Terrier indicates its proficiency in water work. Today, its popularity is declining.

BREED INFORMATION

NAME	Australian Terrier
OFFICIAL RECOGNITION	UK Terrier Group; FCI Group 3;
	KC Terrier Group
COLOUR VARIATIONS	Blue, Steel blue or Dark grey-blue
	with tan; Clear sandy or red

Australian Terrier

HEIGHT 25.4 cm (10 in)

Terrier
GROUP **COAT CARE**

small
SIZE **FEEDING**

CREATED FROM SEVERAL of the terrier breeds, the Australian is a sturdy, low-set dog, fairly long in proportion to its height which is around 25.4 cm (10 in). Weight is usually from 5–6 kg (12–14 lb). The harsh coat is untrimmed and there is a definite ruff around the neck which, with the keen, dark brown eyes, adds to the 'hard-bitten', rugged appearance. The undercoat is short and soft-textured. In blues and greys,

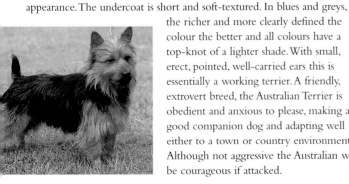

the richer and more clearly defined the colour the better and all colours have a top-knot of a lighter shade. With small, erect, pointed, well-carried ears this is essentially a working terrier. A friendly, extrovert breed, the Australian Terrier is obedient and anxious to please, making a good companion dog and adapting well either to a town or country environment. Although not aggressive the Australian will be courageous if attacked.

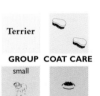

BREED FACT:
The Australian Terrier was introduced to Britain in 1903 but only gained Kennel Club recognition in the 1930s.

Left
First shown in Australia in 1899, this breed has keen eyesight and quick reflexes, making it a good vermin hunter.

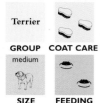
Terrier	
GROUP	**COAT CARE**
medium	
SIZE	**FEEDING**

Bedlington Terrier

HEIGHT 41 cm (16 in)

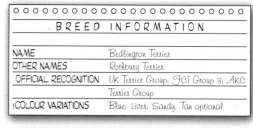

BREED INFORMATION	
NAME	Bedlington Terrier
OTHER NAMES	Rothbury Terrier
OFFICIAL RECOGNITION	UK Terrier Group; FCI Group 3; AKC Terrier Group
†COLOUR VARIATIONS	Blue; Liver; Sandy. Tan optional

BREED FACT:

The name, Bedlington, comes from a mining village in Northumberland, which is called Bedlington.

RENOWNED FOR looking rather like a lamb, the Bedlington is very much a terrier in spirit, and was originally used in the north of Britain to catch rabbits. This breed will not look for a fight but is a spirited, game character, full of confidence at all times and of courage when roused.

Standing around 41 cm (16 in) high and weighing 8–10 kg (17–23 lb), the breed's expression in repose is mild and gentle, with small, bright, deep-set eyes which ideally appear triangular. Blues have a dark eye, blue and tans a lighter one with amber lights, while the eye of livers and sandies is light hazel. This is an intelligent and good-tempered dog,

with an affectionate nature. The distinctive coat is described as thick and linty, standing well out from the skin, but it should not be wiry. The narrow skull is covered with a silky top-knot, which is almost white in colour.

Terrier	
GROUP	**COAT CARE**
large	
SIZE	**FEEDING**

Bull Terrier

HEIGHT 53-56 cm (21-22 in)

BREED INFORMATION	
NAME	Bull Terrier
OTHER NAMES	English Bull Terrier
OFFICIAL RECOGNITION	UK Terrier Group; FCI Group 3; AKC Terrier Group
COLOUR VARIATIONS	White; Brindle; Black; Red; Fawn;

KNOWN AS THE GLADIATOR of the canine race, the Bull Terrier is full of fire and courage but is of even temperament and amenable to discipline. The breed came about through English breeders of the late nineteenth century crossing old fighting dogs which carried Bulldog blood with terriers, among them White English Terriers, which are now extinct, and even Dalmatians.

Strongly built, muscular and with an egg-shaped head when viewed from the front, the Bull Terrier, although requiring firm

BREED FACT:

In the 1850s, James Hinks of Birmingham in the West Midlands was the first person to standardise breed type for the Bull Terrier.

handling and careful training, is a very friendly, affectionate dog, which is good with children. It should never be encouraged to fight. In Britain there are no official height or weight limits but there should be the impression of maximum substance for the size of dog. Generally height is 53–56 cm (21–22 in) and weight 24–28 kg (52–62 lb).

Border Terrier

HEIGHT 25-28 cm (10-11 in)

```
 BREED INFORMATION
NAME                  Border Terrier
OFFICIAL RECOGNITION  UK Terrier Group; FCI Group 3;
                      AKC Terrier Group
COLOUR VARIATIONS     Red; Wheaten; Grizzle/tan; Blue/tan
```

Terrier
GROUP **COAT CARE**
small
SIZE **FEEDING**

BREED FACT:
In the past, the Border Terrier has also been called the Coquetdale or Reedwater Terrier, after areas in which the breed was known.

THIS ESSENTIALLY WORKING terrier comes originally from the border country between England and Scotland, and is a game, active breed fully capable of following a horse and expected to go to ground after a fox. The Border Terrier Club was formed in 1920, the same year in which the breed gained English Kennel Club recognition.

The head is described as being like that of an otter, the eyes dark, with a keen expression, the v-shaped, moderately thick ears dropping forward close to the cheek. No height is specified for the Border Terrier in the English Kennel Club's breed standard but the weight can range from 5.1 kg (11.5 lb) in bitches to 7.1 kg (15.5 lb) in dogs. In general, height is 25–28 cm (10–11 in). The Border Terrier is courageous in work and a loyal companion but requires patient, firm handling.

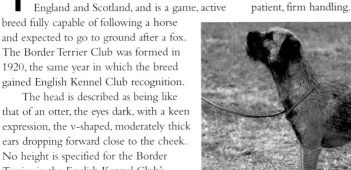

Left
The topcoat of the Border Terrier is dense and harsh with a thick undercoat. As a result, it only needs moderate grooming.

Miniature Bull Terrier

HEIGHT up to 35.5 cm (up to 14 in)

```
 BREED INFORMATION
NAME                  Miniature Bull Terrier
OFFICIAL RECOGNITION  UK Terrier Group; FCI Group 3;
                      AKC Terrier Group
COLOUR VARIATIONS     White; Brindle; Black; Red; Fawn;
                      Tri-colour
```

Terrier
GROUP **COAT CARE**
small
SIZE **FEEDING**

BREED FACT:
Like the Bull Terrier, in the past the Miniature Bull Terrier has been used for dog fighting. It also makes an excellent ratter.

LESS well-known than the Bull Terrier is the Miniature Bull Terrier which follows the same breed standard. In Britain, the only difference is that the height should not exceed 35.5 cm (14 in), but there should still be an impression of substance. Under FCI rules both the Bull Terrier and Miniature are classified as the same breed, but the former is referred to as 'Standard'. The weight of the Miniature is about 11–15 kg (24–33 lb).

The eyes appear narrow and are obliquely placed, triangular and well sunken. They should either be 'black' or as dark brown as possible so as to appear black, giving a piercing glint. The small, thin ears are placed closely together and can be held stiffly erect so that they point upwards.

On pure whites, skin pigmentation and markings on the head are not to be penalised. In coloured dogs, the colour should predominate and, all other things being equal, brindle is preferred.

Left
The Miniature Bull Terrier is not good with small children, but makes a good watchdog or urban companion.

Terrier
GROUP · COAT CARE
small
SIZE · FEEDING

Cairn Terrier

HEIGHT 28-31 cm (11-12 in)

BREED INFORMATION	
NAME	Cairn Terrier
OFFICIAL RECOGNITION	Uk Terrier Group; FCI Group 3; AKC Terrier Group
COLOUR VARIATIONS	Cream; Wheaten; Red; Grey or nearly black

BREED FACT:
When first exhibited in 1909, the Cairn Terrier was shown under the name of 'Short-haired Skye Terrier'.

Right
The Cairn Terrier is easier to obedience train than many other terriers, but care should be taken when it is with young children.

THE CAIRN TERRIER has long been known in the Highlands and Islands of Scotland and it may indeed have originated on the Isle of Skye, where it was used to work the cairns of that island. A true earth dog, recognised by the English Kennel Club under this name in 1910, this workman-like breed stands well forward on the forepaws and is deep in rib and free in movement. The coat is very important and must be weather resistant, double-coated with profuse, harsh outercoat and short, soft undercoat. Brindling is permissible on all colours listed above but the Cairn should not be black, white or black and tan. Dark points on ears and muzzle are very typical.

Of fearless and gay disposition, the Cairn is assertive but not aggressive. Its height varies roughly from 28–31 cm (11–12 in) but height must be in proportion to weight which ranges ideally from 6–7.5 kg (14–16 lb).

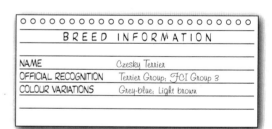

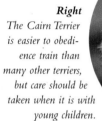

Terrier
GROUP · COAT CARE
medium
SIZE · FEEDING

Czesky Terrier

HEIGHT 28-35.5 cm (11-14 in)

BREED INFORMATION	
NAME	Czesky Terrier
OFFICIAL RECOGNITION	Terrier Group; FCI Group 3
COLOUR VARIATIONS	Grey-blue; Light brown

BREED FACT:
The Czesky Terrier was not registered in Britain until 1990 so there are understandably still limited numbers in this country.

IN THE CZECH REPUBLIC, Dr Frantisek Horak crossed the Sealyham, Scottish and possibly the Dandie Dinmont Terriers in the development of the Czesky Terrier, his aim being to create a breed which could work like a German Hunting Terrier, but had short legs for work underground. Although something of a favourite in the Czech and Slovak Republics, Sealyham blood was introduced in the 1980s because breeders felt the breed had strayed from its original conformation.

Rather long in proportion to its height, this is a sturdy, low-set dog, hardy and tough with plenty of stamina. This agile breed is not aggressive but friendly and companionable. The wavy grey-blue or light brown coat with its silky sheen is clipped, except on the upper part of the head, the legs, the rib cage and the belly, requiring skilful technique. Height is 28–35.5 cm (11–14 in) and the ideal weight is 7–8 kg (15.5–17.5 lb).

Dandie Dinmont Terrier

HEIGHT 20-28 cm (8-11 in)

Terrier
GROUP   COAT CARE
small
SIZE   FEEDING

DEVELOPED IN THE seventeenth century for hunting otter and badger, the breed gained fame, and also its name, from Sir Walter Scott's novel, *Guy Mannering*, which was published in 1814. The first club for this breed was formed in 1876.

With a long, low, weaselly body, the Dandie is different from most other terriers. The distinctive head has a silky covering and the eyes are large, wise and intelligent. Game and workmanlike, the breed is determined, persistent, sensitive and dignified, a good companion and guard. Regular coat care is necessary for this breed which has a weatherproof, double coat with a hard topcoat and soft linty undercoat. Colours are quaintly described as pepper and mustard, again taken from Scott's book, the former ranging from dark bluish-black to light silvery-grey, the latter from reddish brown to fawn. Both have a light-coloured top-knot. Weight ranges from 8–11 kg (18–24 lb) and height is usually 20–28 cm (8–11 in).

BREED FACT:
The name Dandie Dinmont arose from the fictional sporting farmer of the same name in Sir Walter Scott's book, *Guy Mannering*.

Left
The Dandie Dinmont is the most docile of the Terriers and can be trusted with children. It is undemanding and easy to look after.

Smooth Fox Terrier

HEIGHT 38.5-39.5 cm (15 in)

Terrier
GROUP   COAT CARE
medium
SIZE   FEEDING

DEVELOPED TO HUNT badger both above and below ground, the Fox Terrier reached the peak of popularity towards the end of the nineteenth century, the English Fox Terrier Club having been formed in 1876 when the original breed standard was drawn up. Short-backed, but covering a lot of ground, the breed should be made like a well made hunter.

One of the most lively and alert members of the Terrier Group, the Fox Terrier is quick of movement, keen of expression and on the very tiptoe of expectation. Though very adaptable, being friendly, forthcoming and fearless, the breed can be rather sharp with other dogs. The coat is straight, flat and smooth but hard and dense. Weight ranges from 6.8–8.2 kg (15–18 lb) and although no height is specified by the English Kennel Club, height is generally 38.5–39.5 cm (around 15 in).

BREED FACT:
The extinct Cheshire and Shropshire Terriers are in the make-up of the Smooth Fox Terrier we know today.

Left
The Smoth Fox Terrier is a particularly agile and energetic breed, which needs persistent obedient training.

Terrier
GROUP

COAT CARE

medium

SIZE

FEEDING

BREED FACT:
When used for sporting pursuits the Wire Fox Terrier was known as the Rough-haired Terrier.

Wire Fox Terrier

HEIGHT up to 39 cm (up to 15.5 in)

BREED INFORMATION	
NAME	Wire Fox Terrier
OFFICIAL RECOGNITION	UK Terrier Group; FCI Group 3; AKC Terrier Group
COLOUR VARIATIONS	White predominates, with black, black/tan or tan markings

ANOTHER LIVELY, mischievous breed, the Wire Fox Terrier shares its origin with the Smooth. The breed is bold, vociferous, and

Johnson

Right
This breed is more popular than the Smooth Fox Terrier, although it is stubborn and can be snappy.

on tiptoe at the slightest provocation. A well trimmed Wire is a particularly smart dog, the dense, wiry coat has an undercoat of short, softer hair and the crisp hair on the jaws is of sufficient length to give an appearance of strength to the foreface. Colours are as described above, but brindle, red, liver or slate-blue markings are undesirable.

The dark eyes are full of fire and intelligence and as near circular in shape as possible, while the small, v-shaped ears have flaps which fold neatly over and drop forward close to the cheeks. The height of dogs should not exceed 39 cm (15.5 in) and the ideal weight in show condition is 8.25 kg (18 lb). The height and weight of bitches is slightly less.

Terrier
GROUP

COAT CARE

medium

SIZE

FEEDING

Glen of Imaal Terrier

HEIGHT 35-36 cm (14 in)

BREED INFORMATION	
NAME	Glen of Imaal Terrier
OTHER NAMES	Irish Glen of Imaal Terrier
OFFICIAL RECOGNITION	UK Terrier Group; FCI Group 3
COLOUR VARIATIONS	Blue; Brindle; Wheaten

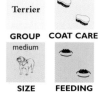

BREED FACT:
The Glen of Imaal was also used as a Turnspit dog, propelling the dog wheel to roast meat on the kitchen roasting spit.

THIS IS AN OLD BREED confined to the scenic but bleak Glen of Imaal in Ireland's County Wicklow. Often pitted against others in dog fights, the Glen had to keep down the rat population as well as hunt the fox and badger. Generations of hard work have made this breed the game, spirited dog it is today.

Active, agile and silent when working, although this terrier has great courage when called upon, the breed is otherwise gentle and docile. Longer than it is high, the Glen of Imaal should be a maximum height of 35–36 cm (14 in) and its weight is generally about 15.5–16.5 kg (34–36 lb). The medium length, harsh-textured coat with its soft undercoat may be tidied to present a neat outline and can be found in blue, brindle and wheaten of all shades.

BREED INFORMATION

NAME	Irish Terrier
OTHER NAMES	Irish Red Terrier
OFFICIAL RECOGNITION	UK Terrier Group; FCI Group 3; AKC Terrier Group
COLOUR VARIATIONS	Red; Red-wheaten; Yellow-red

Irish Terrier

HEIGHT 46-48 cm (18-19 in)

Terrier
GROUP **COAT CARE**
medium
SIZE **FEEDING**

ESTABLISHED IN IRELAND from the nineteenth century the Irish is one of the oldest Terrier breeds. The Black and Tan Terrier was used to bring a certain refinement to the body, which has plenty of substance but is free of clumsiness. The breed has heedless, reckless pluck and, blind to all consequences, will rush headlong at an adversary, earning the breed the epithet: 'the Daredevils'. They have the courage of a lion and will fight to their last breath and yet they are good tempered, notably with humans.

The harsh, wiry, whole-coloured coat has a broken appearance and should not be so long as to hide the body outline. The coat on the foreface gives an appearance of additional strength. The height for dogs is 48 cm (19 in) and for bitches 46 cm (18 in), while weight is generally 11–12 kg.

BREED FACT:
The Irish Terrier was shown in Ireland in 1875 and the Irish Terrier Club was formed in 1879.

BREED INFORMATION

NAME	Kerry Blue Terrier
OTHER NAMES	Irish Blue Terrier
OFFICIAL RECOGNITION	UK Terrier Group; FCI Group 3; AKC Terrier Group
COLOUR VARIATIONS	Any blue, black points optional

Kerry Blue Terrier

HEIGHT 46-47 cm (18-19 in)

Terrier
GROUP **COAT CARE**
medium
SIZE **FEEDING**

ORIGINATING IN IRELAND, this breed was first known as the Irish Blue Terrier and both the Bedlington and the Bull Terrier have played their part in the Kerry's make-up. There is a tradition in Ireland that the breed is ancient and indigenous, descending, in part, from the Wolfhound.

It was said in 1922 that the Kerry's temperament was 'well nigh faultless, if a slight tendency to demolish the cat population be excepted'. This is a fearless watchdog and excellent companion with a certain disciplined gameness. The breed enjoys water and is easily trained, and the coat soft, silky, plentiful and wavy but needing regular trimming. The true colour can develop up to the age of 18 months. The best weight for a male is 15–16.8 kg (33–37 lb), and height 46–47 cm (18–19 in). Bitches are smaller.

BREED FACT:
According to Irish legend, the ancestors of the Kerry Blue Terrier swam ashore from a wrecked ship at Tralee.

Terrier

GROUP COAT CARE

medium

SIZE FEEDING

Lakeland Terrier

HEIGHT up to 37 cm (up to 14.5 in)

BREED INFORMATION	
NAME	Lakeland Terrier
OFFICIAL RECOGNITION	UK Terrier Group; FCI Group 3; AKC Terrier Group
COLOUR VARIATIONS	Black/tan; Blue/tan; Red; Wheaten; Red grizzle; Liver; Blue; Black

BREED FACT:

The Lakeland Terrier took its name when a breed club was formed in 1912, and was recognised by the English Kennel Club in 1928.

Right
The Lake Terrier has never been as popular as some of the other breeds, despite performing well in the show-ring.

DEVELOPING IN ENGLAND'S Lake District and known originally by other names relating to local areas, this is one of the oldest working breeds of Terrier. Farmers hunted foxes in the mountains with only a couple of hounds and Lakeland Terriers.

A tough, quick-moving breed, the Lakeland is bold, self-confident and friendly with a gay, fearless demeanour. Smart and workmanlike, the expression is keen, with dark or hazel eyes and moderately small v-shaped ears carried alertly. The dense, hard, weather-resistant coat has a good undercoat and requires regular stripping, although pet dogs professionally trimmed twice a year can be fairly easily kept tidy between times.

Height should not exceed 37 cm (14.5 in) and an average weight for dogs is 7.7 kg (17 lb) with bitches at an average of 6.8 kg (15 lb).

Terrier

GROUP COAT CARE

medium

SIZE FEEDING

Manchester Terrier

HEIGHT 38-41 cm (15-16 in)

BREED INFORMATION	
NAME	Manchester Terrier
OTHER NAMES	Black and Tan Terrier
OFFICIAL RECOGNITION	UK Terrier Group; FCI Group 3; AKC Terrier Group

BREED FACT:

The Manchester Terrier is an extremely good ratter given half the chance, a sport in which the breed excelled in the nineteenth century.

Right
The Manchester Terrier was used in all manner of field sports.

THIS BREED TAKES ITS NAME from the city of Manchester. In the 1870s, it was a popular rat catcher and also used for rabbit coursing. Possibly crossed with the Whippet, the breed goes back to the old hunting terrier but in contrast to many of the British terriers has a smooth coat and is now more a companion than a working dog.

Always jet black with a rich mahogany tan, this is an elegant breed, sound and with substance. The small, dark, almond-shaped eyes sparkle, while small v-shaped ears are carried well above the topline of the head and hang close to the head above the eyes. Keen, alert, gay and sporting, the Manchester Terrier is both discerning and devoted, a faithful friend fitting into either a town or country environment. Height ranges from 38–41 cm (15–16 in) and weight varies from 5–10 kg (11–22 lb).

Norfolk Terrier

HEIGHT 25-26 cm (10 in)

Terrier
GROUP **COAT CARE**
small
SIZE **FEEDING**

USED IN THE NINETEENTH century for fox and badger hunting, and extensively for ratting and rabbiting, the Norfolk and Norwich Terriers are very similar; Norfolks actually having been known previously under the name of 'Norwich', and recognised by that name in 1932. In 1964, the English Kennel Club separated the two breeds and there are now subtle differences in their breed standards, notably ear carriage. The v-shaped ears of the Norfolk drop forward close to the cheek.

An alert, fearless breed, the Norfolk is one of the smallest terriers, described by the standard as a 'demon' for its size, standing ideally 25–26 cm (10 in). Weight usually falls between 5–5.5 kg (11–12 lb). Compact and strong, this is a low dog of good substance and bone.

BREED FACT:
Breeds involved in the ancestry of the Norwich Terrier include red Cairn Terriers, Glen of Imaals and Dandie Dinmonts.

Left
The hard, wiry coat of the Norfolk Terrier is longer and rougher on the neck and shoulders and needs regular stripping.

Norwich Terrier

HEIGHT up to 25 cm (up to 10 in)

Terrier
GROUP **COAT CARE**
small
SIZE **FEEDING**

WITH A HISTORY tying in closely with that of the Norfolk Terrier, the Norwich is another loveable breed with a tremendously active and hardy constitution. Gay and fearless, the standard for both breeds tells enthusiasts that honourable scars from fair wear and tear are not to be unduly penalised.

The mouth is tight-lipped, the jaws clean and strong and the rather large teeth are strong also. The ears on the Norwich are erect

and set well apart on top of the skull, and the expressive eyes are small, dark, bright and keen. The hard, wiry coat which lies close to the body has a thick undercoat and on the neck forms a ruff, which frames the face. Colours, height and approximate weight are the same as those of the Norwich. In both breeds, white marks or patches on the coat are considered undesirable.

BREED FACT:
To remember the difference between Norwich and Norfolk Terriers, the ears of the Norwich stand up like the cathedral spire.

Left
The Norwich is one of the smallest of the Terriers, but it extremely energetic. It is good with older children.

Terrier	
GROUP	**COAT CARE**
medium	
SIZE	**FEEDING**

Parson Jack Russell Terrier

HEIGHT 35 cm (13 in)

Right
The long legs of the Parson Jack Russell Terrier are a distinguishing feature of the breed.

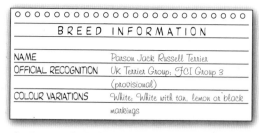

BREED INFORMATION	
NAME	Parson Jack Russell Terrier
OFFICIAL RECOGNITION	UK Terrier Group; FCI Group 3 (provisional)
COLOUR VARIATIONS	White; White with tan, lemon or black markings

A SPORTING PARSON in Devon, Reverend John Russell, developed the Parson Jack Russell Terrier which is akin to the Wire Fox Terrier with legs sufficiently long to accompany horses on a hunt and yet sufficiently small to burrow and bolt foxes. This is an intelligent breed which needs plenty to occupy its mind; it can become destructive if left alone for long periods.

A workmanlike breed, active and agile, the Parson is built for speed and endurance. The skin must be thick and loose and the coat colour is entirely white or white with tan, lemon or black markings, preferably confined to the head or the root of the tail. The coat texture is harsh, close and dense, whether rough or smooth. An ideal height is 35 cm (14 in) for dogs and 33 cm (13 in) for bitches and weight is generally 5–8 kg (12–18 lb).

Terrier	
GROUP	**COAT CARE**
medium	
SIZE	**FEEDING**

Scottish Terrier

HEIGHT 25.4-28 cm (10-11 in)

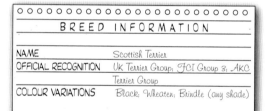

BREED INFORMATION	
NAME	Scottish Terrier
OFFICIAL RECOGNITION	UK Terrier Group; FCI Group 3; AKC Terrier Group
COLOUR VARIATIONS	Black; Wheaten; Brindle (any shade)

U NTIL THE MID-NINETEENTH century, any dog going to ground after a fox in Scotland was called a 'Scottish Terrier' but the breed we know by that name today was then called a Broken-haired or Aberdeen Terrier.

Active and agile, despite being thick set and short legged, the Scottie, as the breed is familiarly known, is courageous and highly intelligent. Described as loyal, faithful, dignified, independent and reserved, the breed is bold, but never aggressive. Requiring regular attention, the close-lying, double coat makes a weather resistant covering and the outercoat is harsh, dense and wiry. Height ranges from 25.4 to 28 cm (10–11 in) and weight from 8.6–10.4 kg (19–23 lb). The skull is long and, because of this length, it can be fairly wide, yet still retain a narrow appearance. The almond-shaped, dark brown eyes are set under eyebrows and have a keen expression.

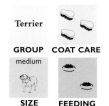

Terrier
GROUP   **COAT CARE**
medium
SIZE   **FEEDING**

Sealyham Terrier

HEIGHT up to 31 cm (up to 12 in)

BREED INFORMATION	
NAME	Sealyham Terrier
OFFICIAL RECOGNITION	Uk Terrier Group; FCI Group 3; AKC Terrier Group
COLOUR VARIATIONS	White; White with lemon, brown, blue or badger pied markings on head/ears

WITH A NAME DERIVED from Sealyham, Haverfordwest, in the county of Pembrokeshire in Wales, the origins of the breed which developed between 1850 and 1891 are undeniably Welsh. A Captain Edwardes, who lived in Sealyham, decided to promote his ideal terrier and in doing so utilised various different terriers and the Welsh Corgi creating a breed which was successful in quarrying fox and badger.

In general outline, the breed is oblong rather than square, giving the impression of great substance in small compass. Sturdy, game and workmanlike, the Sealyham is both alert and fearless, yet has a friendly disposition. The coat is one which requires stripping and trimming, the undercoat being weather resistant and the topcoat long, hard and wiry. The colour is always white but there can be certain coloured markings on the head and ears. Height should not exceed 31 cm (12 in) and weight ranges from 8.2–9 kg (18–20 lb).

BREED FACT:
The Sealyham Terrier was first shown in Haverfordwest in 1903 and in 1908 the Sealyham Terrier Club of Haverfordwest was formed.

BREED INFORMATION	
NAME	Skye Terrier
OFFICIAL RECOGNITION	Uk Terrier Group; FCI Group 3; AKC Terrier Group
COLOUR VARIATIONS	Black; Dark or light grey; Fawn; Cream. All with black points

Skye Terrier

HEIGHT 25-26 cm (10 in)

Terrier
GROUP   **COAT CARE**
medium
SIZE   **FEEDING**

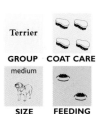

OFF THE NORTH-WEST coast of Scotland is the Isle of Skye from which this breed is generally believed to have hailed. One of the oldest of Scottish breeds, the Skye Terrier has been known for four centuries, used as an earth dog to bolt fox and badger and to hunt otter and weasel.

With males ideally standing 25–26 cm (10 in) and bitches slightly smaller, the breed is twice as long as it is high. In fact from tip of nose to tip of tail a dog should measure 103 cm (41.5 in). Although no weight is specified in the English Kennel Club's standard, it is usually 8.5–10.5 kg (19–23 lb). This is a one-man dog, distrustful of strangers but never vicious. Strong in quarters, body and jaw, the ears can be pricked or dropped. Colours are varied and the long, hard double coat needs attention.

BREED FACT:
In 1858, the Skye Terrier known as Greyfriars Bobby was famed in Edinburgh for his 14-year vigil beside his master's grave until he, too, died.

Left
The Skye Terrier is an intensely loyal one-man dog, which is not ideal around children.

Terrier
GROUP

COAT CARE

medium
SIZE

FEEDING

Soft-Coated Wheaten Terrier

HEIGHT 46-49 cm (18-19.5 in)

BREED INFORMATION

NAME	Soft Coated Wheaten Terrier
OTHER NAMES	Irish Soft Coated Wheaten Terrier
OFFICIAL RECOGNITION	UK Terrier Group; FCI Group 3; AKC Terrier Group
COLOUR VARIATIONS	Clear wheaten, like ripening wheat

BREED FACT:

There is a theory that the Soft Coated Wheaten Terrier was the parent breed of the Irish and Kerry Blue Terriers.

Right

As its name suggests, the distinguishing feature of this breed is its soft, curly, silky coat, the colour of ripening wheat.

BRED FOR OVER TWO hundred years as a farm dog in Munster, Ireland, the Soft Coated Wheaten Terrier was first registered as a breed by the Irish Kennel Club in 1937 and by the English Kennel Club in 1943. This is a natural terrier with strong sporting instincts, a hardy dog of strong constitution.

The natural, soft, silky coat is the shade of ripening wheat and falls in loose curls or waves. Although abundant all over the body, the coat is especially profuse on the head and legs and there is no seasonal change in length or texture. The coat does not shed but needs careful grooming. This medium sized terrier stands 46–49 cm (18–19.5 in) high and weighs 16–20.5 kg (35–45 lb), with bitches somewhat less. This delightful, affectionate and intelligent companion is good tempered and full of confidence and humour.

Terrier
GROUP

COAT CARE

medium
SIZE

FEEDING

Staffordshire Bull Terrier

HEIGHT 35.5-40.5 cm (14-16 in)

BREED INFORMATION

NAME	Staffordshire Bull Terrier
OFFICIAL RECOGNITION	UK Terrier Group; FCI Group 3; AKC Terrier Group
COLOUR VARIATIONS	Red; Fawn; White; Black; Blue; Brindle; Brindle/white

BREED FACT:

The Staffordshire Bull Terrier was not recognised by the English Kennel Club until 1935, despite being bred in the UK in the nineteenth century.

THE STAFFORDSHIRE BULL Terrier is a product of a cross between the Bulldog and a Terrier, combining the temperament of the two breeds. Bred originally for bull- and bear-baiting, which was prohibited by law in England in 1835, the Staffordshire Bull Terrier continued to fight against other dogs until this, too, was outlawed.

Traditionally of indomitable courage and tenacity, the breed is bold and fearless and needs firm handling when in the company of other dogs. Muscular, active and agile, the Stafford has great strength for its size but this intelligent breed is very affectionate, especially with children. The smooth, short coat comes in a variety of colours, but black and tan or liver are undesirable. Height should be related to weight, with heights from 35.5–40.5 cm (14–16 in) and weight from 11–17 kg (24–38 lb).

BREED INFORMATION

NAME	Welsh Terrier
OFFICIAL RECOGNITION	UK Terrier Group; FCI Group 3; AKC Terrier Group
COLOUR VARIATIONS	Preferably black/tan; Or black, grizzle and tan

Welsh Terrier

HEIGHT up to 39 cm (up to 15.5 in)

Terrier
GROUP **COAT CARE**
medium
SIZE **FEEDING**

DESCENDED FROM the rough-coated black and tan Fox Terrier, the Welsh Terrier was used in Wales for hunting fox, badger and otter. There may be some common origin with the Lakeland Terrier, going back to before the Roman invasion. This breed has a happy, volatile temperament and is an affectionate dog, obedient and easily controlled. It usually fits in well in a family situation. Although not aggressive, this dog is game and fearless, well able to hold its own when necessary.

In appearance the Welsh Terrier is workmanlike, well balanced, smart and compact with a hard, wiry topcoat, very close and abundant, which requires regular trimming. It covers a fine undercoat. Although black and tan is the preferable colour, the Welsh may be black, grizzle and tan but must have no black pencilling on the toes, nor black below the hocks. Height should not exceed 39 cm (15.5 in) and weight varies only slightly, from 9–9.5 kg (20–21 lb).

BREED FACT

The first show for Welsh Terriers took place in 1884 and was held at Pwllheli in North Wales.

Left
The Welsh Terrier has an outgoing, friendly nature, which makes it a pleasant companion, although it is also a useful vermin hunter.

BREED INFORMATION

NAME	West Highland White Terrier
OFFICIAL RECOGNITION	UK Terrier Group; FCI Group 3; AKC Terrier Group
COLOUR VARIATIONS	White

West Highland White Terrier

HEIGHT 28 cm (11 in)

Terrier
GROUP **COAT CARE**
medium
SIZE **FEEDING**

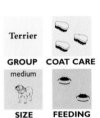

A HIGHLY POPULAR REPRESENTATIVE of this group is the West Highland White Terrier, fondly known as the Westie, and believed to have come from Argyll in Scotland. The breed seems to have been developed in the 1880s from a strain of white and cream-coloured Cairns, the lightest colours having been selectively bred to create this breed. Along with the Scottish Terrier, the 'Westie' is well known through an advertisement for Scotch whisky.

Full of self-esteem, this hardy, active and game little dog has a varminty appearance with dark eyes, small, erect ears and jauntily carried tail. The breed is alert, courageous and self-reliant, but makes a friendly and charming companion. Needing regular attention, the white coat is double, with an outercoat of long hair and a short, soft undercoat resembling fur. Height is approximately 28 cm (11 in) and weight is usually 7–10 kg (15–22 lb).

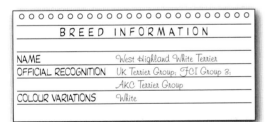

BREED FACT:

West Highland White Terriers were selectively bred for their colour so that they would be easily visible in the heather on Scottish moors.

Left
The Westie was used for hunting in the past and still enjoys chasing after cats, rabbits or other small creatures.

The Toy Group

MANY TOY BREEDS have been carefully bred for centuries by a process of selective miniaturisation. Favourites of the courts and of noble families, they were kept as small lap dogs and companion dogs but in the majority of cases their ancestry can be traced back to other breeds, which were often larger.

Above
The Affenpinscher is a lively, energetic breed, brimming with character.

Right
This beautifully groomed Yorkshire Terrier won Best of Breed at Crufts.

Below
The Pekingese can trace its ancestry back to the Tang Dynasty (618-907).

VISUAL RECORDS

THERE IS A WEALTH of visual records concerning the Toys because many were included in portraits, often on the lap of their prosperous master or mistress and from these we can see how little some of the breeds have changed, such as Hogarth's pet Pug, painted in 1745.

Early writers seem not to have been as enamoured of the Toy breeds as they were of the larger, sporting breeds. Dr Caius, a notable writer on canine matters in the sixteenth century described them thus: 'These dogges are little, pretty, and proper, and fyne, and sought to satisfie the delicatenesse of daintie dames and wanton women's wiles, instruments of folly for them to play and dally withall, to tryfle away the treasure of time, to withdraw their mindes from their commendable exercises'. Dr Caius seems to have overlooked the fact that many of the breeds classified as Toys may

well be diminutive in size, but not in spirit. Indeed it can be amusing to watch one of these tiny dogs taking to task a dog many times greater in size, although of course it is only amusing if the owners exercise great care, for accidents can and do happen.

Thanks to ancient records kept by civilisations of the Far East we obtain insight into breeds of dog in that region. Several which had their origins there were brought to Europe as trade developed. Now this area has become important for the breeding of Toy dogs and even the Papillon, although it clearly carries a French name, very probably came from the Orient.

Few of the Toy Group have been kept other than as pets, but many have been developed and bred down in size from breeds which have indeed 'earned their keep'. Toys have long been thought of as ladies' dogs but as times have changed, so have opinions, and many a gent gets as much pleasure and enjoyment from a Toy dog as does a lady.

Whilst all are small in stature, the Chihuahua being the smallest and the Cavalier King Charles Spaniel at the larger end of the scale, all are small enough to curl up comfortably in a small corner of the sitting room or to sit on one's lap. There is plenty of choice where coat is concerned – the Chinese Crested has virtually none at all, while the Maltese and Yorkshire Terrier have long, flowing coats to keep even the busiest hands occupied with grooming for hours if these dogs are to be kept in full show coat.

Small breeds always seem full of fun and packed with character, and the Affenpinscher with its monkey-like expression, or the perky little Griffon Bruxellois, cannot help but bring a smile to one's face and liven up any moment of the day.

Affenpinscher
HEIGHT 24-28 cm (9.5-11 in)

```
○ ○ ○ ○ ○ ○ ○ ○ ○ ○ ○ ○ ○ ○ ○ ○ ○ ○ ○ ○ ○ ○ ○
  B R E E D   I N F O R M A T I O N
```

NAME	Affenpinscher
OTHER NAMES	Monkey Dog
OFFICIAL RECOGNITION	Uk Toy Group; FCI Group 2; AKC Toy Group
COLOUR VARIATIONS	Black prefered, grey shading allowed

Toy

GROUP   **COAT CARE**

small

SIZE   **FEEDING**

BREED FACT:
Affe, the prefix of the breed name Affenpinscher, can be translated as monkey and even the breed standard calls for a monkey-like expression.

ORIGINATING IN GERMANY and one of the oldest of the Toy breeds, the Affenpinscher is a lively character, full of mischief, known as 'The Black Devil'. The expression is mischievous and monkey-like, the temperament lively and self-confident, indeed there is a certain comic seriousness about this breed. The Affenpinscher is a loyal companion, watchful of strangers and fearless toward aggressors. Although only small with a height of 24–28 cm (9.5–11 in) and weighing 3–3.5 kg (7–8 lb), the breed is not delicate in any way.

The untrimmed rough, harsh, black coat, sometimes with grey shading, is short and dense on some parts of the body and shaggy on others. Badger pied markings on the head and ears are acceptable. The

hair on the head stands away from the skull, framing the dark, sparkling eyes, the nose and chin. This is a suitable breed for a town or country lifestyle.

Left
This endearing nlittle terrier has a monkey-like appearance.

Australian Silky Terrier
HEIGHT 23 cm (9 in)

```
○ ○ ○ ○ ○ ○ ○ ○ ○ ○ ○ ○ ○ ○ ○ ○ ○ ○ ○ ○ ○ ○ ○
  B R E E D   I N F O R M A T I O N
```

NAME	Australian Silky Terrier
OTHER NAMES	Silky Terrier
OFFICIAL RECOGNITION	Uk Toy Group; FCI Group 3; AKC Toy Group
COLOUR VARIATIONS	Blue/tan; Grey-blue/tan; Cream.

Toy

GROUP   **COAT CARE**

small

SIZE   **FEEDING**

BREED FACT:
Before the Second World War, the Australian Silky Terrier was virtually unknown outside Australia.

AT ONE TIME known as 'The Sydney Silk', the Australian Silky Terrier originated, as the name implies, in Australia, with a background combining the Australian and Yorkshire Terriers from which breeds many qualities have been retained. Despite being classified in the Toy Group, this breed should have sufficient substance to suggest ability to hunt and kill domestic rodents.

Although a Toy, the breed is very Terrier-like – keen, alert and active with a temperament which is

friendly, quick and responsive. The eyes are small, round and as dark as possible, imparting a keen, intelligent impression, whilst the v-shaped ears are set high on the skull and are pricked, but have no long hair. Height is around 23 cm (9 in) and weight should be about 4 kg (8–10 lb). The long, straight, glossy coat is not difficult to maintain with a few minutes' daily brushing, the smart parting giving a well groomed appearance.

Left
The colouring of the Australian Silky Terrier should always include black points.

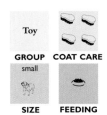

Toy
GROUP

COAT CARE

small
SIZE

FEEDING

BREED FACT:
The Bichon is believed to have been descended from the old French water dog, the Barbet.

Bichon Frise

HEIGHT 23-28 cm (9-11 in)

○ ○
BREED INFORMATION

NAME	Bichon Frise
OTHER NAMES	Bichon à poil frisé; 'Tenerife Dog'
OFFICIAL RECOGNITION	UK Toy Group; FCI Group 9; AKC
	Non-Sporting Group
COLOUR VARIATIONS	White

THE VERY GLAMOROUS, pure white Bichon Frise is thought to have originated in the Mediterranean area where it has probably been known since the Middle Ages. Happy, lively

Right
Bichon Frise puppies have pink noses, which turn black as they grow older.

little dogs, their temperament is friendly and outgoing and this breed likes to be the centre of attention, becoming an integral part of the family unit.

The dark, alert eyes are full of expression, the nose is black, soft and shiny, and the hair accentuates the rounded appearance of the head. A generous amount of grooming is needed to maintain the soft, corkscrew curls of the coat in tip-top condition and the Bichon can be presented un-trimmed or may have the muzzle and feet slightly tidied up. Height is from 23–28 cm (9–11 in) and weight from 3–6 kg (7–12 lb). Dark pigment is desirable under the white coat, but up to the age of 18 months cream or apricot markings are acceptable.

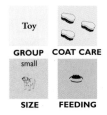

Toy
GROUP

COAT CARE

small
SIZE

FEEDING

BREED FACT:
Blondus (1388–1463) wrote of the Bolognese: 'queens gave them small portions of their own food in golden vases'.

Bolognese

HEIGHT 25.5-30.5 cm (10-12 in)

○ ○
BREED INFORMATION

NAME	Bolognese
OTHER NAMES	Bichon Bolognese
OFFICIAL RECOGNITION	UK Toy Group; FCI Group 9
COLOUR VARIATIONS	Pure white, without markings

THE BOLOGNESE is likely to have been developed from the Bichons of southern Italy even though the name is taken from the northern city of Bologna. A breed such has this has been recorded since the thirteenth century and was popular among the aristocracy during the Renaissance.

Suitable for hot climates, the long, flocked white coat has no undercoat and covers the entire head and body, without curl. The large, round eyes are dark with well-

Right
Although the Bolognese probably originated from Italy, it is no longer a popular breed there.

pigmented rims and lips, and the eyes and nails are black, as is the large nose. The feet are oval and even the pads of the feet are black, in keeping with the other dark pigmentation. This breed is intelligent and forms a close companionship with its owner but is tends to be rather reserved in temperament. Its height ranges from 25.5–30.5 cm (10–12 in) and its weight roughly from 3–4 kg (5–9 lb).

Cavalier King Charles Spaniel

HEIGHT 31-33 cm (12-13 in)

Toy

GROUP · COAT CARE

small

SIZE · FEEDING

THE ORIGIN OF THE Cavalier King Charles Spaniel goes back several centuries but it was only in 1928 that the breed was separated from the slightly smaller, shorter-nosed King Charles. One of the many joys of this popular breed is in its varied colouring: black and tan, ruby (which is a rich red), Blenheim (with rich chestnut markings on pearly white), and tri-colour combining black, white and tan. The coat is long and silky, free from curl with plenty of feathering and it should be totally free from trimming. This absolutely fearless breed of little spaniel is gay, friendly and not aggressive in any way, but is also sporting and affectionate, making an ideal and very popular companion, always seeming to show pleasure by a constantly wagging tail. Also good with children, the Cavalier is easy to care for and weighs from 5.4–8.1 kg (12–18 lb), its height generally being 31–33 cm (12–13 in).

BREED FACT:
Despite not receiving separate Kennel Club status until 1944, by 1970 the Cavalier King Charles Spaniel found itself among the top 10 most popular breeds.

Left
The recent popularity of the Cavalier King Charles Spaniel has led to in-breeding and a tendancy towards heart conditions.

Chihuahua

HEIGHT 15-23 cm (6-9 in)

Toy

GROUP · COAT CARE

small

SIZE · FEEDING

TAKING ITS name from a Mexican city and state, the Chihuahua probably has roots in South America and is said to have been sacred to the Aztecs. Best known for being the smallest dog breed in the world, the preferred weight is 1–1.8 kg (2–4 lb) and should never exceed 2.7 kg (6 lb).

Although small, dainty and compact, this is an alert little dog, gay, intelligent and spirited, not snappy or withdrawn. The well-rounded 'apple dome' head has a saucy expression with large, round eyes and large, flaring ears set on at an angle of about 45. There are two coat varieties – long and smooth – but each is easy to keep clean and well groomed. Not especially suitable for very small children, this is a happy lap dog and one which is usually willing to announce the approach of strangers.

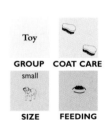

BREED FACT:
The Chihuahua was a religious symbol of the ancient Toltec tribes and is the smallest breed of dog in the world.

Left
Originally, the Chihuahua would have been larger and more robust, but is now known for its miniature size.

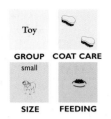

Toy	
GROUP	**COAT CARE**
small	
SIZE	**FEEDING**

Chinese Crested Dog

HEIGHT 23-30 cm (9-13 in)

BREED FACT:
In the 1830s, London's Zoological Gardens featured what must have been a thoroughly fascinating exhibition of hairless dogs.

SAID TO HAVE BEEN OWNED by Chinese families during the Han Dynasty, the Chinese Crested Dog is a very distinctive breed of which there are two varieties: hairless and powderpuff. The hairless is warm to the touch and should have no hair at all on its body, just a crest on the head, plume on the lower two-thirds of the tail and 'socks' covering the long feet. The powderpuff has a soft veil of long hair. This is a fastidious breed and neither variety has a doggy odour. There are also two rather distinct types: one racy and fine boned, the other heavier in body and bone.

This good tempered breed is active and graceful with a height ranging from 23–30 cm (9–13 in) and weight preferably not exceeding 5.5 kg (12 lb). Moisturising cream is usually used on the hairless variety to keep the skin supple.

Toy	
GROUP	**COAT CARE**
small	
SIZE	**FEEDING**

Coton de Tuléar

HEIGHT 25-32 cm (10-12 in)

BREED FACT:
The Coton de Tuléar was popular as a trade commodity and this led to the breed's extinction in Reunion.

THE COTON DE TULÉAR is very little known in Britain but is related to the French Bichons and Italian Bolognese, possibly having arrived in the Mascarene Islands with French troops and been raised in Reunion. Until reintroduced to Europe and America some 20 years ago it seems hardly to have been known at all, although for centuries it was kept by wealthy families in Tuléar, southern Madagascar.

Like the Bolognese, the breed has a single coat and is usually white, but a little lemon or grey colour on the ears is acceptable. In texture the coat is like cotton, long, fine, slightly wavy and needing regular, careful attention. Lively, boisterous and intelligent the Coton is loyal and friendly, standing between 25–32 cm (10–12 in) and weighing 5.5–7 kg (12–15 lb).

Right
The lively Coton de Tuléar deserves to be more popular, but is still comparatively rare in Europe and America.

BREED INFORMATION

NAME	English Toy Terrier
OTHER NAMES	Toy Manchester Terrier; Black-and-Tan Toy Terrier
OFFICIAL RECOGNITION	UK Toy Group; FCI Group 3
COLOUR VARIATIONS	Black and tan

English Toy Terrier

HEIGHT 23-33 cm (9-13 in)

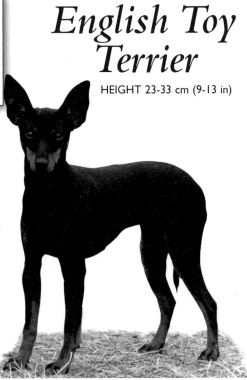

Toy	
GROUP	**COAT CARE**
small	
SIZE	**FEEDING**

BREED FACT:
During the nineteenth century, the English Toy Terrier became particularly popular as a town dog.

THE ENGLISH TOY TERRIER'S ancestry goes back to the Black and Tan Terrier which can be traced back at least as far as the early sixteenth century. This is a sleek, cleanly built dog, alert and with both Toy and Terrier characteristics, a breed which historically could perform very satisfactorily in the rat pit.

The combination of colours is striking; the black parts are ebony, and the tan a rich chestnut, their distribution very carefully set down in the breed standard. Ears are the shape of candle flames, with slightly pointed tips. The tail is thick at the root and tapers to a point. Height can be from 23–33 cm (9–13 in) and weight varies considerably, though it should never exceed 5.5 kg (12 lb). This friendly and intelligent dog makes a charming companion.

Left
The smooth, glossy coat of the English Toy Terrier requires minimal care.

BREED INFORMATION

NAME	Griffon Bruxellois
OTHER NAMES	Belgian Griffon, Petit Brababcon
OFFICIAL RECOGNITION	UK Toy Group; FCI Group 9; AKC Toy Group Clear red;
COLOUR VARIATIONS	Black*; Black and rich tan*

Griffon Bruxellois

HEIGHT 18-20 cm (7-8 in)

Toy	
GROUP	**COAT CARE**
small	
SIZE	**FEEDING**

BREED FACT:
The coachmen of Brussels used Griffons for ratting and the breed has been known as the Belgian Street Urchin.

A PERT, MONKEY-LIKE EXPRESSION typifies the delightful Griffon Bruxellois of which there are two varieties – rough-coated and smooth – and both are heavy for their size. The smooth variety goes by the name Petit Brabancon and needs only regular grooming with a hound glove, while the rough coat requires stripping about twice a year. While in the UK all these small Griffons compete together, under FCI rules there are three separate breeds, of which the third is called the Belgian Griffon which is black with a rough coat. Although in Britain the colour most frequently seen is red; black and black with rich tan are also found.

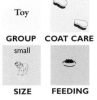

Left
In Belgium, griffon means wire-haired, but there is also a smooth-coated variety of Griffon Bruxellois.

Toy

GROUP   **COAT CARE**

small

SIZE   **FEEDING**

Havanese

HEIGHT 23-28 cm (9-11 in)

Right

The Havanese is little known outside its Cuban homeland (where it has appeared on stamps), despite its appealing appearance.

BREED INFORMATION	
NAME	Havanese
OTHER NAMES	Bichon Havanais; Bichon Habanero
OFFICIAL RECOGNITION	UK Toy Group; FCI Group 9
COLOUR VARIATIONS	Any colour or combination of colours

THOUGHT TO HAVE developed originally in the Mediterranean regions, sadly the Havanese is now rare in Cuba, which is considered the breed's homeland, and as yet only a few are kept here in Britain. This is a small but sturdy breed, slightly longer than it is high with a profusely feathered tail, which is carried over the back.

The soft, silky coat is wavy or slightly curled and should not be scissored into shape but rather allowed to develop naturally. The coat can be any colour or combination of colours; dogs which are brown in shade are allowed to have correspondingly brown

pigment on their nose and eye rims, and their eyes can be slightly lighter. Otherwise eyes should be dark and pigment solid black. Height is 23–28 cm (9–11 in) and weight 3–6 kg (7–13 lb). This breed has a friendly, outgoing temperament and is lively, affectionate and intelligent.

Toy

GROUP   **COAT CARE**

small

SIZE   **FEEDING**

Italian Greyhound

HEIGHT 33-38 cm (13-15 in)

BREED INFORMATION	
NAME	Italian Greyhound
OTHER NAMES	Piccolo Levriero Italiano
OFFICIAL RECOGNITION	UK Toy Group; FCI Group 10; AKC Toy Group
COLOUR VARIATIONS	Black; Blue; Cream; Fawn; Red

PERHAPS THE FIRST BREED which was ever developed as a lap dog, the Italian Greyhound claims a background going back to the days of Pompeii, but it did not come to Britain until the seventeenth century. Described as a Greyhound in miniature, more slender in all proportions, this is an elegant, graceful and quick-moving dog. The many colours of this breed may be broken up with white.

The Italian Greyhound may appear rather aloof, but it is intelligent, affectionate and vivacious, a dog which, though small, enjoys plenty of exercise. With short, fine hair, a velvet pad or even a piece of silk can be used for daily grooming to give a glossy sheen. The skin is fine and supple and this comfort-loving breed will be only too happy to settle into something soft and warm. Height is roughly 33–38 cm (13–15 in) and weight 2.7–4.5 kg (6–10 lb).

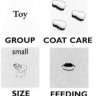

BREED INFORMATION

NAME	Japanese Chin
OTHER NAMES	Chin; Japanese Spaniel
OFFICIAL RECOGNITION	Uk Toy Group; FCI Group 10; AKC Toy Group
COLOUR VARIATIONS	Black/white; Red/white

Japanese Chin

HEIGHT 21-25 cm (9-10 in)

Toy

GROUP COAT CARE

small

SIZE FEEDING

THE JAPANESE CHIN originated in China but ended up in Japan as an exchange of gifts between the Empresses of the two countries. This breed uses its paws to wash its face very much in the manner of a cat, indeed the word chin means cat-like. Queen Alexandra was enamoured of this elegant, aristocratic breed, with its happy, gentle and good natured temperament.

The Chin has a look of astonishment, peculiar to the breed, and its long, soft, profuse coat is silky and absolutely free from curl or wave. The large, dark eyes are set far apart and the well-feathered ears are also set wide apart. Colours are limited to black and white or red and white, the brighter and clearer the red the better. Height is usually from 23–25 cm (9–10 in) and an ideal weight is 1.8–3.2 kg (4–7 lb), the daintier the better.

BREED FACT:
In 1881, the breed now known as the Japanese Chin was shown at Alexandra Palace in the toy spaniel class.

Left
The Japanese Chin has a surprisingly deep bark for its size; it makes a good house-hold companion.

BREED INFORMATION

NAME	King Charles Spaniel
OTHER NAMES	English Toy Spaniel
OFFICIAL RECOGNITION	Uk Toy Group; FCI Group 9; AKC Toy Group
COLOUR VARIATIONS	Black/tan; Tri-colour; Blenheim

King Charles Spaniel

HEIGHT 25–27 cm (10–11 in)

Toy

GROUP COAT CARE

small

SIZE FEEDING

KNOWN IN SOME COUNTRIES as the English Toy Spaniel, this breed was a great favourite of King Charles II from whom the breed took its name. This breed is closely related to the Cavalier King Charles

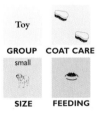

Spaniel and has the same variety of splendid colours.

A compact and cobby dog with very large, wide-set, dark eyes, the King Charles is a happy, intelligent toy spaniel, with a distinctive domed head. The bite is typically slightly undershot. A devoted companion, its temperament is reserved but gentle and affectionate, and the breed is both clean and quiet in habit. The long, silky, straight coat with its slight wave is not especially difficult to keep in good order. Weight ranges from 3.6–6.3 kg (8–14 lb) and height is usually 25–27 cm (10–11in).

BREED FACT:
A similar spaniel to the King Charles was found hidden in the robes of Mary, Queen of Scots when she went to her execution.

Left
It is easy to see why King Charles II was so devoted to the breed which is named after him – they are gentle and affectionate.

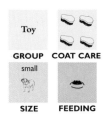

Toy

GROUP | COAT CARE

small

SIZE | FEEDING

Löwchen

HEIGHT 25-33 cm (10-13 in)

BREED INFORMATION	
NAME	Löwchen
OTHER NAMES	Little Lion Dog
OFFICIAL RECOGNITION	Uk Toy Group; FCI Group 9
COLOUR VARIATIONS	Any colour or combination of colours

ALTHOUGH THE LÖWCHEN may be related to the Bichon Frise, the origin of the breed remains obscure. Because the Löwchen is trimmed, leaving a full mane and tail plume resembling those of a lion, the additional name 'Little Lion Dog' is frequently used.

This is a friendly, happy little dog, both active and playful, very intelligent and with no sign of aggression, a good companion for children and an excellent house pet. Its height is 25–33 cm (10–13 in) and weight generally 4–8 kg (9–18 lb). To keep this breed looking like a lion as the name implies requires skill and attention on the part of the owner, as the short hair on the hindquarters and legs does not grow like that naturally but needs careful management.

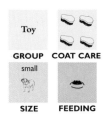

Toy

GROUP | COAT CARE

small

SIZE | FEEDING

Maltese

HEIGHT up to 25.5 cm (up to 10 in)

BREED INFORMATION	
NAME Maltese	OTHER NAMES Bichon Maltais
OFFICIAL RECOGNITION	Uk Toy Group; FCI Group 9; AKC Toy Group
COLOUR VARIATIONS	Pure white (slight lemon markings permissible)

*Right
The Maltese is a lively
and intelligent little
dog, with plenty
of character and an
outgoing nature.*

MOST PROBABLY TAKEN to the island of Malta by Phoenician traders more than 2,000 years ago, it is likely that the breed remained pure, although today's Maltese may be the result of crossing between miniature spaniels and the Miniature Poodle.

The Maltese is well known for the striking contrast between its white coat and dark eyes and eye rims. However, the long, silky coat of good length needs plenty of care if it is to be kept in the best condition and looking smart, for although the coat does not shed, it easily becomes matted. The head hair is usually tied up on top with a neat bow. The Maltese is a sweet tempered breed which is intelligent, alert and full of fun. Height should not exceed 25.5 cm (10 in) and weight is usually about 2–3 kg (4–6 lb).

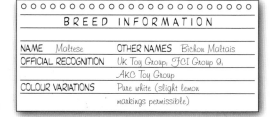

Miniature Pinscher

HEIGHT 25.5-30 cm (10-12 in)

Toy **GROUP**   **COAT CARE**

small **SIZE**   **FEEDING**

A STURDY, COMPACT and elegant little dog the Miniature Pinscher has a smart outline, and moves with a precise hackney gait. Originating in Germany the breed started to gain popularity in Britain after the Second World War. Pinscher is the German word for terrier and although now kept as a companion dog the breed has great ability as a ratter and is often willing to challenge much larger dogs.

Naturally well groomed, fearless and alert, this is a self-possessed breed with a spirited presence, well suited to a small home. The ears may be erect or dropped and the colours are black, blue or chocolate with clearly defined tan markings, all these colours having pencilling on the toes.

Alternatively the breed may be solid red of various shades. Height is 25.5–30 cm (10–12 in), with weight usually 4–5 kg (10–12 lb), and historically the tail has been docked short.

BREED FACT:
Despite the similarity in name, it is believed there is unlikely to be any really close relationship between the Miniature Pinscher and the Dobermann Pinscher.

Left
The Miniature Pinscher was originally used for hunting and killing vermin, but now makes an alert, spirited companion.

Papillon

HEIGHT 20-28 cm (8-11 in)

Toy **GROUP**   **COAT CARE**

small **SIZE**   **FEEDING**

T HE EXTRAORDINARY long-fringed, butterfly-like ears are the reason behind the breed's name, papillon being French for butterfly, but there is also a drop-eared variety called the Phalène, named after a night moth which drops its wings. On the Continent both varieties are called Continental Toy Spaniels.

A dainty breed with alert bearing and intelligent expression, the markings on the head should be symmetrical, a clearly defined blaze often resembling the body of a butterfly. Showing no aggression, always alert, lively, intelligent and friendly, this breed makes a fascinating and charming companion, and the abundant coat is reasonably easy to keep in good order. Height is 20–28 cm (8–11 in) and males, when finished with ruff and hind fringes, can appear rather longer than they are high. The weight of this breed is usually 4–4.5 kg (9–10 lb).

BREED FACT:
Papillons are said by some to have extra-sensory perception, and some believe the breed to be descended from the Spanish Dwarf Spaniel.

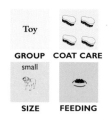
Toy

GROUP   **COAT CARE**

small

SIZE   **FEEDING**

BREED FACT:
The Pekingese first came to Britain in 1860 following the overthrowing by the British of China's Summer Palace.

Right
The Pekingese is not easy to train, but is ideal for those who like an independent, intelligent dog.

Pekingese

HEIGHT 15-23 cm (6-9 in)

WITH ANCESTRY which can be traced back to China's Tang Dynasty, the Pekingese is a true aristocrat of dignified quality. Somewhat leonine in appearance, the expression is alert and intelligent, the personality fearless and loyal. Although aloof, the breed shows no timidity or aggression but is well able to stand its ground against others when necessary.

The head of the Pekingese is large, proportionately wider than it is deep. Heavy bone and a well built body are essentials of the breed, the weight of which should not exceed 5 kg (11 lb) for dogs and 5.5 kg (12 lb) for bitches. Height is usually from 15–23 cm (6–9 in). Movement is slow with a characteristic dignified, rolling gait and the long coat with its pro-

fuse mane and feathering on the ears, legs, tail and toes needs a great deal of care and attention. Black pigment is essential on the nose, lips and eye rims.

BREED INFORMATION	
NAME	Pekingese
OFFICIAL RECOGNITION	UK Toy Group; FCI Group 9; AKC Toy Group
COLOUR VARIATIONS	All colours and markings, except albino and liver

Toy

GROUP   **COAT CARE**

small

SIZE   **FEEDING**

BREED FACT:
Despite its size, the Pomeranian is allied to larger spitz breeds, like the Keeshond, and is descended from Arctic sled-hauling dogs.

Pomeranian

HEIGHT 22-28 cm (8.5-11 in)

THE SMALLEST OF THE spitz breeds, the Pomeranian now weighs from 1.8–3.5 kg (4–5.5 lb), bitches being slightly larger than

BREED INFORMATION			
NAME	Pomeranian	OTHER NAMES	Zwergspitz
OFFICIAL RECOGNITION		UK Toy Group; FCI Group 5; AKC Toy Group	
COLOUR VARIATIONS		All colours, no black or white shadings	

dogs, although dogs called by this name were often much larger in years gone by. The height of this breed is now usually 22–28 cm (8.5–11 in).

With a foxy outline to the head and nose and bright eyes, this breed has an intelligent expression and epitomises liveliness and an extrovert temperament. Abundant in coat, it has a soft, fluffy undercoat and a long, perfectly straight outercoat which can be found in a wide variety of colours. Although small in size, because of the coat this breed requires care and dedication to maintain its attractiveness and good, clean condition, but for those prepared to put in the necessary work this is a vivacious companion with a sweet temperament.

```
○ ○ ○ ○ ○ ○ ○ ○ ○ ○ ○ ○ ○ ○ ○ ○ ○ ○ ○ ○ ○ ○ ○ ○
     B R E E D   I N F O R M A T I O N
```
NAME	Pug
OTHER NAMES	Mops; Carlin
OFFICIAL RECOGNITION	UK Toy Group; FCI Group 10; AKC Toy Group
COLOUR VARIATIONS	Sliver; Apricot; Fawn; Black

Pug

HEIGHT 25-28 cm (10-11 in)

Toy
GROUP COAT CARE
small
SIZE FEEDING

TODAY'S PUG'S DISTANT ancestors come from the Far East where they were miniaturised from mastiffs some 2,400 years ago, but in the sixteenth century they found their way to Holland via the Dutch East India company and later arrived in Britain. They became prized companions and this dignified breed has since been popular with both royalty and aristocracy.

This is a dog of great charm and intelligence with an even tempered, happy, lively disposition. The large head has clearly defined wrinkles and eyes described as globular in shape, making for a thoroughly expressive face. With well-knit proportions and hardness of muscle, the legs are very strong, straight and of moderate length. The high-set tail is curled tightly over the hip, and all this is fitted into an ideal weight of 6.3–8.1 kg (14–18 lb). Height range is generally 25–28 cm (10–11 in).

BREED FACT:
The Pug is an excessively short-nosed breed and is said to have a tendency to snort and rumble like an old man.

Left
The Pug is strong-willed and not easy to train. However, it is worth the effort as it makes a rewarding companion and a good family dog.

```
○ ○ ○ ○ ○ ○ ○ ○ ○ ○ ○ ○ ○ ○ ○ ○ ○ ○ ○ ○ ○ ○ ○ ○
     B R E E D   I N F O R M A T I O N
```
NAME	Yorkshire Terrier
OFFICIAL RECOGNITION	UK Toy Group; FCI Group 3; AKC Toy Group
COLOUR VARIATIONS	Dark steel-blue with tan

Yorkshire Terrier

HEIGHT 22.5-23.5 cm (9 in)

Toy
GROUP COAT CARE
small
SIZE FEEDING

POSSIBLY AN ORIGINAL result of crossing the Maltese with local terriers, the Yorkshire Terrier, though only weighing up to 3.1 kg (7 lb), is a hardy character, full of fun and very much a toy terrier at heart. Spirited, yet with an even disposition, this is an alert breed with dark, sparkling eyes giving a sharp, intelligent expression. Height is usually 22.5–23.5 cm (around 9 in).

The magnificent sight of a Yorkshire Terrier in full show coat is outstanding. Their owners have put in a tremendous amount of work to get the coat looking at its best, and when not being exhibited it is usually kept in 'wraps'. Thus the pet 'Yorkie' rarely looks quite like those which attain top honours in the ring. Colour is important and should be dark steel-blue, not silver-blue. All tan hair should be darker at the roots than in the middle, shading to still lighter at the tips.

BREED FACT:
The smallest Yorkshire Terrier on record stood only 6.3 cm (2.5 in) high and weighed 113 g.

Left
Although the coat of a pet Yorkshire Terrier does not need much maintenance, that of a show dog requires a great deal of work.

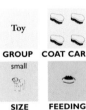

The Utility Group

THE UTILITY GROUP is probably the most disparate group, as the breeds within it are largely those which do not fit comfortably into any of the other group categories. When the various breeds began to be divided there was an initial division between Sporting and Non-Sporting breeds and it is from the latter that the Utilities were eventually drawn out into a group of their own.

DIFFERENT GROUPS
HAVING SAID THAT, there is regular controversy in the Group regarding which breeds should or should not be included, and only in 1999 the Leonberger was taken out to join the newly revised Working Group. In other countries some of the breeds fall into different groups, in part because there are often more actual groups making it possible to split the breeds further. However, the Shih Tzu, for example, regularly finds itself in the Toy Group in other countries, includ-

ing the USA, while in some countries the Tibetan Terrier finds itself being judged with the Terrier Group rather than with the Utility Group.

In general the Utility breeds were not developed for any specific purpose or, if they were, their original purpose has fallen into decline; the Dalmatian, once used as a coach dog; the Poodle once a water dog and the Bulldog, used for bull-baiting, are prime examples.

Indeed the Utility Group is rather a 'mixed bag', but all the breeds seen together make for interesting observation as they differ so greatly in style, size, personality and so many other ways. Some are as small as 23–25.5 cm (9–10 in), while others like the Japanese Akita and Dalmatian are at the larger end of the scale in the canine world. Some have easy temperaments, others are more difficult to control, and undoubtedly some are among the most spectacular of breeds. The Lhasa Apso and Shih Tzu are indeed eye-catching with their long, flowing coats, the Poodles quite spectacular, especially in show-trim, while the Chow Chow and Shar Pei are unique in their own way.

Unlike several rather similar breeds of dog within other groups, it is not really possible to directly compare many of the breeds in the Utility Group with any others. Of course, one can compare the different sizes of Poodle against each other, but technically these differ only by size. To find a comparison between the Boston Terrier and Tibetan Terrier is difficult in anything other than the fact that they share, for some inexplicable reason, the word 'Terrier'. Several dogs within the Group are Spitz breeds, and although they vary, they share a common ancestry. For size, colour or temperament, those considering one of the breeds within this Group have endless choice and, in effect, the decision depends on one's preference.

Above
The Corded Poodle is now a rare breed; it has been superseded by the Standard Poodle.

Right
This Japanese Akita is the Group winner at Crufts. It is a powerful breed that was originally developed as a fighting dog.

Right
The Tibetan Spaniel is not related to other spaniels and its origins are shrouded in a certain amount of mystery.

Boston Terrier

HEIGHT 38-43 cm (15-17 in)

Utility
GROUP **COAT CARE**
small/med.
SIZE **FEEDING**

BREED FACT:
Despite its small stature, the short, square muzzle identifies the Boston Terrier as a member of the Bull breeds.

THE RESULT OF CROSSING the British Bulldog with the white English Terrier, as the name implies, the Boston Terrier is a native of America where a specialist breed club was formed in 1891. A lively, intelligent, determined and strong-willed breed, the Boston is a compactly built dog, varying substantially in size.

With a short head and short, low-set tail, either tapering or screw, the breed should be well balanced, no feature standing out so prominently that the dog appears badly proportioned. The coat is short and smooth and the colours preferably brindle with white markings or alternatively black with white markings. Weight is divided into three categories, Lightweight: under 6.8 kg (15 lb), Middleweight: 6.8–9 kg (15–19 lb) and Heavyweight: 9.1 kg (20 lb) or above but under 11.4 kg (25 lb). Although no height guide is given in the British breed standard, this is usually 38–43 cm (15–17 in).

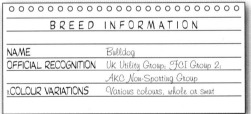

Left
The short, smooth coat of the Boston Terrier is lustrous and fine in texture. It has bright markings and an alert expression.

Bulldog

HEIGHT 31-36 cm (12-14 in)

Utility
GROUP **COAT CARE**
medium
SIZE **FEEDING**

BREED FACT:
For one of the oldest of Britain's indigenous breeds, The Bulldog Club (England) was formed in 1864.

THE BULLDOG IS DESCENDED from the old bull-baiting dogs although shape and substance have changed greatly with the passage of time. Even as far back as the 1630s it was classified as a Bulldog, and after the days of bull-baiting were over the breed was still an active participant in the dog pits. The breed's first appearance as a show dog was in 1860 and from then on the breed has changed not only in shape but also in personality.

Conveying an impression of determination, strength and dignity, the

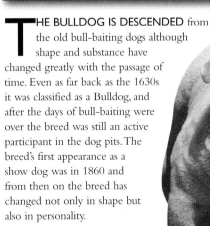

Bulldog is a magnificent breed and despite the fierce appearance it has a most affectionate and loyal nature but is alert, bold, and courageous. Thick-set and low in stature, the dog is broad and powerful, the head massive in size but no feature should be to excess. The fine-textured, short coat comes in various colours and although no height is specified, the weight for dogs should be 25 kg (55 lb) and for bitches 22.7 kg (50 lb).

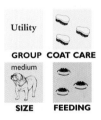

Left
Although the popular view of the Bulldog is one of ferocious tenacity, it is, in fact, an affectionate and gentle breed.

Utility

GROUP   COAT CARE

large

SIZE   FEEDING

Canaan Dog

HEIGHT 50-60 cm (20-24 in)

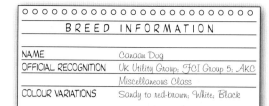

○ ○

BREED INFORMATION

NAME	Canaan Dog
OFFICIAL RECOGNITION	UK Utility Group; FCI Group 5; AKC Miscellaneous Class
COLOUR VARIATIONS	Sandy to red-brown; White; Black

BREED FACT:

A Canaan Dog, with a gold collar, was believed to have been kept tethered to the throne of Queen Jezebel.

ONE OF THE BREEDS more recently introduced to Britain, the Canaan Dog is widely accepted as Israel's national breed with origins going back to the pariah dog, the feral dog of the Middle East. By selective breeding a distinct breed type is evolving, and although only small numbers have been registered in Britain during recent years there are some interesting bloodlines which should prove valuable to the breed.

An alert, intelligent, confident and vigilant breed, the Canaan Dog is aloof with strangers but steady and loyal to its owners. Medium sized, the height is from 50–60 cm (20–24 in) and weight 18–25 kg (40–45 lb). The straight, harsh coat is of medium length but the high-set tail curled over the back is bushy. Colours can be sand to red-brown, white, black or spotted, with or without a symmetrical black mask.

Utility

GROUP   COAT CARE

large

SIZE   FEEDING

Chow Chow

HEIGHT 46-56 cm (18-22 in)

○ ○

BREED INFORMATION

NAME	Chow Chow
OFFICIAL RECOGNITION	UK Utility Group; FCI Group 5; AKC Non-Sporting Group
COLOUR VARIATIONS	Black; Red; Blue; Fawn; Cream; White

IN CHINA, THIS BREED'S HOMELAND, the Chow Chow was used both as a guard and for hunting and, regrettably, also as food. It came to Britain towards the end of the eighteenth century. This is a unique breed with a blue-black tongue, black roof to the mouth and short, stilted movement. Leonine in appearance, various different colours are acceptable and there are two coats

types – rough and smooth – the former more frequently seen and needing daily grooming.

A compact dog, its height ranges from 46–56 cm (18–22 in) and its weight is usually from 20–32 kg (45–70 lb). The oval eyes should be of medium size and clean, and the ears small, thick and slightly rounded at the tips. Both a quiet companion and a good guard, the Chow Chow is independent and yet loyal, with a tendency to be a 'one-man' dog, although it is rather aloof in temperament.

BREED FACT:

That the Chow Chow was used as food in China is well known, but less well known is the fact that its skin was used for clothing.

```
○○○○○○○○○○○○○○○○○○○○○○○○○○○
    BREED  INFORMATION
NAME                  Dalmatian
OTHER NAMES           Dalmatinac
OFFICIAL RECOGNITION  UK Utility Group; FCI Group 6;
                      AKC Non-Sporting Group
COLOUR VARIATIONS     White/black spots; White/liver brow
```

Dalmatian

HEIGHT 56-61 cm (22-24 in)

Utility

GROUP   **COAT CARE**

large

SIZE   **FEEDING**

ALTHOUGH THE BREED can possibly be traced back to India in the distant past, it is generally believed to have originated in Yugoslavia. The Dalmatian's development has been primarily in England where the breed was exceptionally popular as a carriage dog during the Regency period. The Dalmatian was a familiar sight running both beside and under all types of carriage, including those of the gentry, the mail coach and even fire engines.

Distinctively spotted with black or liver-brown spots on a white background, the coat is short, hard and dense, looking both sleek and glossy. The spots should not run together but should be round and well defined. Symmetrical in outline and free from coarseness, the height of this well-balanced dog is from 56.9–61 cm

(22–24 in) while weight is generally 23–25 kg (50–55 lb). An outgoing, friendly breed, neither shy nor hesitant, the Dalmatian is capable of great endurance and so needs plenty of exercise.

BREED FACT:

In London, the Dalmatian often ran with fire engines and their crew, and was often called the 'Firehouse Dog'.

Left
The Dalmation used to be known as the Coach or Carriage Dog – a reflection of its working duties until the end of the nineteenth century.

```
○○○○○○○○○○○○○○○○○○○○○○○○○○○
    BREED  INFORMATION
NAME                  French Bulldog
OTHER NAMES           Bouledogue Français
OFFICIAL RECOGNITION  UK Utility Group; FCI Group 9;
                      AKC Non-Sporting Group
COLOUR VARIATIONS     Brindle; Pied; Fawn
```

French Bulldog

HEIGHT 30.5-31.5 cm (12 in)

Utility

GROUP   **COAT CARE**

medium

SIZE   **FEEDING**

THERE HAS LONG BEEN some dispute as to the origin of this breed, the French claiming it as one of their old native breeds while in the

UK it is believed to be descended from the British Bulldog, bred from some of the smaller specimens which have been produced over time.

A vivacious, deeply affectionate and intelligent breed, whatever the origin, the 'Frenchie', as the breed is fondly known, is a real charmer, full of courage and yet with clown-like qualities. Bat ears and a short undocked tail are essential features. Sturdy, compact and solid with good bone, the French Bulldog has a large, square, broad head, though no point is exaggerated. The short, fine and lustrous coat can be brindle, pied or fawn and an ideal weight for dogs is 12.7 kg (28 lb) and for bitches 10.9 kg (24 lb). Height is generally about 30.5–31.5 cm (12 in).

BREED FACT:

The French Bulldog appeared in England, and was first shown there, around the turn of the twentieth century.

Utility

GROUP **COAT CARE**

medium

SIZE **FEEDING**

BREED FACT:
The size of the German Spitz varies greatly and, over time, its weight has ranged from 2.3–20 kg (5–45 lb).

Right
The German Spitz can be difficult to obedience train and is often relectrant to be groomed. However, it makes a loyal, affectionate companion.

German Spitz

HEIGHT 23-38 cm (9-15 in)

BREED INFORMATION	
NAME	German Spitz
OTHER NAMES	Deutscher Spitz
OFFICIAL RECOGNITION	UK Utility Group; FCI Group 5
COLOUR VARIATIONS	All colour varieties and markings

ALTHOUGH KNOWN FOR many years in a wide variation of sizes, in the UK there are now two recognised sizes of German Spitz, taking the names Klein and Mittel. Klein is the smaller size, measuring 23–29 cm (9–11.5 in) and Mittel from 30–38 cm (12–15 in). In both cases, there is a marked difference of appearance between dogs and bitches. In all respects other than size, the two types are identical and neither has any restrictions on colour other than that butterfly pigment is not acceptable. In Germany there is also a Giant Spitz.

Of happy disposition, the German Spitz is intelligent, active and alert. Independence and devotion to the family are characteristic of the breed. The double coat has a soft, woolly undercoat and long, harsh, straight topcoat. This is not a trimmed breed and the coat needs care and attention.

 Utility

GROUP **COAT CARE**

large

SIZE **FEEDING**

BREED FACT:
The Japanese Akita is one of several Spitz dogs from Japan where *Akita Inu* means 'large dog'.

Japanese Akita

HEIGHT 61-71 cm (24-28 in)

BREED INFORMATION	
NAME	Japanese Akita
OTHER NAMES	Other names: Akita
OFFICIAL RECOGNITION	UK Utility Group; FCI Group 5; AKC Working Group
COLOUR VARIATIONS	Any colour

A HIGHLY POPULAR BREED in Japan, the Japanese Akita was developed some 300 years ago as a fighting dog, later to hunt bear, wild boar and deer. Its origins can be traced to other spitz-type dogs from polar regions which ended up in the northern, mountainous areas of Japan.

A large, powerful, alert and substantial breed with heavy bone structure, the Japanese Akita is dignified, courageous and aloof. The breed needs careful handling as there is a tendency to show dominance over other dogs. It has a soft, dense undercoat and coarse, straight outercoat standing off the body and in the UK this comes in any brilliant, clear colour, including white, brindle and pinto. Markings are well defined, with or without a mask or blaze. Height ranges from 61–71 cm (24–28 in) and weight is generally somewhere from 34–50 kg (75–110 lb).

BREED INFORMATION

NAME	Japanese Shiba Inu
OTHER NAMES	Shiba
OFFICIAL RECOGNITION	UK Utility Group; FCI Group 5
	AKC Non-Sporting Group
COLOUR VARIATIONS	Red; Black; Black/tan; Brindle;

Japanese Shiba Inu

HEIGHT 36.5-39.5 cm (14.5-15.5 in)

Utility

GROUP   COAT CARE

medium

SIZE   FEEDING

BREED FACT:
The Japanese Shiba Inu's name has been translated as 'Little Brushwood Dog' and 'Little Turf Dog'.

A JAPANESE BREED which has rapidly become popular and well-established in the UK is the Shiba Inu, a small, well-balanced, sturdy dog of spitz type, slightly longer than it is high. Lively and friendly in character, this breed is bright, active, keen and alert, often doing sudden things which take an owner by complete surprise. The Shiba, however, is docile and faithful and is understandably one of the most popular breeds in its homeland.

The triangular head is characteristic, while the eyes and ears are relatively small. Colours of this double-coated breed, with a thick curled or sickle-like tail, can be striking, in red, black, black and tan, brindle, or white with a red or grey tinge. Average height is from 36.5–39.5 cm (14.5–15.5 in) and weight usually 8–10 kg (18–22 lb).

Left
The head of the Japanese Shiba Inu looks like a blunt triangle when viewed from above.

BREED INFORMATION

NAME	Japanese Spitz
OTHER NAMES	Nihon Supittsu
OFFICIAL RECOGNITION	UK Utility Group; FCI Group 5
COLOUR VARIATIONS	Pure white

Japanese Spitz

HEIGHT 30-36 cm (12-14 in)

Utility

GROUP   COAT CARE

medium

SIZE   FEEDING

BREED FACT:
Although there are similarities in appearance, many believe that Samoyed blood has never been introduced to the Japanese Spitz breed.

E VEN THE JAPANESE themselves seem confused about the origin of the Japanese Spitz, with theories varying considerably and too widely to outline here, though one simple theory is that the breed has been in Japan for centuries. A recent study concludes that various white spitz-type dogs are descended from the now-extinct German White Spitz.

This is an affectionate and companionable breed that can be slightly wary at first meeting with strangers but is alert, intelligent, bold and lively. The dark, rather oblique eyes of moderate size are oval shaped, and the small, angular ears stand erect. The profuse pure white coat is straight and stand-off, with a dense under-coat, so care and attention are needed. The bushy tail is curled over the back. Dogs are 30–36 cm (12–14 in) high and bitches slightly smaller. This is not a heavy breed, weighing about 5–6 kg (11–13 lb).

Left
The Japanese Spitz is inclined to bark a great deal, although selective breeding has reduced this tendency to some extent.

Utility

GROUP   COAT CARE

large

SIZE   FEEDING

Keeshond

HEIGHT 43.2-45.7 cm (17-18 in)

BREED INFORMATION	
NAME	Keeshond
OTHER NAMES	Wolfspitz; Dutch Barge Dog
OFFICIAL RECOGNITION	UK Utility Group; FCI Group 5; AKC Non-Sporting Group
COLOUR VARIATIONS	A mixture of grey and black

BREED FACT:
The Keeshond is the Dutch national breed, used originally as a barge- and watchdog, and also known as the Dutch Barge Dog.

Right
The Keeshond requires firm handling and thus is not ideal for an inexperienced dog owner. However, it is an excellent watchdog and loyal companion.

D URING UNREST IN HOLLAND before the French Revolution, a dog owned by Cornelius de Gysalaer, whose nickname was 'Kees', became the symbol of the patriots, giving the breed its name. Subsequently the breed fell into decline but it was revived in Holland in the 1920s.

With a fox-like head and small, pointed ears this breed has an alert expression, the head surrounded by a large ruff, complemented by a well-feathered tail curled over the back. Intelligent and adaptable, the Keeshond is friendly and an ideal companion, making a good guard as the breed has a marked guarding tendency. The harsh, off-standing coat needs regular grooming to maintain condition and ideal size is 45.7 cm (18 in) for dogs and 43.2 cm (17 in) for bitches. Weight is generally around 25–30 kg (55–66 lb).

Utility

GROUP   COAT CARE

small

SIZE   FEEDING

Lhasa Apso

HEIGHT 25.4 cm (10 in)

BREED INFORMATION	
NAME	Lhasa Apso
OFFICIAL RECOGNITION	UK Utility Group; FCI Group 9; AKC Non-Sporting Group
COLOUR VARIATIONS	Many

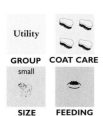

BREED FACT:
Tibetans likened the Lhasa Apso to the mythological Snow Lion which is white, not golden as was originally believed by early travellers to Tibet.

A NATIVE OF TIBET, the Lhasa Apso was originally kept in monasteries, giving a warning bark to monks if intruders managed to get past the huge Tibetan Mastiffs tethered outside. Also kept by families and traders, the breed was a bringer of good fortune, always a gift and never sold as it is believed to be the reincarnation of monks who have sinned in previous lives. First known in Britain in 1854, several were shown around the turn of the century but it was not until 1928 that the breed re-emerged, with direct imports from Tibet.

Only 25.4 cm (10 in) in height the Apso is really a large dog in a small frame, generally weighing 6.5–8.5 kg (14.5–19 lb). Although gay and assertive, the character of the breed is rather special and needs some understanding, being aloof with strangers. The extremely long double coat of virtually any colour needs constant attention as it does not moult but mats naturally as protection against the elements.

Mexican Hairless

HEIGHT 33-57 cm (13-22.5 in)

Utility	
GROUP	**COAT CARE**
small	
SIZE	**FEEDING**

BREED INFORMATION

NAME	Mexican Hairless
OTHER NAMES	Xoloitzcuintli, Tepeizeuintli
OFFICIAL RECOGNITION	UK Utility Group; FCI Group 5
COLOUR VARIATIONS	Several solid colours, with some pink spotting allowed

THE MEXICAN HAIRLESS does not yet have an official breed standard in Britain and is therefore not eligible for exhibition. Although the breed first arrived here 12 years ago there are only nine living in the UK. It is anticipated that the Mexican Hairless will be divided into those under 33 cm (13 in) and those over, although in other countries there are three sizes: Toy, Miniature and Standard and these vary considerably in size, up to 57 cm (22.5 in) with weight varying between 4 and 14 kg (9 and 31 lb).

Also known as the Xoloitzcuintli and Tepeizeuintli, the breed appears to have remained unchanged for thousands of years, a living link to old pre-Columbian civilisations. Usually a hairless breed, some are born with coats but it is not anticipated that these will be allowed to be shown. Like that of the Chinese Crested Dog, the skin feels hot to the touch.

BREED FACT:
The most usual alternative name for the Mexican Hairless, *Xoloitzcuintli*, combines the word *Xolotl*, an Aztec god, and *itzcuintli*, the word for dog.

Left
The high body temperature of the Mexican Hairless means that its skin always feels hot when it is touched.

Miniature Schnauzer

HEIGHT 33-35.6 cm (13-14 in)

Utility	
GROUP	**COAT CARE**
medium	
SIZE	**FEEDING**

BREED INFORMATION

NAME	Miniature Schnauzer
OTHER NAMES	Zwergschnauzer
OFFICIAL RECOGNITION	UK Utility Group; FCI Group 2; AKC Terrier Group
COLOUR VARIATIONS	Pepper and salt; Black; Black/silver

OF GERMAN ORIGIN, the Miniature Schnauzer comes from the same root stock as the Schnauzer but it is believed that Affenpinscher blood was also included to bring down size, while retaining Terrier characteristics. The Miniature Schnauzer first appeared in the showring in 1899.

A sturdily built, robust breed, nearly square in outline, the Miniature Schnauzer has a keen expression and alert attitude. With medium sized, dark, oval eyes and arched, bushy eyebrows, this is a stylish and adaptable breed kept primarily as a companion dog. The harsh, wiry coat with dense undercoat needs regular attention. Pepper and salt colours, pure black or black and silver, as well as the stubby moustache and chin whiskers enhance the smart appearance. Ideal height for dogs is 35.6 cm (14 in) and for bitches 33 cm (13 in), while weight is generally 6–7 kg (13–15 lb).

BREED FACT:
In German, *schnauze* means nose or snout, and indeed the powerful muzzle and black nose with its wide nostrils are a feature.

Left
Once used for hunting vermin, the Miniature Schnauzer now makes an excellent guard dog and an obedient companion.

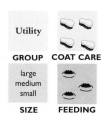

Utility	
GROUP	**COAT CARE**
large medium small	
SIZE	**FEEDING**

Poodle

STANDARD: HEIGHT over 38 cm (over 15 in)
MINIATURE: HEIGHT 28-38 cm (11-15 in)
TOY: HEIGHT under 28 cm (under 11 in)

BREED INFORMATION	
NAME	Standard, Miniature, Toy Poodle
OTHER NAMES	Grand-Caniche, nain, miniature.
OFFICIAL RECOGNITION	UK Utility Group; FCI Group 9; AKC Non-Sporting Group
COLOUR VARIATIONS	White; Cream; Brown; Apricot; Black

BREED FACT:

In Paris, especially on Pont Neuf, small Poodles were trained to soil people's shoes, so that their masters could profit from cleaning them.

ALTHOUGH THE POODLE is divided by size into three different varieties in Britain, the history of the breed is common to them all. Under FCI rules there are four sizes, a Medium size (Caniche moyen) fitting in between the Miniature and Standard varieties.

Despite being widely accepted as a French breed, development of the Poodle began in Germany as the Water Dog or Pudel. Originally a large gundog, in Germany, these dogs were used to pull milk carts, so becoming stronger and heavier, while in France, where they were used mainly as companion dogs, the breed became smaller. The smaller Poodles also have a great reputation as circus dogs, especially in France, and the breed is renowned for being able to learn tricks with ease. At one time the Corded Poodle was exhibited, strikingly different in appearance from the curly coat seen today.

All Poodles, whatever their size, should be well balanced and elegant looking, with a very proud carriage. They are gay spirited and good tempered, their heads long and fine with a strong, well-chiselled foreface. Colours are white, cream, apricot, brown, black, blue and silver and in all cases clear colours are preferred. The profuse, curly coat does not moult and for exhibition at shows it is recommended that dogs are shown in traditional lion clip, although puppies are shown in what is termed 'puppy trim'. Standard Poodles are to be over 38 cm (15in), their weight approaching 19 kg (42 lb) or sometimes more; Miniature Poodles are under 38 cm (15 in) but over 28 cm (11 in) and weigh about 12–14 kg (26–30 lb); Toy Poodles are under 28 cm (11 in) and usually weigh about 6.5–7.5 kg (14–16.5 lb).

Above
The Miniature Poodle became smaller as the breed was used as a companion and lapdog.

Above Right
Standard Poodles were used as cart dogs in Germany, and so became stron and large.

Right
This Toy Poodle has an excellent, proud carriage, with his head held high.

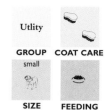

BREED INFORMATION

NAME	Schipperke
OFFICIAL RECOGNITION	Uk Utility Group; FCI Group 1; AKC Non-Sporting Group
COLOUR VARIATIONS	Black; Other whole colours permissible.

Schipperke

HEIGHT 22-33 cm (9-13 in)

Utility

GROUP small

COAT CARE

SIZE **FEEDING**

BREED FACT:
The Schipperke is reputed to have been very popular among shoemakers who paraded their dogs on Sundays.

the name translates to mean little captain. Belgium's Queen Maria Henrietta acquired a Schipperke at a show in Brussels in 1885, later helping to give the breed a fashionable career as a companion.

Weighing about 5.4–7.3 kg (12–16 lb), according to the British breed standard, the Schipperke is a small, cobby, active dog with a sharp, foxy expression. Under FCI rules it is grouped in two sizes: 3–5 kg (6.5–11 lb) and 5–8 kg (11–17.5 lb). Height varies from about 22–33 cm (9–13 in).

Intensely lively and alert, this is an amenable breed, intelligent and faithful. The dense, harsh coat is smooth on the head but erect and thick around the neck, forming a mane and frill, while on the back of the thighs are culottes. The colour is generally black, but other whole colours are allowed.

COMING ORIGINALLY from Flanders, the compact little Schipperke was used in Belgium and Holland to guard canal boats,

BREED INFORMATION

NAME	Schnauzer
OTHER NAMES	Standard Schnauzer
OFFICIAL RECOGNITION	Uk Utility Group; FCI Group 2; AKC Working Group
COLOUR VARIATIONS	Pure black; Pepper and salt

Schnauzer

HEIGHT 45.7-48.3 cm (18-19 in)

Utility

GROUP medium

COAT CARE

SIZE **FEEDING**

BREED FACT:
In Germany, the multi-purpose Schnauzer was a ratter, a drovers' dog, a carting dog, a stock tender and a guard.

OF GERMAN ORIGIN, the Schnauzer appears to have been derived from the black Poodle, wolf-grey Spitz and old German Pinscher, thereby combining working and terrier stock. Known in some countries as the Standard Schnauzer, in Britain the Schnauzer has not achieved the popularity of the Miniature version, but this is an ideal dog for those who are active and prepared to devote time to the coat.

Primarily a companion dog, the Schnauzer is strong and vigorous, capable of great endurance. Sturdy of build and robust, the breed has a keen expression and an alert attitude. The harsh, wiry coat, short enough for smartness, can be pure black or pepper and salt, shades ranging from dark iron grey to light grey. The neat, v-shaped ears are high-set and drop forward to the temple. Size averages 45.7–48.3 cm (18–19 in) and weight is usually 14.5–15.5 kg (32–34 lb).

Left
The Schnauzer has a strong, dense topcoat over an even denser undercoat. As a result, the breed neeeds regualr stripping.

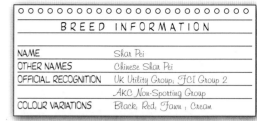

BREED INFORMATION

NAME	Shar Pei
OTHER NAMES	Chinese Shar Pei
OFFICIAL RECOGNITION	UK Utility Group; FCI Group 2
	AKC Non-Sporting Group
COLOUR VARIATIONS	Black; Red; Fawn; Cream

Shar Pei

HEIGHT 46-51 cm (18-20 in)

Utility

GROUP — COAT CARE
medium

SIZE — FEEDING

BREED FACT:
'Shar Pei' can be translated as 'sand skin'. This refers to the texture of the coat and not to the colour.

THE SHAR PEI HAILS from China where a great deal of written material was destroyed around 255 BC, making it difficult to separate fact from fiction where its ancestry is concerned. However, it is believed that the breed can be traced back to the Han Dynasty (206 BC–AD 220). The Tibetan Mastiff and Chow Chow are probably involved in the background of the Shar Pei, as are some other Molosser breeds and even, perhaps, the Pyrenean Mountain Dog.

On the South China coast, the Shar Pei was used for fighting but soon became a multi-purpose dog, used also for hunting and guarding game. Now primarily a companion dog, its temperament is calm and independent, and it is a very affectionate breed. A frowning expression and loose skin are characteristic but must never be taken to excess. The distinctive coat, found in a variety of solid colours, is short, bristly and harsh to the touch. Height is 46–51 cm (18–20in) and weight usually 16–20 kg (35–45 lb).

BREED INFORMATION

NAME	Shih Tzu
OFFICIAL RECOGNITION	UK Utility Group; FCI Group 9;
	AKC Toy Group
COLOUR VARIATIONS	All colours

Shih Tzu

HEIGHT up to 26.7 cm (up to 10.5 in)

Utility

GROUP — COAT CARE
small

SIZE — FEEDING

Left
The head hair of the Shih Tzu should be tied back to keep it in order.

BREED FACT:
Among other differences, the nose of this breed is shorter than that of the Lhasa Apso and, though the dog is technically slightly taller, the legs are, in fact, shorter.

THE SHIH TZU'S ROOTS lie in both Tibet and China, the Lhasa Apso and Pekingese both having been involved in the breed's make-up. When dogs arrived in Britain in 1930 confusion arose between the Shih Tzu and Lhasa Apso, causing much heated debate. Later even more dilemma was created in the USA when Shih Tzus were imported from England, but registered as Lhasa Apsos and subsequently bred from.

Sturdy, standing not more than 26.7 cm (10.5 in) and weighing 4.5–8.1 kg (10–18 lb), this is an intelligent, active, alert breed, both friendly and independent. It is described as having a chrysanthemum-like face, because hair grows upward on the nose; the long dense coat with its good undercoat requires considerable care and it is recommended that head hair is tied up. All colours are allowed and a white blaze on the forehead and white tip to the tail are highly desirable in parti-colours.

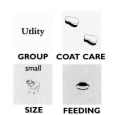

Tibetan Spaniel

HEIGHT 25.4 cm (10 in)

Utility

GROUP **COAT CARE**

small

SIZE **FEEDING**

BREED FACT:
In 1938 the trade agent of Gartok presented a Tibetan Spaniel to Sir Edward and Lady Wakefield.

LIKE THE HISTORIES of all Tibetan and oriental breeds, that of the Tibetan Spaniel is veiled in a certain haze. It is said the breed may be the ancestor of the Japanese Chin and the Pekingese, while another belief is that they were used to turn prayer wheels in Tibetan monasteries. Certainly the breed was known in Britain prior to the close of the last century and undoubtedly the name 'Spaniel' is a misnomer.

With a rather special temperament, the Tibetan Spaniel is aloof with strangers, but highly intelligent, gay and assertive, alert, loyal and yet independent. Slightly longer than it is high, this small active dog measures about 25.4 cm (10 in) in height and weight is ideally 4.1–6.8 kg (9–15 lb). All coat colours and colour mixtures are acceptable and the top coat is silky in texture, of moderate length on the body and with a mane, which is more apparent in dogs than bitches.

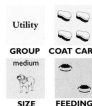

Tibetan Terrier

HEIGHT 35.6-40.6 cm (14-16 in)

Utility

GROUP **COAT CARE**

medium

SIZE **FEEDING**

BREED FACT:
The Tibetan Terrier has large, flat feet, which have undoubtedly helped the breed to survive in rough, mountainous country.

ANOTHER TIBETAN BREED, the Tibetan Terrier is used, among other purposes, for herding stray animals and retrieving lost articles from steep mountain passes. This breed is a good deal larger and longer in the leg than the Lhasa Apso and the Tibetan Spaniel. An active companion of nomadic tribes this sturdy breed is generally square in outline, a lively, good natured, loyal companion dog with many engaging ways.

Its temperament is outgoing, alert, intelligent and game and, although sparing of affection to strangers, the breed is in no way fierce. The bite of the Tibetan Terrier may be either scissor or reverse scissor. The long double coat requires regular attention and most colours are acceptable, except chocolate and liver. The well-feathered tail is carried in a gay curl over the back. Dogs stand some 35.6–40.6 cm (14–16 in) in height, while bitches are slightly smaller. Height is not specified in the British breed standard but is generally 8–14 kg (18–30 lb).

The Working Group

For centuries dogs have worked with man, in many cases doing something as simple and instinctive as protecting their own territory. Breeds developed a wide variety of uses and with the passage of time, coupled with the introduction of foreign breeds to this country, the Working Group grew larger and larger in Britain. By 1998 this group comprised over 50 different breeds. In consequence, from January 1999 the group was split, several of its breeds moving into the newly created Pastoral Group. Additionally the Leonberger joined the ranks of the Working breeds from the Utility Group where many thought this large dog had never really belonged. Hence the number of different breeds in this Group has been brought into line with those of others.

INTELLIGENCE

Above
The Rottweiler needs firm training and sensible handling.

Above right
The Siberian Husky is ideally suited to very cold climates.

Below
Dogs have worked alongside man for thousands of years.

ALL ARE SUFFICIENTLY intelligent to be trained and a high proportion of breeds remaining in the Working Group are sizeable, both in height and stature. Their functions in life differ considerably, several used as watch- and guard dogs, others originally for fighting, while the Great Dane was used to hunt boar and stag. The Giant Schnauzer and Bouvier des Flandres mainly herded cattle, although the latter, like other Working dogs, is now involved in security work. Then there are the breeds which work in water, dragging nets and retrieving, while others toil in snowy terrain, the Saint Bernard doing rescue work, and others like the Alaskan Malamute and Siberian Husky representing several breeds involved in heavy haulage work. In Switzerland, Belgium, Holland and Newfoundland, dogs pulled smaller carts, none the less coming to the aid of mankind in his toils.

Although many of the dogs which fall within this group are used now just for exhibition purposes and for companionship, rather than the work for which their breeds were developed, in a number of cases, especially abroad, these breeds still carry out their work, provid-ing invaluable service to man. Among them are dogs much loved and admired the world over.

As with the majority of group classifications, there is a wide variety of dogs in the Working Group, but none within this group can be considered small dogs. There are gentle giants such as the St Bernard and Newfoundland and that majestic dog the Great Dane – indeed, were these dogs not amenable to training they would be very difficult to handle. Also in this group fall some of the Bull breeds which are enormously strong. The large ones, especially, need careful handling as one can be dealing with a dog whose overall weight can be well in excess of one's own. Added to this such dogs are powerful in every way, so it is of the utmost importance that they know who is their boss.

Coats vary from the short-coated Bull breeds to the more substantially-coated ones such as the Portuguese Water Dog and Pyrenean Mountain Dog. The breeds within this group all have active minds as they were bred to work in all manner of ways, some of them to guard their property and owners, so it is important to fully understand a working dog's original function before deciding whether a particular breed will be well-suited to one's own lifestyle – town or country, active or sedentary, and so on.

BREED INFORMATION

NAME	Alaskan Malamute
OFFICIAL RECOGNITION	UK Working Group; FCI Group 5; AKC Working Group
COLOUR VARIATIONS	Light grey to black; Gold, to red to liver. White underbody; White

Alaskan Malamute

HEIGHT 58-71 cm (23-28 in)

Working

GROUP **COAT CARE**

large

SIZE **FEEDING**

BREED FACT:
In 1927, the American Kennel Club issued an official breed standard for the Alaskan Malamute.

ONE OF THE OLDEST ARCTIC sled dogs, the breed name comes from the Eskimo settlement of Malamute. To survive in Alaskan temperatures and pull heavy loads at steady speeds the Alaskan Malamute needs to be powerful and heavily boned, but never short on the leg. Weight ranges from 38–56 kg (85–125 lb) and height 58–71 cm (23–28 in).

Affectionate, friendly, loyal and a devoted companion, this is not a 'one-man' dog. This breed has a tendency to show aggression toward other dogs and its size and strength, coupled together, necessitate firm, careful handling. The broad head and obliquely set eyes add to the dignified appearance of this thickly-coated dog, ranging in colour from light grey to black or from gold through shades of red to liver, always with certain white markings. The only solid colour permissible is all white.

Left
The Alaskan Malamute is a very powerful, deep chested dog with a masses of stamina. It enjoys activity and exercise of all kinds.

BREED INFORMATION

NAME	Beauceron
OTHER NAMES	Berger de Beauce; Bas Rouge
OFFICIAL RECOGNITION	UK Working Group; FCI Group 1
COLOUR VARIATIONS	Black/tan; Harlequin

Beauceron

HEIGHT 63-70 cm (24.5-27.5 in)

Working

GROUP **COAT CARE**

large

SIZE **FEEDING**

BREED FACT:
The first specific description of a dog that matches the description of the Beauceron is in a manuscript of 1587.

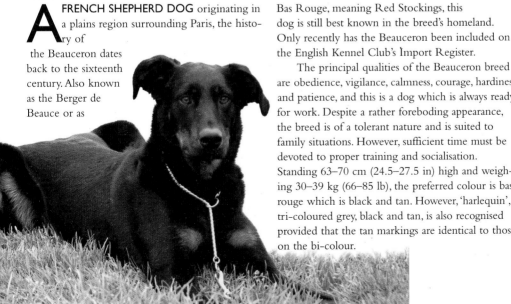

A FRENCH SHEPHERD DOG originating in a plains region surrounding Paris, the history of the Beauceron dates back to the sixteenth century. Also known as the Berger de Beauce or as Bas Rouge, meaning Red Stockings, this dog is still best known in the breed's homeland. Only recently has the Beauceron been included on the English Kennel Club's Import Register.

The principal qualities of the Beauceron breed are obedience, vigilance, calmness, courage, hardiness and patience, and this is a dog which is always ready for work. Despite a rather foreboding appearance, the breed is of a tolerant nature and is suited to family situations. However, sufficient time must be devoted to proper training and socialisation. Standing 63–70 cm (24.5–27.5 in) high and weighing 30–39 kg (66–85 lb), the preferred colour is bas rouge which is black and tan. However, 'harlequin', tri-coloured grey, black and tan, is also recognised provided that the tan markings are identical to those on the bi-colour.

Left
The Beauceron has a double dewclaw on the hind legs and a rough, short, dense coat.

Working

GROUP   **COAT CARE**

large

SIZE   **FEEDING**

Bernese Mountain Dog

HEIGHT 58-70 cm (23-27.5 in)

BREED INFORMATION	
NAME	Bernese Mountain Dog
OTHER NAMES	Berner Sennenhund
OFFICIAL RECOGNITION	UK Working Group; FCI Group 2
	AKC Working Group
COLOUR VARIATIONS	Jet black with reddish-brown and white

BREED FACT:

The Bernese is a dog which has evolved from mastiff-type dogs and local dogs which guarded flocks, and is a breed capable of withstanding mountain conditions.

Right

Despite its size the Bermese Mountain Dog has a sweet, affectionate nature, which makes it an ideal family dog.

ONE OF four varieties of mountain dog introduced to Switzerland by Roman soldiers 2,000 years ago, the Bernese was used as a draught dog by the weavers of Berne. A strong, sturdy working dog, compact in build and standing some 58–70 cm (23–27.5 in) high and weighing 40–44 kg (88–97 lb), this breed enjoys pulling light carts.

This is a farm dog, active, alert and a devoted family member. Temperament is self-confident, good natured, friendly and fearless. The strong skull and black colouring with rich, reddish-brown on the cheeks, over the eyes and on all four legs and the chest, with a long, quite wavy coat and natural sheen, makes the Bernese a really impressive dog. Its feet are short, round and compact, and the tail of this breed is bushy. The dog carries it raised up when alert or moving.

Working

GROUP   **COAT CARE**

large

SIZE   **FEEDING**

Bouvier des Flandres

HEIGHT 59-68 cm (23-27 in)

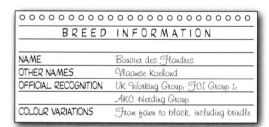

BREED INFORMATION	
NAME	Bouvier des Flandres
OTHER NAMES	Vlaamse Koehond
OFFICIAL RECOGNITION	UK Working Group; FCI Group 1;
	AKC Herding Group
COLOUR VARIATIONS	From fawn to black, including brindle

DESCENDED FROM FLEMISH cattle dogs, in French Bouvier means herdsman, or might also be translated as oxherd or cattle herder. Found originally in south-west Flanders and northern France, the Bouvier des Flandres was originally used for driving cattle but in more recent times has been used in security work.

A compact, powerfully built dog, the breed is well-boned and has strongly muscled limbs, giving the impression of great power without clumsiness.

The Bouvier's lively appearance reveals intelligence, energy and audacity and the harsh beard is highly characteristic, giving a forbidding impression to this calm, sensible dog. The abundant, thick coat, ranging in colour from fawn to black, and including brindle, is coarse to the touch and is meant to be unkempt-looking. Height is 59–68 cm (23–27 in) and weight 27–40 kg (59–88 lb).

BREED FACT:

The Bouvier des Flandres was first shown in Brussels in 1910. In the First World War, it was used as a messenger and ambulance dog.

BREED INFORMATION

NAME	Boxer
OFFICIAL RECOGNITION	UK Working Group; FCI Group 2; AKC Working Group
COLOUR VARIATIONS	Fawn or Brindle (may have some white)

Boxer

HEIGHT 53-63 cm (21-25 in)

Working GROUP — large SIZE

COAT CARE — FEEDING

BELIEVED TO BE descended from Bulldog and Great Dane type dogs, the Boxer was developed in Germany towards the close of the nineteenth century and gained recognition as a guard dog in 1926. In Britain, the Boxer is shown with its high set ears hanging naturally by the head, but in some countries they are cropped.

Full of stamina, this is a fearless and self-assured breed, but it is equable in temperament and biddable too. The Boxer is loyal to its owner and family and friendly at play, but has a guarding instinct and is distrustful of strangers so needs careful training. With an appearance of great nobility this dog has a square build, is strong boned and has powerful, well-developed muscles. The short, glossy coat is smooth and tight to the body, and the colour fawn or brindle. Height ranges from 53–63 cm (21–25 in) and weight from 25 to 32 kg (55–70 lb).

BREED FACT:
The official breed standard for the Boxer was issued in Germany in 1905 and the name may be derived from *bullen-beisser* which means bull biter.

Left
The Boxer requires energetic, experienced owners. However, once trained, it makes a gentle, affectionate family dog.

BREED INFORMATION

NAME	Bullmastiff
OFFICIAL RECOGNITION	UK Working Group; FCI Group 2; AKC Working Group
COLOUR VARIATIONS	Brindle; Fawn; Red

Bullmastiff

HEIGHT 61-68.5 cm (24-27 in)

Working GROUP — large SIZE

COAT CARE — FEEDING

THE OLD ENGLISH Mastiff and also the Bulldog are the breeds behind the Bullmastiff which has been known since 1860 as a guard dog, one which helped gamekeepers to apprehend poachers. However the breed was not officially recognised by the English Kennel Club until 1924.

A powerful, active and high-spirited breed, the Bullmastiff needs firm handling but is amenable to discipline and is very reliable. The short coat is hard and weather resistant and can be any shade of brindle, fawn or red. A black muzzle, however, is essential. Height is 61–68.5 cm (24–27 in) and weight 41–59 kg (90–130 lb) indicating the powerful build and great strength of this breed. The skull is large and square viewed from any angle, and the skull circumference may equal the height of the dog when measured from ground to top of shoulder.

BREED FACT:
The Bullmastiff, legendary for its bravery and courage, was originally developed to overtake and capture intruders without mauling or killing them.

Working **GROUP** • **COAT CARE**

large **SIZE** • **FEEDING**

Dobermann

HEIGHT 65-69 cm (25.5-27 in)

BREED FACT:
The breed name was taken from Louis Dobermann, a tax collector, who wanted his clients to pay!

BREED INFORMATION	
NAME	Dobermann
OTHER NAMES	Dobermann Pinscher
OFFICIAL RECOGNITION	UK Working Group; FCI Group 2; AKC Working Group
COLOUR VARIATIONS	Black; Brown; Blue; Fawn

THE DOBERMANN was created in Germany, with the aim of producing a giant terrier that had the aptitude of a guard dog. A satisfactory type of the breed had been bred by 1890 but Otto Galler helped to improve the breed still further and added Pinscher to the name. In Germany, the National Dobermann Club was formed in 1900.

Capable of great speed and needing sensible handling, the Dobermann is intelligent with a firm character, bold, alert and obedient. Standing ideally 65–69 cm (25.5–27 in) high and weighing in the region of 30–40 kg (66–88 lb), this is a medium sized, tough breed, muscular and elegant with a well-set body and proud carriage. The short, thick, close-lying coat is easy to care for and the colours are black, brown, blue or fawn, with rust red markings, sharply defined.

Working **GROUP** • **COAT CARE**

large **SIZE** • **FEEDING**

Dogue de Bordeaux

HEIGHT 58-69 cm (23-27 in)

BREED INFORMATION	
NAME	Dogue de Bordeaux
OTHER NAMES	French Mastiff
OFFICIAL RECOGNITION	UK Working Group; FCI Group
2COLOUR VARIATIONS	Golden; Fawn; Mahogany

FIRST USED IN FRANCE FOR guarding and hunting boar and bear, the Dogue de Bordeaux also goes under the name of French Mastiff. Because for centuries the Bordeaux region of France was ruled by English kings, it is likely that the English Mastiff was used in matings with the large guard dogs of the region. The Spanish Mastiff may also have been included in this cross-breeding and the outcome was a powerful mastiff, which was then decidedly ferocious.

BREED FACT:
A completely fearless breed, the Dogue de Bordeaux does not tolerate intruders. It was used for animal-baiting and dog fighting.

The head is huge and gives a pugnacious appearance, and the skull is broad, with an abrupt stop. Height ranges between 58 and 69 cm (23–27 in) and weight from 36–45 kg (80–100 lb) though it is often somewhat more. Colours include golden, fawn and mahogany with a distinct black or red mask. Although large and powerful, the breed is calm by nature.

Eskimo Dog

HEIGHT 51-68 cm (20-27 in)

Working

GROUP **COAT CARE**

large

SIZE **FEEDING**

BREED FACT:
The dog was the only means of transport for Inuits living in Canada's Northwest Territory and the Eskimo Dog was used for this purpose.

A N ALL-PURPOSE HAULAGE DOG, the breed was traditionally used by the Eskimo (now known as the Inuit) tribe and falls between the larger Alaskan Malamute and smaller Siberian Husky in size. Expected originally to catch any prey, forming part of the dogs' own food ration, the Eskimo Dog is not a breed to keep with other livestock or dogs.

Early socialisation of this dog is essential and traditional training methods are not always successful. With its powerful body, heavy impenetrable coat, and large bushy tail, there is a marked contrast in size between dogs and bitches, the former standing 58–68 cm (23–27 in) high and weighing 34–47.6 kg (75–105 lb) while bitches stand 51–61 cm (20–24 in) high with a weight of 27–41 kg (60–90 lb). All known dog colours or combinations of colours are acceptable in this breed.

Left
The Eskimo Dog is an energetic working dog but is not a good domestic companion. It is a pack animal and needs firm handling.

Giant Schnauzer

HEIGHT 60-70 cm (23.5-27.5 in)

Working

GROUP **COAT CARE**

large

SIZE **FEEDING**

BREED FACT:
At Munich in Germany, around 30 black dogs were shown as 'Russian Bear Schnauzers' in the year 1909.

I N THE BAVARIAN HIGHLANDS, the Giant Schnauzer was used by drovers to herd cattle and for many years the breed was known as the Munchener Dog. Classified in Germany as a Working dog in 1925, the Giant Schnauzer is generally less well-known than this breed's smaller cousins, the Miniature and Standard Schnauzers, both of which are classified in the Utility Group. An imposing, powerfully built and robust breed, the good natured Giant Schnauzer is versatile, being strong, hardy, intelligent and vigorous. Resistant to weather and capable of great speed and endurance, regular exercise is necessary. Height ranges from 60–70 cm (23.5–27.5 in) and weight is generally from 32–35 kg (70–77 lb). The harsh, wiry coat with its undercoat needs trimming. Colours are pure black or pepper and salt, on which a dark facial mask is essential.

Left
Despite its size and strength, the Giant Schnauzer is good natured, friendly and reliable.

Working

GROUP   **COAT CARE**

large

SIZE   **FEEDING**

Great Dane

HEIGHT 71-76 cm (28-30 in)

BREED INFORMATION

NAME	Great Dane
OTHER NAMES	Deutsche Dogge, German Mastiff
OFFICIAL RECOGNITION	UK Working Group; FCI Group 2; AKC Working Group
COLOUR VARIATIONS	Brindle; Fawn; Blue; Black

BREED FACT:

In Germany, the Great Dane has been the country's national dog since 1876. The breed came to Britain the following year.

Right

The Great Dane is truly a gentle giant. Despite its daunting size, it makes am excellent family companion if it has been well-trained.

DESPITE THE NAME, the Great Dane hails from Germany, where the breed is known as the Deutsche Dogge or German Mastiff and is the country's national dog. It was used in the seventeenth century to hunt boar and stags.

Although this is a large breed, some 71–76 cm (28–30 in) high and weighing 46–54 kg (100–120 lb) at minimum in maturity, the Great Dane is friendly and outgoing. Elegantly built, the Great Dane looks ready to go anywhere and do anything. The head gives the impression of great length and the strength of the jaw and the wide open nostrils give a blunt look to the nose. The short, dense, sleek-looking coat comes in brindle, fawn, blue, black and harlequin, which is a pure white ground with all black or all blue patches.

Working

GROUP   **COAT CARE**

large

SIZE   **FEEDING**

Leonberger

HEIGHT 65-80 cm (26-32 in)

BREED INFORMATION

NAME	Leonberger
OFFICIAL RECOGNITION	UK Working Group; FCI Group
COLOUR VARIATIONS	Light yellow; Golden to red-brown

FROM LEONBERG IN GERMANY comes one of Britain's more recent introductions, the Leonberger. Although not quite so heavy as its ancestors, this magnificent breed was originally produced using Newfoundlands and Saint Bernards, the monks of the Hospice of St Bernard having helped the creator of this new breed.

This dog stands some 65–80 cm (26–32 in) high. The slightly wavy, fairly long hair ranges in colour from a light yellow, through golden to a red-brown, preferably with a black mask, and there can be dark or even black points on the coat. The skull is fairly wide and the dark, intelligent, medium sized eyes show no haw and have a good natured expression. This faithful, intelligent and amenable watchdog, with webbed feet and strong movement, was slow to gain popularity in Britain but has many valuable merits. Neither timid nor aggressive the Leonberger has a self-confident, equable temperament.

BREED FACT:

In 1840, Heinrich Essig, Mayor of Leonberg, aimed to create a breed resembling the lion in Leonberg's Coat of Arms.

Mastiff

HEIGHT 70-76 cm (27.5-30 in)

Working
GROUP   COAT CARE
large
SIZE   FEEDING

RECOGNISED AS THE OLDEST British breed, the Mastiff is believed to have been brought to Britain in the sixth century BC; it was used to fight against bears, bulls and lions. Mercifully, the baiting of these animals was abolished in Britain in 1835 – subsequently the Mastiff lost popularity and became virtually extinct during the Second World War, though it was later revived.

Powerfully built, with a massive body, broad skull and head of generally square appearance the Mastiff breed is a combination of grandeur and courage: calm and affectionate to owners, but capable of guarding. While no height or weight is specified for this breed, it is a particularly large dog demanding suitably correct diet and exercise. The short coat is close-lying and the colour is

apricot-fawn, silver-fawn, fawn or dark fawn-brindle, always with black on the muzzle, ears, nose and around the eyes. Height is around 70–76 cm (27.5–30 in) and weight 79–86 kg (175–190 lb).

BREED FACT:
The name, Mastiff, is likely to have come from the Anglo-Saxon word 'masty', meaning powerful, one of the words used to describe the breed's characteristics.

Left
The exact origin of the Mastiff is obscure, but it probably came from south-west Asia and spread into Tibet, China and Japan.

Neapolitan Mastiff

HEIGHT 65-75 cm (26-29 in)

Working
GROUP   COAT CARE
large
SIZE   FEEDING

THE NATIVE MASTIFF of Italy, the Neapolitan is another ancient breed descended from the Roman fighting, war and circus mastiffs. The breed was used for guarding and dog fighting but is now owned for security and companionship.

This strongly built dog has a very majestic bearing and is a devoted and loyal guard of both owner and property. Despite this, it is reputed to be of reliable temperament, attacking only upon command. The skin fits rather loosely over the body, but although this a feature of the breed it should not be excessive. The coat is short, dense, even, fine and of hard texture with good sheen; the colours are black, blue, grey and brown, varying from fawn to red. The height of males is from 65 to 75 cm (26–29 in) and weight 50–70 kg (110–154 lb), bitches being somewhat less.

BREED FACT:
Since ancient times, the Neapolitan Mastiff has been found in Campania, which is in central Italy, but it was not exhibited at shows until 1947.

Working

GROUP   **COAT CARE**

large

SIZE   **FEEDING**

Newfoundland

HEIGHT 66-71 cm (26-28 in)

BREED INFORMATION	
NAME	Newfoundland
OFFICIAL RECOGNITION	Uk Working Group; FCI Group 2; AKC Working Group
COLOUR VARIATIONS	Black; Brown; Landseer (white with black markings)

BREED FACT:

It is not known when the breed arrived in Newfoundland, but in 1732 fishermen used large bear-like dogs to help drag nets and pull carts.

Right

The water-loving Newfoundland is an exceptionally gentle, obedient breed, which makes a loyal, affectionate companion.

MANY BELIEVE THE ANCESTOR of the Newfoundland is the Tibetan Mastiff. The Newfoundland is a large draught and water dog with a natural lifesaving instinct and, in France, Newfoundlands are now used in teams to assist in emergency sea rescue work. In England, the breed was first shown in 1860 and recognised by the Kennel Club in 1878.

A devoted companion with an exceptionally gentle, docile nature, the Newfoundland is noble, majestic and powerful. With massive bone through-out, there is an appearance of strength and great activity. The large feet are webbed and the coat is double, flat and dense, as well as being oily and water-resistant, hence requiring regular grooming. Permitted colours are black, brown or Landseer, which is white with black markings. Average height for dogs is 71 cm (28 in) and for bitches 66 cm (26 in), and their weights are 64–69 kg (140–150 lb) and 50–54.5 kg (110–120 lb) respectively.

Working

GROUP   **COAT CARE**

medium

SIZE   **FEEDING**

Pinscher

HEIGHT 43–48 cm (17–19 in)

BREED INFORMATION	
NAME	Pinscher
OTHER NAMES	German Pinscher
OFFICIAL RECOGNITION	Uk Working Group; FCI Group 2; AKC
COLOUR VARIATIONS	Fawn (Isabella) to stag red

BREED FACT:

With legs too long to go to ground, in Germany the Pinscher was used to control vermin, to watch, guard and to drove livestock.

ORIGINALLY A MULTI-PURPOSE dog belonging to German farmers, the Pinscher is medium sized and stands some 43–48 cm (17–19 in) in height at the withers, weighing in the region of 11–16 kg (25–35 lb). With elegant, flowing outlines this is a strong, well-muscled dog with a short, dense, glossy coat which requires little attention. Colours range from fawn to stag red, or may be black and blue with carefully distributed red-dish tan markings.

The high-set, v-shaped ears fold down close to the head. The head is strong but not heavy and when viewed both from above and from the side resembles a blunt wedge. The tail is high-set and is customarily docked to three joints. Bearing in mind that the word Pinscher means terrier, this high-spirited, self-possessed breed is alert, good natured and playful. A loyal dog which is both watchful and fearless, making a good guard.

Portuguese Water Dog

HEIGHT 43-57 cm (17-22.5 in)

Working GROUP — **COAT CARE**

SIZE large — **FEEDING**

BREED FACT:
The Portuguese Water Dog was used to carry messages from boat to boat by swimming to and fro.

USED ONCE AS A hunting dog, the Portuguese Water Dog is now used by fishermen in the breed's homeland. A keen guard, it can be easily trained to swim from boats and to retrieve lost nets thanks to its great diving skills. This energetic breed needs to be robust and strongly muscled on the shoulders.

Brave and tireless, the Portuguese Water Dog has a pleasant disposition and, although self-willed, is very obedient to its owner. There are two distinct types of coat, neither of which has undercoat. Hair can either be fairly long, loosely waved and with a slight sheen, or short, fairly hard and dense with compact curls lacking lustre. Both are usually clipped over the hindquarters and on the tail, with a plume left at the end. Height and weight range considerably, from 43–57 cm (17–22.5 in) and 16–25 kg (35–55 lb).

Left
Originally, the hair of the Portugese Water Dog was clipped to leave its hind legs free while swimming; now it is clipped for showing.

Rottweiler

HEIGHT 58-69 cm (23-27 in)

Working GROUP — **COAT CARE**

SIZE large — **FEEDING**

BREED FACT:
Rottweilers are reputed to have guarded livestock during the march of the Roman Soldiers across Europe, leading to the breed's arrival in Germany.

UNEXCELLED AS A GUARD dog and used frequently in police and security work all across Europe, the Rottweiler is one of Germany's foremost and most popular working breeds. Thought to be descended from a combination of Molossus breeds, Roman cattle dogs and the Bullenbeisser, the breed's name is taken from the town of Rottweil in Germany.

The very appearance of the Rottweiler displays the boldness and courage that is inherent in the breed, while the calm gaze should indicate good humour and even temperament. Self-assured and fearless, the breed should be good natured, not nervous, aggressive or vicious. However, this is a courageous breed with natural guarding instincts so it must be trained well and sensibly handled. Compact and powerful in form, height ranges from 58–69 cm (23–27 in) and weight is usually from 41–50 kg (90–110 lb). The black coat has clearly defined tan markings, including a spot over each eye, on the cheeks and around each side of the muzzle.

Left
Contrary to its reputation, the Rottweiler breed is biddable and loyal when handled firmly.

Working
GROUP

COAT CARE

large

SIZE

FEEDING

BREED FACT:
A St Bernard named Barry was responsible for saving the lives of 40 travellers but the 41st struck out at him in fear, resulting in the dog's death.

Right
Keeping the massive St Bernard in a household requires both large amounts of space and money.

St Bernard

HEIGHT 61-71 cm (24-28 in)

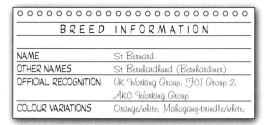

BREED INFORMATION

NAME	St Bernard
OTHER NAMES	St Bernhardhund (Bernhardiner)
OFFICIAL RECOGNITION	UK Working Group; FCI Group 2; AKC Working Group
COLOUR VARIATIONS	Orange/white; Mahogany-brindle/white;

THIS TRUSTWORTHY, BENEVOLENT breed has long been associated with the Hospice of St Bernard in the Swiss Alps but earlier dogs were by no means so heavy as the breed we know today. It is believed that the first dogs were bred at the hospice between 1660–70, since when the breed has been responsible for saving many lives of travellers lost and stranded on the mountains. The name, St Bernard, was first used in England in 1865.

A dog of great substance, there is no set height for the breed but the taller is considered the better, provided that symmetry is maintained. In general, height is 61–71 cm (24–28 in) and weight can be anywhere from 50–91 kg (110–200 lb). Clearly for a breed of this size substantial feeding is important, particularly during the growing stage. Steady, kindly, intelligent and courageous, the St Bernard is distinctly marked and there are two coat types: rough and smooth.

Working
GROUP

COAT CARE

large

SIZE

FEEDING

Right
Popular as a show dog and racing dog in North America, the Siberian Husky is becoming better known in Britain.

BREED FACT:
The Siberian Husky is a dog which is indifferent to cold and snow, a great jumper and a clever digger.

Siberian Husky

HEIGHT 51-60 cm (20-23 in)

BREED INFORMATION

NAME	Siberian Husky
OFFICIAL RECOGNITION	UK Working Group; FCI Group 5; AKC Working Group
COLOUR VARIATIONS	All colours and markings.

ORIGINATING IN NORTH-EAST ASIA, the Siberian Husky is a medium sized, working sled dog, quick and light on its feet, and capable of great endurance. Originally used by the Chukchi peoples, a Siberian Eskimo tribe which herded reindeer, by the turn of this century sled-dog racing had become popular in Alaska and in 1909 the breed made an appearance in the All Alaska Sweepstakes Race. Under the FCI the Siberian Husky is however considered an American breed.

A breed with moderate bone structure, height ranges from 51–60 cm (20–23 in) and weight from 16–27 kg (35–60 lb), the bitches feminine but not weak, the dogs masculine but never coarse. This friendly, alert and outgoing breed is an agreeable companion and willing worker, one which does not display guard dog traits. The breed's medium length, double coat is found in a wide range of colours and fascinating markings, and the eyes can be one each of two different colours.

```
○ ○ ○ ○ ○ ○ ○ ○ ○ ○ ○ ○ ○ ○ ○ ○ ○ ○ ○ ○ ○ ○ ○ ○
       BREED  INFORMATION
```

NAME	Tibetan Mastiff
OTHER NAMES	Do-Khyi
OFFICIAL RECOGNITION	UK Working Group; FCI Group 2
COLOUR VARIATIONS	Black; Black/tan; Brown; Gold; Grey/blue; Grey/tan

Tibetan Mastiff

HEIGHT 61-66 cm (24-26 in)

Working

GROUP **COAT CARE**

large

SIZE **FEEDING**

BREED FACT:
Tibetan Mastiffs marked with tan above the eyes can reputedly see danger days in advance, considered by Tibetans a tremendous advantage in lonely terrain.

USED PRIMARILY as a watch and guard dog, protecting flocks from predators and families from intruders, the Tibetan Mastiff's homeland is in the high Himalayan ranges. In Tibet these dogs are kept heavily chained and are encouraged to be ferocious, but a different lifestyle in the West somewhat tempers this behaviour. However, the breed is meant to be aloof and protective so an understanding of this rather special temperament, coupled with sensible handling, are both important.

An impressive, powerful, well-built animal, the Tibetan Mastiff has a solemn but kindly appearance and can be a loving companion, being especially fond of children. Males carry noticeably more coat than females and both moult seriously in the warmer months. The minimum height for dogs is 66 cm (26 in) and for bitches 61 cm (24 in). Weight can vary considerably but is usually 64–82 kg (140–180 lb).

Left
Most European mastiffs are descended from the Tibetan Mastiff. It is well-established in Europe but still uncommon.

287

Other Breeds

BESIDES THE BREEDS recognised by the English Kennel Club, there are many other dog breeds located throughout the world; indeed it is estimated that there are between 700 and 800 recognised breeds worldwide. However, those recognised in one country are not necessarily recognised in another. Breeds recognised by the English Kennel Club are generally found in many other countries and, in the main, are recognised by other leading authorities in dog breeding, although there are always exceptions.

THE FEDERATION Cynologique Internationale (FCI) recognises over 300 dog breeds, while the American Kennel Club gives its recognition to over 140 breeds. In addition to these breeds, many other dogs are recognised by the smaller official and semi-official bodies that exist in individual countries.

With headquarters in Belgium, the FCI is an international federation, originally founded by canine societies in Germany, Austria, Belgium, France and the Netherlands in 1911. The FCI is now the World Canine Organisation and includes 77 members and contract partners (one member per country). Each of these issue its own pedigrees and trains its own judges. The FCI recognises 329 breeds of pedigree dogs, although each breed remains the 'property' of specific countries, and breed standards are compiled by the countries which are designated 'owners' of any given breed, not by the FCI itself.

Right
Hungarian Pumis are working dogs which are mainly used to drive cattle.

Centre Right
An early Korean painting of a dog.

Far Right Top
The Tosa is a large Japanese dog that was originally bred for fighting.

Far Right Bottom
The Catalan Sheepdog breed standard was formulated in 1929.

Contrary to widespread opinion, the FCI is not a registry and does not itself issue any pedigrees, unlike the English Kennel Club which can provide pedigree information for dogs registered under its auspices. The American Kennel Club, known as the AKC, was founded in 1884 and now records the parentage of more than one million dogs annually.

In this section of the book, many breeds are incorporated which are either not known or not registered in Britain, but it would not be possible to include each and every breed. Instead they have been restricted largely to those recognised by the FCI and AKC, with a few others which the author considers are particularly deserving of mention. So often the reader has no opportunity of seeing some of the breeds outlined here,

but it is to be hoped that through this book more people throughout the world will at least learn of the existence of some of the rare breeds.

Besides alternative names in use for many of the breeds, breed standards also differ from country to country, and it is often the case that there are subtle differences between the standards recognised in different parts of the world. For this reason, some of the heights and weights of individual breeds indicated here may be slightly different according to the country in which a breed resides.

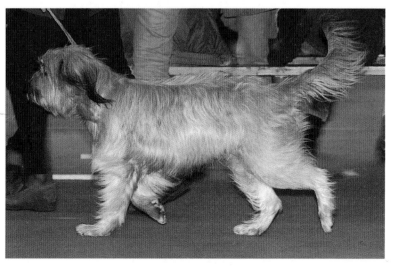

Gundog

GROUP COAT CARE

large

SIZE FEEDING

ARGENTINA
Dogo Argentino
HEIGHT 61-69 cm (24-27 in)

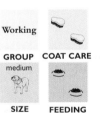

Above and Right
The Argentine hunting dog is known as the Dogo Argentino.

DEVELOPED IN ARGENTINA in the 1920s by Dr Antonio Martinez, this relatively modern breed was selectively created using the blood of old-style Spanish fighting dogs, the Spanish Mastiff, Great Dane, Bulldog, Boxer and an old-style bull terrier. The aim was to produce a breed which would be a fearless hunter of puma and jaguar, but the Dogo Argentino has also been used for wild boar and mountain lion, as it can hunt tirelessly over highly difficult terrain. A dog such as this breed will appeal to those involved in the fighting sports that are still in existence in some countries.

The breed has a fearless and aggressive disposition, which has led to its being banned in some countries, including Britain, although some of its aggressive tendencies seem to be declining in certain strains. This bold, brave and loyal dog certainly needs to be trained by a knowledgeable handler and should be obedience trained. The short, sleek white coat deflects the heat and the ears are surgically adjusted to increase the aggressive appearance. The breed stands 61–69 cm (24–27 in) high, weighs 36–45 kg (80–100 lb) and needs plenty of open spaces for exercise purposes.

Working

GROUP COAT CARE

medium

SIZE FEEDING

AUSTRALIA
Kelpie
HEIGHT 43-58.5 cm (12-23 in)

THE KELPIE ORIGINATED around 1870 and by 1890 had become well established, playing a major part in Australia's sheep and wool industry and usually bred by ranchers and farmers. Descended from British Collies, this dog was created to cope with harsh, hot, landscape and to handle the reputedly unruly Merino sheep kept on extensive acreage. This is a gathering dog, which uses eye, bark and bite or grip to move stock. In the bush they are often worked unsupervised, with their handlers relying on the dog's own wit and spirits. A keen, active breed, always ready for work, legend has it that the Kelpie must carry Dingo blood.

With its mild, tractable disposition, this is a lithe, active breed, showing hard muscle condition and standing from 43–58.5 cm (17–23 in) in height, weighing in the region of 11–20 kg (25–45 lb). The widely spaced ears are pricked, running to a fine point at the tip but strong at the base. The moderately short coat is flat, straight and weather resistant with a dense undercoat and can have a fair amount of ruff, with mild breeching on the thighs and sufficient tail coat to form a brush. Colour varies through black, blue, red (from chocolate to light red) and tan (from dark to cream). All these can be with or without tan markings and may have minimal white markings.

BREED INFORMATION

NAME	Alpine Dachsbracke
OTHER NAMES	Alpenländische Dachsbracke
OFFICIAL RECOGNITION	FCI Group 6
COLOUR VARIATIONS	Usually stag red

AUSTRIA
Alpine Dachsbracke

HEIGHT 34-42 cm (13-16.5 in)

Hound
GROUP COAT CARE
medium
SIZE FEEDING

DATING BACK TO the middle of the nineteenth century, the dog was produced as the result of hunters crossing local brackes with Standard Smooth-haired Dachshunds. This is a slow-moving, cold-trail follower, but a highly efficient one, used often to trail a wounded deer so that it is not allowed to die a slow and painful death. This robust, industrious breed is well able to work at high altitude. It is deservedly popular amongst hunters, and also used for rabbit and fox. Longer in leg than a Dachshund, this breed's compact forefeet are rugged. The muzzle and nose are rather large for the overall size of the head, and the round eyes have a lively expression. Height ranges between 34 and 42 cm (13–16.5 in) and the weight is 13–18 kg (33–40 lb). The coat is dense and coarse but not wiry, and the colour is usually stag red, although some dogs are black and tan or red with black ticking.

Left
The Alpine Dachsbracke's dense coat protects it from the extreme weather found at high altitude.

BREED FACT:
This dog is a highly efficient trailing breed, and can easily follow a scent that is quite old, or has 'gone cold'.

BREED INFORMATION

NAME	Austrian Black and Tan Hound
OTHER NAMES	Österreichische Glatthaarige
	Bracke, Brandlbracke
OFFICIAL RECOGNITION	FCI Group 6
COLOUR VARIATIONS	Black with fawn markings

Austrian Black and Tan Hound

HEIGHT 48-56 cm (19-22 in)

Hound
GROUP COAT CARE
large
SIZE FEEDING

ACKNOWLEDGED TO BE A TRUE descendent of the Celtic Hound, as with all breeds of older origin there is no authentic history for the Austrian Black and Tan Hound until the middle of the nineteenth century, before which no controlled breeding took place. A universally popular hunting dog, this hound is especially suitable for heavy work on high mountains, as well as on flat ground. It is used in hunting for tracking wounded game, especially hare, by giving tongue. This is a medium-sized, strong breed which has a long cast, supple body and sensitive black nose. The long, tapering tail is slightly bent and the ears are of medium length, hanging flatly and rounded at the tips. The smooth, close-fitting hair is dense, full and springy, with a silky sheen and is about 2 cm (under 1 in) in length. Colouring is understandably important for this breed which is black with small, clearly defined light to dark fawn markings. The two fawn marks above the eyes, known as Vieraugl, must be present. Height is from 48–56 cm (19–22 in).

Left
This hound is popular for its tracking abilities and is recognised as a descendant of the Celtic Hound.

Working

GROUP COAT CARE

medium

SIZE FEEDING

Austrian Short-haired Pinscher

HEIGHT 36-51 cm (14-20 in)

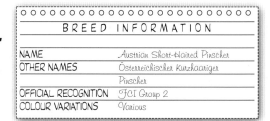

BREED INFORMATION	
NAME	Austrian Short-Haired Pinscher
OTHER NAMES	Österreichischer Kurzhaariger Pinscher
OFFICIAL RECOGNITION	FCI Group 2
COLOUR VARIATIONS	Various

> **BREED FACT:**
> These dogs have an excellent sense of smell and strong muzzles, making them good tracking animals.

THE AUSTRIAN SHORT-HAIRED Pinscher was developed to drive livestock and to guard farmers' homes, but using its powerful muzzle, it is also a talented hunter of vermin. Dogs much like these can be seen in eighteenth-century paintings. Still found primarily in Austria, this breed is related to the German Pinscher and is an extremely good watchdog, always willing to bark at strange sounds. This breed does not always get on well with other dogs, reputedly having a tendency to bite.

The head is somewhat pear-shaped, with a reasonably short muzzle, and the ears, which vary widely, are slightly pricked. The feet are compact and the toes well-arched. Standing 36–51 cm (14–20 in) high, and weighing 12–18 kg (26–40 lb), this breed has a short, hard topcoat and an undercoat which is also short but very dense.

Hound

GROUP COAT CARE

large

SIZE FEEDING

Styrian Coarse-haired Hound

HEIGHT 45-53 cm (17.5-21 in)

BREED INFORMATION	
NAME	Styrian Coarse-Haired Hound
OTHER NAMES	Steirische Rauhhaarbracke, Peintinger Bracke
OFFICIAL RECOGNITION	FCI Group 6
COLOUR VARIATIONS	Red and fawn

THE CREATION OF THE Styrian Coarse-haired Hound was begun in Styria in 1870, when Karl Peintinger crossed the Hanoverian Scent Hound with a coarse-haired male Istrian Hound which reputedly excelled in hunting qualities and appearance. The best puppies from this litter were reared, and selective breeding then continued, producing a rough-coated, weather-resistant dog. Rarely seen outside Austria and neighbouring Slovenia, this breed is kept primarily by hunters for use with wild boar. It is still usually bred for hunting abilities rather than show

Right
This is a superb working dog that does not make a good pet or show dog.

purposes and is not frequently kept as a companion. Its work consists not only of hunting while giving tongue but often also in tracking wounded animals in difficult mountain terrain.

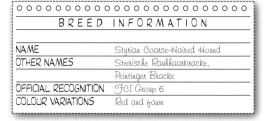

This is a passionate, tough, hunting dog, a firm and determined tracker of medium size with strong muscles. The expression is serious but not vicious, the eyes have a brown iris and the nose leather is black. The rough coat is not shaggy and is without gloss, harsh and coarse, while that on the head is shorter than on the body, and there is a moustache. Colours are red and fawn, and there may be a white mark on the chest. Height is 45–53 cm (17.5–21 in) and weight is in the general range of 15–18 kg (33–40 lb).

Tyrolean Hound

HEIGHT 42-51 cm (16-20 in)

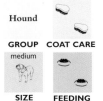

Hound
GROUP   **COAT CARE**
medium
SIZE   **FEEDING**

THIS IS ANOTHER BREED descended from the Celtic Hound and represents the purest type of game-hunting hounds. Around the year 1500, Emperor Maximilian I used this hound for hunting in the Tyrol and, according to his diary, took his lead hounds from them. Pure breeding from particular strains began in 1860, leading to official recognition of the Tyrolean Hound in 1908. Many types of Hound were originally native to the Tyrol but now only the red and the black and tan colour varieties remain. This is an ideal working dog for hunting hare and fox in wood and mountains, and also for tracking wounded game.

This medium sized dog is a steady, passionate, hunting hound with a fine scenting ability. It works independently and hunts with endurance, giving tongue clearly and following scent firmly. The broad ears are set on high, as is the tail, and the large dark brown eyes are not deep set. The thick double coat has a coarse undercoat, with hairy belly, the buttocks are well-feathered and the tail coated with dense brush. There are two colour types - red, and black and tan – both of which can have white markings in specified areas.

Left
As a descendent of the Celtic Hound, the Tyrolean Hound received official breed recognition in 1908.

BELGIUM
Griffon Bruxellois

HEIGHT 18-20 cm (7-8 in)

Hound
GROUP   **COAT CARE**
small
SIZE   **FEEDING**

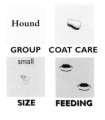

UNDER FCI REGULATIONS, the breed now known in both the UK and the USA as the Griffon Bruxellois is divided into three separate breeds, which are the Griffon Belge, the Griffon Bruxellois and the Petit Brabançon. All three types of dog are classified within FCI Group 9.

The Belgian Griffon is black or black and tan with long, wiry hair. The dog was bred with English Toy Spaniels to reduce its size. The Griffon Bruxellois, also known as the Brussels Griffon, has a harsh, wiry, coat of clear red, which is longer than the Belgian Griffon's and is perhaps the most familiar in the UK. The third variation, the Petit Brabançon, can be red, black, or black and tan ,and has a short, tight coat. It has a Pug-like face with semi-erect ears.

> **BREED FACT:**
> Other Austrian breeds include the Schipperke, a breed of dog which is registered under FCI and Kennel Club rules.

Left
The Belgian Griffon has long, wiry hair around its short muzzle and is not a good ratting terrier.

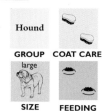

Hound
GROUP

COAT CARE

large
SIZE

FEEDING

BOSNIA
Coarse-haired Hound

HEIGHT 46-55 cm (18-22 in)

BREED INFORMATION	
NAME	Bosnian Coarse-haired Hound, Barak
OTHER NAMES	Bosanski Ostrodlaki Gonic-Barak
OFFICIAL RECOGNITION	FCI Group 6
COLOUR VARIATIONS	Various

Right
Bosnian hunters bred the Coarse-haired Hound to have a strong sense of smell to work as a gamedog.

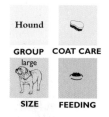

IN THE NINETEENTH CENTURY, hunters in Bosnia developed the Bosnian Coarse-haired Hound-Barak, and requiring an efficient scent hound, they used whatever dogs were available in its creation. In 1965, the breed was registered with the FCI under the name Illyrian Hound, and the breed standard has been altered little since then. However, the name has changed to that used today. This is a robust dog with an expression described as serious, severe but playful, undoubtedly enhanced in appeal by the pronounced, bushy eyebrows.

Slightly longer than it is high, this dog stands 46–55 cm (18–22 in) and weighs 16–24 kg (35–53 lb). A lively breed with courageous and persistent temperament, this is a typical scenthound ,and one that makes a good watchdog. The long, hard, shaggy coat has a tousled appearance and there is dense undercoat, which is good insulation in the tough weather conditions of the area. Basic colours are wheaten, reddish yellow, earthy grey or blackish but there are white markings or colours which can be combined in bi-colour or tri-colour.

Hound
GROUP

COAT CARE

large
SIZE

FEEDING

BRAZIL
Fila Brasiliero

HEIGHT 61-76 cm (24-30 in)

BREED INFORMATION	
NAME	Cão de Fila
OFFICIAL RECOGNITION	FCI Group 2
COLOUR VARIATIONS	All brindle or solid colours

Above and Right
This dog's size is reminiscent of the Spanish Mastiff, with which it shares its breeding.

THE MASSIVE FILA BRASILIERO is descended from early Spanish and Portuguese Mastiffs as well as from Bloodhounds, clearly apparent in the breed's appearance today. It was used for tracking and to hunt large game, although it holds the quarry at bay rather than attacking. In history this breed was used successfully to track Brazilian slaves and now has a variety of working tasks, including herding cattle, guarding flocks and

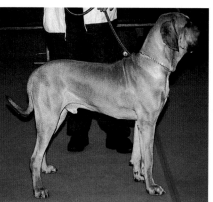

homes, and hunting large cats. Some Portuguese herding dogs and Bulldogs are thought to have been used in the development of this bold breed.

This is an exceedingly loyal breed but it can be aggressive with strangers and unfamiliar dogs, so it is banned in some countries and needs early socialisation with other dogs. Weight is 61–76 cm (24–30 in) and weight 41–50 kg (90–110 lb). The short, smooth coat is thick and tight and comes in a variety of brindle and solid colours, but not white or light grey.

Brazilian Terrier

HEIGHT 33.5–40.5 cm (14–16 in)

Hound
GROUP **COAT CARE**
medium
SIZE **FEEDING**

THE BRAZILIAN TERRIER has been in existence for about a hundred years, one of two main breeds which were developed in Brazil. This feisty little dog is a pack hunter which wears down its prey by surrounding it and terrorising it into submission. It is reputed to be an excellent rat dog. The breed is always eager to learn and in general has a charming personality, making it a good companion and house dog.

The height of the Brazilian Terrier is 35.5–40.5 cm (14–16 in) and its weight is 6.5–9 kg (14–20 lb). The short, smooth coat of the dog is tricolour with black saddle and tan markings on a white grounding.

Brazil has another dog breed, known as the **Brazilian Greyhound**, which is probably a cross between the English Greyhound and a Foxhound.

BHUTAN
Damchi

HEIGHT 33–43 cm (13–17 in)

Toy
GROUP **COAT CARE**
medium
SIZE **FEEDING**

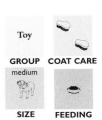

THIS CHARMING BREED is somewhat similar to the Tibetan Spaniel and lives in Bhutan, where people are particularly fond of pets. A Damchi named *Khomyto*, meaning 'my little baby', was owned by the former King of Bhutan, and the breed has been featured on postage stamps of the country. Although resembling the Tibetan Spaniel, the Damchi is slightly larger and more sturdy, with a slightly longer muzzle and less cushioning on the cheeks. A few of these dogs live in Germany with a breeder who took them back with her from India, but it seems unlikely that the true breed can now survive in Europe unless new blood is introduced from Bhutan.

Left
The Bhutanese Damchi is revered in Bhutan but its survival abroad is in danger if new blood is not introduced.

Terrier

GROUP

COAT CARE

small

SIZE

FEEDING

BRITAIN

Jack Russell Terrier

HEIGHT 25-30.5 cm (10-12 in)

BREED INFORMATION

NAME	Jack Russell Terrier
OFFICIAL RECOGNITION	Australian Kennel Club
COLOUR VARIATIONS	White; White and black; White and brown; Tri-colour

THE JACK RUSSELL TERRIER is famous worldwide but not recognised by the English Kennel Club, although some countries have given the breed recognition, including Australia. This dog was developed in the south of England in the late nineteenth century as a white terrier, and was used to work fox, both above ground and below. The Reverend John Russell had terriers who bolted foxes from dens so that the hounds they trailed could run, hence the breed's name came into being. This breed is very popular in Britain.

The Jack Russell is an excellent ratter and is very much a working terrier in the truest sense of the word, alert, confident, feisty and exuberant. The double, weatherproof coat can be broken or smooth but with no strong tendency to curl or wave. In size there is some lack of uniformity, for an accepted size by some authorities is 25–30.5 cm (10–12 in) with weight from 4–7 kg (9–15 lb), while in the USA, for example, dogs under 30.5 (12 in) and over 38 cm (15 in) are disqualified and more nearly resemble the breed recognised in Britain as the Parson Jack Russell, as they are generally longer in the leg.

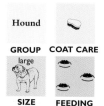

Hound

GROUP

COAT CARE

large

SIZE

FEEDING

Harrier

HEIGHT 46-56 cm (18-20 in)

BREED INFORMATION

NAME	Harrier
OFFICIAL RECOGNITION	FCI Group 6; AKC Hound Group
COLOUR VARIATIONS	Any colour

THE FIRST HARRIER pack in England was established by Sir Elias de Midhope in 1260 and the breed was mainly bred in the west of the country, although it was also used as popular pack hound in Wales. Ancestors of this dog include the Beagle and Bloodhound, with Foxhound blood being introduced later. Although there are many working Harriers in Britain this breed is not recognised by the English Kennel Club. It is recognised in the USA and by the FCI. This is a sturdily built scenting pack hound, its running gear and scenting ability being of particular importance. In the USA, where the

breed has been known since colonial times, it is stated that 'the Harrier should, in fact, be a smaller version of the English Foxhound'.

Its height is 46–56 cm (18–22 in) and weight 22–27 kg (48–60 lb), the expressive head being rather

narrower than that of a Beagle, and the eyes having good binocular vision. Slightly longer than it is high, the breed has as much substance as possible, without being coarse, and the chest is deep. This proficient working hound also makes a fine companion.

Terrier

GROUP | COAT CARE
small
SIZE | FEEDING

British Terriers

HEIGHT 25-34 cm (10-13.5 in)

BREED FACT:
These dogs all originated in Great Britain and have a mixture of terrier blood in them,.

OTHER BRITISH breeds which are not recognised by the English Kennel Club include the **Lucas Terrier** created by Sir Jocelyn Lucas, who bred Sealyham bitches and Norfolk Terrier dogs together. Longer than it is high with large, gentle looking eyes, this terrier has a hard mouth, but it is an adaptable, friendly dog reputed to be good with children. Height is 25–30 cm (10–12 in) and weight 4.5–6 kg (10–14 lb).

The **Patterdale Terrier** is found primarily in the Lake District and in Yorkshire where it is used to hunt rat, fox and rabbit and is bred more for its working appearance than its appearance. Height is

less than 32 cm (12.5 in) and weight 5–6 kg (12–13 lb). This is a hard-bitten terrier, willing to work and reputed to be quiet both indoors and out.

The **Plummer Terrier** is a compact, sprightly little ratter standing some 29–34 cm (11.5–13.5 in) high and weighing in the range of 5.5–7 kg (12- 15 lb). This breed was created by Brian Plummer in the 1980s.

Although the **Rat Terrier** is not recognised by the AKC, it is best known in the USA. It is a fearless hunter standing 25.5–33 cm (10–13 in) high, with a short, shiny coat. The dog has dark, round eyes, a slightly pointed muzzle and v-shaped ears.

Left
The Rat Terrier is the result of the cross of blood between Smooth Fox and Manchester Terriers and was an indispensable rat catcher in town and country.

CROATIA
Sheepdog
HEIGHT 40-51 cm (16-20 in)

Working

GROUP | COAT CARE
large
SIZE | FEEDING

THE CROATIAN SHEEPDOG was developed in northern Croatia from shepherd dogs of that region, the latter having probably descended from dogs from that general region and from Greek and Turkish dogs. Larger than the rather similar Hungarian breed, the Mudi, this dog is fairly commonly found in Croatia's countryside where it is used mainly for flock guarding.

This is a breed which tends not to get on well with other dogs and one which is not ideally suited to urban living. Early socialisation is important because the breed is wary of

strangers, though it does respond positively to obedience training. Also used in security work, the Croatian Sheepdog can vary in height from 40–51 cm (16–20 in) and weighs 13–16 kg (29–35 lb). The thick, soft, wavy coat is generally 8–13 cm (3–5 in) in length and the colour is black, sometimes with white on the feet which are quite small and elongated. The ears are pricked, triangular in shape and carried erect.

Left
The Croatian Sheepdog does not adapt well to urban life and tends to be wary of strangers.

Hound
GROUP

COAT CARE

large
SIZE

FEEDING

Posavac Hound

HEIGHT 43-59 cm (16-20 in)

○○○○○○○○○○○○○○○○○○○○○○○○

BREED INFORMATION

NAME	Posavac Hound
OTHER NAMES	Posavki Gonic, Posavatz Hound
OFFICIAL RECOGNITION	FCI Group 6
COLOUR VARIATIONS	Yellow, Fawn and Red

ALTHOUGH THE history which lies behind all the Balkan hounds is now lost, it would appear that traders brought dogs into the region from Egypt via the Adriatic ports and undoubtedly hunting hounds thrived in the former Yugoslavia. Now categorised as a Croatian breed, the Posavac Hound has adapted to the hilly environment as it is sure-footed with compact, narrow feet, and its tough coat is dense and short.

The dark eyes are alert, portraying the character of this breed which is a lively hound with good scenting abilities, used for hunting small game and also deer. Its gentle nature also makes this a good companion dog. Wide-ranging in height, the Posavac stands from 43–59 cm (17–23 in) and weight ranges from 16–20 kg (35–45 lb).

Right
Like all Balkan hounds, the Posavac Hound's bloodline and history is unknown.

Hound
GROUP

COAT CARE

large
SIZE

FEEDING

CZECH REPUBLIC AND SLOVAKIA
Pointing Griffon

HEIGHT 58-66 cm (23-26 in)

○○○○○○○○○○○○○○○○○○○○○○○○

BREED INFORMATION

NAME	Bohemian Wire-haired Pointing Griffon
OTHER NAMES	Czesky Fousek
OFFICIAL RECOGNITION	FCI Group 7
COLOUR VARIATIONS	Liver or liver and white, may have ticking

Above and Right
The Wire-haired Pointing Griffon has a gentle expression with deep-set eyes.

THE CZESKY FOUSEK, a native Bohemian gundog, is a close relation of the Drahthaar and Sticelhaar. It was very popular during the First World War, but was subsequently almost lost as a breed. Revived by introducing some German Short-haired and Wire-haired Pointer blood, today's Czesky Fousek closely resembles these breeds. Very much a multi-purpose worker, best in the hands of experienced hunters, this is a breed which points, sets and also retrieves, either from land or from water and it would appear that the original breed worked with wildfowl as far back as the fifteenth century.

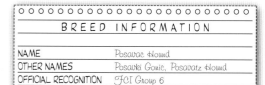

This breed needs regular exercise, but still makes a good companion to man. The dog is reputed to be amenable with children, although some dogs of this breed can be headstrong and need firm control and training. Size of dog varies substantially, with height from 58–66 cm (23–26 in) and weight anything between 22 and 34 kg (48.5–75 lb). The rough outercoat is of medium length with a soft undercoat and the deep-set, dark eyes portray a gentle expression.

Czechoslovakian Wolfdog

HEIGHT 60-75 cm (24-29.5 in)

Working
GROUP **COAT CARE**
large
SIZE **FEEDING**

THIS IS A COMPACT, wolf-like breed. Breeding began in 1955 when the German Shepherd Dog was crossed with the Carpathian Timber Wolf, the aim being to improve still further upon the GSD's working ability. Breed

recognition was received in 1982, but the Czechoslovak Wolfdog needs extremely firm, patient handling. Some dogs are afraid of strangers. However, the breed develops a close affinity with its handler, although it does not take well to others and is therefore not a suitable breed to use in police work.

This is a lively breed with a memorable howl. The thin, triangular ears stand erect and are highly mobile and, in overall appearance, there are many wolf-like characteristics. The topcoat is straight and close and a thick undercoat is always developed in the winter months. Height is 60–75 cm (24–29.5 in) and weight 20–35kg (44–77 lb).

BREED INFORMATION

NAME	Czechoslovakian Wolfdog
OTHER NAMES	Ceskoslovensko Vlcak, Czech Wolfdog
OFFICIAL RECOGNITION	FCI Group 1 provisional
COLOUR VARIATIONS	Wolf-like colours

BREED INFORMATION

NAME	Broholmer
OTHER NAMES	Danish Broholmer
OFFICIAL RECOGNITION	FCI Group 2
COLOUR VARIATIONS	Light or brownish yellow; Black. White marking permissible

DENMARK

Broholmer

HEIGHT 70 cm (27.5 in)

Working

GROUP **COAT CARE**
large

SIZE **FEEDING**

THE BROMHOLER WAS developed from a cross between English Mastiffs and local dogs in Germany. English royalty had given Mastiffs as gifts, while the German royalty had given their German Mastiffs to the Danes. King Frederik VII and his consort, Countess Danner, owned several Bromholers, and one of their paintings depicts the two of them with one of these dogs. The breed was first established in the early nineteenth century when it was moderately popular in Denmark, especially as a guard dog in homes of the wealthy. Numbers dwindled severely in the Second World War so that, in 1974, this was a breed which was targeted for revival by the 'Committee for National and Forgotten Breeds'.

This breed is a large one, standing at about 70 cm (27.5 in) in height and weighing in the region of 41–59 kg (90–130 lb). The coat is short and harsh, and the colour can be light or brownish yellow, or black. Some white markings on the coat are also permissible.

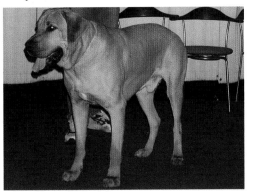

Above

This is a relatively new breed that has introduced blood of the Timber Wolf and also the German Shepherd Dog.

Left

The Broholmer is a large breed that developed from Mastiff blood and has been rebred successfully in the last 30 years.

Hound

GROUP | COAT CARE

large

SIZE | FEEDING

Old Danish Pointer

HEIGHT 051-58 cm (20-23 in)

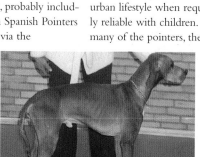

BREED INFORMATION	
NAME	Old Danish Pointer
OTHER NAMES	Gammel Dansk Hønsehund, Old Danish Bird Dog
OFFICIAL RECOGNITION	FCI Group 7
COLOUR VARIATIONS	White and liver, some ticking allowed

THE OLD DANISH POINTER was developed in the eighteenth century from various local dogs of Bloodhound descent, probably including the St Hubert Hound, and from Spanish Pointers which had been taken to Denmark via the Netherlands. Created as a retriever, close-working skills were also developed so that now the breed is used for tracking, pointing and retrieving game, as well as companionship. The breed was verging on extinction by the end of the Second World War and even today is rarely seen outside its homeland. However this is a popular field trail participant with an excellent nose.

Owners of the breed describe this dog as a quiet, friendly family friend, which readily adapts to an urban lifestyle when required to do so and is generally reliable with children. More substantially built than many of the pointers, the chest and thighs are broad, the fore- and hindquarters well-muscled. The head is rather deep and there is a certain breadth to the muzzle. The ears are long, pendant and rounded at the tip. The coat is short, dense and tight with an undercoat for insulation, and the colour is white and liver, with a small amount of ticking allowed.

Right
The adaptable Old Danish Pointer faced extinction in the 1950s but has now increased in numbers.

Hound

GROUP | COAT CARE

large

SIZE | FEEDING

FINLAND

Finnish Hound

HEIGHT 56-63 cm (22-25 in)

BREED INFORMATION	
NAME	Finnish Hound
OTHER NAMES	Suomenajokoira, Finsk Stovare
OFFICIAL RECOGNITION	FCI Group 6
COLOUR VARIATIONS	Tri-colour

THE FINNISH HOUND is the result of breeding in the nineteenth century in which French, German and Swedish hounds were involved. As a result of this, the Finnish Hound has become the country's most popular working breed. Used for deer and hare hunting, the breed follows scent but it does not retrieve. Usually it leads huntsmen to gamebirds and woodcock which have been shot in dense cover. Now it is popular as a companion dog as well as for hunting.

The Finnish Hound needs plenty of physical activity and seems perfectly happy to sleep outdoors during the summer months. The breed has a placid nature and is reputed to be good with children, although males often find it difficult to get on well with other male canines. The fairly harsh coat has a some length to it but it is still effectively short and does not need much attention to keep it in good order. The pendant ears are high-set and the head noble. Height is around 56–63 cm (22–25 in) and weight 20–25 kg (45–55 lb).

Right
Although used for deer and hare hunting, the Finnish Hound does not retrieve.

Reindeer Herder

HEIGHT 48-56 cm (19-22 in)

Working
GROUP COAT CARE
large
SIZE   FEEDING

THE FINNISH Reindeer Herder goes back in its origin to the Finnish Lapphund, which was used by Sami people in north Norway, Sweden, Finland and Russia. A good shepherd's working dog, the breed's principal use was to drive reindeer as it is well-able to cope with the area's harsh climatic conditions. In the twentieth century, German Shepherd Dogs were

introduced to breeding programmes with the aim of improving upon the breed's herding character. The current breed standard was drawn up in 1966 by the Chairman of the Finnish Kennel Club.

Although use of the snowmobile reduced the need for these canine reindeer herders, their use is again coming to the fore, helped by a well-organised breeding programme. This is a sturdy, confident, spitz-like breed with strong, powerfully muscled forelegs. Although remarkably similar to the rather smaller Finnish Lapphund, the muzzle is thick and short. The thick coat is of moderate length, and the hair straight and rough, giving good insulation. Height is 48–26 cm (19–22 in) and weight 27–30 kg (60–66 lb).

Left
The thick coat helps the Finnish Reindeer Herder protect itself against the harsh climate that it works in.

Karelian Bear Dog

HEIGHT 48-58 cm (19-23 in)

Working
GROUP COAT CARE
large
SIZE   FEEDING

THE ORIGINS OF the Karelian Bear Dog lie in Finland and also Russia, where it was once regarded as a national treasure. Legendary as a bear fighter, this dog was bred by farmers in the Karelia region near the Finnish-Russian border where they hunted birds, rodents and large game. It was the ability to offer protection from bears which earned the breed its name and even today the dogs are kept by hunters in Russia, Finland, Sweden and Norway, s a companion and for protection.

The Karelian Bear Dog, when not engaged in the hunt, is a friendly breed, easy to train but best in the hands of people with plenty of energy and space for exercise. Still rare, it is becoming

popular as a companion and has a striking coat of straight, stiff, guard hairs with a thick, soft undercoat; the colour is black, white or a combination of the two. The bushy tail curls over in a tight ring. Height is around 48–58 cm (19–23 in) and the weight 20–23 kg (44–50 lb).

BREED FACT:

This dog is still used today by elk hunters in Scandinavia, but is becoming popular to keep as a companion.

Left
The Karelian Bear Dog's feats as a bear fighter are legendary, but these dogs also hunted vermin, birds and large game.

Hound
GROUP

COAT CARE

large
SIZE

FEEDING

FRANCE
Anglo-Français de Petite Vénerie

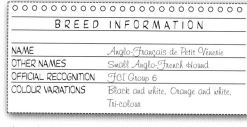

BREED INFORMATION	
NAME	Anglo-Français de Petit Vénerie
OTHER NAMES	Small Anglo-French Hound
OFFICIAL RECOGNITION	FCI Group 6
COLOUR VARIATIONS	Black and white, Orange and white, Tri-colour

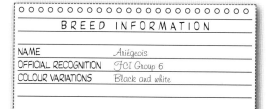

T HIS BREED, ORIGINALLY known as the Petit Anglo-Français, only came about during the first half of the twentieth century, by crossing the French Poitevin, Porcelaine and the Beagle or Beagle-Harrier, so it is the result of recent planned breeding programmes. As a pack hound, this breed is still developing but it is full of voice, drive and tenacity, used for scent trailing small game, including rabbit, pheasant and quail.

The first breed standard was formulated in 1978 and height ranges from 48–56 cm (19–22 in) with weight from 16–20 kg (35–44 lb). Eyes are fairly deeply set, the nose pointed and head well rounded. The coat is smooth but rough-coated puppies were produced in the breed's early days. Although a little reserved, the Anglo-Français de Petit Vénerie is an obedient, willing dog which is amenable as a household pet as well as when used for the hunt.

Right and Above
This is a recent addition to the French hunting-pack breeds and is used in all manner of hunting.

Hound
GROUP

COAT CARE

large
SIZE

FEEDING

Ariégeois

HEIGHT 53-62 cm (21-24 in)

BREED INFORMATION	
NAME	Ariégeois
OFFICIAL RECOGNITION	FCI Group 6
COLOUR VARIATIONS	Black and white

A N EXCELLENT WORKING harrier, the Ariégeois was first recognised in 1912 and appears to have been the result of crossing other French breeds, including the Bleu de Gascogne and the Gascon Saintongeois, as well as local briquet hounds. The breed was virtually extinct until a club that promoted it was formed in 1908. Primarily a hunting-pack hound, the breed hails from Ariége in south-west France and at one time was distinguished from the Petit Bleu de Gascogne only by colour.

Used to follow hare and other small game, the breed uses its nose and voice while doing so. The dark eyes are gentle in expression, the long, lean head set off by long, low-set ears. The skin is supple and loose on the body, covered by fine, close hair. Height is 53–62 cm (21–24 in) and weight 25–30 kg (55–66 lb).

BREED FACT:
This dog is bred from harriers and French briquet hounds.

BREED INFORMATION

NAME	Barbet
OTHER NAMES	Griffon d'Arrêt à Poil Laineux
OFFICIAL RECOGNITION	FCI Group 8
COLOUR VARIATIONS	Black; White; Grey; Chestnut; Fawn

Barbet

HEIGHT 46-56 cm (18-22 in)

Gundog
GROUP COAT CARE
large
SIZE FEEDING

AN ANCIENT EUROPEAN water-dog, the Barbet has most proba-bly played an important part in the development of several other water-dogs. Once a very common water dog in Europe, the breed was used not only to retrieve water fowl from water, but also fallen arrows. Today it is used both as a gundog and frequently as a companion, but a lot of work is involved in keeping the coat clean so the breed is not usually kept as a house dog. The distinctively curled coat is highly water-proof and even the head and tail are covered with dense hair. The long, pendant ears add to the kindly expression of this attractive gundog breed.

Left
The Barbet has a weather-proof coat which requires considerable mainte-nance if used as a show dog.

BREED INFORMATION

NAME	Basset Artésien Normand
OFFICIAL RECOGNITION	FCI Group 6
COLOUR VARIATIONS	Tri-colour; Fawn/white

Basset Artésien Normand

HEIGHT 25-36 cm (10-14 in)

Hound
GROUP COAT CARE
small
SIZE FEEDING

DESCENDED FROM THE Old French Bloodhound and the St Hubert Hound, this breed is an ancestor of the Basset Hound better known in Britain. The Basset Artésien Norman originated, as the name implies, in Normandy but was divided in type, some with straight legs, other crooked. Since the formation of a breed society in 1910 it has been standardised and streamlined, blending attributes from both. The Second World War saw the breed's serious decline but it was saved from extinction.

Used to trail deer and small game such as rabbit and hare, the breed's short legs allow it to follow small animals on foot and to penetrate dense vegetation where larger dogs cannot go. Height is only 25–36 cm (10–14 in) and weight 14.5–15.5 kg (32–34lb), but this breed is still rather less heavy than its cousin, the Basset Hound.

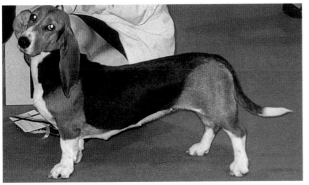

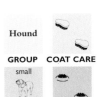

Left
The dog's short legs allow it to follow small animals into dense undergrowth and flush them out.

Hound

GROUP   **COAT CARE**

large

SIZE   **FEEDING**

Beagle-Harrier

HEIGHT 45-50 cm (18-20 in)

> **BREED FACT:**
> The Beagle-Harrier is an excellent working dog and has a gentle temperament, making it a good companion.

Bottom

The Berger is one of France's oldest dog breeds, and makes a good watch-dog.

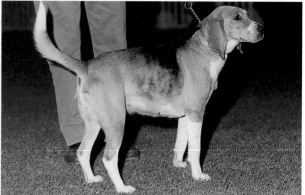

A TIRELESS AND enthusiastic worker, the Beagle-Harrier was developed in the late 1920s and 1930s with the aim of amalgamating all the virtues of the Beagle and Harrier. Still very rarely seen outside France, this dog is mainly kept in small packs and is still used to hunt hare, which was the prime purpose when the breed was developed, although it now also hunts fox, wild boar and deer.

This is a gentle breed which enjoys the company of other dogs as well as that of people. Temperament is sound and the Beagle-Harrier is fairly easy to train. Its size falls between those of its ancestors with height from 45–50 cm (18–20 in) and weight 20–25 kg (44–55 lb), the back a little longer than that of the Beagle. The breed is usually tri-coloured and is often black-blanketed.

Working

GROUP   **COAT CARE**

large

SIZE   **FEEDING**

Berger de Picardie

HEIGHT 55-66 cm (21.5-26 in)

P ERHAPS THE OLDEST of the French shepherd dogs, the Berger de Picardie arrived with the Celts in AD 800. This herding dog was found on the farms of north-east France. Its numbers were greatly diminished by trench warfare in the Somme, and consequently even today it is still a rare breed

This is a good guard dog for farms and also a talented herder of both sheep and cattle. A substantial dog, ranging in height from 55–66 cm (21.5–26 in) and weighing between 23 and 32 kg (50–70 lb), this is a fairly long-legged dog with high, erect ears and thick eyebrows, although these do not shield the eyes. The thick, weatherproof coat needs care but is very appropriate for the lifestyle for which this breed is suited. Although it has a rather assertive disposition, the breed responds easily to obedience training and is renowned for reliability as a family member.

BREED INFORMATION

NAME	Billy
OFFICIAL RECOGNITION	FCI Group 6
COLOUR VARIATIONS	White; Cafe-au-lait; White with orange or lemon

Billy

HEIGHT 58-70 cm (23-27.5 in)

NAMED AFTER THEIR creator who lived at Chateau de Billy in Poitou, these pale-coloured hounds shares its ancestry with that of the Poitevins, a combination of Montemboeuf and Ceris with some Larye. Foxhound blood has also been introduced, but this has been minimal. Selection was made primarily for colour, usually all white, lemon and white or cafe-au-lait and white; all can have a blanket or mottling on their short,

glossy coat. The expressive eyes have dark rims, adding to the breed's aesthetic appeal.

Most packs of Billys hunt roe deer, but some also specialise in hunting wild boar, so the breed needs both courage and sagacity. These are fast hounds which are full of cry and are known sometimes to quarrel with other pack members. They thrive on exercise and are good at obedience work. Their height is 58–70 cm (23–27.5 in) and weight 25–33 kg (55–73 lb).

Left
Billys have a mixed background, sharing their ancestry with the Foxhound and also the Poitevin. They tend to be quarrelsome.

BREED INFORMATION

NAME	Braque de l'Ariège
OTHER NAMES	Ariège Pointer
OFFICIAL RECOGNITION	FCI Group 7
COLOUR VARIATIONS	White with orange or chestnut

Braque de l'Ariège

HEIGHT 60-67 cm (24-26 in)

THE BRAQUE DE L'ARIÈGE is a hard and fast working Pointer, descended from the heavier Pointer, as can be found in the paintings of Oudry. This breed was developed during the twentieth century by introducing the Saint-Germain Pointer, a more lightly built dog. Today's Braque can scent and flush game while on a fast trot and yearns for both physical and mental activity.

If not given stimulus, this breed can be both noisy and destructive; because of this it should be acquired as a puppy so it adapts to the lifestyle of its owners. Height is 60–67 cm (24–26 in) and weight 25–30 k (55–65 lb), making this the largest of modern French Pointers.

BREED FACT:
This Braque needs to be stimulated; it grows bored easily and tends to be destructive.

Gundog
GROUP

COAT CARE

large
SIZE

FEEDING

Braque d'Auvergne

HEIGHT 55-63 cm (22-25 in)

BREED INFORMATION	
NAME	Braque d'Auvergne
OTHER NAMES	Auvergne Pointer
OFFICIAL RECOGNITION	FCI Group 7
COLOUR VARIATIONS	Black and white, Charcoal and white, both with ticking

Right and Above
This dog is of Maltese origin; it is believed to have arrived in France following Napoleon's rout of Malta.

WITH ROOTS in southern and central areas of France, the Braque d'Auvergne is nowadays a rare Pointer which is thought to have been taken to France by cavalrymen driven from Malta by Napoleon Bonaparte. The coat on this breed is short and glossy, and it is allowed to have white with black mottling and patches. Height is 55–63 cm (22–25 in) and weight 22–28 kg (49–62 lb).

Gundog
GROUP

COAT CARE

large
SIZE

FEEDING

Braque du Bourbonnais

HEIGHT 55.5-56.5 cm (22-22.5 in)

BREED INFORMATION	
NAME	Braque de Bourbonnais
OTHER NAMES	Bourbonnais Pointer
OFFICIAL RECOGNITION	FCI Group 7
COLOUR VARIATIONS	White with liver, reddish or orange mottling

FIRST DESCRIBED by an Italian traveller in the Bourbonnais region of France in 1598, this breed has a long history as a French pointing dog. Used originally for game hunting, it is now both a companion and a highly versatile gundog. Tracking, pointing and retrieving from land, water or marshland all fall within the working sphere of this breed, which was revived following near extinction during the Second World War years.

Well-balanced in temperament and sturdy in build with a deep, broad chest, the breed's height is 55.5–56.5 cm (around 22 in) and weight 18–26 kg (40–57 lb). The easily manageable coat is dense and often of an oily nature, but not glossy.

Right
This handsome dog has a soft mouth and is commonly used for retrieving game.

BREED INFORMATION

NAME	Braque Français, Type Gascogne (Grand Taille)
OTHER NAMES	French Gascony Pointer, French Setter
OFFICIAL RECOGNITION	FCI Group 7
COLOUR VARIATIONS	White with chestnut patches and mottling

Braque Français, Type Gascogne

HEIGHT 56-69 cm (22-27 in)

Gundog **GROUP** **COAT CARE**
large **SIZE** **FEEDING**

BREED FACT:
All Braques make superb game and gun dogs, although some types need more training than others.

FROM SOUTHERN FRANCE'S Gascony region, the Braque Français, Type Gascogne, or French Gascony Pointer, has descended from Spanish and Italian Pointers and was saved from extinction at the turn of the twentieth century. Although the breed favours air scent it also follows ground scent and is an avid tracker, responding best to gentle methods of training. Kept primarily as a working dog by French hunters, its numbers are still limited.

An enthusiastic breed, this is a good household companion, taking pleasure from both human and canine company and thoroughly enjoying exercise. The coat is rather thick, and rougher on the back than on the head, the nose brown to complement the breed's colouring. Sizes varies considerably, with height from 56–69 cm (22–27 in) and weight from 20–32 kg (45–71 lb).

Left
This dog is noted for its gentle nature and enthusiasm for working and companionship, human and canine.

BREED INFORMATION

NAME	Braque Français, Type Pyrénées (Petite Taille)
OTHER NAMES	French Pyrenean Pointer, Small-sized French Setter
OFFICIAL RECOGNITION	FCI Group
COLOUR VARIATIONS	White with chestnut patches

Braque Français, Type Pyrénées

HEIGHT 48-65cm (18.5-23 in)

Gundog **GROUP** **COAT CARE**
large **SIZE** **FEEDING**

THE BRAQUE FRANÇAIS, Type Pyrénées, more easily referred to perhaps as the French Pyrenean Pointer, is a rather refined version of the French Gascony Pointer, somewhat shorter on the leg, and a dog which works extremely well in thick cover. This agile breed was developed near France's Spanish border in the region of the Pyrénées and is descended from the now-extinct Southern Hound and the Spanish Pointer.

This breed is by instinct an air hunter, reaching skyward to sniff for the smallest scent. Rarely seen outside France it is not a numerically strong breed but is a good companion which suits many lifestyles, in the country or otherwise. The hair is somewhat shorter and finer than that of the Gascony but the colouring is the same. Height is 48-65 cm (18.5–23 in) and weight 17–22 kg (37–55 lb).

Left
A very rare dog, this is not often found outside France, although efforts are being made to increase numbers.

Gundog

GROUP

COAT CARE

large

SIZE

FEEDING

BREED FACT:
Like most Braques, the St-Germain will respond best to gentle discipline during its training as a gundog.

Braque St-Germain

HEIGHT 54-62 cm (21-24 in)

○ ○

BREED INFORMATION

NAME	Braque St-Germain
OTHER NAMES	St Germain Pointer
OFFICIAL RECOGNITION	FCI Group 7
COLOUR VARIATIONS	White with orange markings

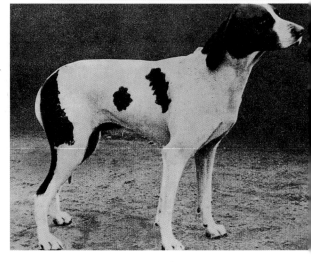

A DOG OF SIMILAR appearance to the Braque St-Germain dates back to the time of King Louis XV, so the breed is believed to be one with a long history. During the French Revolution numbers declined, but by crossing survivors with the French Gascony Pointers it was revived.

This breed is used to point and retrieve on land but is now also used as a companion as well as a working gundog.

Docile and obedient, the Braque St-Germain responds best to gentle training, as do many similar breeds as this has a slightly nervous disposition. With a short coat, which is distinctively marked, the breed is 54–62 cm (21–24 in) in height and weighs 18–26 kg (40–57 lb).

Below

One of France's oldest breeds, this has recently been the subject of a breeding programme to boost numbers.

Hound

GROUP

COAT CARE

large

SIZE

FEEDING

Chien d'Artois

HEIGHT 52-58 cm (20.5-23 in)

○ ○

BREED INFORMATION

NAME	Chien d'Artois
OTHER NAMES	Artois Hound, Briquet
OFFICIAL RECOGNITION	FCI Group 6
COLOUR VARIATIONS	Tri-colour

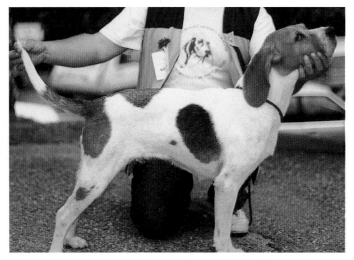

IT IS LIKELY THAT this breed's alternative name, Briquet, may have been derived from the word *braquet*, which means small hound. Certainly this is one of the oldest of French scenthounds, but it was on the verge of extinction in the nineteenth century. French hunting scenes of the fifteenth century show hounds very similar in type to the Chien d'Artois, which hunted in packs and were used for small game, their relatively short legs making them capable of working in thick undergrowth.

Largely due to the breed's popularity, some breeders made indiscriminate use of British gundogs which were crossed with the purebred hound of this breed, but as the twentieth century moved forward, a true type was re-established. This short-haired breed with a rather thick skin stands 52–58 in (20.5–23 in) high and weighs 18–24 kg (40–53 lb).

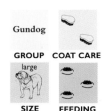

BREED INFORMATION

NAME	Epagneul Bleu de Picardie
OTHER NAMES	Blue Picardy Spaniel
OFFICIAL RECOGNITION	FCI Group 7
COLOUR VARIATIONS	Blue and black (blue roan) with white ticking and tan patches

Epagneul Bleu de Picardie

HEIGHT 56-61 cm (22-24 in)

Gundog
GROUP **COAT CARE**
large
SIZE **FEEDING**

USED TO retrieve snipe from marshland in north-east France, the Epagneul Bleu de Picardie has a deep chest with ample room for lung expansion. This gundog was developed from a cross between the Blue Belton English Setter and the Picardy Spaniel. Resembling a setter in many ways, this breed is broader in the skull than others of the more commonly known setters.

The ears are low-set and covered in silky hair which is waved, the heavy body coat is a blue-black with white ticking. This is a quiet breed but needs a great deal of physical exercise because of its high level of stamina. A fun loving, responsive and obedient breed which adores human companionship, it is especially good with children. Height is 56–61 cm (22–24 in) and weight 19.5–20.5 kg (43–45 lb).

Left
This French Spaniel resembles a Setter in many ways and developed from a cross of Setter and Spaniel.

BREED INFORMATION

NAME	Epagneul français
OTHER NAMES	French Spaniel
OFFICIAL RECOGNITION	FCI Group 7
COLOUR VARIATIONS	White with brown

Epagneul Français

HEIGHT 53-61 cm (21-24 in)

Gundog
GROUP **COAT CARE**
large
SIZE **FEEDING**

A VERY ELEGANT FRENCH Pointer, the Epagneul Français is related to the Small German Munsterlander and the Dutch Partridge Dog. The breed's history most probably goes back to the Barbary coast, from where its ancestors were taken to Spain and subsequently to France. Others believe it to have developed in Scandinavia. This is another breed of dog called a spaniel, but it is more like a setter in many respects and is used to flush and retrieve game birds.

Quite tall and powerfully built, this is a typical working gundog. It is a quiet breed and responds to gentle training. Although a fairly popular companion dog, the breed is rarely seen outside its homeland but is a dog which gets on well with others and loves

exercise. The short, flat coat is feathered, the tail and ears covered in longer hair and this breed can cope well in cold conditions. Height is 53–61 cm (21–24 in) and weight 20–25 kg (44–55 lb).

Left
The roots of this elegant breed are obscure.

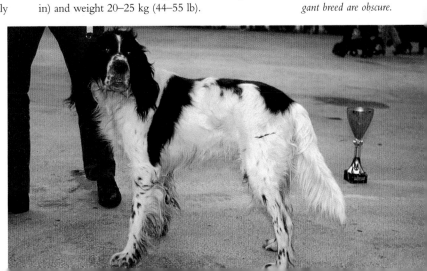

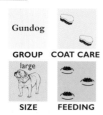

Gundog

GROUP **COAT CARE**

large

SIZE **FEEDING**

Epagneul Picard

HEIGHT 56-61 cm (22-24 in)

BREED INFORMATION	
NAME	Epagneul Picard
OTHER NAMES	Picardy Spaniel
OFFICIAL RECOGNITION	FCI Group 7
COLOUR VARIATIONS	Brown with white and tan.

Below

A preservation society has been set up to increase the numbers of this soft-natured dog.

IT IS LIKELY THAT the Epagneul Picard has descended from the Chien d'Oysell which is now an extinct breed, and that the present-day breed carries the blood of fourteenth century Spanish spaniels. During the nineteenth century the breed almost disappeared but was revived in Normandy and Picardy in the early twentieth century. Historically used for waterfowl, this dog is used for setting and retrieving game in marshland or on plains.

Although it has tremendous powers of endurance the Epagneul Picard is content with moderate exercise and makes a good companion, though the breed is rarely found outside France and Belgium. There is heavy body hair with feathering on the ears, legs and tail and the expressive amber coloured eyes tone complement the coat colour.

Gundog

GROUP **COAT CARE**

large

SIZE **FEEDING**

Epagneul de Pont-Audemer

HEIGHT 57-58 cm (20-23 in)

BREED INFORMATION	
NAME	Epagneul de Pont-Audemer
OTHER NAMES	Pont-Audemer Spaniel
OFFICIAL RECOGNITION	FCI Group 7
COLOUR VARIATIONS	Liver and white, Liver

THIS THOROUGHLY attractive spaniel is related to the Barbet and to old French spaniels, and may well originally have had connections with the Irish Water Spaniel too. The breed became virtually extinct during the Second World War but was revived afterwards by the deliberate introduction of Irish Water Spaniel blood. Used to flush and retrieve game, the breed works well and with exuberance in marsh and wetlands; it kept mainly by serious hunters. Still rare, there is a preservation society in France which will ensure that the breed survives.

The Epagneul Pont-Audemer is responsive and has a docile temperament, getting on well with other dogs and being very reliable. This is a substantial breed, standing some 51–58 cm (20–23 in) high and weighing 18–24 kg (40–53 lb). Its profuse shiny coat is wavy but not oily, and there are long fringes on the low set ears. The kindly eyes with liver pigmentation express a charming character.

Français Tricolore

HEIGHT 62-72 cm (24-28 in)

BREED INFORMATION

NAME	Français Tricolore
OTHER NAMES	French Tricolour Hound
OFFICIAL RECOGNITION	FCI Group 6
COLOUR VARIATIONS	Tri-coloured

ONE OF THE LARGE French hound breeds, these dogs mainly hunt red and roe deer and sometimes wild boar. Like other breeds within this group, the Français Tricolore has been derived from various crosses including the Poitevins, Billys, Bleus de Gascogne, Gascon-Saintongeois and Foxhounds. The breed was not recognised until 1965. It is now the second most popular of the French hounds, and is used to hunt small game.

Sturdy but elegant, the Français Tricolore covers all sorts of terrain at great speed and is able to work for a long while thanks to its great strength and stamina. Standing 62–72 cm (24–28 in) high and weighing 34.5–35.5 kg (76–78 lb) the dog's smooth coat is rather fine, and the skin is fine too. These tri-coloured hounds have a black blanket and the tan may be bright or copper-toned. A grizzle-coloured coat is permissible, although any tan or blue mottling should not be obvious.

Left and Above
This popular breed originally hunted deer.

Français Blanc et Noir

HEIGHT 65-72 cm (25.5-28 in)

BREED INFORMATION

NAME	Français Blanc et Noir
OTHER NAMES	French White and Black Hound
OFFICIAL RECOGNITION	FCI Group 6
COLOUR VARIATIONS	Black and white with some tan

JUST AS ROBUST and vigorous as the similar Français Tricolore, the striking appearance of the Français Blanc et Noir makes this a very majestic breed. In its creation, the English Foxhound, Bleu de Gascogne and other French hounds were used. As a scenthound, this breed is mainly used to hunt small game, its rather long tail, which is strong at the base, is carried high when alert. This glamorous hound has a devoted following and has been used to hunt wolves in Quebec, where the people have tried to keep alive the traditional French style of hunting.

Standing 65–72 cm (25.5–28 in) high and weighing 34.5–35.5 kg (76–78 lb), this breed has a smooth, strong, close coat which is black and tan in colour, black blanketed or with smaller black marks. Some blue mottling is permitted, with tan mottling only on specific areas. This breed has a kindly disposition, loves children and is easy to obedience train, but is not suitable for city life.

Left
Despite its name, the Français Blanc et Noir has a distinct tan shade in its coat.

Hound
GROUP

COAT CARE

large
SIZE

FEEDING

Grand Anglo-Français Tricolore

HEIGHT 62-72 cm (24-28 in)

DESCENDED PRINCIPALLY from tricoloured Poitevins and Foxhounds, the combination of breeding has given this breed the orthodox colouring of a black blanketed tri-colour. Indeed the Foxhound has also strongly influenced the breed in many ways, such as in its compact stature with low-set hocks and in not having such a sculptured head as the Poitevin. A very popular large French hound breed, the Grand Anglo-Français Tricolore is often kept as a companion dog but still thoroughly enjoys hunting in a pack in the pursuit of large game.

Right
This large dog thrives as a hunting dog and requires an immense amount of exercise.

This double-coated breed has a short, thick topcoat and a softer, fine undercoat. It stands 62 0 72 cm (24–28 in) and weighs 34.5–35.5 kg (76–78 lb).

Grand Blanc et Noir

HEIGHT 62-72 cm (24-28 in)

Hound
GROUP

COAT CARE

large
SIZE

FEEDING

Right
Not a good dog for a pet, the Grand Blanc et Noir is used to hunt deer.

UNTIL 1957, the Grand Anglo-Français Blanc et Noir was grouped together with other similar Anglo-Français and Français hound breeds which were known as *Batards*, or crossbreeds. This was followed by the region of France in which the cross was originally made, which made for a group of very unwieldy and clumsy breed names; so even though these closely associated breeds may still seem somewhat difficult to differentiate, the nomenclature is in actual fact now more clear. Almost identical to the Grand Français Tricolore, this breed is closely related to the Bleu de Gascogne and Gascon Saintongeois. Rarely kept as a companion animal, the breed is mainly used to hunt red and roe deer in addition to wild boar. Height and weight ranges are exactly the same as those for the Grand Tricolore.

Grand Gascon Saintongeois

HEIGHT 63-71 cm (25-28 in)

THE HOMELAND OF THE now extinct Saintongeois breed is in France's Midi region, but the Grand Gascon-Santongeois was developed by crossing this with the Grand Bleu de Gascogne and the Ariégeois. The breed is a good hunter with excellent voice and nose, and also possesses strong perseverance. Used to hunt large game such as roe deer, this is a popular pack hound, particularly near the Pyrenées, but is rarely seen outside France.

A breed that gets on well with other canines, this dog is of sound temperament and tends to be gentle with children. It can be kept in the home if adjusted to this lifestyle from a puppy but it needs regular exercise; it is, however, quite easy to train in obedience work. Height is 63–71 cm (5–28 in) and weight 30–32 kg (66 -71 lb). Colour is mainly black and white but the head has tan cheeks; tan hairs mingle with black on the ears.

Left
A popular pack hunter, especially in the south-west of France around the Pyrenées, this breed is still rare outside France.

Griffon d'Arrêt à Poil Dur

HEIGHT 58-60 cm (20-24 in)

ALTHOUGH THE Griffon d'Arrêt à Poil Dur is classified as a French breed, its point of origin is actually Dutch. However, a major part of the breed's development took place in France. This breed is very well adapted to work in swampy country as its harsh coat affords the dog excellent protection. A wonderful swimmer and retriever, this is a willing and intelligent breed which is easy to train.

Outgoing in personality, loyal and trustworthy, this Griffon breed stands 50–60 cm (20–24 in) and is slightly longer than it is tall. With an alert, friendly expression, its eye colour ranges through all shades of yellow and brown, but the eyes must not protrude and the haw should not show. Nose colour is always brown. One of the features of this breed is the double coat, which has an outer coat of medium length, straight and wiry, never curly or woolly. The undercoat is a fine, thick down, providing both insulation and water resistance. The round, firm feet have tightly closed, webbed toes.

BREED FACT:
The Griffon has a stable temperament; it is rarely irritable but some male dogs may snap at other males.

Left
Originally a Dutch breed, this is a particularly loyal and trustworthy dog.

Hound

GROUP

large

SIZE

COAT CARE

FEEDING

Griffon Fauve de Bretagne

HEIGHT 45-56 cm (19-22 in)

Right
This ancient breed has
soft hair covering its ears.

○○○○○○○○○○○○○○○○○○○○○○○○○○

BREED INFORMATION

NAME	Griffon Fauve de Bretagne
OTHER NAMES	Fawn Brittany Griffon
OFFICIAL RECOGNITION	FCI Group 6
COLOUR VARIATIONS	Red; Wheaten; Gold; Fawn

THE FAUVE DE BRETAGNE is one of four breeds named by King Charles IX, all of them wire-haired and more hardy than other French hounds. The original breed type is preserved in today's Griffon Fauve de Bretagne, which was created by introduction of the Briquet Griffon Vendéen. The Griffon Fauve was used to hunt the wolf and is most probably also related to the Welsh Foxhound. This hound has excellent powers of scent and working ability is still important, although the breed is now commonly employed as a gundog rather than a pack hound.

With a hard coat but ears covered with soft hair, the head has pronounced eyebrows. This is a strongly built breed and a tenacious hunter. Height is 48–56 cm (19–22 in) and weight 18–22 kg (40–48.5 lb).

Hound

GROUP

large

SIZE

COAT CARE

FEEDING

Griffon Nivernais

HEIGHT 53-64 cm (21-24 in)

○○○○○○○○○○○○○○○○○○○○○○○○○○

BREED INFORMATION

NAME	Griffon Nivernais
OTHER NAMES	Chiens de Pays
OFFICIAL RECOGNITION	FCI Group 6
COLOUR VARIATIONS	Grey; Black; Fawn

THE GRIFFON NIVERNAIS is very close to the large, dark coloured and shaggy haired Canis Segusien, which lived with the primitive cavemen who painted on the walls at Lascaux. This breed goes back to the rough-coated hounds bred for centuries in the highlands of southern France. The dogs were used in densely wooded hilly areas to control wolves and wild boar. Rangier in build than the Vendéen, the Griffon Nivernais is a long-backed hound with rather large, long feet. A pack of just four or five will follow their quarry over difficult terrain at a steady pace, hunting wild boar with expertise. The breed is ready to follow anything that moves and is not well suited to obedience work. The unkempt, shaggy coat is strong, hard and never woolly nor curly. Height is 53–64 cm (21–24 in and weight 23–25 kg (50–55 lb).

Briquet Griffon Vendéen

HEIGHT 50-55 cm (20-22 in)

BREED INFORMATION

NAME	Briquet Griffon Vendéen
OTHER NAMES	Medium Griffon Vendéen
OFFICIAL RECOGNITION	FCI Group 6
COLOUR VARIATIONS	Tri-colour; Orange and white; Cream

LIKE SO MANY breeds, the Briquet Griffon Vendéen fell drastically in number during the Second World War and in France even now it is not at all a well-known breed. The Briquet was originally developed from the Grand Griffon Vendéen for the purpose of hunting small game; it requires experienced handling as the breed has a tendency to be rather stubborn.

As a watchdog, this breed is reasonably adept, and it also makes a good gundog which can be worked in all weather conditions, in water and on varied terrain. An energetic, lively, decisive and intelligent breed, although some can be rather snappy, they are generally good with children. The waterproof, dense, wiry coat is never soft nor woolly and the large, black nose is surrounded by whiskers. This breed makes also makes a good guard dog in the home and can adapt to urban life if introduced to it at an early age. This is a thick-boned, muscular gundog standing 50–55 cm (20–22 in) high and weighing 22–24 kg (48–53 lb).

Left
Although prone to stubbornness and snapping from time to time, this Griffon generally gets on well with children.

Poitevin

HEIGHT 58-71 cm (23-28 in)

BREED INFORMATION

NAME	Poitevin
OTHER NAMES	Haut-Poitou
OFFICIAL RECOGNITION	FCI Group 6
COLOUR VARIATIONS	Tri-colour; Orange/white; Badger pied

THE POITEVIN WAS ORIGINALLY derived from three different strains of Staghound but a shortage of hounds led to inbreeding so new blood was introduced in 1844 by way of the Foxhound from England. Again after the Second World War, similar new blood was needed but after this Foxhounds were discarded from breeding programmes. After three generations, the breeders claimed that the Foxhound influence was barely perceptible in the dog, but the Poitevin remains a difficult breed to rear and maintain successfully.

This is an excellent hunter with many hunting attributes; formerly it hunted wolf and now fox. The breed is still rare but has been described as 'a masterpiece of breeding'; its appearance is so sculptured that it almost appears breakable. Despite this, the dog combines strength, elegance and lightness of foot. The breed's height is generally around 58–71 cm (23–28 in) and the weight is roughly 29.5–30.5 kg (65–67 lb). The short, glossy coat is tri-colour with a black saddle or with large black patches, but can also be orange and white or badger pied.

Left
Despite its delicate appearance, the Poitevin combines strength with agility.

Hound
GROUP

COAT CARE

large
SIZE

FEEDING

Porcelaine
HEIGHT 53-58 cm (21-23 in)

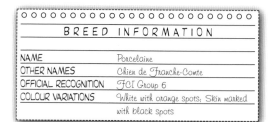

○○○○○○○○○○○○○○○○○○○○○○○○○○○○

BREED INFORMATION

NAME	Porcelaine
OTHER NAMES	Chien de Franche-Comte
OFFICIAL RECOGNITION	FCI Group 6
COLOUR VARIATIONS	White with orange spots; Skin marked with black spots

Below
The Porcelaine has a distinctive white coat with skin spots showing through it.

THIS IS A DISTINGUISHED hound and the details of its structure indicate a race of great antiquity; indeed the breed is descended from the 'Royal White Hounds'. Originally from the Franco-Swiss border, the breed was first called after the region, Franche-Comte. The modern name of Porcelaine come from the breed's colour, character and style. There is a delicacy and translucence about this breed which has a quiet dignity but, despite this, is one of the best breeds for hunting the hare.

Sensible both in character and build, an outstanding feature of this breed is the skin which is fine and elastic and must be mottled with black; this colour shows through the fine white coat, giving a blue glazed appearance. There are small orange markings on the coat, but never grouped together or forming a saddle. Although the breed stands 53–58 cm (21–23 in) in height and weighs 25–28 kg (55–62 lb), it is often said to be delicate and difficult to rear. Found mainly in France, Switzerland and Italy, this is a biddable breed which is easy to manage.

Hound
GROUP

COAT CARE

large
SIZE

FEEDING

Petit Bleu de Gascogne
HEIGHT 50-60 cm (20-23 in)

○○○○○○○○○○○○○○○○○○○○○○○○○○

BREED INFORMATION

NAME	Petit Bleu de Gascogne
OTHER NAMES	Small Blue Gascony Hound
OFFICIAL RECOGNITION	FCI Group 6
COLOUR VARIATIONS	Black or mottled

IN THE 1970S THE Petit Bleu de Gascogne was considered perhaps the rarest of the hound breeds in France. It is still not numerous and found mainly in the south-west of France. The Petit has a more refined head than the Grand Bleu and its ears are thicker and more curled. This breed is also more rare than its cousin, from which it has been selectively bred down in size. The breed has an excellent nose and is used to hunt hare and rabbit.

Right
This breed has been seriously reduced in numbers and is now found mostly in south-west France.

Despite being called a 'small' hound, it stands some 50–60 cm (20–23 in) high and weighs in the region of 18–22 kg (40–48 lb). The coat, although easy to manage, is dense and thick, providing protection in all weathers; this working

hound is well suited to life in the country. A determined breed, the Petit Bleu is fairly easy to train in obedience and enjoys the company of other dogs.

Other French Breeds

MANY OF THE FRENCH hunting breeds share distinct similarities in their breeding, with some varying basically only in size or in colour. The majority are kept primarily for sporting use rather than for the showing but, none the less, are registered with the FCI. Other French FCI breeds not detailed in the previous sections are the Basset d'Artois or Artois Basset (Group 6), the Braque Dupuy, or Dupuy Pointing Dog (Group 7), the Français Blanc et Orange, or French Orange and White Hound (Group 6), the Grand Anglo-Français Blanc et Orange, or Great Anglo-French White and Orange Hound (Group 6), the Griffon à Poil Laineux, or French Woolly-haired Pointing Griffon (Group 7), the Griffon Bleu de Gascogne, or Blue Gascony Griffon (Group 6) and the Petit Gascon Saintongeois, which is also called the Small Gascon Saintongeois (Group 6).

The following breeds are also recognised in Britain but certain clarifications, as outlined here, are necessary when found in other countries.

BEAUCERON AND BRIARD

Under FCI rules, the Beauceron breed is divided by colour into different acceptable categories, which are black and tan and also harlequin, the Briard is divided by colour into slate, fawn and grey.

BRITTANY

Under the FCI the Brittany is divided by colour into white and orange and all other colours.

FRENCH BULLDOG

UNDER THE FCI the French Bulldog is divided by colour: a) fawn, brindle or not brindle, or with limited patching; b) fawn, brindle or not brindle, with medium to predominating patching = pied.

PAPILLON AND PHALÈNE

BOTH ARE CATEGORISED under the FCI as the Continental Toy Spaniel and are divided thus: a) Papillon (with erect ears) 1.5–2.5 kg and 2.5–4.5 kg; b) Phalène (with drooping ears) 1.5 kg–2.5 kg and 2.5 kg–4.5 kg.

POODLE

UNDER THE FCI RULES, the Poodle is divided into four sizes: Standard, Medium, Miniature and Toy; and for each size there are five different colour categories: white, brown, black, grey and apricot.

PYRENEAN SHEEPDOG

Under the FCI there are two distinct breeds, one the Long Haired Pyrenean Sheepdog, and the other the Smooth Faced Pyrenean Sheepdog.

Top
The Pyrenean Sheepdog is a hardy breed, well-adapted to coping with working on rough terrain and in all weathers.

Centre
The Briard was originally bred as a sheep-dog and is registered with the British Kennel Club.

Bottom
The Griffon Bleu de Gascogne is a useful hunting dog, working well in packs.

BREED FACT:
Many French dogs began life as gun- and gamedogs, but are now frequently kept purely for pleasure.

Utility

GROUP   **COAT CARE**

large

SIZE   **FEEDING**

GERMANY

Eurasier

HEIGHT 48-60 cm (19-23.5 in)

Right
The Eurasier has attendancy towards wariness of people and tends to timidity.

THE EURASIA IS A SPITZ breed but was not developed until the 1950s. This happened in Germany and involved crossing the Chow Chow, Samoyed and German Wolfspitz. The intention was to develop a breed similar to the Russian Laïka, to be used for pulling sleds although now the breed is also kept as a companion dog. The Eurasia tends to select just one family member as a pack leader and is reluctant to respond to any other people, hence it is not ideal as a family companion.

Although some authorities say the breed seldom barks, others consider it makes an excellent watchdog because of its wariness of strangers. Shyness and timidity are accepted behavioural problems and it is a breed which tends to be a little snappy. With height at 48–60 cm (19–23.5 in) and weight 18–32 kg (39.5–70 lb), this can be a reasonably large dog with a long muscular neck. The long, abundant, straight coat is found in a variety of colours but white and pinto are not permitted. The ears are typically spitz-like and the dense tail curls over the back. The feet are large, making them ideal for gripping ground.

Hound

GROUP   **COAT CARE**

medium

SIZE   **FEEDING**

German Hound

HEIGHT 00-00 cm (00-00 in)

Right and Bottom
This dog is an excellent tracker and fast mover, owing to its long legs.

FROM COMMON German Celtic hounds of different types comes the German Hound, also known frequently as Deutsche Bracke. Its predecessors were the Westphalian Bracke and the Sauerlander Holzbracke. Popular for tracking fox, hare, rabbit and boar this breed works best on a hot scent and works with a beautiful bell-like voice. The breed's long legs allow it to run quickly covering much ground. Because of the breed's superb nose it can also work in the same manner as a Bloodhound,

working on the cold trails of wounded animals.

The size of the German Hound varies quite considerably, with height from 41–53 cm (16–21 in) and weight 14.5–23 kg (32–50 lb). The breed is typically hound-coloured in tri-colour, black, white and tan, the coat short, smooth, hard and dense.

German Hunting Terrier

HEIGHT 00-00 cm (00-00 in)

BREED INFORMATION	
NAME	German Hunting Terrier
OTHER NAMES	Deutscher Jagterrier
OFFICIAL RECOGNITION	FCI Group 3
COLOUR VARIATIONS	Black/tan; Brown/tan; Red

Terrier

GROUP · COAT CARE · medium · SIZE · FEEDING

NOT UNTIL THE 1920s did Bavarian breeders begin to create the German Hunting Terrier. This they did by crossing the Welsh Terrier with the old English Black and Tan Terrier and subsequently the English Fox Terrier was introduced. Used for working with vermin and small game, breeding is still based upon ability to work, indeed this is a breed which seems perfectly happy to work all day if required and perhaps this is the reason why it is kept primarily by gamekeepers and hunters.

It is a strong-willed and resourceful breed which needs both mental and physical activity and, being of a somewhat independent nature, can be quite difficult as a companion dog. Prepared to work both above and below ground, the German Hunting Terrier is capable of tracking and retrieving either on land or in water. This fairly small dog stands about 40.5–41.5 cm (16 in) high and weighs 9–10 kg (20–22 lb). The coat is usually hard and rough, but smooth-coated specimens of the breed do exist. With a terrier-like expression and demeanour, the jaw is robust and this breed's teeth are exceptionally large for its size.

Left
The German Hunting Terrier is of an independent nature and needs the stimulus of being a working dog.

German Spaniel

HEIGHT 00 cm (0 in)

BREED INFORMATION	
NAME	German Spaniel
OTHER NAMES	Deutscher Wachtelhund, German Quail Dog
OFFICIAL RECOGNITION	FCI Group 8
COLOUR VARIATIONS	Brown and white; Brown

Working

GROUP · COAT CARE · large · SIZE · FEEDING

BREED FACT:
Spaniels were originally bred in Great Britain as gundogs to work in dense undergrowth and flush out their quarry.

THE GERMAN SPANIEL was developed in the late nineteenth century with the aim of recreating the Stober, a breed known during the early years of the eighteenth century and noted for its ability for following scent. What remained of the Stober was bred by hunters in Germany with English Cocker Spaniels and other sporting spaniels. A new breed was created but it is still rare and really known only within Germany. Effectively this is an all round bird dog, one which can retrieve from water as well as from dense undergrowth. The German name, Wachtelhund, actually means quail dog although the breed is also used for hare and fox.

This breed loves to follow scent and will do so with enormous persistence. Kept primarily by hunters, it has a vibrant personality and stands some 40-51 cm (16-20 in) high, weighing 20-30 kg (44-66 lb). Resembling other of the larger spaniels in general appearance, the eyes are dark brown and almond shaped, the ears well-feathered and pendant, the face smooth. On the body, the hair is long, thick and wavy, while the undercoat is waterproof with insulating qualities. The feet look larger than they actually are because they have tufts of hair growing between the toes.

Left
An adept retriever, the German Spaniel will also follow a scent with great persistence.

Hound
GROUP

COAT CARE

large
SIZE

FEEDING

Hanoverian Hound

HEIGHT 51-61 cm (20-24 in)

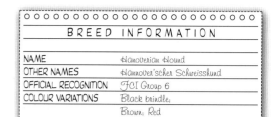

○○○○○○○○○○○○○○○○○○○○○○○○○○○○○

BREED INFORMATION

NAME	Hanoverian Hound
OTHER NAMES	Hannover'scher Schweisshund
OFFICIAL RECOGNITION	FCI Group 6
COLOUR VARIATIONS	Black brindle;
	Brown; Red

THE GAMEKEEPER of the city of Hanover crossed the tracking dogs of St Hubert with lighter built Celtic dogs to create the Hanoverian Hound. The breed has a reputedly unfailing nose and is used primarily for tracking because of the breed's great ability in this field. This breed is able to follow cold trails left by wounded animals and is kept mainly as a tracker, rather than as a companion. It is used often by game wardens and by foresters and is not only used for tracking game, but also people. It used to work in packs, but now mainly works alone.

Although a calm, relaxed hound, the Hanoverian is dedicated to its task and becomes obsessive when working. This large breed has heavy, pendulous lips and flat, pendant ears giving a somewhat solemn appearance. The coat is short, thick and shiny, and the colours are grey and brown, red and brown, yellow and red, dark yellow or blackened brown, with or without a black mask. Height ranges from 51–61 cm (20–24 in) and weight from 38–44 kg (84–99 lb).

Right
Historically the Hanoverian Hound was a pack dog, but now it is used on its own for tracking.

Terrier
GROUP

COAT CARE

medium
SIZE

FEEDING

Kromfohrländer

HEIGHT 38-43 cm (15-17 in)

○○○○○○○○○○○○○○○○○○○○○○○○○○○○○

BREED INFORMATION

NAME	Kromfohrländer
OFFICIAL RECOGNITION	FCI Group 9
COLOUR VARIATIONS	White with tan

BREED FACT:
This dog is on the verge of extinction; the breed will need careful protection if it is to survive.

THERE IS A FASCINATING history to the Kromfohrländer which came about as a result of American soldiers who, passing through Krumme Furche in Westphalia, gave a lady a fawn coloured dog which had been travelling with them. Keeping this dog, she bred it with her own dog which was something like a Griffon Fauve de Bretagne. Five litters were born from such a mating and formed the basis of this breed, named after the region in Germany where it originated.

Although it was recognised in 1953, again the breed is all but on the verge of extinction. Originally bred solely as a companion animal, it makes a good watchdog and is rather terrier-like in character. This is a good tempered breed, fond of children and agreeable with other dogs. It is also reasonably easy to train in obedience work.

There are two coat varieties, wire-haired which is short, rough and rather wiry, with dense undercoat; and smooth-haired in which the coat is long, smooth and straight. The dark, oval eyes are slightly slanted, and the expression very alert. Height is 38–43 cm (15–17 in) and weight 11.5–12.5 kg (25–27 lb).

Right
A biddable dog, the Kromfohrländer was only recognised in 1953.

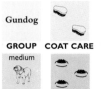

Gundog
GROUP **COAT CARE**
medium
SIZE **FEEDING**

BREED INFORMATION

NAME	Pudelpointer
OTHER NAMES	Poodlepointer
OFFICIAL RECOGNITION	FCI Group 6
COLOUR VARIATIONS	Liver; Chestnut; Black

Pudelpointer

HEIGHT 54-65 cm (21.5-25.5 in)

THE PUDELPOINTER was developed in Germany by Baron von Zedlitz, to produce a breed with ideal tracking, pointing and retrieving abilities, one which could be used both on land and in water. The dogs he used comprised seven poodles and almost a hundred of various pointers. Today all such dogs have to pass field tests on land and in water before they can be registered and, understandably, the Pudelpointer is therefore usually kept only by serious hunters. Even its homeland this is a rare breed but makes a good gundog and companion. The ideal type is the build of a large, heavy

Pointer with a coat which is not too long but harsh and wiry, brown in colour, or dried-leaf colour. The ears are flat and close-fitting, more pointed than rounded, and with a covering of hair. The large, round eyes are fiery with the expression of a bird of prey and are yellow to yellow-brown. The feet are round with tight toes and the pads are robust. The dog's height is 54–65 cm (21.5–25.5in) and the weight is around 20–30 kg (44–66 lb).

Left and Below
The Pudelpointer is a hunting dog that requires serious training in the field.

BREED INFORMATION

NAME	Small Munsterlander
OTHER NAMES	Kleiner Munsterländer Vorstehhund, Heidewachtel
OFFICIAL RECOGNITION	FCI Group 7
COLOUR VARIATIONS	Brown and white

Small Munsterlander

HEIGHT 48-56 cm (19-22 in)

Gundog
GROUP **COAT CARE**
medium
SIZE **FEEDING**

USED ORIGINALLY FOR tracking, pointing and retrieving, ancestors of the Small Munsterlander were ancient hawking dogs and European gundogs which had been bred together. As a bird dog it was used with hawk and net but having fallen into serious decline as a breed it was not redeveloped until early in the twentieth century. Now it is still used as a gundog, but also as a good companion dog.

This is a breed with a happy disposition and an endearing personality

and at work it is a willing retriever with natural inclination. In general appearance it resembles the Large Munsterlander but is substantially smaller. The smooth coat is close-fitting with just a little wave and there is feathering, especially on the tail and on the pointed ears. Although reasonably small in size, this is a well-boned breed with good muscling, especially on the thighs. Height is 48–56 cm (19–22 in) and weight 14.5–15.5 kg.

Left
This ancient breed fell into decline in the nineteenth century but has recently been redeveloped and its numbers are rising.

Other German Breeds

OTHER GERMAN BREEDS recognised by the FCI are the German Broken-coated Pointer, known as the Deutscher Stichelhaariger Vorstehhund which is in Group 7 and the Westphalian Dachsbracke, or Westfälische Dachsbracke in Group 6.

Another German breed is the **German Wolfspitz** which also originated in Germany and stands 46 cm (18 in) and weighs in the region of 23 kg (50 lb). This double-coated breed has a long, thick, stand-off coat which is always wolf-grey in colour.

The following breeds are also recognised by the British Kennel Club but certain clarifications, as outlined here, are needed for these breeds when found in other countries:

BOXER

Under the FCI the Boxer is divided by colour in to fawn and brindle.

DACHSHUNDS

Under the FCI, in addition to the six varieties of Dachshund recognised in Britain, there is also a Rabbit Dachshund, of which there are the usual three coat varieties: smooth-, long- and wire-haired.

DOBERMANN

Under the FCI the Dobermann is divided by colour in to black with rust red markings and brown with rust red markings.

GERMAN SPITZ BREEDS

Under the FCI, the German Spitz (in addition to the Keeshund and Pomeranian which also come under the same auspices) is divided into three sizes: Giant Spitz; Medium Size Spitz and Miniature Spitz.

GREAT DANE

Under the FCI the Great Dane is divided by colour in to fawn and brindle.

MINIATURE PINSCHER

Under the FCI the Miniature Pinscher is divided by colour in to red-brown to stag-red and black with red-brown markings.

PINSCHER

Under the FCI the Pinscher is dived by colour in to red-brown to stag red and also black with red-brown markings.

GIANT SCHNAUZER, SCHNAUZER AND MINIATURE SCHNAUZER

Under the FCI, all three of the above Schnauzer breeds are divided by colour: pepper and salt (which is blackened sand with sand-coloured markings) and black. However, the Miniature Schnauzer has two further divisions: black and silver and white.

WEIMERANER

Under the FCI the Weimeraner is divided by coat in to short-haired and long-haired.

BREED INFORMATION	
NAME	Greenland Dog
OTHER NAMES	Grønlandshund
OFFICIAL RECOGNITION	FCI Group 5
COLOUR VARIATIONS	All colours except albino

GREENLAND
Greenland Dog
HEIGHT 56-64 cm (22-25 in)

Working

GROUP **COAT CARE**

large

SIZE **FEEDING**

BREED FACT:
This is another spitz-type dog which has the same heavy coat as the Eskimo Dog to withstand the cold.

CLASSIFIED AS A working husky dog, the Greenland Dog is akin to other northern dogs which are used for transportation and seems to be traced back to dogs which accompanied people from Siberia some 12,000 years ago. Such people went on to become today's Inuits and may well have used local wolves for breeding. This another spitz-type dog but unfortunately, like many others, numbers have diminished in recent years due to other means of transport being introduced to Arctic regions.

The Greenland Dog, though slightly taller than the Eskimo Dog, is not so heavy. Aloof and independent, the breed

can be affectionate with those it knows well and is devoted to its owners. Now the breed is used in hunting, sled racing and is a popular hiking companion in Scandinavia. Height is 56–64 cm (22–25 cm) and weight 30–32 kg (66–70 lb), the coat moderately long, straight, thick and stand-off, with a heavy undercoat. The bushy tail, curled over the back, is used to protect the face while sleeping so that all that can be seen are the small, triangular, pricked ears.

Left
The Greenland Dog is used in sled racing as well as hunting.

BREED INFORMATION	
NAME	Drentse Partridge Dog
OTHER NAMES	Dutch Partridge Dog
OFFICIAL RECOGNITION	FCI Group 7
COLOUR VARIATIONS	White with brown or orange markings; Tri-coloured

HOLLAND
Drentse
HEIGHT 55-65 cm (21.5-25.5 in)

Gundog

GROUP **COAT CARE**

large

SIZE **FEEDING**

Left
The Partridge Dog is a loyal companion as well as a superb hunting dog.

THE DRENTSE PARTRIDGE Dog originated in the sixteenth century from the Spioenen (also called Spanjoelen) which went to Holland from Spain, via France. Called Partridge Dogs, in the eastern part of Holland they were kept purebred and in 1943 the breed was officially recognised. Related primarily to the Small Munsterlander and Épagneul Français, this is an ideal breed for Dutch sportsmen who wish to hunt without too much physical effort. The dog hunts within range of the gun keeping closely in touch with the hunter, and when pointing waits for the hunter to come near. Capable of hunting all sorts of game in water and in fields, this is also a good retriever of lost game.

Well proportioned, with bodily power and ability to develop necessary speed, the Drentse Partridge Dog stands 55–65 cm (21.5–25.5 in) and weighs in

the region of 21–23 kg (45–50 lb). The coat is not really long, but dense and not curly, rather longer on the forechest. The close-hanging ears are covered with longer, wavy hair. This obedient, loyal, intelligent breed is a valued hunting companion and family pet.

Working

GROUP   **COAT CARE**

large

SIZE   **FEEDING**

Dutch Shepherd Dog

HEIGHT 55-62 cm (23-24.5 in)

Right
This dog was bred to be a good all-round farming dog.

THE DUTCH SHEPHERD DOG evolved early in the nineteenth century in the southern part of Holland, in Brabant, and in Belgium which was then part of the same country. It is an all-purpose farm dog, working originally as a guard, drover, livestock dog and for carting. Although not numerically strong, this is a competent working dog, now used for herding and as a guard, police and security dog.

There are three different coat types: short, wire and rough, but all are considered to be the same breed and all have a woolly undercoat. The short variety has quite a hard coat with ruff, trousers and feathered tail. The long coat is long all over the body, straight, close-lying and harsh, without curls or waves, while the rough is a thick, hard, tousled coat and notably the upper and under lips are to be well furnished with hair, and the eyebrows rough and off-standing. The prick-ears are high-set and rather small This is an affectionate, obedient, tractable breed which is alert, faithful and reliable. Height is 55–62 cm (22–24.5 in) and weight 29.5–30.5 kg (65–67 lb).

Gundog

GROUP   **COAT CARE**

medium

SIZE   **FEEDING**

Frisian Pointer

HEIGHT 48-53 cm (19-21 in)

THE FRISIAN Pointer has been bred since the seventeenth century in Friesland, a northern Dutch province, although written records only go back as far as the nineteenth century. It is likely that the breed's ancestors are those spaniels which were taken to Holland from France in the sixteenth century. Despite being a good hunting dog, a fine pointer and a soft-mouthed retriever, as well as lovely companion breed, the Frisian Pointer fell from popularity in the nineteenth century and has never really recovered,

Right
This Pointer has many strong points; it is an amenable companion and a useful working dog.

and is still rarely seen outside Holland.

This is a calm and reliable dog, placid and faithful, which seems always happy to please and is reputed to be good with children. The coat is long and smooth, while the undercoat is dense, especially in winter, and the tail carries long feathering. The colours indicated above can have ticking or roaning. The ears are fairly low-set and described as trowel-shaped, and although the muzzle narrows it is not pointed. Height is 48–53 cm (19–21 in) and weight 15–20 kg (33–44 lb).

Frisian Water Dog

HEIGHT 53-58 cm (21-23 in)

Hound
GROUP **COAT CARE**
medium
SIZE **FEEDING**

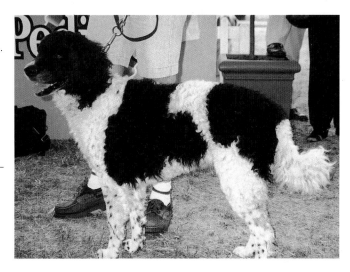

DEVELOPED IN FRIESLAND some 400 years ago, the Frisian Water Dog used to specialise in killing otters and was therefore highly prized by fishermen. Otters, however, came to be kept under control so the breed's uses diversified into hunting small mammals and guarding farms. Although a rare breed and only infrequently found outside Holland, this dog is still kept for hunting purposes as it is a good gundog and can both flush and retrieve on land and in water.

The Frisian Water Dog is also kept as a companion but is a strong-willed breed with guarding instincts, so firm training is needed from an early age. The coat is of coarse, thick, curly hair and covers the entire body with the exception of the head, so coat care is important. The body shape is rather square and the chest very broad, while the fairly large, rounded feet have particularly thick pads. Height is 53–58 cm (21–23 in) and weight 15–20 kg (33–44 lb).

Hollandse Smoushond

HEIGHT 35-42 cm (14-17 in)

Hound
GROUP **COAT CARE**
medium
SIZE **FEEDING**

IN THE LATE nineteenth century a similar dog, the German Coarse-haired Pinscher, was popular throughout Germany but the Germans had a preference for the black puppies which born and destroyed those which were red or yellow, although these were then common in litters. A Dutch merchant, Abraas, bought some of the rejected puppies and took them to Holland where they were sold in Amsterdam as gentlemen's stable dogs. Their numbers declined, especially during the war years but in the 1970s Mrs Barkman re-created the Hollandse Smoushond through selective breeding. Nowadays the Hollandse Smoushond breeds true to type and is equally typical in temperament. Very much a terrier, this is an excellent ratter and is always alert, but affectionate and friendly, with no nervousness. Standing 35–42 cm (14–17 in) high and weighing 9–10 kg (20–22 lb) the breed has small, expressive bright eyes with black pigmentation and triangular ears set rather high and adding to its charm. The medium length coarse coat is rough and wiry, with eyebrows, moustache and beard.

BREED FACT:
The Frisian Water Dog was bred to hunt otters, but now they are used as gundogs and retrievers.

Left
Selective breeding has saved this dog breed from extinction; it remains an excellent stable dog and ratter.

Working
GROUP   **COAT CARE**

large
SIZE   **FEEDING**

Saarloos Wolfdog

HEIGHT 60-75 cm (24-29.5 in)

○○○○○○○○○○○○○○○○○○○○○○○○○

BREED INFORMATION

NAME	Saarloos Wolfdog
OTHER NAMES	Saarlooswolfhond, Saarloos Wolfhound
OFFICIAL RECOGNITION	FCI Group 1
COLOUR VARIATIONS	Wolf-grey; Agouti; Brown. Sometimes

THE SAARLOOS WOLFDOG was created in 1921 by Leendert Saarloos who crossed a German Shepherd Dog with a part wolf dog carrying Canadian timber wolf blood. Selectively breed for several decades this breed is rather easier to train than the similar Czech Wolfdog, but it is still a pack oriented breed and still has the wolf-like wariness of its ancestor so can be shy. The breed was officially recognised in 1975 but is little known outside the Netherlands. The harsh coat has some length but is not too long and has a dense undercoat and the tail is densely feathered. The neck is broad and powerful and erect ears. Its weight is 36–41 kg (79–90 lb) and height is 60–75 cm (24–29.5 cm), and this dog stands on rather long legs with feet which turn slightly outwards.

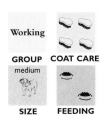

Working
GROUP   **COAT CARE**

medium
SIZE   **FEEDING**

Schapendoes

HEIGHT 43-51 cm (17-20 in)

○○○○○○○○○○○○○○○○○○○○○○○○○

BREED INFORMATION

NAME	Schapendoes
OFFICIAL RECOGNITION	FCI Group 1
COLOUR VARIATIONS	All colours

Above
The Saarloos Wolfdog has the blood of the Canadian timber wolf in its breeding.

THE ORIGIN OF THE Schapendoes is not actually known, but this breed is certainly related to the Briard, Bergamasco and to the Bearded Collie, while it also bears some resemblance to the Puli and Polish Lowland Sheepdog. Originally used as a herding dog on the moors the breed still carries this instinct strongly, and although brave it can sometimes be a little anxious, although this is heavily penalised in the conformation ring. Instead these dogs should really be excited. The Schapendoes makes a

good watchdog because, despite its vigilance, this breed is not aggressive, indeed it is reputed to make a wonderful companion for children.

An agile jumper, this dog has a great deal of energy and is very playful. The coat is long, dense, harsh and wavy and comes in a variety of hues, any colour being acceptable although the preferred ones are blue-grey to black, with lighter-coloured feet. The head is flat and relatively wide, the ears placed high and hanging loosely beside the head. Height is 43–51 cm (17–20 in) and weight 13.5–18.5 kg (30–40 lb).

> **BREED FACT:**
> The Schapendoes makes an ideal family pet as it is gentle with children.

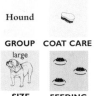

BREED INFORMATION

NAME	Hungarian Greyhound
OTHER NAMES	Magyar Agar
OFFICIAL RECOGNITION	FCI Group 10
COLOUR VARIATIONS	Any colour

HUNGARY
Hungarian Greyhound

HEIGHT 64-70 cm (25-27.5 in)

Hound
GROUP   COAT CARE
large
SIZE   FEEDING

IT WAS DURING THE TENTH century that ancestors of the Hungarian Greyhound went with the Magyars to the countries which have now become Hungary and Romania, following which the English Greyhound and Asian sighthounds played a part in the breed's development. Originally used to hunt small game, this breed is now used for hare coursing and for long-distance racing. A quiet, retiring breed, it also makes a good companion animal and is similar in many ways to the Greyhound known in Britain. It usually gets along well with other dogs and rarely bites or snaps.

When coursing the Hungarian Greyhound works by sight like other sighthound breeds, its expressive, oval eyes clear and bright. The coat is short and smooth, providing little protection from the elements, but is noticeably longer during the cold winter months. Height is 64–70 cm (25–27.5 in) and weight 22–31 kg (49–68 lb).

Left and Below
This fast dog is used as a race dog as well as a hare courser.

BREED INFORMATION

NAME	Mudi
OTHER NAMES	Hungarian Mudi
OFFICIAL RECOGNITION	FCI Group 1
COLOUR VARIATIONS	Usually black, sometime white or black and white

Mudi

HEIGHT 36-51 cm (14-20 in)

Working
GROUP   COAT CARE
medium
SIZE   FEEDING

USED ORIGINALLY for flock guarding, herding and boar hunting, the Mudi is now primarily owned by cattle breeders for herding and as a watchdog. Compared to other Hungarian breeds the Mudi is very rare and would be in danger of extinction were it not for a handful of dedicated breeders. This is an efficient, adaptable breed rarely seen outside its homeland.

Conformation was stabilised early in the twentieth century, standards having been written down in accordance with the breed's original traits, as until the 1930s all Hungarian herdsmen's dogs were classified together. This lively dog is high-tempered and smart, primarily a worker and very much aware of its own territory which it defends boldly. First and foremost a working breed, it is important that owners involve their Mudis in some sort of activity such as obedience, agility or as some kind of service dog. Easy to train, the Mudi can live with other domestic animals and gets attached to its own family. The fairly long, curly hair is not difficult to look after as it is 'dirt-proof' and only needs brushing. Height is 36–51 cm (14–20 in) and weight 8–13 kg (18–29 lb).

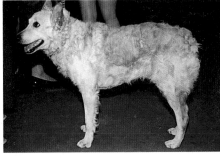

Left
Dedicated breeding is restoring the numbers of this breed, which is used for herding cattle and as a watchdog.

Working

GROUP **COAT CARE**

medium

SIZE **FEEDING**

Pumi

HEIGHT 33-48 cm (13-19 in)

○○○○○○○○○○○○○○○○○○○○○○○○○○○

BREED INFORMATION

NAME	Hungarian Pumi
OFFICIAL RECOGNITION	FCI Group 1
COLOUR VARIATIONS	Grey; Black; White; Cream

Top and Right
With a very distinct look and an amiable disposition, the Pumi is an endearing dog.

THE ATTRACTIVE Pumi was created from a cross between the Hungarian Puli, which has a corded coat, and the softer coated German Spitz. Mentioned by name in 1815 it was not divided from the other Hungarian herdsmen's dogs until the 1930s. The Pumi was used mainly to drove cattle rather than to guard them, but is a breed which watches its own territory carefully and a gives a noisy report on anything unusual. The Pumi is a working dog and benefits from activity in life.

The head and ears of this breed give the Pumi a very special look. The erect ears have unusual drooping points with tufts of hair. Although this breed can be slightly reserved with strangers it is a sociable, jolly dog which loves being at home surrounded by familiar faces. Rather terrier-like in appearance, the coat is quite harsh and curly and must be one solid colour all over. Whatever the coat colour, the eyes must be dark and the pigment black or dark grey. The height is 33–48 cm (13–19 in) and the weight around 10–15 kg (22–33 lb).

Hound

GROUP **COAT CARE**

large

SIZE **FEEDING**

Transylvanian Hound

HEIGHT 00-00 cm (00-00 in)

○○○○○○○○○○○○○○○○○○○○○○○○○○

BREED INFORMATION

NAME	Transylvanian Hound
OTHER NAMES	Erdélyi Kopó
OFFICIAL RECOGNITION	FCI Group 6
COLOUR VARIATIONS	Black and tan; Tri-colour

THIS FAVOURED HOUND is believed to have arrived in the Transylvanian mountains with those who travelled from Russia and from the Balkans to conquer new territory. It has remained much the same for over 1,000 years and was once prized by Hungarian nobility and kings. Unfortunately those dogs in what is now Romania were killed on government orders in 1947 because they, just like the Hungarian Greyhound, which suffered the same fate, provided a reminder of Hungarian occupation. Some representatives of the Transylvanian Hound survived in Hungary and in Slovakia and serious attempts are being made to revive the breed.

Originally this dog was used to hunt bear and is still used as a hunting dog today, and also as a watch dog. A substantially built animal, its size varies greatly, with height from 45–65 cm (18–26 in) and weight 22–35 kg (48–77 lb). The head somewhat resembles that of a heavy-headed Dobermann and the brown, oval eyes have a look of concern. The coat is short but dense and the colour is black and tan or tri-coloured.

HUNGARIAN PULI

Under the FCI the Hungarian Puli is divided by colours of white or black, grey and fawn.

ICELAND
Iceland Sheepdog

HEIGHT 31-41 cm (12-16 in)

Working

GROUP **COAT CARE**

medium

SIZE **FEEDING**

THE ICELAND Sheepdog is the country's only indigenous breed and most probably a direct descendent of the Buhund which was introduced to the country by Scandinavians. Unfortunately, before effective treatment was available for tapeworm, dogs were badly infested and were banned from the capital, Reykjavik. The Iceland Sheepdog was developed for herding and this instinct still survives today. Because of its alertness, the breed makes a good watchdog but is also naturally loving and can also be a very devoted companion.

Not a large herding dog, standing 31–41 cm (12–16 in) and weighing 9–14 kg (20–30 lb), this breed is none the less sturdy and with well-developed double dew claws, similar to those of the Norwegian Lundehund. The Iceland Sheepdog has an alert expression, emanating from medium sized, dark brown eyes. The coat is of medium length, coarse, thick and standing-off from the body. Colours are various, described as above, and may be with or without markings.

Left and Below
Iceland's only indigenous breed has strong herding instincts and is a good watchdog as it is naturally alert.

IRELAND
Kerry Beagle

HEIGHT 55-61 cm (22-24 in)

Hound

GROUP **COAT CARE**

large

SIZE **FEEDING**

ONE OF THE MOST ANCIENT of Irish dog breeds, the Kerry Beagle is believed to have descended from the Old Southern Hound and probably goes back to a dog referred to as gadhar in old Irish texts. This dog was used to find scent game by ground scent and to 'start' the game, then followed by larger hounds. The Kerry Beagle today seems to have been cross-bred with the French hounds, Chien d'Ariège and St Hubert but detailed pedigrees go back to 1794. Still used for hunting hare, this breed always fans out in a large circle when casting and now also takes part in drag trials. It has only recently been recognised by the Irish Kennel Club.

With its broad head and long ears, the eyes of the Kerry Beagle are bright and intelligent, varying in their shade of brown. This is a breed which always suggests vigilance, endurance and speed. Height is about 56–61 cm (22–24 in) with weight up to 27 kg (60 lb). Although black and tan has been considered the classic colour, the coat can be blue mottled and tan, black, tan and white or just tan and white. The 'music' of a Kerry Beagle pack can be heard for miles around.

Above and Left
This Irish hound has very loud cry when hunting in its pack.

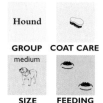
Hound

GROUP **COAT CARE**

medium

SIZE **FEEDING**

Istrian Short-haired Hound

HEIGHT 46-54 cm (18-21.5 in)

BREED INFORMATION	
NAME	Istrian Short-haired Hound
OTHER NAMES	Istarski Kratkodlaki Gonic,
	Istrian Setter
OFFICIAL RECOGNITION	FCI Group 6
COLOUR VARIATIONS	White with yellow or orange markings

THE ISTRIAN HOUND was developed by crossing the Phoenician sighthounds with European scenthounds and it hails from the Balkan region bordering Italy and Austria. It is believed that original breeding may have taken place by monks for certainly it is known that smooth-coated hounds were sent from the country now known as Slovenia to French monasteries. Able to track blood even several days old, the Istrian Hound is much admired for its ability in blood trailing, with game including fox, hare, rabbit and wild boar.

The smooth coat is short and fine and one of the principal distinctions between this and the other similar breeds is the coat coloration. The main colour is white with yellow or orange markings, primarily on the ears. The ears are broad and hang flatly on the side of the head, and the eyes are dark and oval. Height is 46–54 cm (18–21.5 in) and weight 16–23.5 kg (35–52 lb).

Right
An excellent nose allows this Hound to trail game well.

Hound

GROUP **COAT CARE**

medium

SIZE **FEEDING**

Istrian Coarse-haired Hound

HEIGHT 46-58.5 cm (18-23 in)

BREED INFORMATION	
NAME	Istrian Coarse-haired Hound
OTHER NAMES	Istarski Ostrodlaki Gonic
OFFICIA RECOGNITION	FCI Group 6
COLOUR VARIATIONS	White with yellow or orange markings

Right
The Coarse-haired Hound hunts for fox, rabbits, hare and even wild boar.

THE CREATION OF this breed, like that of its smooth-haired cousin, goes back to Phoenician sighthounds and European scenthounds but in the mid-nineteenth century blood of the French Griffon

Vendéen was introduced in an aim to improve the breed's voice. This created a rather different hound, slightly larger and a more weather resistant animal because of the coat. The temperament is also rather different, this breed being more difficult to train because of its willfulness, hence taking more patience in training and being kept usually as a hunting animal rather than as a companion dog. Again renowned for blood trailing, the Istrian Coarse-haired Hound hunts fox, hare, rabbit and wild boar.

Of the same colour as the short-haired dog, the wiry coat is 5–8 cm (2–3 in) long, with a woolly undercoat. The forepart of the lower jaw is rounded, and the ear broaden in the middle but hang without fold. Height is 46–58.5 cm (18–23 in) and weight 16–25.5 kg (35–56 lb).

ITALY
Cane Corso

HEIGHT 56-71 cm (22-28 in)

Working

GROUP   COAT CARE

large

SIZE   FEEDING

BREED FACT:
The Cane Corso shows its Mastiff blood in its massive size and strong head.

THE CANE CORSO is a recreation of the Cane di Macellaio which was an old Italian herding breed living in Sicily. This old breed was certainly used to drove cattle to the slaughterers and it is likely that it was also used for fighting purposes. This is a highly trainable breed, now often used as a guard dog or as a companion, as the breed's temperament is reputed to be sound. However, it can be aggressive with strangers so needs firm and sensible handling and benefits from early socialisation.

This mastiff does not have such loose skin as some similar breeds but the head is broad and the skull wide, with a square muzzle. The ears are triangular or cropped as fashion demands in countries where this is permissible. This large dog, standing 56–71 cm (22–28 in) and varying in weight from 36–63.5 kg (80–140 lb), is muscular, with a large body and powerful motion when running. Many shades of brown and brindle colours are acceptable in the thick, dense, harsh coat.

Left
This large dog requires careful training and sensible handling as it is very powerful.

Cirneco
dell'Etna

HEIGHT 16.5-50 cm (16.5-19.5 in)

Hound

GROUP   COAT CARE

medium

SIZE   FEEDING

SIMILAR IN APPEARANCE to the Pharaoh and Ibizan Hounds, the Cirneco dell'Etna is considerably smaller but has identical roots in Egypt. It is believed to have arrived in Sicily some 2,000 years ago, since when it has bred true to type due largely to its isolation. Although primarily a sighthound, the breed is also capable of tracking by scent and uses sound too, while hunting. Rabbit and hare are the breed's speciality but being a silent breed it can also hunt feathered game.

Also used as a watchdog, the Cirneco is content to sleep outdoors in warm weather but, as it needs plenty of exercise, it is not always a suitable breed for a town. This breed is not easy to train and needs careful introduction to other dogs and children, but is a lively and friendly companion. It height is 42–50 cm (16.5–19.5 in) and weight 8–12 kg (18–26 lb) and the short, glossy coat has a rustic appearance but is without feathering.

Left
With the appearance of a small Pharoah Hound, this dog is hard to train and needs a great deal of stimulus and exercise.

Working
GROUP

COAT CARE

medium
SIZE

FEEDING

Romagna Water Dog

HEIGHT 41-49 cm (16-19.5 in)

BREED INFORMATION	
NAME	Romagna Water Dog
OTHER NAMES	Lagoto Romagnolo
OFFICIAL RECOGNITION	FCI Group 8 (provisional)
COLOUR VARIATIONS	Shades of white; Various shades of brown; Orange

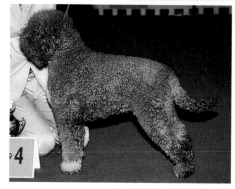

Right
The dense coat of this breed requires clipping at least once a year to prevent felting.

THE ROMAGNA Water Dog is an ancient breed of water retrieving dog, used in the lowlands of Comacchio and the marshlands of Ravenna. Because the marshlands were drained and changed to arable land, the dog also changed from being a water-dog to a truffle dog, and is an excellent worker both in flat open country and on hills.

This sturdy, robust breed has a dense, curly coat of woolly texture with a visible, waterproof undercoat. If not cut, the hair has a tendency to 'felt' so the coat must be completely clipped at least once a year in addition to which the felting and undercoat needs periodic removal. Skin pigmentation is light to dark brown, complementing the coat colour which can be dingy white or white, white with liver-brown or orange markings, liver-brown roan, liver-brown or orange. Even the head and cheeks are thickly covered with hair. Height is 41–49 cm (16–19.5 in) and weight 11–16 kg (24–35 lb). This is a keen, affectionate dog, a loyal companion and good at giving warning.

Utility
GROUP

COAT CARE

small
SIZE

FEEDING

Volpino Italiano

HEIGHT 27-30 cm (11-12 in)

BREED INFORMATION	
NAME	Volpino Italiano
OTHER NAMES	Cane de Quirinale
OFFICIAL RECOGNITION	FCI Group 5
COLOUR VARIATIONS	White; Fawn; Black

Right
The Italian Volpino shows many of the characteristics of the Spitz-type breeds.

SOME CONSIDER THE VOLPINO to be a descendent of the German Spitz, while others believe the Volpino is its ancestor. the breed was completely developed in Italy, the name meaning little fox. This was a favourite among Italy's womenfolk for many centuries, indeed some of the dogs wore ivory bracelets as a symbol of the owner's love.

Although small, some 27–30 cm (11–12 in) high and weighing 4–5 kg (9–11 lb), this is a good watch-dog which can be trained in obedience, though it has a tendency to bark if not controlled properly. Not much exercise is necessary but the coat needs careful attention. This is a good natured, loyal breed, rather suspicious of strangers. The head is stronger than the Pomeranian and the eyes larger; but the ruff is less dense, but the tail curls over the back and the small, triangular ears are erect like those of any spitz.

JAPAN
Hokkaïdo

HEIGHT 45·5-51.5 cm (18-20.50 in)

Utility

GROUP | COAT CARE

large

SIZE | FEEDING

THE HOKKAÏDO IS BELIEVED to have originated from the medium sized Japanese dogs which accompanied migrants from Honshu, Japan's main island, to Hokkaïdo around 1140. The breed was designated as a 'natural monument' in 1937 and took on the name of the area. Another name for this breed is the Ainu-ken because the Ainu who were the former inhabitants of Hokkaïdo used to breed these same dogs to hunt bears and other animals.

The physique of this sturdily built, well-boned breed enables it to withstand severe cold and heavy snowfalls. It is a dog of noteworthy endurance kept primarily as a companion and watchdog, often kept outside in Japan, attached to a rope or a chain. It is an alert, bold breed and can be highly vocal.

Being one of the spitz breeds, this dog has typically spitz-like ears and tail. Its outercoat is harsh and straight, the undercoat soft and dense and the hair on the tail is fairly long and off-standing. Height is 45.5 cm–51.5 cm 18–20.5 in) and weight 20–30 kg (45–65 lb).

Left
This is a strong and sturdy breed with great powers of endurance.

Japanese Terrier

HEIGHT 32.5-33.5 cm (13-13.5 in)

Terrier

GROUP | COAT CARE

small

SIZE | FEEDING

THE JAPANESE TERRIER was created by mating Smooth-haired Fox Terriers, exported to Nagasaki from Holland in the seventeenth century, to small pointers or small native dogs. They were kept primarily as lap-dogs in Japanese ports such as Kobe and Yokohama but, being terriers, they make good ratters and are good at retrieving too. Planned breeding began around 1920 and by 1930, type had become fixed. Not a numerically strong breed, even in its homeland, this is a resourceful little dog which makes an amusing companion. Because numbers are declining a preservation society has been formed in Japan to help this and other Japanese breeds. The high-set ears have natural folds and the medium sized dark eyes look thoroughly alert amid the head of shiny black hair with black nose. The rest of the coat is predominantly white with random speckling and all of it is short. Standing 32.5–33.5 cm (13 in) high and weighing 4.5–6 kg (10–13 lb) this smart breed deserves to live on.

Left
Sadly, this is another dog breed who is in decline but a preservation society has been set up in Japan to boost numbers.

Gundog

GROUP   **COAT CARE**

medium

SIZE   **FEEDING**

Kai

HEIGHT 46-58 cm (18-23 in)

BREED FACT:

The Kai is an ancient breed that developed in an isolated area, so has several unusually primitive characteristics.

Right

The breed is now used as a watchdog but is also becoming popular as a companion.

BREED INFORMATION

NAME	Kai
OTHER NAMES	Kai Inu, Tora Inu
OFFICIAL RECOGNITION	FCI Group 5
COLOUR VARIATIONS	All brindle colours, preferably well-defined

DEVELOPED AS A hunting dog in the province of Kai on the Japanese island of Honshu, this is an ancient breed, although not recognised until 1934. Its homeland is surrounded by mountains so the Kai remained geographically isolated and was used by professional big game hunters for deer and wild boar. A competent watchdog and legendary for its courage, the Kai was once thought too primitive to be a family pet, but in recent years it has proved to be a good family companion. It is, however, reserved with strangers but is generally friendly with people and not aggressive with other dogs. Falling in size between the Akita and Shiba Inu, ranging from 46–58 cm (18–23 in) in height and weighing 16–18 kg (35–40 lb), the Kai is a sturdy, muscular dog of exceptional courage and agility. The tail may be carried over the back, or in a sickle position. The brindle coat of the Kai has given this breed the nickname, Tora Dog, as tora means tiger. Well-defined brindle is strongly preferred but some white is allowed in specified places.

Gundog

GROUP   **COAT CARE**

medium

SIZE   **FEEDING**

Kishu

HEIGHT 43-51 cm (17-22 in)

Below

The Kishu was once designated a national treasure in Japan.

BREED INFORMATION

NAME	Kishu
OFFICIAL RECOGNITION	FCI Group 5
COLOUR VARIATIONS	Various solid colours

THE KISHU ORIGINATED from the medium sized dogs which existed in Japan in ancient times and became established as a breed in mountainous districts in Kishu, taking the name of the region in which it was bred. This breed is used for hunting, primarily wild boar but at one time it was also used for deer. Unfortunately following the First World War this breed's popularity fell somewhat when the larger, stronger German Shepherd Dog came to people's notice in Japan. In 1934 the Kishu was designated a 'natural monument'. Very much one of the spitz group of breeds, the closest relatives of the Kishu are the Shikoku and Ainu dogs.

Originally Kishu coats were marked with conspicuous colours such as red, sesame or brindle but from 1934 only solid colours were allowed and by 1945 marked coats had completely disappeared. Now white coats are also found in this breed. The coat is short, straight and coarse with a thick undercoat and fringing on the tail and cheeks. Height is 43–51 cm (17–22 in) and weight 18.5–27.5 kg (40–60 lb).

```
○ ○ ○ ○ ○ ○ ○ ○ ○ ○ ○ ○ ○ ○ ○ ○ ○ ○ ○ ○ ○ ○ ○ ○
     B R E E D   I N F O R M A T I O N
```

NAME	Shikoku
OTHER NAMES	Kochi-ken
OFFICIAL RECOGNITION	FCI Group 5
COLOUR VARIATIONS	Sesame; Black sesame; Red sesame

Shikoku

HEIGHT 43-55 cm (17-21.5 in)

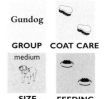

Gundog

GROUP **COAT CARE**

medium

SIZE **FEEDING**

BREED FACT:
As a breed, this dog tends to dominate others but still shows deference towards its master.

THE SHIKOKU goes back to medium sized dogs which existed in Japan in ancient times and was bred mainly as a hunting dog, primarily for boar in the mountainous Kochi district. There used to be three varieties of this breed – Awa, Hongawa and Hata – each name relating to the place in which it was bred. These tough dogs are agile enough to run through mountainous terrain and are characterised by their sesame-coloured coats. In 1937 the breed took its present name and was designated a 'natural monument'.

This enthusiastic hunter is docile towards its master but rather stubborn and has a tendency to dominate other breeds. Typical of the spitz breeds, the small, triangular ears incline slightly forward and are firmly pricked, while the tail is set-on high, either vigorously curled or curved like a sickle. The relatively small, triangular eyes are set wide apart, and dark brown in colour. The outercoat is rather harsh and straight, the undercoat soft and dense, with fairly long hair on the tail. Height is 43–55 cm (17–21.5 in) and weight roughly 15–20 kg (38–44 lb).

Below

The Tosa was bred as a fighting dog and has a reputation for deep-seated aggression.

```
○ ○ ○ ○ ○ ○ ○ ○ ○ ○ ○ ○ ○ ○ ○ ○ ○ ○ ○ ○ ○ ○ ○
     B R E E D   I N F O R M A T I O N
```

NAME	Tosa
OTHER NAMES	Tosa Inu, Tosa Fighting Dog, Japanese Fighting Dog, Japanese Mastiff, Tosa-Ken, Tosa-Token
OFFICIAL RECOGNITION	FCI Group 2
COLOUR VARIATIONS	Solid red or fawn

Tosa

HEIGHT 62-65 cm (24-25.5 in)

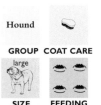

Hound

GROUP **COAT CARE**

large

SIZE **FEEDING**

BRED ORIGINALLY in Tosa, in Japan's Kochi prefecture, the Tosa is a result of crossing Shikoku Fighting Dogs with Bull Dogs (1872), Mastiffs (1874), German Pointers (1876), Great Danes (1924), Bull Terriers and even Saint Bernards. The aim was to increase the size and strength of the local dogs so that they were not habitually defeated in dog-fighting sports by European breeds. The breed became a stoic fighter which would rarely even whimper or scream, but would fight to the death. Such fights were ceremonial occasions requiring stamina and fighting instinct.

Although now illegal in many countries including Japan, pit fights still take place in rural regions of Japan and the Tosa is still used for these. Banned from many countries because of the breed's fighting instinct, the robust, powerful Tosa stands 62–65 cm (24.5–25.5 in) high and weighs 89.5–90.4 cm (197–200 lb) making it important that owners are skilled handlers, physically able to handle and mentally dominate this large dog. The breed gives no ground and attacks head on. Preferred colours for the short, hard, dense coat are red or fawn, but slight white and red markings are permitted.

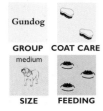

Gundog

GROUP | COAT CARE

medium

SIZE | FEEDING

Korean Jindo Dog

HEIGHT 46-55 cm (18-22 in)

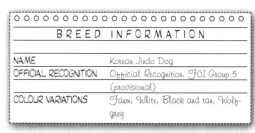

BREED INFORMATION	
NAME	Korean Jindo Dog
OFFICIAL RECOGNITION	Official Recognition: FCI Group 5 (provisional)
COLOUR VARIATIONS	Fawn; White; Black and tan; Wolf-grey

Below and Right
This dog looks to have escaped possible extinction as it has been designated a Korean national treasure.

Bottom
This elegant sighthoud from Mali may be up to 3,000 years old.

THE JINDO IS THE MOST famous of Korea's dogs and is named after the southern Korean island from which the breed originally came. It was only in 1938, during the Japanese Colonial era, that the Jindo was officially recognised and it has been designated Natural Treasure number 53. With its erect ears and sickle shaped tail, the breed stands 46–55 cm (18–22 in) high and weighs 15–19 kg (33–42 lb). The double coat, usually fawn or white, has a soft, dense, light undercoat which is shorter

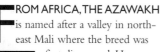

than the outercoat. This dog has an expression of alertness and dignity. It is faithful to its master. The future of this breed now looks bright.

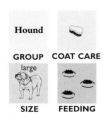

Hound

GROUP | COAT CARE

large

SIZE | FEEDING

Azawakh

HEIGHT 60-74 cm (23.5-29 in)

BREED INFORMATION	
NAME	Azawakh
OTHER NAMES	Tuareg Sloughi, Azi
OFFICIAL RECOGNITION	FCI Group 10
COLOUR VARIATIONS	Various

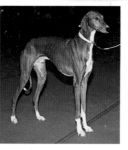

FROM AFRICA, THE AZAWAKH is named after a valley in northeast Mali where the breed was first discovered. However, this sight hound has lived for a long while across most of North Africa, acting as companion and protector of the Tuareg Bedouins, as well as assisting them in hunting. Even as puppies these dogs learn to chase animals and are socialised by spending time with young pack members who are already able to chase away or kill any intruder. It has been suggested from images that the Azawakh has existed for as long as 3,000 years but its genetic relationship with other sight hounds is still not certain. These dogs were introduced to Europe and to the United States during the twentieth century.

Proud, alert and attentive, the Azawakh has a natural tendency to guard and is instinctively reserved with strangers although gentle with loved ones. Muscles are visible under the breed's dry, fine skin and there is a pronounced fineness of outline and a dancing gait. Standing 60–74 cm (23.5–29 in) high and weighing 17–25 kg (37–55 lb) the smooth, taught skin is covered by a short, silky coat. Colours vary but include cream to dark red, white, chocolate, black, brindle and grizzle. White markings are allowed.

MOROCCO
Aidi

HEIGHT 53-61 cm (21-24 in)

Gundog

GROUP   **COAT CARE**

large

SIZE   **FEEDING**

FOR CENTURIES IN MOROCCO the Aidi has been used as a guard by nomads to protect their livestock from predators. The good scenting powers of this breed have also been used for hunting

purposes, as it is an efficient tracking animal, although other dogs such as the Sloughi are used to actually bring down the prey. This is a typical mountain dog which is well-adapted to the region's harsh weather conditions – high temperatures during the daytime and extremely cold temperatures at night.

The Aidi is also a capable watchdog and is easy to train, although it has a great deal of energy and is alert, highly strung and curious about things, so needs plenty to keep it occupied. Although sometimes kept as a companion, the breed is not yet really considered a household dog. Standing 53–61 cm (21–24 in) high and weighing 23–24 kg (50–55 lb), this is a relatively lean but well-muscled and deep-chested dog, doubtless related to several of the other livestock breeds. The strong coat of varying colours is about 5 cm (2 in) in length.

Left
The Aidi is well-adapted to the country's rugged, terrain and inhospitality.

NORWAY
Halden Hound

HEIGHT 51-64 cm (20-250 in)

Hound

GROUP   **COAT CARE**

large

SIZE   **FEEDING**

THE HALDEN HOUND was developed in the south of Norway in the area near Halden. Local hounds along with the English Foxhound have been used in its makeup, the breed standard not being fixed until the 1950s. This is not a pack hound but hunts individually with its owner. It is used primarily for hare hunting and also as a companion dog but is little known in countries outside Norway.

With its placid disposition this is an affectionate dog which is rarely snappy, but it should be carefully supervised when initially introduced to children. Of generous size, this breed's height is 51–64 cm (20–25 in) and it weighs 23–29 kg (51–64 lb). The legs are muscular and well-boned and the oval feet have well-arched toes. Because the coat is smooth, shiny and

very fine, the Halden Hound should be protected from the extreme cold. Typically hound-like in appearance the ears are pendant and in length reach to the middle of the muzzle, while the eyes have a serene expression. The tri-coloured coat has predominant black and tan markings on a white ground.

Left
This sleek dog is of an affectionate nature and settles with children if introductions are handled well.

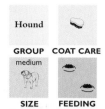

Hound
GROUP　**COAT CARE**
medium
SIZE　**FEEDING**

Hygen Hound

HEIGHT 47-58 cm (18.5-23 in)

BREED INFORMATION	
NAME	Hygen Hound
OTHER NAMES	Hygenhund
OFFICIAL RECOGNITION	FCI Group 6
COLOUR VARIATIONS	Black and chestnut; Yellow and red; Chestnut

Top and Right
A strong hunting dog, this Hound has a mixture of blood which comes from dogs bred all over Europe.

DEVELOPED IN THE 1830s for hare hunting, the Hygen Hound, named after its first breeder, is a retrieving dog which came about by crossing hounds from northern Germany with those dogs from Scandinavia. These included the Ringerike Hound which is now extinct. The breed is still used mainly as a hunter of small game at which it excels, but it is not a very popular companion animal.

This is rather a short-backed hound with medium sized brown eyes which have an earnest expression and a black nose with wide nostrils. Although a reliable watchdog and a breed which gets along reasonably well with other dogs, it does have a reputation for a tendency to snap and to bite. The breed needs plenty of exercise and although seemingly con-

tent to live outdoors, needs protection from excessive cold because of its short coat which is smooth, shiny and dense. Height is 47–58 cm (18.5–23 in) and weight 20–24 kg (44–53 lb).

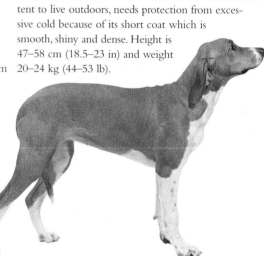

Hound
GROUP　**COAT CARE**
medium
SIZE　**FEEDING**

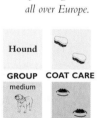

Norwegian Hound

HEIGHT 47-57 cm (18.5-22.5 in)

BREED INFORMATION	
NAME	Norwegian Hound
OTHER NAMES	Dunker
OFFICIAL RECOGNITION	FCI Group 6
COLOUR VARIATIONS	Various

THE NORWEGIAN HOUND, or Dunker as it is also known, was developed to hunt and retrieve hares, mainly by scent, and it is a breed which can work over a variety of terrain. Norwegian breeder, Wilhelm Dunker, bred the Russian Harlequin Hound, which carried the merle gene, with other strong, reliable scenthounds creating a breed with a straight, hard dense coat which is not too short and of interesting colour. It may be black or blue marbled, with pale fawn or white markings. A warm brown or predominant black colouring is less desirable, but acceptable.

This is described as a rectangular dog and it is important that the depth of the chest is half the

Right
Bred as a retriever and to hunt by scent, this Hound works well over rough ground.

height at the withers. The clean, noble head is of good length and not wedge-shaped, with parallel planes. The rather large, round eyes are dark but wall eyes are permitted in blue marbled dogs. The overall impression is bright, with a calm, earnest expression. The moderately wide ears hang close to the head and are moderately long. Height is 47–57 cm (18.5–22.5 in) and weight 16–22 kg (35–49 lb).

Another Norwegian breed is the **Black Norwegian Elkhound,** also known as the Norsk Elghund (Sort). This is generally a little smaller than the better-known Elkhound, standing some 46–51 cm (18–20 in) high and weighing 17.5–18.5 kg (38–41 lb), although some can be just a little heavier. Although similar in structure, the chest is less deep than that of the Elkhound and the coat, short and thick, is not quite so dense.

BREED INFORMATION

NAME	Peruvian Hairless Dog, Inca Hairless
OTHER NAMES	Perro sin pelo del Perú
OFFICIAL RECOGNITION	FCI Group 5
COLOUR VARIATIONS	Various

PERU

Hairless Dog

HEIGHT 59 cm (23 in)

Hound
GROUP **COAT CARE**
large
SIZE **FEEDING**

THE PERUVIAN HAIRLESS DOG is believed to have some connection with sighthound breeds taken to the Americas by the Conquistadors. However, taking into account statues dating back to before that time, other authorities believe that it is descended from the Mexican Hairless Dog, also known as the Xoloitzcuintli while still others even say the breed evolved from North American timber wolves. The Peruvian dog was probably introduced to the area by Ecuadorian sea-traders.

Looking rather like a small deer in structure, there are three sizes of this breed, varying widely and weighing 4–8 kg (9–18 lb), 8–12 kg (18–26 lb) and 12–25 kg (26–55 lb) respectively. The breed is hairless and needs to be oiled for the prevention of sunburn, but there is a little longer hair on the head

and coated specimens do appear from time to time. The ears are erect and not very large, and the eyes are expressive and gentle.

Another Peruvian breed is the Inca Orchid but some people consider this the same breed as the Peruvian Hairless. In the Inca Orchid there are two varieties – hairless and coated – though the Incan nobility favoured the latter, keeping them as pets. In these, the coat can be as short as that of a Dobermann or as long as that of a Collie. Both have both speed and strength, they are gentle, quiet and clean.

Below
The bald skin of this dog needs to be oiled to prevent it from suffering from sunburn.

BREED INFORMATION

NAME	Polish Hound
OTHER NAMES	Ogar Polski
OFFICIAL RECOGNITION	FCI Group 6
COLOUR VARIATIONS	Tan with black or dark grey

POLAND

Polish Hound

HEIGHT 56-66 cm (22-26 in)

Hound
GROUP **COAT CARE**
large
SIZE **FEEDING**

ALTHOUGH IT IS LIKELY that the history of the Polish Hound goes back to the St Hubert Hound which may have been bred with German hounds, little is really known of the breed's history, although a similar but

smaller hunting dog, the Polski Pies Gonczy, died out during the Second World War. The Polish Hound came close to extinction itself in the war years but Polish hunters managed to keep the breed alive because it is a exceptionally good tracking animal, and therefore very useful.

Of strong and compact build, this hound has a rather heavy, nobly chiselled head and has powerful bone structure, being built for power and endurance rather than speed. Its height is 56–66 cm (22–26 in) and its weight 25–32 kg (55–71 lb). The medium length coat is thick with a dense undercoat, and the body colour is black or very dark grey, while the head, ears, legs and thighs are varied shades of tan. Small specific areas of white are also permitted. On the trail this dog's voice is sonorous and pure.

Left and Below
The Polish Hound relies on its strength and abilities of endurance rather than speed when hunting.

Working

GROUP **COAT CARE**

large

SIZE **FEEDING**

Tatra Shepherd Dog

HEIGHT 61-87 cm (24-34 in)

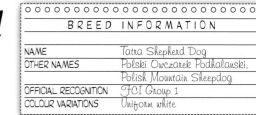

○○○○○○○○○○○○○○○○○○○○○○○○○○○○

BREED INFORMATION

NAME	Tatra Shepherd Dog
OTHER NAMES	Polski Owczarek Podhalanski, Polish Mountain Sheepdog
OFFICIAL RECOGNITION	FCI Group 1
COLOUR VARIATIONS	Uniform white

Above
The Tatra lived with the sheep it guarded in the mountains, protecting them from wolves.

BELIEVED TO HAVE ancestry going back to great Asian mastiffs which arrived in Europe more than 1,000 years ago, and related to a number of mountain sheepdogs such as the Hungarian Kuvasz, Slovakian Kuvac and Bergamasco, the Tatra Mountain Sheepdog is a heavily muscled, well-boned herd guarding mountain dog, now used also as a companion animal. This is an aloof, guarding breed but it has been used to pull carts and has even been employed for police and military work. In its natural habitat this dog lives and travels with

the flock and even has its coat shorn at the same time as the flock animals.

A very large breed standing 61–87 cm (24–34 in) high and weighing 45–69 kg (99–152 lb) although some apparently weigh less, the Tatra Mountain Dog is happy to protect its owner or flock from dangerous predators such as the wolf, or even from humans. This intelligent breed with its long, thick, straight or slightly waved hair and profuse ruff thrives in a cold climate and is characteristically a calm dog with a rather independent nature.

Another Portuguese breed recognised provisionally by the FCI is the Polish Greyhound, known also as the Chart Polski. This is in the Short-haired Sighthound section of Group 10 but, being only provisionally accepted, is excluded from CACIB awards.

Working

GROUP **COAT CARE**

large

SIZE **FEEDING**

PORTUGAL
Cão Fila de São Miguel

HEIGHT 48-60 cm (18.5-23.5 in)

○○○○○○○○○○○○○○○○○○○○○○○○○○○○

BREED INFORMATION

NAME	Cão Fila de São Miguel
OTHER NAMES	Cattle Dog of the São Miguel Island (Azores), Cow Dog
OFFICIAL RECOGNITION	FCI Group 1 (provisional)
COLOUR VARIATIONS	Fawn, Grey and Yellow brindle

THE CÃO DE Fila São Miguel is linked to the extinct Fila da Terciera and has been known since the beginning of the nineteenth century. Now re-established and recognised, it is mainly found in the island of St Miguel in the Azores where the breed is very

Right
Sharp and protective in temperament, these dogs are very loyal to their masters.

popular and used extensively as a cattle dog and for herding. Strong in temperament, this is an excellent watchdog with a massive, strong, square head and ears which are usually cropped to have rounded tips. When uncropped they are of medium size, triangular,

pendant and a little away from the cheeks.

This breed has a very sharp temperament but is docile with its master. It is highly intelligent with a great capacity to learn. Because of the breed's function as a cattle dog it bites at the heels but with no intention of doing harm to the animals; however, when handling stray cattle this dog sometimes bites higher up. Height ranges from 48–60 cm (18.5–23.4 in). The coat is smooth, dense and short with strong texture and slight fringing. The range of brindle colours may have specific white markings.

Castro Laboreiro Dog

HEIGHT 51-61cm (20-24 in)

Working
GROUP   COAT CARE
large
SIZE   FEEDING

ALTHOUGH THE HISTORY of the Castro Laboreiro Dog is not entirely clear, it is likely that root stock included small, dark, smooth-coated Estrela Mountain Dogs and that these may possibly have been crossed with local breeds, possibly including those of mastiff-type. The Estrelas would have moved to Portugal's flat northern lowlands for winter grazing. On the northern tip of Portugal is a small village called Castro Laboreiro, meaning village of labourers, from which the breed took its name. This sizeable dog, a good

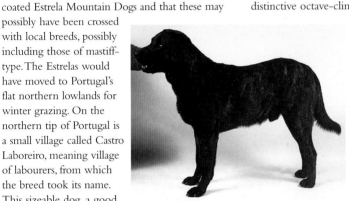

all-weather guardian, still works to protect sheep and cattle from predators and is even tough enough to combat wolves. It makes a good watchdog with a distinctive octave-climbing, chromatic vocalisation.

In general the breed tends to be threatening at first meeting but these dogs' dedication to their masters is proverbial. With a short, heavy, hard and rather dull coat, the eyes have a somewhat severe expression and the medium sized ears are pendant. Height is 61–61 cm (20–24 in) and weight usually 23–34 kg (50–75 lb) although some can weigh as much as 91 kg (90 lb).

BREED FACT:
These dogs can be intimidating on first encounter, but they are known for their loyalty to their master.

Left
Named after a village in northern Portugal, this breed makes a good guard dog.

Portuguese Pointer

HEIGHT 52-56 cm (21-22.50 in)

Gundog
GROUP   COAT CARE
large
SIZE   FEEDING

THE PORTUGUESE Pointer has definitely been in Portugal since the twelfth century, having initially been bred in the royal kennels and those of the gentry, and used to point wounded game and for falconry and the fowling net. From the twelfth to eighteenth century this breed was also popular with lower classes of society who used it widely to point and retrieve game.

Many eventually found their way to England where they played a part in the development of the English Pointer. A standard for the breed was drawn up in 1932. A solidly built dog with superb working ability, demonstrating agility and lightness of movement, this is a natural hunter which searches for game methodically, demonstrating both pleasure and passion. When pointing the dog is indifferent to anything around and when delivering game, from land or water, the dog does not destroy it. Good with children and other dogs, this Pointer is easy to train in obedience. The smooth, firm coat needs little attention but it does require plenty of exercise. Height is 52–56 cm (20.5–22 in) and weight 16–27 kg (35–60 lb).

Left and Below
Originally used to point to wounded game and birds, these dogs are easy to train.

Working

GROUP   COAT CARE

large

SIZE   FEEDING

Portuguese Sheepdog

HEIGHT 42-55 cm (16.5-21.5 in)

BREED INFORMATION	
NAME	Portuguese Sheepdog
OTHER NAMES	Cão da Serra de Aires, 'Monkey Dog'
OFFICIAL RECOGNITION	FCI Group 1
COLOUR VARIATIONS	Yellow; Chestnut; Grey; Fawn; Wolf

Below
*The Podego
Portugês is similar to
its Spanish counter-
part in appearance.*

FOR A LARGE PART of the twentieth century the Portuguese Sheepdog was kept as a companion and herding dog by poor shepherds in Portugal's southern regions, but by the 1970s it had neared extinction. Coming to the attention of dog owners with more funds available in the 1970s, the breed was certainly one of great appeal and now its future seems assured although it is still little known outside Portugal. Particularly in the Alentejo area this breed is used to guard and drive flocks and herds, including sheep, cattle, goats, horses and pigs. An exceptionally intelligent and lively

dog, this is a breed with perceptible hardiness and prudence, very devoted to the shepherd and flock but with a tendency to avoid strangers. The breed's monkey-like attitude and looks have earned it the local name, 'monkey dog'. The long coat is smooth or slightly wavy and forms a long beard, moustache and eyebrows, not covering the eyes. Its texture of coat is like that of a goat, and there is no undercoat or wool. Height is 42–55 cm (16.5–21.5 in) and weight 12–18 kg (26.5–30.5 lb).

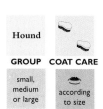

Hound

GROUP   COAT CARE

small,
medium
or large

according
to size

SIZE   FEEDING

Podengo Portugês

HEIGHT 20-56 cm (8-22 in)

BREED INFORMATION	
NAME	Podengo Portugês
OTHER NAMES	Portuguese Warren Hound
OFFICIAL RECOGNITION	FCI Group 5
COLOUR VARIATIONS	Yellow; Tan; Dark grey; White with markings

THE PODENGO PORTUGUÊS, although classified as one breed, has three sizes – large, medium and small – and two coat types: smooth-haired and wire-haired. It is an ancient breed and is popular primarily in northern Portugal, although the large variety, standing 56–71 cm (22–28 in) high and weighing around 30 kg (66 lb), is now rare. The two larger sizes are generally used for hunting rabbit and hare, while the smaller version is used for flushing game and for ratting. It is likely that the breed developed from dogs such as the Pharaoh Hound when they spread to the Iberian Peninsula, but small Iberian wolves may also have played a part in its development. The small Podengo has been bred down from the larger varieties with attention paid primarily to size rather than to coat or colour.

The size of the smallest variety is 20–31 cm (8–12 in) with a weight of 4–6 kg (9–13 lb), while the medium sized dog can be up to 56 cm (22 in) and the large even taller. Colours seem relatively unimportant and the coats may be solid or marked with white. Wire-haired dogs have rather long hair, especially on the body, with a feathered face, muzzle and well-covered ears. The triangular ears are upright, mobile and turn forward in order to catch sound. All like plenty of exercise and can be kept as companion dogs, the small variety being a popular house pet.

Rafeiro of Alentejo

HEIGHT 64-74 cm (25-29 in)

Working

GROUP **COAT CARE**

large

SIZE **FEEDING**

BREED INFORMATION

NAME	Rafeiro of Alentejo
OTHER NAMES	Rafeiro do Alentejo
OFFICIAL RECOGNITION	FCI Group 2
COLOUR VARIATIONS	Black; Wolf-grey; Tawny; Yellow
	Tawny or yellow may have white mark

THE RAFEIRO OF ALENTEJO is an excellent watchdog used on farms and dwellings in Portugal's Alentejo and is much appreciated as a protector of herds. The breed is most vigilant at night time, but is always threatening toward strangers.

With height at 64–74 cm (25–29 in) and weight 35–50 kg (77–110 lb), this is a large breed, slightly longer than it is high and one which is powerful and rustic. The head is bear-like, wider on the top of the skull and narrower at the base, but in proportion with the body size. The small, dark eyes have black pigmented lids and a calm expression, while the ears are set-on high and hang folded at the sides. Movement is heavy, slow and rolling. The coat may be short but is preferably of medium length, heavy, dense, straight and covering the body evenly, right down to the space between the toes. The colours of black, wolf-grey, tawny or yellow have white markings or alternatively a white coat can be marked with any of these colours and can be dappled, streaked or brindled.

The following breeds are also recognised in Britain but certain clarifications, as outlined here, are necessary when found in other countries.

ESTRELA MOUNTAIN DOG
Under the FCI the Estrela is divided by coat into smooth-haired and long-haired.

PORTUGUESE WATER DOG
Under the FCI the Portuguese Water Dog is divided by coat into curly and wavy.

RUSSIA

Black Russian Terrier

HEIGHT 00 cm (0 in)

Terrier

GROUP **COAT CARE**

large

SIZE **FEEDING**

BREED INFORMATION

NAME	Black Russian Terrier
OTHER NAMES	Tchiorny Terrier; Black Terrier;
	Chornyi Terrier
OFFICIAL RECOGNITION	FCI Group 2
COLOUR VARIATIONS	Black; Black with grey hairs

OFFICIALLY RECOGNISED in the 1940s, the Black Russian Terrier was developed at the Red Star Army Kennels in the Soviet Union. Breeds used in its creation included the Giant Schnauzer, Rottweiler and Airedale Terrier although there may have been other breeds too. This new breed was used in scientists' attempts to prove a genetic theory relating to 'acquired characteristics', but the theory was subsequently disproved.

Now used primarily as a protector and guard dog the breed is an aggressive one. Although the strong head is always well-covered with hair and has rough, bushy eyebrows, the length of coat varies considerably from 4–10 cm (1.5–4 in). It is rough, harsh, abundant and thick, forming a mane on neck and withers. The harsh undercoat should also be well-developed. Height is 63–74 cm (25–29 in) and weight ranges considerably from 37–55 kg (80–120 lb). The breed, which has large, well-arched, rounded feet is mainly found in Russia but there are a few in other countries too.

Above
The Rafeiro needs careful handling and can often be aggressive towards strangers.

BREED FACT:
A relatively new breed, the Black Russian Terrier is primarily used as a guard dog and protector.

Working

GROUP

COAT CARE

large

SIZE **FEEDING**

Caucasian Shepherd Dog

HEIGHT 64-72 cm (24.5-28 in)

BREED FACT:
With firm training and discipline, this breed can become an excellent companion dog.

Below Right and left
Commonly used as a guardian of livestock, this is a sturdy and powerful dog.

○○○○○○○○○○○○○○○○○○○○○○○○○○○

BREED INFORMATION

NAME	Caucasian Shepherd Dog
OTHER NAMES	Kavkazskaïa Ovtcharka, Caucasian Mountain Dog
OFFICIAL RECOGNITION	FCI Group 2
COLOUR VARIATIONS	Many combinations

THIS BREED comes from the Caucasus Mountains near the Georgian Republic. It is a large, strong dog with a bear-like appearance which has lived with human companions for several hundred years, though it is possible that its original history dates back to a Mastiff-Spitz cross several thousand years ago. This is Russia's most popular Ovtcharka, now found at many dog shows in Russia and elsewhere in Europe, although the breed's original use as a livestock guardian is on the decline. In the 1960s the Caucasian Sheepdog was used in Germany for patrol along the Berlin Wall where there were 7,000 dogs. Due to challenging climatic conditions these dogs lived in isolation for many centuries, resulting in a natural, healthy and instinctive breed which protected flocks of sheep from both human and animal predators. The breed has a reputation for aggressiveness but with strict discipline and careful socialisation it can become a good companion dog. With height ranging from 64–72 cm (24.5–28 in) and weight from 45–70 kg (99–154 lb), this is a sturdy, well-boned, strong and powerful breed and with deeply set eyes the breed has binocular vision. The coat is thick, dense and coarse.

Hound

GROUP **COAT CARE**

large

SIZE **FEEDING**

Central Asian Shepherd Dog

HEIGHT 60-65 cm (23.5-25.5 in)

○○○○○○○○○○○○○○○○○○○○○○○○○○○

BREED INFORMATION

NAME	Central Asia Shepherd Dog
OTHER NAMES	Sredneasiatskaïa Ovtcharka, Middle Asian Ovtcharka
OFFICIAL RECOGNITION	FCI Group 2
COLOUR VARIATIONS	All colours.

THE CENTRAL ASIAN Shepherd Dog is of greater than average size, with a robust constitution and a strong distrust of strangers. Used as a livestock guardian this dog does not make a good companion animal. The breed is probably descended from Asian mastiffs and has certainly been guarding flocks in central Asia for several hundred years, indeed possibly thousands. It has inhabited a wide region from Russia's Ural mountains eastward to Siberia, and various central Asian republics. Besides being powerful and very sturdy, the Central Asian Sheepdog is athletic and alert. Its character is self-esteemed and imperturbable and this dog has a great memory. The massive head has a broad, flat skull with well developed cheeks but the brow is not pronounced and the lips are thick and overhanging. The coat is straight with medium coarse guard hair and well developed undercoat, but on the muzzle, front of forelegs and hindlegs it is short and smooth. There are two coat varieties: long 7–8 cm (3 in) and shorter 3–5 cm (1.5–2 in). There is no maximum height but dogs must be not less than 65 cm (25.5 in) and bitches not less than 60 cm (23.5 in). Weight ranges from 37–50 kg (80–110 lb).

East Siberian Laika

HEIGHT 56-64 cm (22-25 in)

Gundog
GROUP   COAT CARE
large
SIZE   FEEDING

BREED FACT:
Laikas were breed from spitz-type breeds that were hunters and working dogs.

THE EAST SIBERIAN LAIKA was developed in the nineteenth century by selective breeding of Siberian Spitz dogs who were working sled dogs and also those who were hunters. Now the breed is used as a large game hunter, working with the gun, finding the game and holding it until the hunter arrives, the dog barking meanwhile. The breed can also be used to hunt birds in this way.

This is an even tempered breed and due to its calm personality it can make a fine companion dog. It is also possible to train the East Siberian Laika in obedience work. Well insulated, with a short, dense coat and waterproof undercoat, even the ears and paws are well-covered. This dog also uses its tightly curled tail to keep itself warm. Height is 56–64 cm (22–25 in) and weight 18–23 kg (40–50 lb).

Left
The East Siberian Laika is still used today for hunting and giving tongue.

Russian-European Laïka

HEIGHT 51-61 cm (20-24 in)

Hound
GROUP   COAT CARE
medium
SIZE   FEEDING

Left
This typical spitz-type breed is strong enough to hunt moose and boar.

THE RUSSIAN-EUROPEAN Laika was created by Russian breeders who wished to increase the aggressive nature and power of the Karelian Bear Laika by crossing it with the Utchak Sheepdog. This produced a fearless bear hunter, but one which also hunts moose, boar and wolf. This is an excellent breed for a forest ranger but the breed does not do well in urban situations or with routine human contact so it would not make a suitable companion dog.

With pricked ears and a curled tail, although this uncurls when relaxed, this is indeed a spitz breed, with small, brown fiery eyes giving an alert expression. The muzzle is straight and tapers towards the nose. Height varies from 51–61 cm (20–24 in) and weight is roughly 18.5–23 kg (40–50 lb). The reasonably short coat is straight and stiff, and the colour white with black markings.

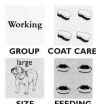

Working

GROUP | COAT CARE

large

SIZE | FEEDING

South Russian Shepherd Dog

HEIGHT 58-65 cm (23-25.5 in)

BREED INFORMATION	
NAME	South Russian Shepherd Dog
OTHER NAMES	South Russian Ovcharka;
	Ioujnorousskaïa Ovtcharka
OFFICIAL RECOGNITION	FCI Group 1
COLOUR VARIATIONS	White and various pastel colours

THE SOUTH RUSSIAN SHEPHERD Dog most probably descends from the Tibetan Mastiff and arrived in Russia centuries ago, having come with invaders from Asia. Originally white dogs were used to protect flocks in Russia and the Ukrane but around 200 years ago smaller Spanish sheepdogs were crossed with these. The breed we know today has long been favoured by the Russian Army as a guard dog. Although mainly known in Russia, a few individuals have found their way to other countries where they are much prized and admired.

This is a robust dog of greater than average size and speed, a protective breed with a genuine distrust of strangers. A well-boned, well-muscled dog, the South Russian Shepherd Dog manages well in different climatic conditions. There is no maximum height specified but dogs are penalised if they fall below the lowest limit with dogs from 60–65 cm (23.5–25.5 in) and bitches 58–62 cm (23–24.5 in). However, some are taller than this. Weight range is generally 55–75 kg (121–165 lb). The long coat is coarse and slightly wavy, with a well developed undercoat. White is the most common colour but the colour can also be light fawn, grey or blue, indeed any light pastel colour with or without white.

Right
The South Russian was used by the Red Army as a guard dog.

Gundog

GROUP | COAT CARE

medium

SIZE | FEEDING

West Siberian Laika

HEIGHT 53-62 cm (21-24 in)

BREED INFORMATION	
NAME	West Siberian Laika
OTHER NAMES	Zapadno-Sibirskaïa Laïka
OFFICIAL RECOGNITION	FCI Group 5
COLOUR VARIATIONS	White; White/black; Tan; Red; Black

OF THE RUSSIAN LAIKA breeds, the West Siberian is the most popular and most numerous. It is a well-established breed which has been used mostly for large game. Such sizeable prey as reindeer, elk and bear all fall within its sphere as a hunter although it can also be used for birds and small game. The most likely explanation for the development of this breed is that hunters in the Ural mountains bred it specifically for the work they required it to carry out. Apart from hunting large game, it is well able to pull enormous weights as a sled dog.

This is a breed which has been used in Russia's medical experimentation work, as well as in space research. With its pricked ears and small brown eyes it has an alert, willing expression. The thick skin, short, thick hair and dense undercoat ensure the necessary insulation. Height is 53–62 cm (21–24 in) and weight 18–23 kg (40–50 lb).

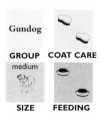

Right
Before opinion changes, this dog was used in medical research in Russia.

Other Russian Breeds

THE MOSCOW TOY TERRIER is an attractive little breed, loveable for its excellent temperament, outstanding trainability and general good health. Many dogs died in Russia during the Second World War but a limited surviving population became the base for a modern Moscow Toy Terrier, although the breed is vary rare. Average height is 20–28 cm (8–11 in) but even smaller dogs are preferred and these can be 15 cm (6 in). The most valued colour is red sable, but this breed can also be black, tan or red. There are two coat varieties, long and short, and the most distinguishing feature of the former is the long hair which falls down to the shoulders from the pricked or semi-pricked ears. The tail is docked.

The origin of the **Russian Hound** is not really known but it is believed that they descended from

Laikas. This hound stands some 56–69 cm (22–27 in) high and weighs 18–32 kg (40–70 lb). Colours are yellow and red, with a black saddle and small white markings, while the coat is short and dense.

Another Russian breed is the **Russian Spaniel**, believed to have been developed from European spaniel breeds, it is a good house pet, faithful and reliable with children and makes a good watchdog. Height is 38–43 cm (15–17 in) and weight 13–18.5 kg (28–40 lb). The coat is silky with fringing.

Top Left
The Moscow Toy Terrier is a rare breed; the long-haired variety has head hair falling over the shoulders.

BREED INFORMATION

NAME	Slovakian Chuvach
OTHER NAMES	Slovensky Cuvac, Slovak Cuvac, Slovensky Kuvac, Tatransky Cuvac
OFFICIAL RECOGNITION	FCI Group 1
COLOUR VARIATIONS	Always white

SLOVAKIA

Chuvach

HEIGHT 55-70 cm (22-27.5 in)

Working

GROUP   COAT CARE

large

SIZE   FEEDING

THE SLOVAKIAN CHUVACH is remarkably similar to the Hungarian Kuvasz and the breeds certain share a similar ancestry. However, the Slovak breed came close to extinction until a veterinary surgeon decide to make an effort to keep the breed alive. His breeding programme commenced after the Second World War and met with success, the breed being internationally recognised in 1969. It is said that this breed originally evolved as a result of a wolf and Greyhound being crossed. Like other similar breeds the Slovakian Chuvach has an ability to kill wolves.

A livestock guardian, this large breed is also popular as a companion as it has a sound, equable temperament and thoroughly enjoys the company of family members. This is, however, a large breed with a thick white coat with dense undercoat, and is there-

fore a dog which needs regular attention. Height generally ranges from 55–70 cm (22–27.5 in) with weight 30–45 kg (66–99 lb) although some are known to be a little larger, weighing up to 48 kg (105 lb).

Left
Although primarily a guard dog, this breed has an equable temperament and will make a good companion to a family.

Hound

GROUP **COAT CARE**

medium

SIZE **FEEDING**

Slovakian Hound

HEIGHT 40-50 cm (16-20 in)

```
BREED INFORMATION

NAME                    Slovakian Hound
OTHER NAMES             Slovensky Kopov, Black Forest
                        Hound
OFFICIAL RECOGNITION    FCI Group 6
COLOUR VARIATIONS       Black and tan
```

ORIGINALLY USED FOR HUNTING wild boar and small vermin, the Slovakian Hound was created by Czech and Slovak hunters following the Second World War. This they did by selectively breeding indigenous mountain dogs to develop a breed capable of working in difficult and rough mountain territory. This is an excellent tracker with a good voice, and is still used against wild boar. Now that Slovakia is independent this breed has stimulated a certain national pride and is now found also at shows, although primarily in the Czech and Slovak Republics.

Standing 40–50 cm (16–20 in) high and weighing 15–20 kg (33–44 lb), the breed is smooth-coated and well-muscled. The medium sized ears are pendant and the deep-set eyes have black eyelids. The feet are oval with well-arched toes. Its temperament is said to resemble that of the Dobermann, despite the fact that this breed has not really played any significant role in the development of the Slovakian Hound.

Right
This is a relatively new hunting dog that has become the source of a degree of nationalist pride in Slovakia.

Hound

GROUP **COAT CARE**

large

SIZE **FEEDING**

Wire-haired Pointing Griffon

HEIGHT 56-68 cm (22-27 in)

```
BREED INFORMATION

NAME                    Slovakian Wire-haired
                        Pointing Griffon
OTHER NAMES             Slovensky Hrubosrsty Stavac (Ohar)
OFFICIAL RECOGNITION    FCI Group 7
COLOUR VARIATIONS       Silver, mouse, or roe grey
```

Right
Despite its recent creation, the Slovensky Pointer has been registered by the FCI.

THE CREATION OF THE Slovensky Pointer did not begin until after the Second World War when the Czesky Fousec was crossed with the German Wire-haired Pointer.

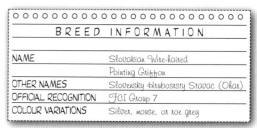

Descendants were then bred with the Weimeraner and by 1975 this new breed had received recognition in Czechoslovakia, followed a few years later by the FCI. Good in all weather conditions, this dog is used for both setting and pointing and is easy to handle. They are still not often seen outside the Czech and Slovak Republics but some have gone to Switzerland for search and rescue work.

This new breed seems certainly to have combined the most pleasing features of all breeds involved in its make-up. The hard, straight coat has a close, fine undercoat affording a protective layer and there is soft hair over the eyes and around the mouth, forming a distinctive beard. The pendant ears are large, rounded and high-set, and the amber eyes of almond shape. Height is 56–68 cm (22–27 in) and the weight range 25–35 kg (55–77 lb).

SOUTH AFRICA
Boerboel

HEIGHT 61-66 cm (24-26 in)

Hound

GROUP **COAT CARE**

large

SIZE **FEEDING**

BREED FACT:
Some native dogs in South Africa were named after their physical characteristics.

ALTHOUGH NOT YET recognised, there is a strong and dedicated following of the Boerboel in South Africa which already has provision made for it on South Africa's 'Foundation Stock' register. There is some dispute over the breed's origin but it appears that these dogs are descendants of the old Boer Hund, a powerful, fleet-footed animal which was invaluable to the farmer. The Boer Dogs were used to hunt leopard and baboon and were the result of a cross between the Mastiff and Bulldog.

A big, strong and sturdy dog with powerful muscles, for comparison's sake the Boerboel is sturdier, heavier and bigger in the body than the Boxer, but shorter in the leg than the Great Dane, with height ranging from 61–66 cm (24–26 in). The whole character of the dog is reflected in the head which is big, strong and broad between the ears. The lips are loose and fleshy but the top lips should not hang too low, nor be coarse and thick. The short, smooth coat can be of various colours but breeders are trying to achieve a single colour dog with little or no white. The eyes can be light brown, yellow brown or dark brown, but not blue or blue-grey.

Other South African breeds include the indigenous dogs of the Ba-Ntu people, dogs which went with them in their migrations south from the Congo basin many centuries ago. Pure strains are becoming scarce but a project is underway to ensure their survival.

The **I-Baku** and **I-Twina** breeds were once called Kaffir Dogs but now the use of this name is forbidden by law. The I-Baku, with its attractive coat and markings, appears to be a breed of the Xhosa speaking people, I-Baku meaning floppy ears or big in the Xhosa language. In rural Natal the I-Twina is well known and considered a living representative of the Iron Age dog. Athletic in build, although prone to obesity if not sensibly and carefully fed, this sighthound is an intelligent dog, naturally obedient and highly adaptable.

Another breed, the **Venda**, like the I-Twina has a tall, slender physique with large bat or semi-erect ears, somewhat resembling the dogs of ancient Egypt. It seems likely that the origin of the Venda goes back to North African dogs, possibly with East African or European breeds more recently introduced to the bloodlines.

Below
This sturdy breed may well have developed from Boar Hunds, which were farm dogs.

Working

GROUP

COAT CARE

medium

SIZE

FEEDING

SPAIN
Catalan Sheepdog

HEIGHT 45-55 cm (17.5-21.5 in)

BREED INFORMATION	
NAME	Catalan Sheepdog
OTHER NAMES	Gos d'Atura Catalá, Catalonian Sheepdog
OFFICIAL RECOGNITION	FCI Group 1
COLOUR VARIATIONS	Several, with hairs in different tones

IT IS BELIEVED that the Catalan Sheepdog is related to the Portuguese and Pyrenean Sheepdogs and this breed is enjoying increased popularity both inside Catalonia and elsewhere, the standard having been formulated in 1929. The true essence of this breed manifests itself in the driving of flocks, obeying the shepherd, but the dogs also use initiative and direct the flock with marvellous ease. Thanks to its great bravery and courage, the Catalonian Sheepdog can also be used for guarding.

This sedate, yet active, intelligent dog has a noble expression and a hardy, pleasant character. It is really devoted to the shepherd and flocks but is wary of strangers, making the breed appear unsociable. This vigilant dog is resistant to all weathers and able to work in extreme conditions. The long coat is flat or slightly wavy, rough and with abundant undercoat on the back half of the body. The beard, moustaches, tuft and eyebrows do not affect the dog's sight. Height is 45–55 cm (17.5–21.5 in), weight 17.5–18.5 kg (39–41 lb) and this breed has double dew claws on the hind feet.

Utility

GROUP

COAT CARE

large

SIZE

FEEDING

Majorca Mastiff

HEIGHT 56-58 cm (22-23 in)

BREED INFORMATION	
NAME	Majorca Mastiff
OTHER NAMES	Perro Dogo Mallorquin (Ca de Bou)
Perro de Presa Mallorquin, Mallorquin Bulldog	
OFFICIAL RECOGNITION	FCI Group 2
COLOUR VARIATIONS	Tan; Yellow; Lion-golden

BREED FACT:

As with most Sheepdogs, the Catalan relishes the outdoor life and is wary of strangers.

THE MAJORCA Mastiff, as the name implies, is a mastiff-type breed, though it is not so large as some. The breed was developed between the thirteenth and sixteenth centuries. Later, dog fighting became a popular sport in the Balearic islands and this breed played an active part in the sport, being a highly prized fighter. Fighting was mercifully abolished, but the Majorcan Mastiff suffered a consequent decline in numerical strength. However, breeders on the Spanish mainland took an interest in the

breed which was subsequently exhibited at shows.

In further developing a dog suitable for exhibition purposes the breed now has a more stable temperament and can be both biddable and affectionate, although one should never forget that it has the history of a fighter and is very powerful and alert. The coat is hard and short without undercoat, and the neck is thick and strong and the jaws powerful. Height is 56–58 cm (22–23 in) but this breed is higher at the hips than at the shoulders. The weight is 35.5–36.5 kg (78–80 lb).

Right
Dummy text Dummy text Dummy text Dummy text Dummy text Dummy text

Majorca Shepherd Dog

HEIGHT 62-73 cm (24-29 in)

Working
GROUP | COAT CARE
large
SIZE | FEEDING

Left
The Majorcan Sheepdog originates in mainland Europe.

DOGS ARRIVED ON the Balearic islands from mainland Europe and it was from these that the Majorca Sheepdog evolved, the local farmers selectively breeding for working ability rather than for appearance. It was originally used as a farm guard but is now used in security work as well as being a companion breed. In North America it is also employed to keep the coyote under control and also for guarding wealthy homes.

This tenacious guard has an ability to work well in high temperatures which is unusual for such a dark-coated dog with smooth hair that is short and hard. This very substantial dog has a long, powerful back, and in height is 62–73 cm (24–29 in), weighing 35–40 kg (77 -88 lb). The upper lips hang slightly over the lower ones and the ears somewhat resemble those of a Labrador, but are slightly larger.

Pyrenean Mastiff

HEIGHT 60-70 cm (23-28 in)

Hound
GROUP | COAT CARE

large
SIZE | FEEDING

IN APPEARANCE the Pyrenean Mastiff somewhat resembles a combination of the Pyrenean Mountain Dog and the Spanish Mastiff. Both of these dogs can trace their ancestry back to large Asiatic mastiffs, as the Phoenicians had acquired their own dogs in Assyria and Sumatra but sold some in

Spain when trading there. The Pyrenean Mastiff has primarily been used to move and to protect sheep in the region from which the breed took its name. The wolf was a troublesome predator and the dogs wore spiked collars to protect their necks.

This is a reliable, obedient companion, understandably protective, and it did not receive specific breed recognition until late in the nineteenth century. Markings are symmetrical on the large, strong head which sits on a strong but supple neck with loose skin and a dewlap. The thick, dense coat is fairly rough and around the throat and neck it is slightly longer than elsewhere. Height is 71–80 cm (28–31 in) and weight 55–75 kg (212–165 lb).

Hound
GROUP

COAT CARE

large
SIZE

FEEDING

Below
Owing to it geograph-
ical isolation, this is
one of the oldest and
purest Hound breeds.

Spanish Greyhound

HEIGHT 60-70 cm (23-28 in)

ALTHOUGH THE HISTORY of the Spanish Greyhound dates back to Roman times, the breed probably did not arrive on the Iberian Peninsular until much later. Various sighthounds, the Sloughi among them, were bred together during the Muslim invasion, explaining why some of the breed have wire-haired coats and others smooth. This is a superb hunter, noble but without sophisti-cation, and it is still used for sport in its homeland, as well as for racing when it is sometimes crossed with the English Greyhound.

The Spanish Greyhound needs plenty of exer-cise and can be rather difficult to train in obedience. Although a somewhat aloof breed, it can provide great friendship as a companion. In head, the breed closely resembles the English Greyhound, but the muscle structure is closer to that of a Sloughi. The breed has dark, oval eyes and rose-shaped ears and the long tail is usually carried low. The wire-haired coat is now rare. Height is 60–70 cm (23–28 in) and weight 20–30 kg (44–66 lb).

BREED INFORMATION	
NAME	Spanish Greyhound
OTHER NAMES	Galgo Español
OFFICIAL RECOGNITION	FCI Group 10
COLOUR VARIATIONS	Cream; Black; Gold; Tiger; Chestnut and white

Hound
GROUP

COAT CARE

medium
SIZE

FEEDING

Spanish Hound

HEIGHT 46-56 cm (18-20 in)

DESCENDED FROM THE white Talbot Hound, ancestors of the Spanish Hound are largely the same as those of the Bloodhound, but because it lived in isolation on the Iberian peninsular the breed remained pure. There have, however, been two sizes of the breed although the smaller, the Lebrero, is now all but extinct. When tracking game, which it does willingly for hour upon hour, this breed usually works alone, with just human companionship. The breed is still used as a gundog, and also as a companion and watchdog.

White is the predominant colour with either red or black markings on the short coat. The eyes are chestnut in colour and the nose blends with the colour of the hair surrounding it. Although not tall, standing 46–56 cm (18–20 in) high, this is a sturdy breed weighing 20–25 kg (45–55 lb). Longer than it is high, this reasonably long-headed breed has long, pedant ears. The breed is rather temperamental and caution should be exer-cised with strangers, children and other dogs.

BREED INFORMATION	
NAM	Spanish HoundE
OTHER NAMES	Sabueso Español
OFFICIAL RECOGNITION	FCI Group 6
COLOUR VARIATIONS	Black and white; Red and white

Spanish Mastiff

HEIGHT 72-77 cm (28.5-30.5 in)

BREED INFORMATION

NAME	Spanish Mastiff
OTHER NAMES	Mastín Español, Mastín de la Mancha, Mastín de Extremadura
OFFICIAL RECOGNITION	FCI Group 2
COLOUR VARIATIONS	Any colour

Utility
GROUP COAT CARE
large
SIZE FEEDING

THE SPANISH MASTIFf has guarded sheep at least the fifteenth century, accompanying the merino livestock on its seasonal moves. This is an obedient guard, sure of itself and aware of its own enormous power, very determined when facing harmful animals or strangers. An intelligent animal, the breed is mainly used as guard dogs. This Mastiff's sheer size makes it unpopular as a household pet, indeed there is no upper limit to size, and those which are greatest are prized most highly.

The minimum height for dogs is 77cm (30.5 in) and for bitches 72cm (28.5 in), weight generally ranging from 55–70 kg (121–154 lb). The breed is longer than it is high, and balance and functional harmony are important both when standing and on the move. The big, strong head is shaped like a truncated pyramid, broad at the base, and the medi-um sized, triangular ears hang close to the head when at rest but are partially pricked at the top when attentive. The ears are not cropped. Solid colours are appreciated most but combined colours, brindles or parti-colours are possible. The coat is thick and dense.

Left
This heavy breed of Mastiff does not make an ideal family dog.

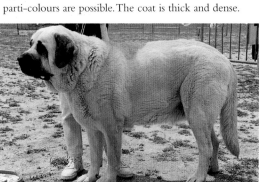

Norrbottenspitz

SWEDEN

HEIGHT 40-43 cm (16-17 in)

BREED INFORMATION

NAME	Norrbottenspitz
OTHER NAMES	Norrbottenspets, Pohjanpystykorva
OFFICIAL RECOGNITION	FCI Group 5
COLOUR VARIATIONS	White with yellow, red or brown

Hound
GROUP COAT CARE
medium
SIZE FEEDING

THE NORBOTTENSPITZ is a small spitz breed which is thought to have descended from the spitz dogs owned by the Vikings. It also somewhat resembles the Norwegian Lundehund. The breed has mainly been used in hunting and in aiding farm work but is now all but extinct due to other working breeds having been introduced to Sweden during the latter half of the twentieth century.

Height is 40–43 cm (16–17 in) and weight 12–15 kg (26–33 lb). The coat of the Norrbottenspitz is medium-short, thick, coarse and off-standing. The coat is primarily white in colour but with a few coloured spots of yellow, red or fawn.

BREED FACT:
The spitz-type blood in this Swedish dog may come from dogs owned by the Vikings.

Left
Due to other hardier breeds being introduced in to Sweden, this dog is now all but extinct.

Hound

GROUP   COAT CARE

medium

SIZE   FEEDING

Schiller Hound

HEIGHT 53-57 cm (21-22 in)

Below

The Smaland Hound is bred to have a short tail so it can retrieve in dense undergrowth.

BREED INFORMATION

NAME	Schiller Hound
OTHER NAMES	Schillerstövare
OFFICIAL RECOGNITION	FCI Group 6
COLOUR VARIATIONS	Tan with black

THE SCHILLER Hound stems from Sweden's local working hounds but was actually developed in the nineteenth century by the farmer Per Schiller who required a light hound which was fleet of foot. As a result he imported German hounds and bred them with local ones to produce this breed which carries his name and was officially recognised in 1952. This working hound which tracks fox and snow hare, holding the prey at bay until the hunter's arrival, is rarely found outside Sweden, although some are found in other Scandinavian countries. The high-set ears are soft-textured and hang flat at the side of the head. The entire coat is short but develops to a harsh winter coat for protection from the elements. The feet are compact but with elastic toes and large, robust pads which aid the dog in its function. Height is 53–57 cm (21–22 in) and weight 18–24 kg (40–53 lb).

Hound

GROUP   COAT CARE

medium

SIZE   FEEDING

Smaland Hound

HEIGHT 46-50 cm (18-20 in)

BREED INFORMATION

NAME	Smaland Hound
OTHER NAMES	Smålandsstövare
OFFICIAL RECOGNITION	FCI Group 6
COLOUR VARIATIONS	Black and tan

THE HISTORY of the Smaland Hound has been traced back to the Middle Ages and this dog is native to Sweden, having originated in Smaland in the south of Sweden. However, the breed was not recognised by the Swedish Kennel Club until 1921. Bred to work in dense forests to hunt hare and fox, this breed used stamina rather than speed to carry out its work. It is also a good scent hound and hunts effectively in any weather.

Tail amputation is illegal in Sweden so the breed's usually short tail is a result of selective breeding, a result of nineteenth century crosses between the Schillerstövare and local hounds. The coat is short, thick and heavy, as well as being shiny and sleek. In colour it is black with tan markings. Height is 46–50 cm (18–20 in) and weight 15–18 kg (33–40 lb).

Swedish Dachsbrackes

HEIGHT 29-41 cm (11.5-16 in)

BREED INFORMATION

NAME	Swedish Dachsbracke
OTHER NAMES	Drever
OFFICIAL RECOGNITION	FCI Group 6
COLOUR VARIATIONS	Tri-colour; Black/white; Fawn/white

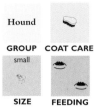

Hound
GROUP

COAT CARE

small
SIZE

FEEDING

THE SWEDISH Dachsbracke, or Drever as it is also commonly known, is a popular short-legged game dog in Sweden. Used to drive game to the gun, it was developed from a combination of local hounds and the Westphalian Dachsbracke, the Swedish Dachsbracke's rather short legs making it slower than many other hounds. A popular companion dog in Sweden as well as being a good tracker, it is, perhaps surprisingly, not well known outside its homeland.

In comparison with its long, low body, the head is rather large, but long and well-proportioned. The legs, though short, are none the less both vertical and parallel, the tail carried in a downward curve. It is a headstrong breed and a willing worker, which expresses itself in clear, alert eyes with close-fitting rims. The coat is short and close-fitting, lying flat on the body and colours are tri-colour, black and white or tan and white. Height is 29–41 cm (11.5–16 in) and weight 14.5–15.5 kg (32–34 lb).

Above

This is a good tracking dog but its short legs make it slower than other hounds.

Swedish Elkhound

HEIGHT 58-64 cm (23-25 in)

BREED INFORMATION

NAME	Swedish Elkhound
OTHER NAMES	Jämthund
OFFICIAL RECOGNITION	FCI Group 5
COLOUR VARIATIONS	Wolf-grey

Hound
GROUP

COAT CARE

large
SIZE

FEEDING

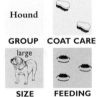

THIS BREED TAKES its alternative name from Sweden's Jämtland district and is now Sweden's national breed. Once used for hunting bear, this is the largest of the Elkhound breeds, several of which are to be found in Scandinavia. With the decline in bear hunting, lynx, wolf and moose took over as the prey of the Swedish Elkhound which is also a good sled dog, shepherd dog, watchdog and is used by the Swedish army. Indeed in Sweden the breed is highly popular both for its working abilities and as a companion animal.

This hardy breed is heavy-set, thick-boned and the broad, capacious chest has flexible ribs. The hind legs are particularly powerful and the neck is lean and long, but robust. The spitz-like head has pricked ears which incline forward and the reasonably small eyes are lively in their expression. The reasonably long coat is hard and close-fitting. Height is 58–64 cm (23–25 in) and weight 29.5–30.5 kg (65–67 lb).

BREED FACT:
Dogs indigenous to the Arctic and Scandinavia were often bred to hunt elk.

Left

The Elkhound is a popular dog with multiple uses; it acts as sled, shepherd and guard dog as well as working for the Army.

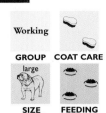

Working

GROUP **COAT CARE**

large

SIZE **FEEDING**

SWITZERLAND
Appenzell Cattledog

HEIGHT 50-58 cm (19.5-23 in)

<table>
<tr><td colspan="2">○○○○○○○○○○○○○○○○○○○○○○○○○○○○○</td></tr>
<tr><td colspan="2">BREED INFORMATION</td></tr>
<tr><td>NAME</td><td>Appenzell Cattledog</td></tr>
<tr><td>OTHER NAMES</td><td>Appenzeller Sennenhund</td></tr>
<tr><td>OFFICIAL RECOGNITION</td><td>FCI Group 2</td></tr>
<tr><td>COLOUR VARIATIONS</td><td>Black or havana brown, with red-rust and white markings</td></tr>
</table>

ALTHOUGH BELIEVED to have been kept by Swiss farmers since the Middle Ages, the first description of an Appenzell Cattledog was in a book entitled Animal Life in the Alps and published in 1853 in which reference was made to 'Spitz type', a feature of which remains clearly in the breed's curled tail. By 1898 it had been designated as a separate breed and a specialist club was formed in 1906. Original breeding took place in the Appenzell region but today this dog is found all over

Top and Right
The Appenzell is a well-established breed, registered in 1898.

Switzerland and in other European countries. A versatile working and family dog, it is used to drive animals, to watch, guard, as a farm dog and for carting.

The Appenzell Cattledog is lively, high-spirited, self-assured, reliable and fearless, although slightly suspicious of strangers. A very substantial dog, its height is 50–58 cm (19.5–23 in) and weight 25–32 kg (55–70 lb). A tri-coloured breed, the base colour is either black or havana brown, the nose colour black or brown accordingly. Although short-coated, there is a thick undercoat.

Working

GROUP **COAT CARE**

medium

SIZE **FEEDING**

Entlebuch Cattledog

HEIGHT 42-52 cm (16.5-20.5 in)

<table>
<tr><td colspan="2">○○○○○○○○○○○○○○○○○○○○○○○○○○○○</td></tr>
<tr><td colspan="2">BREED INFORMATION</td></tr>
<tr><td>NAME</td><td>Entlebuch Cattledog</td></tr>
<tr><td>OTHER NAMES</td><td>Entlebucher Sennenhund, Entlebuch Mountain Dog</td></tr>
<tr><td>OFFICIAL RECOGNITION</td><td>FCI Group 2</td></tr>
<tr><td>COLOUR VARIATIONS</td><td>Tri-colour</td></tr>
</table>

Right
This breed has been known in Switzerland since 1889.

THE ENTLEBUCH CATTLEDOG is the smallest of the four Swiss Mountain- and Cattledogs. The breed originated in Entlebuch, a valley in the area of Lucerne and Berne.

Under the name Entilbucherhund the breed has been known since 1889 but then no difference was made between this breed and the Appenzell Cattledog. From 1926 onward it has been promoted as a pure breed but has developed only slowly. Used as a driving, watch, guard and farm dog this is a versatile and agreeable family dog which is increasing in popularity.

High-spirited, self-assured and fearless, the breed is good tempered and devoted to familiar people though slightly suspicious of strangers. This cheerful breed, capable of learning, stands 42–52 cm (16.5–20.5 in) high and weighs 25–30 kg (55–66 lb). Double-coated, the topcoat is short, close-fitting, harsh and shiny, and the undercoat is dense. The breed is typically tri-coloured, the basic colour black, with tan, which can be fawn to rust red, and the white markings should be as symmetrical as possible.

BREED INFORMATION

NAME	Grosser Schweizer Sennenhund
OFFICIAL RECOGNITION	FCI Group 2; AKC Working Group
COLOUR VARIATIONS	Jet black with rich rust and white markings

Great Swiss Mountain Dog

HEIGHT 60-72 cm (23.5-28.5 in)

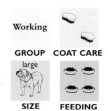

Working
GROUP   **COAT CARE**
large
SIZE   **FEEDING**

TRADITIONALLY ASSOCIATED with the farmers and tradesmen of small Swiss villages, the Great Swiss Hound has also been used successfully as a draught dog. Like other Swiss breeds, it is believed that its ancestry probably goes back to the Roman mastiffs. Breed recognition was achieved in 1910, soon after the breed had been re-discovered, some thinking it to have already become extinct.

Although now used primarily as a companion animal, The Great Swiss Cattledog is a draught breed and this should be evident in its structure, for this is a powerful dog of sturdy appearance. Height is 60–72 cm (23.5–28.5 in) and weight 59–61 kg (130–135 lb). The expression is animated and gentle, with medium sized, dark brown eyes surrounded by black rims. The tri-coloured coat is dense and the undercoat may be thick and is sometimes showing. This is a bold, faithful, willing worker, both alert and vigilant, and it should never be nervous or aggressive.

Left
This is a draught breed, which is evident in the dog's robust and sturdy appearance.

BREED INFORMATION

NAME	Swiss Hounds
OTHER NAMES	Bernese, Jura, Lucerne, Schwyz Hound, Schweiser and Berner, Jura, Luzerner and Schwyzer Laufhund.
OFFICIAL RECOGNITION	FCI Group 6
COLOUR VARIATIONS	This varies according to the breed.

Swiss Hounds

HEIGHT 47-59 cm (18.5-23 in)

Hound
GROUP   **COAT CARE**
large
SIZE   **FEEDING**

THE HISTORY OF the Swiss Hounds dates back to the Middle Ages when these dogs hunted roe deer and small game around the area of Berne in Switzerland. Going even further back in time, they are believed to have descended in the ancient past from hounds of Celtic and Phoenician origin. In the fifteenth century it is known that these hounds were much sought after by Italian dog lovers and in the eighteenth century, the French appreciated them for their aptitude for hunting hare. In 1882. standards were draw up for five Swiss Hounds, but in 1909 when the standards were revised, the fifth, the Thurgovie, was no longer represented.

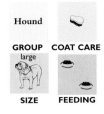

The remaining four – the Bernese, Jura, Lucerne and Schwyz – differ only in skin and coat. All are good working dogs which track and flush and are used with the gun for hare, deer, fox and boar, hunting in an independent manner and giving tongue. These hounds get on well with children and make fine companion animals, showing little aggression towards other dogs unless provoked but firm training is needed. The Swiss Hound stands 47–59 cm (18.5–23 in) high, weighs 15–20 kg (34–44 lb) and has good bone. The head has a gentle expression and the long ears fall in folds.

Left
The origins of the various Swiss Hounds can be traced back to the Middle Ages.

Other Swiss Hounds

ALL VARIETIES OF Swiss Hound have short, dense, smooth coats, very fine on the head and ears. The Bernese has black skin under areas of black coat and white skin, slightly black-mottled, under a white coat. The dog is white with black patches or a black saddle, with light to dark fawn markings in specified areas.

The **Jura Hound** has black skin under areas of black coat, but lighter skin under tan areas. Its colour is fawn with a black blanket, sometimes with a black overlay, or black with fawn markings, and there is sometimes a small white patch on the chest, which may be speckled.

The **Lucerne Hound** has black skin under black coat and lighter skin under the blue speckling. The 'blue' of this variety results from black and white hairs together. It is very heavily speckled with black patches or a black saddle and light to dark fawn markings.

The **Schwyz Hound** has dark grey skin under orange coat and white skin, flecked with black, under white coat. The coat colour is white with either patches or a saddle of orange fawn, sometimes very slightly spotted.

The **Berner Neiderlaufhound** is effectively simply a smaller version of the Swiss Hound.

Top
The Jura Lafhound may be of Celtic and Phoenician origin.

Right
The Swiss Berner Neiderlaufhound is a smaller version of the Swiss Hound.

Hound

GROUP   **COAT CARE**

large
SIZE   **FEEDING**

THAILAND
Thai Ridgeback Dog

HEIGHT 58-66 cm (22-26 in)

BREED INFORMATION	
NAME	Thai Ridgeback Dog
OTHER NAMES	Mah Thai
OFFICIAL RECOGNITION	FCI Group 5 (provisional)
COLOUR VARIATIONS	Light chestnut red; pure black; silver; blue

BECAUSE OF POOR transportation systems, allowing few opportunities to cross with other breeds, the Thai Ridgeback has bred true in isolated populations for several hundred years and can be found in archeological writing in Thailand some 350 years ago. Mainly from the eastern part of Thailand, the breed was used for hunting, to escort carts and as a watchdog. This endearing breed has not long been known outside its homeland but thanks to a dedicated following its future is now assured. The Thai Ridgeback is a tough, active breed with well developed muscles and excellent jumping ability, a medium sized dog with short, smooth hair and a narrow ridge of hair growing in the opposite direction to the rest of the coat along the back. This is a highly important feature and should be clearly defined. Height is 58–66 cm (22–26 in) and weight in the region of 23–34 kg (51–75 lb). The rather large triangular ears incline forward and are firmly pricked.

Right
The Thai Ridgeback must have a narrow ridge of dorsal hair along its spine.

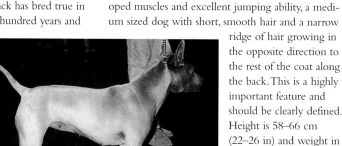

TIBET & CHINA
Tibetan Kyi Apso

HEIGHT 56-71 cm (22-28 in)

Hound		
GROUP	**COAT CARE**	
large		
SIZE	**FEEDING**	

IN ITS HOMELAND OF TIBET, in the region of Mount Kailash, the Tibetan Kyi Apso lives at high altitudes and under challenging and exacting conditions. Lack of available food has made the Kyi Apso a strong, speedy hunter, capable of tackling small rodents and, because of dangerous predators, this dog has developed as a resourceful, agile breed. In Tibet Kyi Apsos are still difficult to locate, even in their primary homeland, which is one of the most sacred places on in the world for both Buddhists and Hindus.

A very few of these dogs now exist in the West, mainly in the USA, where a careful and monitored breeding programme is being conducted under the auspices of the Kyi Apso Club. This large, muscular, light-boned dog moves with a powerful rolling motion and stands some 56–71 cm (22–28 in). The wide head has a flat skull with a tight

muzzle, almond-shaped eyes and v-shaped ears, while the high-set tail has a full curl, is feathered and curls over the back. The long, thick double-coat can be any colour, but sable and black, blue and black and black and white combinations are most common.

BREED FACT:
The hostile environment in which the Kyi Apso has developed has produced a very resilient, hardy dog.

Left
A few of these dogs now exist in the west, and are the subject of a careful and selective breeding programme.

Tibetan Mastiffs

HEIGHT 51-63 cm (20-25 in)

Working		
GROUP	**COAT CARE**	
large		

IN THE WEST many people assume that all large, reasonably heavy Tibetan Dogs are Tibetan Mastiffs, but this is not the case. There are several dogs of smaller stature which work with the nomads of Tibet, many of them herding sheep and goats. It has never been easy to draw a fine line between the various breeds as the Tibetans understandably pay more attention to the function of a dog than to its actual name.

The **Bangara Mastiff** is a distinct breed developed by the Tehri Garhwallas out of the Tibetan Mastiff. Standing 51–63.5 cm (20–25 in) high, this dog has a compact body and is generally used for herding yak and sheep, as well as for guarding them from predators. With its coarse, heavy coat and thick undercoat, the heavily plumed tail is curled to one side, and the colour usually black, tan or apricot.

Rather less heavy as a breed is the **Bhotia**, also known as the Himalayan Sheepdog, which is usually black and tan or black with white. Like the Bangara Mastiff it stands about 51–63.5 cm (20–25 in) high but weighs around 22.5–27 kg (50–60 lb). In India the same standard was used for both these breeds but elsewhere in the world they have not been recognised.

The **Tibetan Hunting Dog** will be a familiar sight to the Tibetan nomads in the mountains and has remained true to its type for many years.

Left
Tibetan Hunting Dogs have not changed since this nineteenth century picture was taken.

Chinese and Tibetan Breeds

OTHER TIBETAN AND CHINESE breeds are many and various but none are registered with the English Kennel Club, FCI or American Kennel Clubs.

Top
This odd little dog looks like a Smooth-coated Pekingese.

Right
It was thought that the Happa was extinct, but this photograph disputes that fact.

The **Happa Dog** is a little-known Chinese breed found sometimes in Tibet, which was originally described as a smooth-coated Pekingese; certainly photographs of specimens of the dogs, presumed long since gone, would bear this out. However, the author, who travels regularly to Tibetan settlements in the Himalayan regions on research expeditions, located a dog, which is pictured here, that the Tibetan monks insisted was a Happa, although it appears to be longer in the leg than those known previously and stands roughly about 25.5 cm (10 in) high.

A Happa Dog, also spelt Hapa, was exhibited in England in 1907 at the first show held by the Pekingese Club. This dog was described as being not unlike a Miniature Bulldog, with a quaint face and large eyes set far apart and with ears like the sails of a 'war junk'. There are no known Happas living in Europe.

Another remote breed is kept by the Khampa tribes of Western Tibet and is usually called the **Tibetan Hound**. Research would indicate, however, that this lean, swift hunting dog appears to be more or less the same as the **Tibetan Hunting Dog**, but with a shorter coat.

Hound	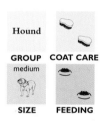
GROUP	**COAT CARE**
medium	
SIZE	**FEEDING**

USA
American Eskimo Dog
HEIGHT 23-48 cm (9-19 in)

○○○○○○○○○○○○○○○○○○○○○○○○○
BREED INFORMATION

NAME	American Eskimo Dog
OFFICIAL RECOGNITION	AKC Non-Sporting Group
COLOUR VARIATIONS	White; Biscuit cream

THE AMERICAN ESKIMO DOG was a favourite among circus performers in the early twentieth century but was not accepted for registration by the American Kennel Club until 1994. Contrary to popular belief, this breed is not descended from working sled dogs. It is a dog which is learns new tasks with ease and is always eager to please. Although the breed does not bite or attack people, it is protective of its home and family.

A picture of strength, alertness and beauty, this a small to medium sized Nordic dog which has three separate size divisions. Toy is 23–30.5 cm (9–12 in), Medium over 30.5–38 cm (over 12–15 in) and Standard over 38–48 cm (over 15–19 in). All should for preference be white but the presence of biscuit-cream colour is also allowed. With a keen, intelligent expression the eyes are slightly oval with black eye rims and white eyelashes. The breed has a stand-off, double coat with a dense undercoat and a longer coat of guard hair growing through it. The hair on the muzzle is short and smooth.

American Foxhound

HEIGHT 53-64 cm (21-25 in)

Hound

GROUP   **COAT CARE**

large

SIZE   **FEEDING**

THE American Foxhound was developed from packhounds which had arrived in America in the 1860s from France, England and Ireland, the latter being of Kerry Beagle type. George Washington was responsible for founding the breed, aiming to produce a dog which was more suitable for America's rugged terrain than was the English Foxhound, although new blood was routinely introduced. Used as the name implies for foxhunting, the methods of hunting fox vary according to region in the USA. In northern areas hunting takes place in the daytime and the fox is killed, but in southern areas hunting is at night and it is the chase which is more important than a kill.

The American Foxhound has a reasonably short but fairly dense coat which is hard and close and any colour is acceptable. The head is fairly long and the pendant ears are set at the level of the eyes which are large and soft, brown or hazel in colour. This is a strong-willed breed and dogs have a very distinctive voice which owners recognise. Height is 53–64 cm (21–25 in) and weight 30–34 kg (65–75 lb).

Below
This breed is more hardy than the English Foxhound.

Staffordshire Terrier

HEIGHT 43-48 cm (17-19 in)

Hound

GROUP   **COAT CARE**

medium

SIZE   **FEEDING**

THE AMERICAN Staffordshire Terrier was at one time the same as the English Staffordshire Bull Terrier, but the American dog was selectively bred for increased bulk, height and weight and recognised as a separate breed in 1936. Despite the reputation of this breed, its courage and the fact that it can inflict severe injury on other dogs, it has a gentle nature and is good with children.

A stocky dog, not long-legged, this is a muscular but agile breed, keenly alive to its surroundings. The ears may be cropped or uncropped, but those left in their natural state are preferred. The tail is low set, tapering to a fine point and is not carried over the back. The coat is short, close, stiff to the touch and glossy. Although any colour is permissible those which have more than 80 per cent white, or are black and tan, or liver are not to be encouraged. Height is 43–48 cm (17–19 in) and weight in the region of 18–23 kg (40–50 lb).

> **BREED FACT:**
> This dog was recognised as a separate breed from the original English dog in 1936.

Left
The American Staffordshire Terrier is an amiable dog which makes an excellent house pet.

Gundog

GROUP   COAT CARE

medium

SIZE   FEEDING

American Water Spaniel

HEIGHT 37.5-45 cm (15-18 in)

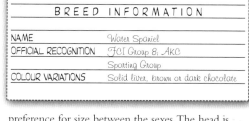

BREED INFORMATION	
NAME	Water Spaniel
OFFICIAL RECOGNITION	FCI Group 8; AKC Sporting Group
COLOUR VARIATIONS	Solid liver, brown or dark chocolate

THE AMERICAN WATER SPANIEL was the first breed which was developed in the USA as an all-round hunter capable of retrieving from boats. It works from a skiff or canoe and also on the ground with relative ease. Prior to recognition by the American Kennel Club in 1940 this breed had never been shown because its owners felt a showring reputation may damage the breed's prowess as a hunter.

An active, muscular dog, emphasis is placed on correct size and symmetry. Slightly longer than it is tall, height is 15–18 in) and weight 30–45 lb), with no preference for size between the sexes. The head is moderate in length with an alert, self-confident and intelligent expression. Eye colour harmonises with that of the coat which is solid liver, brown or dark chocolate, sometimes with a little white on the toes and chest. The coat can range from 'marcel', which is uniform waves, to closely curled, and this breed must have sufficient undercoat to protect against weather, water or punishing cover. The coat may be trimmed to present a well-groomed appearance and the ears may be shaved, but neither is essential.

Right
This Spaniel was bred as a first-rate retriever and will happily work from boats.

Hound

GROUP   COAT CARE

large

SIZE   FEEDING

Black and Tan Coonhound

HEIGHT 58-69 cm (23-27 in)

BREED INFORMATION	
NAME	Black and Tan Coonhound
OTHER NAMES	American Black and Tan Coonhound
OFFICIAL RECOGNITION	FCI Group 6; AKC Hound Group
COLOUR VARIATIONS	Black and tan

IT IS BELIEVED THAT THE BLACK and Tan Coonhound may be related to the Talbot Hound which existed in the eleventh century, but more recent ancestors are the Bloodhound, various Foxhounds and the Irish Kerry Beagle. Although breeding is also focused on coat colour as indicated in the name, the breed's skill at trapping raccoons is also highly important. This is a methodical tracker which keeps its nose to the ground and changes voice to indicate that quarry has been cornered. Besides raccoon and other small animals, this breed will also hunt large game, including bear.

The coat is short, thick and shiny. Owners pay special attention to the coat which is deep black in colour with tan markings on the chest, legs and over the eyes and sides of the muzzle. The gently rounded skull has a long, rectangular muzzle and the long, large ears hang low. Exercise is important for this breed which stands 58–69 cm (23–27 in) high and weighs 23–34 kg (50–75 lb).

Right
Possibly related to the Talbot Hound, this Hound gets its name from its skill at catching raccoons.

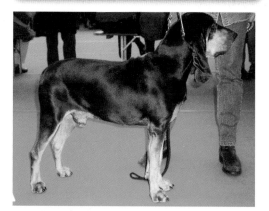

Hound
GROUP   COAT CARE
large
SIZE   FEEDING

BREED INFORMATION

NAME	Plott Hound
OFFICIAL RECOGNITION	AKC
COLOUR VARIATIONS	Any shade of brindle or blue

Plott Hound

HEIGHT 51-64 cm (20-25 in)

THE PLOTTS WERE mountain men who left Germany and emigrated to America with their Hanoverian Hounds. They built homes and raised families all over the Smoky Mountains and their dogs became known as the Plott's hounds. These dogs were used to hunt bear, boar and lion. After several generations a cross was successfully introduced, the tan, black-saddled Blevin. Coonhunters began to take an interest in this breed with its treeing instinct and thus the Plott became classified as a coonhound.

This hunting hound of striking colour traditionally brings big game to bay or tree and is noted for stamina, endurance, agility, determination and aggressiveness when hunting. Powerful, well-muscled and streamlined, the Plott stands between 51–64cm (20–25 in) in height and weighs between

18.5–27 kg (40-60 lb). The ears of the Plott Hound are semi-erectile, hanging gracefully with the inside part rolling forward toward the muzzle. The coat is usually smooth, fine and glossy but thick enough to provide protection from wind and water, although rare specimens can be double-coated. Any shade of brindle colour is preferred but other colours are acceptable.

Other American breeds recognised in Britain include the American Cocker Spaniel. Under the FCI this Spaniel is may be black, colour other than black or parti-colour.

Below
The Plott Hound can have several different coat colours, but brindle is preferred.

BREED INFORMATION

NAME	Louisiana Catahoula Leopard Dog
OTHER NAMES	Cat
OFFICIAL RECOGNITION	None as yet
COLOUR VARIATIONS	Merle, Black and tan

Catahoula Leopard Dog

HEIGHT 51-66 cm (21-26 in)

Hound
GROUP   COAT CARE
large
SIZE   FEEDING

THE LOUISIANA CATAHOULA LEOPARD DOG, founded in America's Deep South, is still popular, respected and well loved in its native state. It is called the 'leopard' dog because of the distinctive spotted patches on the skin. Originally names after a small village in the state of Louisiana, it was made the state's official dog in 1979 and given its full name. The breed's ancestors are thought to be the Mastiffs or Greyhounds which came travelling to the New World on board ships with the explorer Hernando de Soto.

These traditional 'war dogs' were left with local tribes who crossed them with wolves. Later, French Beauceron blood was introduced. Standing 51–66 cm (21–26 in) high, this spotted dog is a muscular, athletic breed with a powerful body. The legs are sturdy and the breed is deep-chested with a decent

lung capacity. The short to medium length coat is blue, grey, black, liver, red or white, with patched leopard patterns preferred. By nature the dogs can be troublesome and stubborn; equally well they are fearless and will attack wild pigs and boar.

Below
The 'cat' has distinctive mottled patches on its skin.

Terrier
GROUP

COAT CARE

large
SIZE

FEEDING

Pit Bull Terrier

HEIGHT 46-56 cm (18-22 in)

Right

The reputation of the Pit Bull Terrier has suffered in recent years but it is now being breed as a companion breed again.

THERE ARE many other American breeds which are not recognised by the American Kennel Club but each have their own specialist clubs and recognition. These include the American Bulldog which is a bold and lively breed descended from the dogs of European immigrants, including English working Bulldogs. Another is the American Pit Bull Terrier, a breed that knows no fear, which was bred for bull-baiting and dog fighting and, as a result of its acknowledged aggressive streak, is now completely banned or restricted in some countries.

This breed resulted from selective crosses between the Staffordshire Bull Terrier and fighting dogs, including the original Bulldog. It requires experienced handling and socialisation from an early age to avoid its latent aggression from coming out. It weighs between 14-36 kg (30-80 lb) and has a powerful body with immense shoulders.

Hound
GROUP

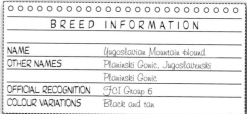
COAT CARE

large
SIZE

FEEDING

FORMER YUGOSLAVIA

Mountain Hound

HEIGHT 46-56 cm (18-22 in)

Below

These hounds have stamina in abundance and either hunt alone or in packs.

THE YUGOSLAVIAN HOUNDS are considered ancient breeds and the Mountain Hound is no exception. Believed to have been descended from European scent hounds and pariah-type sighthounds, the combination of these dogs adapted well to the hunting work required of it in mountainous regions. This hound is used for tracking fox, hare, deer and wild boar. The breed is now still quite rare, its population having declined during recent troubled years.

Although principally a working dog, this a good natured breed, capable of hunting alone or in packs. It has plenty of stamina and agility which make it highly suitable for difficult terrain. With its pendant ears and darkly pigmented eyelids this is a distinctive black and tan coloured dog which sometimes has greyish-white markings on the chest. Although the hair is short, the topcoat is thick and abundant and there is a warm, insulating undercoat. Height is 46–56 cm (18–22 in) and weight 20–25 kg (44–55 lb).

Tricolour Hound

HEIGHT 46-56 cm (18-22 in)

Hound
GROUP small

COAT CARE

SIZE

FEEDING

CLOSELY RELATED to the Mountain Hound, this Tricoloured Hound's ancestry is much the same, being a descendent of European scenthounds and pariah-type sighthounds. However, the Tricoloured Hound used to be commonly found near the border with Greece, although now, this breed too is becoming very rare, even in this region. Reputed for its excellent vision, this is a dedicated worker, used to hunt game, including fox, hare, deer and wild boar.

A breed which will always gladly please its owner, the Tricoloured Hound is an obedient and loving companion as well as a hunter, with a relaxed personality around the home. With a rather wide, flat head, the brownish black eyes have a gentle expression, aided by the black pigment also found on the close-fitting lips. The short, dense, weather-resistant coat is glossy and is tri-colour, black with tan, and white on the face, chest, tail tip, feet and also the legs. Height is 46–56 cm (18–22 in) and weight 20–25 kg (44–55 lb).

BREED FACT:
Most Hounds in the former Yugoslavia are descended from European scent hounds and pariah dogs.

Left
The Tricolour Hound is now increasingly rare, despite its abilities as a working dog.

Yugoslavian Herder

HEIGHT 57-61 cm (22.5-24 in)

Hound
GROUP large

COAT CARE

SIZE

FEEDING

AN ANCIENT LIVESTOCK guarding breed from the mountainous south-eastern region of former Yugoslavia, the Yugoslavian Herder was formerly called the Illyrian Shepherd Dog after this region. Recognised by the FCI in 1939, in 1957 the name was altered because it is in the Sarplanina mountain range that the breed is most common. The breed is believed to have descended from the ancient Molossian dogs of Greece and from the livestock guarding dogs of

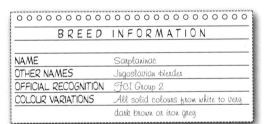

Turkey. The breed is still widely used in its homeland in the protection of flocks.

The minimum height for a dog is 61 cm (24 in) and 57 cm (22.5 in) for bitches. Weight should be (66–99 lb) but this breed looks bigger than it actually is because of its heavy bone and thick coat. The v-shaped ears are dropped and the long tail is carried like a sabre. Although rather smaller than many other livestock guarding breeds, the Sarplaninac has extraordinary strength and large teeth, making it a formidable adversary.

Left and Above
The Yugoslavian Herder is still used to protect sheep in its native country.

Exotic Dog Breeds

THE DOGS INCLUDED on these spreads are all rare or exotic breeds that are little known outside their own countries, and are generally not registered with any kennel clubs.

RARE BREEDS OF SHEEPDOG

THE EXACT ORIGIN of the Greek Sheepdog is not known but this breed is somewhat similar to the Maremma and Kuvasz in appearance, standing about 66 cm (26 in) in height and weighing 36–43 kg (80–94 lb). The coat is thick and the colour can include white. The Greek Sheepdog makes a good hunter and working dog, but it is rarely kept just as a pet. Although not recognised by the FCI, Greek canine enthusiasts are working toward obtaining some official registration for this breed.

HELLENIC HOUND

ALSO KNOWN AS THE Hellinikos Ichnilatis or Greek Harehound, this breed is quite popular in Greece but enjoys little popularity outside its homeland, although is recognised by the FCI. This is a good hunter of hare with an excellent nose and good vocal abilities. In height it stands 46–54.5 cm (18–21.5 in) and its weight is roughly 16–20.5 kg (35–45 lb).

KARST SHEPHERD DOG

ONE OF THE OLDEST BREEDS from former Yugoslavia, the Karst Shepherd Dog, also called the Kraski Ovcar, is now classified as a Slovenian breed in FCI Group 2. Used for guarding and herding flocks, this is a breed with plenty of courage and its wariness of strangers makes it an excellent watchdog. With its family the Karst Shepherd Dog is affectionate and it has a playful personality. Standing 56–61 cm (22–24 in) and weighing 25–40 kg (55–88 lb), its thick, harsh coat is of medium length with an abundant undercoat. The colour is iron grey with shading.

ORIENTAL DOGS

THE KINTAMANI DOG is an Indonesian breed, specific to the

island of Bali and found in the remote regions in the north-east of the island. Breeding takes place primarily in the volcanic mountainous area, from where the puppies are brought down to small towns and villages for sale. Although they vary in substance and size, partly due to their upbringing, all have erect ears and thick, insulating double coats which are found in a variety of colours. Most cherished is a tri-colour – white, yellow and black.

NEW GUINEA SINGING DOG

BROUGHT TO THE attention of the public during the first half of the twentieth century, a pair of New Guinea Singing Dog was taken to Sydney's Taronga Zoo from the Southern Highlands of Papua New Guinea and great debate as to classification, it is now accepted that this most primitive 'domestic dog' was taken to the island at least 6,000 years ago. Due to its isolation, the breed is like a living fossil. Bearing resemblance to the Dingo, the double coat is short and dense with a plush texture. Height varies from 35.5–46 cm (14–18 in). The breed's tonal howl is characteristic and this dog has a complex vocal behaviour and incredible structural flexibility. The breed's intense hunting drive is likely to overwhelm any training and although it is usually gentle and affectionate with people, the breed is aggressive towards other dogs.

WORKING DOGS

ALTHOUGH AN OLD BREED, this is one of the more recent pointing dogs, and the Burgos Pointer resulted most probably from crosses between fairly light-boned pointers and the Perddiguero Navarro. It was originally used for deer hunting, pointing and retrieving and is now still used as a pointer and retriever but primarily of small, fast game such as partridge and hare. The breed works willingly both on land and in water. This easy-going dog which gets along well in a family environment and also with children is now also used as a companion animal. Unless provoked, the Burgos Pointer is unlikely to bite or snap and generally enjoys the companionship of other dogs. The breed has dark eyes with prominent ridges above for protection, long and wide ears and a wrinkled dewlap at the neck. Height is 66–76 cm (26–30 in) and weight 25–30 kg (55–66 lb).

Above
The New Guinea Singing Dog is said to be an extremely primitive domestic breed, probably because of its geographical isolation in Papua New Guinea.

Below Left and Left
Kintamani Dogs are peculiar to Bali in Indonesia, bred in remote villages and sold as family pets.

BREED FACT:

The Burgos Pointer comes from Spain and was bred for working with small fast game like partridge and hare.

coated, powerful breed stands 51–61 cm (20–24 in) high and uses its voice to great effect in the gathering of sheep and to move them forward. The colour is predominantly black, with patches of tan. Although used extensively in New Zealand, it is not a recognised breed, but it does breed true to type. Some have now been imported to the UK where some farmers see the benefits of having a dog which works for them in this special way.

Right
Although not a recognised breed, the New Zealand Huntaway is bred black and tan.

Below
The Rampur Hound is an exceptional Indian hunting dog which can hunt jackal.

THE HUNTAWAY WAS developed in New Zealand by selective breeding of dogs which barked to herd sheep, rather than working them silently. This short-

RAMPUR HOUND
THE RAMPUR HOUND, also known as the Rampur Greyhound or North-Indian Greyhound, was a favourite of the maharajas and was primarily kept in India to hunt the jackal. This breed is also capable of tracking and killing wounded game. Substantially built and smooth-haired, the coat is like that of a newly trimmed horse. The head is broader than that of the English Greyhound and the pointed nose has a characteristic Roman bend. The fairly large ears are high-set and the bite is extremely powerful. The dog has a fine sense of balance and the hare feet have webbing between the toes. A limited number are now in the USA but they are otherwise unknown outside India.

LANDSEER NEWFOUNDLAND
THIS ATRACTIVE BREED is included here because in some countries itis classified as a separate breed to its better-known black and tan cousin. It is of a distinctive black and white colouring, also comes from Canada and shares the same sunny nature. The Landseer has large feet with broadly webbed toes for use in water.

RARE KOREAN DOGS
KOREAN BREEDS faced near extinction until recently but are now being carefully bred. The **Poong San** originates from the Poong San region of North East Korea and bares a strong resemblance to the Alaskan malamute or Siberian Husky.

The **Sapsal** is a rare but protected breed and has been designated Natural Treasure Number 368. The last official records showed only 40 in existence in Korea. This appealing breed has a long coat and a shaggy, cuddly appearance.

Left
The Landseer is black and white in colouring and is sometimes considered to be a separate breed to the traditional Newfoundland type.

Bottom
Tibetan Hunting Dogs were once subject to rigorous and questionable training methods as puppies.

THE TIBETAN HUNTING DOG

THE DOG SHOWN here was photographed early in the nineteenth century but this type of dog has not changed since then and the very same type can still be found in remote regions. This breed is roughly the size of a small Airedale and usually has a creamy grey coat, although some are much darker. Coat is dense, but fairly short, the muzzle is elongated and the drop-ears hang forward. The Tibetan Hunting Dog was used for game, taken on a leash within sight of the game and then slipped. However, the dog did not kill, but barked to distract the quarry's attention until the hunter was able to come up close for the kill.

The training of Tibetan Hunting Dogs was strange; puppies were tied to their dam whist she went after the game. As a result they were dragged along after her, but this seemingly cruel method reputedly made them both fierce and keen. To the author's knowledge, only one has been ever imported to Britain, in the early 1930s, and according to an English breeder who attempted to keep the dog in Tibet, they were 'tiresome in attacking strangers'.

Useful Addresses

Animal Health Trust
PO Box 5, Snailwell Road, Newmarket, Suffolk,
CB8 7DW
Tel: 01638 661111
Fax: 01638 665789

Association of Homoeopathic Veterinary Surgeons
c/o The Natural Medicine Veterinary Surgeon
Centre, 11 Southgate Road, Potters Bar,
Hertforshire, EN6 2QD
Tel: 01707 662058
Fax: 01707 646948

Association of Pet Behaviour Councillors
PO Box 46, Worcester, WR8 9YS
Tel: 01386 751151

Association of Private Pet Cemetries
Tel: 016974 72232 or 01342 712976 .

Asthma Research Council
300 Upper Street, London, N1 2SX
Tel: 0171 226 2260

Battersea Dogs Home
4 Battersea Park Road, London, SW8 4AA
Tel: 0171 622 3626

British Flyball Association
Tel: 01705 468462

British Small Animal Veterinary Association (BSAVA)
Kingsley House, Church Lane, Shurdington,
Cheltenham, Gloucestershire
Tel: 01242 862994
Fax: 01242 863009
E-mail: adminoff@BSAVA.demon.co.uk

British Veterinary Association (BVA)
7 Mansfield Street, London, W1M 0AT
Tel: 0171 636 6541
Fax: 0171 436 2970
E-Mail: BVA@netcomuk.co.uk

Canine Studies Institute
Ascot House, High Street, Ascot, Berkshire, SL5 7JG
Tel: 01344 28269
Fax: 01344 22771

Dog World **(weekly newspaper)**
Somerfield House, Wotton Road, Ashford, Kent,
TN23 6LW
Tel: 01233 621877
Fax: 01233 645669
E-mail: info@dogworld.co.uk

Guide Dogs For the Blind Association
Tollgate House, Banbury Road, Bishops
Tachbrook, Leamington Spa, Warwickshire, CV33
9QJ
Tel: 01962 651226

Hearing Dogs For Deaf People
The Training Centre, London Road (A40),
Lewknor, Oxford, OX9 5RY
Tel: 01844 353898
Fax: 01844 353898
E-mail: info@hearing-dogs.co.uk

Irish Kennel Club
Fottrell House, Harold's Cross Bridge, Dublin 6,
Eire
Tel: 00353 1453 3300
Fax: 00353 1453 3237

Kennel Club
1-5 Clarges Street, Piccadilly, London, W1Y 8AB
Tel: 0171 493 6651
or 0171 629 5828

National Canine Defence League (NCDL)
17 Wakley Street, London,
EC1V 7LT
Tel: 0171 833 7624
Fax: 0171 833 2701

National Dog Tattoo Register
PO Box 3389, Manningtree, Essex, CO11 2LN
Tel: 01206 397510

Our Dogs (weekly newspaper)
5 Oxford Road Station Approach, Manchester,
M60 1SX
Tel: 0161 236 2660
Fax: 0161 236 0892

**Peoples' Dispensary For Sick Animals
(PDSA)**
Head Office, Whitechapel Way, Priorslee, Telford,
TF2 9PQ
Tel: 01952 290999
Fax: 01952 291035

**Petlog (national database for micro-chipped
animals)**
15 Knightsbridge Green, London, SW1X 7QL
Tel: 0171 518 1000
Fax: 0171 581 2865

Pet Plan (dog insurance)
Computer House, Great West Road, Brentford,
Middx., TW8 9DX
Tel: 0181 580 8080 Fax: 0181 580 8001

RSPCA (headquarters)
Causeway, Horsham,
West Sussex, RH12 1HG
Tel: 01403 264181
Fax: 01403 241048
E-mail: enqserv@rspca.org.uk

Search and Rescue Dogs Association
Bannersdale Head, Selside,
Kendall, Cumbria, LA11 9JZ
Tel: 01539 823685

Wood Green Animal Shelter
London Road, Godmanchester,
Huntingdon, Cambs., PE18 8LJ
Tel: 01480 830014

Selected Bibliography

Cunliffe, Juliette, 'Show Training For You and Your Dog', *Popular Dogs*, 1991

Cunliffe, Juliette, 'Popular Sight Hounds', *Popular Dogs*, 1992

Dale-Green, Patricia, *Dog*, Rupert Hart-Davis, 1966

Flamholtz, Cathy J., *A Celebration of Rare Breeds* Vol I (1986) and Vol II (1991), OTR Publications

Fogle, Dr Bruce, *The Encyclopedia of the Dog*, Dorling Kindersley, 1995

Geary, Michael, *Purnell's Pictorial Encyclopedia of Dogs*, Purnell & Sons Ltd., 1978

Glover, Harry, *Standard Guide to Pure Bred Dogs*, Macmillan London Ltd., 1977

Glover, Harry, *Toy Dogs*, David & Charles, 1977

The Irish Kennel Club, *The Native Dogs of Ireland*, 1984

Jackson, Frank, *Crufts: The Official History*, Pelham, 1990

Johnston, George & Ericson, Maria, *Hounds of France*, Saiga Publishing Co Ltd., 1979

Leighton, Robert, *The Complete Book of the Dog*, Cassell & Company Ltd., 1952 edition

Lyon, McDowell, *The Dog in Action*, Howell Book House Inc., 1981

Macgregor, James & Johnston, James, *Illustrated Guide to Hound Breeds*, Kelso Graphics, 1987

Mery, Fernand, *The Life, History and Magic of the Dog*, Grosset and Dunlap, 1968

Ney, Patrick, *An Animal Lover's Scrapbook*, Max Parrish, 1963

Porter, Valerie, *The Guinness Book of Almost Everything You Didn't Need to Know About Dogs*, Guinness Books, 1986

Sloan, A. and Farquhar, A., *Dog and Man*, George H. Doran Company, 1925

Spira, Harold R., *Canine Terminology*, David & Charles, 1986

Stephen, David (General Editor), *Dogs*, Collins, 1973

Vesey-Fitzgerald, Brian, *The Domestic Dog*, Routledge and Kegan Paul, 1957

Vesey-Fitzgerald, Brian (edited by), *The Book of the Dog*, Nicholson & Watson, 1948

Taylor, David BVMS FRCVS, *The British Veterinarian Association Guide to Dog Care*, Dorling Kindersley, 1989

The Complete Book of the Dog, (various contributors), Pelham Books Ltd, 1985

Guinness Books of Records, Guinness Publishing Ltd

The Kennel Club's *Illustrated Breed Standards* – 1989 and 1998

Glossary

Action
Movement. i.e. walking or running.

Anal Glands
Sacs located on each side of the rectum.

Apron
Longer hair below the neck on the chest

Bat ear
An erect ear, broad at base and rounded at the top.

Bay
The prolonged cry of a hunting dog.

Beard
Long hair on muzzle and under jaw.

Belton
Intermingled coloured and white hairs.

Bitch
A female dog.

Blenheim
Used to define the chestnut and white on the King Charles and Cavalier King Charles Spaniels.

Bi-colour
Two coloured.

Blaze
White strip running up the centre of the face.

Brindle
Fine, even mixture of black hairs with those of a lighter colour, usually in stripes.

Candle-flame ears
Flame-shaped ears of the English Toy Terrier.

Couple
Two hounds.

Cross-breeding
Breeding together of two dogs of different breeds.

Dam
The female parent.

Dew claws
The fifth digits, found on the inside of the legs.

Dewlap
Loose skin under throat.

Dock
Amputation of the tail

Double coat
An outercoat which is weather-resistant, and an undercoat for warmth and water-proofing.

Feathering
Longer fringe of hair on ears, tail, legs or body.

Femur
Thigh bone: from hip to stifle joint.

Flecking
The coat ticked with another colour.

Floating ribs
The thirteenth and last ribs, unattached to the others.

Gait
Movement at various speeds.

Game
Wild animals and birds hunted by dogs.

Gestation
The time between conception and birth; usually about 63 days in dogs.

Giving tongue
Baying and barking of a hound pack.

Guard hairs
Longer, stiffer and smoother hairs which grow through the undercoat.

Hare foot
An elongated foot.

Harlequin
Patched or pied colouration. Generally black on white or blue on white.

Heat
Seasonal fertility of female.

Humerus
The largest bone of the forequarters; the arm.

Lachrymal glands
Tear-producing glands, one located at the inner corner of each eye.

Landseer
Black and white colouring; term used for some Newfoundlands.

Lion clip
Traditional clipping of body from last rib, leaving mane on forequarters. Clipping also on legs, back, face and tail, according to breed.

Mask
Dark shading on foreface.

Merle
Colouration of blue-grey, often flecked with black.

Molars
Back teeth in upper and lower jaws (two each side: top; three each side: bottom).

Mottled
Bi-coloured coat pattern with dark, roundish blotches superimposed on a lighter background.

Moult
Shedding of the coat.

Muzzle
The head in front of the eyes (also known as the foreface).

Pack
A number of hounds which are kept together in one kennel.

Pads
The thick skin on underside of the feet that act as protection.

Pedigree
A written record of a dog's breeding history.

Plume
A fringe of long hair hanging from the tail.

Premolars
The teeth between the molars and canines.

Pure breed
A dog with parents of the same breed that are themselves of unmixed breeding.

Ridge
Streak of hair which grows in reverse direction to the main coat.

Roan
Fine mixture of coloured hairs alternating with white ones.

Runt
The smallest, weakest puppy of a litter.

Sable
Black-tipped hairs overlaid on a background of a different basic coat colour.

Saddle
Coat which is of a different quality or colour over the back.

Self coloured
A dog who is one colour, except for lighter shading.

Sickle-like tail
Tail carried up in a semi-circle.

Smooth-haired
Short, close-lying coat.

Soft mouth
A gentle grip on retrieve.

Spayed
Uterus and ovaries have been surgically removed.

Sternum
Bone which forms the floor of the chest.

Top-knot
Longer hair on top of head.

Tricolour
Three coat colours together – black, white and tan.

Undercoat
Coat, usually dense, soft and short, which is concealed by top-coat.

Wheaten
Fawn or pale yellow colour.

Whelps
Unweaned puppies.

Wire-haired
Coat of a harsh, crisp, wiry texture.

Acknowledgments and Picture Credits

With thanks to Carol Ann Johnson for providing many of the images in this book, to Polly Willis, Claire Dashwood, Karen Villabona, Sally MacEachern, Ruth Shane and Harvey de Roemer for valuable editorial and design assistance.

The publishers would like to point out that veterinary practice differs from country to country and that local medical advice should always be sought.

Docking is not recommended by the British Veterinary Association and is now illegal unless performed by a qualified veterinary surgeon.

Anatomical Illustrations by Susie Green: 12 (bl), 13 (b), 14, 16, 18 (b) and **General Illustrations** by Jennifer Kenna and Helen Courtney, courtesy of Foundry Arts 1999

All pictures courtesy of Carol Ann Johnson except:

AKG: 19 (t), 68 (t), 69 (b), 70 (c), 70 (b), 71 (b), 73 (b), 74 (t), 74 (b), 77 (b), 80 (t), 81 (r), 85 (b), 86 (b), 87 (t), 87 (b), 88 (tl), 97 (tr), 108 (b), 109 (t), 110 (c), 110 (b), 112 (tr), 112 (b), 113 (t), 114 (t), 115 (t), 115 (b), 118 (t), 121, 122, 128 (cl), 128 (bc), 130 (t), 130 (b), 131 (tl), 131 (tr), 133 (tr), 137 (b), 140 (l), 141 (t), 143 (r), 152 (t), 152 (b).

Alyce Ingle: 363 (b).

Allan and Isobel Legget: XXXX

Angela Racheal: 271 (tl).

Animal Photography: R. T. Willbie 310 (t), 310 (b), 322 (br), 356 (b). Sally Anne Thompson: 293 (b), 301 (b), 309 (t), 319 (b), 323 (b), 324 (t), 329 (tr), 329 (tl), 341 (bl), 341 (br), 342 (b), 348 (t), 355 (b), 356 (tl), 356 (tr), 358 (tl), 358 (tr).

Ardea: 172 (t). John Daniels 322 (tl), 322 (c). Jean-Paul Ferrero 322 (bl).

Cogis: Fleury/Cogis: 296 (bl), 296 (br), 302 (tr), 311 (b). Francais/Cogis: 291 (t), 291 (b), 293 (t), 297 (t), 298 (t), 307 (t), 307 (b), 311 (tl), 311 (tr), 318 (t), 319 (t), 320 (b), 320 (t), 321 (r), 321 (t), 321 (b), 328 (b), 330 (b), 332 (bl), 334 (b), 334 (t), 337 (br), 337 (bl), 338 (tr), 338 (tl), 339 (bl), 339 (t), 340 (t) 361 (tl), 361 (tr), 363 (t), 364 (b), 366 (bl), 367 (t). Hermeline/Cogis: 298 (b), 327 (tr), 332 (br). Hutin/Cogis: 339 (br). Labat/Cogis: 327 (tl). Lanceau/Cogis: 318 (br). Lili/Cogis: 318 (bl). Nicais/Cogis: 297 (b), 330 (t).

D. G. Philipson, Spanish Water Dog Partnership: 204 (b).

Dorling Kindersley: 208 (b), 292 (b), 294 (t), 301 (t), 302 (b), 312 (b), 314 (t), 315 (b), 315 (t), 333 (t), 333 (b), 335 (t), 337 (t), 341 (t), 343 (t), 344 (t), 344 (b), 346 (b), 348 (b), 357 (b), 365 (t), 368 (t), 369 (t).

Dr Daniel Taylor-Ide: 359 (t).

Dutch Kennel Club: 324 (b).

G. Samson: 217 (tl), 217 (tr).

Harry Baxter: 292 (t), 299 (b), 300 (t), 300 (b), 303 (b), 305 (t), 312 (t), 314 (b), 317 (b), 325 (t), 325 (b), 338 (b), 347 (t), 350 (b), 351 (t), 352 (t), 352 (b), 353 (t), 358 (b). Claudio Celotto 256 (b).

Hellenic Magazine for Dogs: 366 (t).

Martina Krüger: 295 (b).

Milepost 92½: 84 (b).

R. Gould: 190 (b).

Swedish Kennel Club: 355 (t), 355 (b), 354 (t), 354 (b).

Topham Picture Point: 78 (bl), 88 (r), 89 (b), 92 (t), 93 (cr), 94 (t), 103 (c), 103 (b), 105 (b), 110 (t), 129, 131 (b), 132 (t), 136 (br), 137 (cr), 140 (t), 147 (b), 149 (t), 150 (t), 150 (b), 151 (t), 153 (t).

Vos Chiens: 295 (t), 304 (t), 305 (t), 306 (b), 306 (t), 308 (b), 309 (b), 310 (b), 313 (t), 313 (b), 314 (t), 314 (b), 316 (t), 316 (b), 323 (t), 325 (t), 331 (b), 333 (b), 374.

Every effort has been made to contact the copyright holders and we apologise in advance for any ommissions. We will be pleased to insert appropriate acknowledgments in subsequent editions of this publication.

Index